KU-523-871

At the Edge of International Relations

AT THE EDGE OF INTERNATIONAL RELATIONS

Postcolonialism, Gender and Dependency

Edited by
Phillip Darby

PINTER

London and New York

PINTER
A Cassell Imprint
Wellington House, 125 Strand, London WC2R 0BB, England
127 West 24th Street, New York, NY 10011, USA

© Phillip Darby and contributors 1997

Apart from any fair dealing for the purposes of research or private study or criticism or review as permitted under the Copyright, Designs and Patents Act 1988, this publication may not be reproduced, stored or transmitted in any form or by any means or process, without the prior permission in writing of the copyright holders or their agents. Except for reproduction in accordance with the terms of licences issued by the Copyright Licensing Agency, photocopying of whole or part of this publication without the prior written permission of the copyright holders or their agents in single or multiple copies whether for gain or not is illegal and expressly forbidden. Please direct all enquiries concerning copyright to the publishers.

First published 1997

British Library Cataloguing-in-Publication Data
A catalogue record for this book is available from the British Library.

ISBN   1-85567-438-6

Library of Congress Cataloging-in-Publication Data
At the edge of international relations : postcolonialism, gender and
  dependency / edited by Phillip Darby.
      p.   cm.
    Includes bibliographical references and index.
    ISBN 1-85567-438-6 (hardcover)
    1. Developing countries—Foreign relations.   2. World
politics—1945–   3. International relations.   4. Afro-Asian
politics. I. Darby, Phillip.
D887.A88 1997
327'. 09724—dc20   96-21544
                                                             CIP

9 7 1 6 8 7 4

Cover illustration by courtesy of Phillip Darby

Typeset by Ben Cracknell Studios

Printed and bound in Great Britain by Biddles Ltd, Guildford and King's Lynn

Contents

Contributors and acknowledgements

This book emerged from a composite culture reinforced by scholarly collaboration and personal friendship. All the contributors studied international relations at the University of Melbourne and went on to do postgraduate work here. All but two have taught for a time in international relations at the University of Melbourne. Seven of us are presently attached to the University of Melbourne. Paul James now lectures at Monash University, where he holds an Australian Research Council Fellowship. Pam Stavropoulos lectures at Macquarie University. Albert Paolini lectures at Latrobe University. Sekai Nzenza is resident in Zimbabwe where she writes fiction. All the contributors have undertaken research in Asia and Africa, some of us jointly. It is relevant, I believe, to point out that we have worked together over several years – and in some cases much longer. I hope the book bears the mark of this cooperative engagement.

Collectively we wish to thank Kirsty Major for laying the ground for this book through her commitment to rethinking approaches to international studies. We also acknowledge with pleasure the help of Mary Mackinnon (Economics, McGill), who insisted that the new be subjected to the same critical scrutiny as the old, and Patrick Wolfe (History, Melbourne), who extended our thinking in significant ways. At Cassell we are grateful to Janet Joyce for the confidence she showed in the project from the outset and to Nicola Viinikka, who was prepared to extend her taste for the unorthodox to international relations. In the Department of Political Science at Melbourne we owe much to Rita Corelli and Wendy Ruffles for their administrative and other support, and to Craig Lonsdale, who collated the typescript and smoothed out many of the wrinkles in the individual contributions. Personally, I must thank Albert Paolini and Grant Parsons, who played a key role in shaping the overall conception of the project and acted as associate editors throughout.

We gratefully acknowledge the financial support of the Political Science Department, the Faculty of Arts and the William Buckland Foundation through the School of Graduate Studies, all at the University of Melbourne.
P.G.C.D.

Introduction

PHILLIP DARBY

This book is addressed to two broad constituencies of readers: students of
international relations and students of postcolonial politics concerned with
questions of dependency, gender and culture. The orientation of the two
constituencies is very different. In the former category, there are likely to be
many who are reluctant to depart from the established meanings of the
international and are therefore resistant to the presuppositions of the book.
In international relations, disciplinary boundaries remain strong and they
continue to have a powerful influence on the design and content of
university courses. For this reason, the book will appeal mainly to those
interested in looking beyond the established agenda and who are prepared
to countenance a good deal less fixity about how to approach global
politics than is customarily conceded. Readers primarily concerned with
postcolonial politics, on the other hand, are unlikely to need convincing
about the significance of the issues canvassed in this book. Instead, doubts
may be expressed about the appropriateness of making international
relations a reference point of analysis. Why, critics might ask, should
approaches grounded in a new political sensibility have to wrestle with the
constraints of disciplinary orthodoxy?

In writing this book, our hope is that the one school of thought might
better understand the claims of the other; that there might be some
engagement between established and emergent approaches. This commitment to a fuller exchange between different formations of knowledge is,
however, more of a background presumption than a focal point of
argument. It would be beyond the scope of this book to investigate the
closures and evasions of the various bodies of knowledge and it would be
tedious simply to rehearse our basic contention in different contexts. In any
case, with respect to international relations, the ground has been well
covered by writers such as Richard Ashley, James Der Derian, R. B. J.
Walker and others. The immediate objectives of the book are therefore
more grounded. They are to bring together alternative approaches to and
episodes in global politics, to debate how they might be conceptualized
and to consider their international significance. For the most part, the
individual chapters do not directly address disciplinary constructs or
the demarcation of international relations as a field of study. Our aim is
not to interrogate in any detail international relations as it is presently

constituted, but to examine ways of thinking about global issues which might fall within the province of a broader conception both of what constitutes the international and of the meaning of relationships.

The book is 'at the edge' in two senses: with regard to subject matter and with regard to approach. On the first count, the book is fundamentally concerned with the Third World. It takes as its principal focus the Third World's relationship with the First World – how much it has figured in global politics, the terms in which it has been treated, the possibilities of change. To this end, the chapters in the first part of the book critically examine the major discourses which position Third World states and societies in a global framework. The chapters in the second and third parts of the book take up issues of identity, social change, development and violence which straddle the traditional divide between domestic and international politics. Throughout, the book attempts to take account of the perspectives and interests of non-European peoples and it asserts that they should be accorded a more prominent place in the purview of international relations.

On the second count, the book is concerned to reconceptualize or at least to assess the utility of new ways of conceptualizing the politics of North–South relations. This involves expanding established conceptions of the political, disrupting received distinctions between the external and the internal and drawing on source material not usually taken into account – as for instance imaginative literature. The rationale of reconceptualization is that established ways of seeing lock the Third World into a subordinate and derivative position *vis-à-vis* the First World and inhibit thinking about systemic change. Yet it is crucial to our approach to consider the limits of new ways of seeing – otherwise strategies of change may have little purchase on either the international politics of the North–South engagement or the position of the Third World dispossessed.

These introductory remarks setting out the postulates of the book need some immediate elaboration to ensure that issues which we will want to see as contestable are not assumed to be set in stone. Generic categories such as the Third World, the non-European world or the South are clearly problematical. For many years formulations of this kind have served to order discussion of international political and economic relations. Recently, however, there has been a spate of criticism – much of it directed to the concept of the Third World.[1] In the main the arguments run along more or less familiar lines. The terminology and its associations are ethnocentric. The tendency is to homogenize peoples and countries. The restructuring of global politics and markets brought about by the end of the cold war and the rise of East Asia calls for new categories of reference.

There is, of course, much force in these and related contentions. The process of 'worlding' – meaning setting apart certain parts of the world from others through practices of naming – may appear as, and can encourage, a reworking of earlier tropes about Oriental passivity and decline, or Africa as darkness and blankness. Nomenclature inevitably carries historical associations – the Third World with the ideas about economic backwardness and non-alignment of the 1960s; the South with the failure of attempts to secure a new economic and political order in the 1970s. Viewed through one of the lenses of contemporary postcolonialism, all such conceptualizations carry the connotation of a binaristic contest between 'us' and 'them', 'self' and 'other'. As such, they are indicative of a discursive mapping of the global order which works to perpetuate the subjugation of the 'them' and the 'other'.

But are not the risks of dispensing with constructs such as the Third World or the South even greater? That elements or aspects of what we take to be characteristic of the South are present in the North, and vice versa, hardly provides a basis for rejecting larger commonalities and differences and thus, potentially at least, homogenizing peoples and politics all over the globe. Our starting-point in this book is that there were believed to be and in many respects still are commonalities between Third World societies anchored in their colonial experience, economic deprivation, power status and racial consciousness. Further, that these same criteria set shadow lines of demarcation between North and South – the word 'shadow' denoting their fluid and shifting nature. Grouping countries and peoples in this way should be taken not as the outcome of some ineluctable politics of othering, or as a measure of an innate sense of difference, but as a recognition of historical processes and situational positioning. Nor should it be understood as implying something fixed in time and for all purposes. Placement must be responsive to the claims of mobility, and in any case it will be dependent upon the criteria employed.

To put the argument in a different way, worlding represents a strategic move to ensure the visibility of the problems and perspectives of people too often overlooked or marginalized in dominant discourses – which means, of course, discourses of the dominant. A few remarks about the treatment of colonial societies and later ex-colonial states in disciplinary international relations will establish the ease with which global paradigms displace consideration of the interests of people without standing in the international system and alternative ways of thinking about the processes at work. It is a remarkable fact that the second expansion of Europe and its colonial consequences have attracted little systematic interest within the discipline. In the standard texts, imperialism receives some treatment as a historical category for the enhancement of power, reaching back almost unchanging to classical times. What is missing, however, is any sustained analysis of the processes and consequences of the nineteenth-century subjugation of Africa and Asia. What is more, in the period of imperial rule colonial issues intruded very little into international politics. Imperial relations were not international relations and they fell outside the main concerns of the discipline. As a result, international relations distanced itself from the processes which helped shape the future of more than two-thirds of the world's peoples and their response to this situation. After independence, Afro-Asian states fared little better. Overshadowed by the politics of the cold war, their place in international relations was basically determined by their relationship to the central balance. The terms of reference were external to them. In consequence, the interests which they pursued and the flags of identity that they flew had to be chosen in the light of prevailing norms. We have now entered an era characterized by a form of one-worldism which goes under the catch-cry of 'the new world order'. If we are to believe the enthusiasts, the global divisions of the past are being swept aside as more and more countries embrace neo-liberal market economics and as the pressures for democratization become irresistible. This latest manifestation of Western universalism may not mesh with what appears to be happening at grass roots (where history is perhaps still in the process of being made), and it certainly leaves much out of account. But unless safeguards are in place, it is likely that the Third World will remain only as a reflection in the mirror of what was once the First.

In short, while it is easy to argue against the concept of the Third World, it is hard to do without it. This is not only because of different historical experiences and unequal processes of exchange, but because it provides a conceptual tripwire against the colonizing tendencies of much contemporary Western discourse. If today the Third World is at the edge of international relations, it is better having a voice there than being silenced through an illusory incorporation into the centre.

The matter of reconceptualization raises more vexatious issues and it is appropriate to develop my earlier remarks in a different way. Recent developments in the humanities and social sciences have involved critiques of the foundational assumptions of old disciplines and the establishment of new configurations of knowledge, directed to different purposes. The situation with respect to international relations is that new formations concerned with global issues have developed both within the disciplinary domain and outside it. In the former case, the new formations directly challenge established knowledge. Here I would cite feminist and postmodernist approaches, both of which drew their original inspiration from elsewhere but have now been domesticated, so to speak. It may be that over time an accommodation is reached between old and new so that the radical edge of the new becomes blunted. There are grounds for arguing that this has been the situation with respect to feminist approaches to international relations, and this issue will be taken up in the book. In the latter case, mostly the new formations do not engage with established knowledge and often they proceed in relative ignorance of it. An obvious illustration is cultural studies. In many instances, however, whether a body of thought is deemed to be inside or outside disciplinary international relations will be a matter of argument and interpretation. To some degree this has always been so. Think for example of the development discourse, which has for years been perched somewhat precariously at the edge of international relations. But this situation has become more common now that disciplinary boundaries have lost their old sanctity, and new configurations, often with their own language, methodology and publishing houses, go their own way – sometimes to be picked up and taken into international relations and sometimes not. On this basis, one might argue that academe is becoming not so much interdisciplinary as multi-discursive.

It is perhaps rash to attempt to position some of the discourses with which this book is concerned, but it will at least drive home the point about indeterminancy. Dependency theory, initially beyond the pale, made a belated entry into the discipline but then interest waned. Postcolonialism has so far made little impact in international relations. For the most part, the two bodies of knowledge pass like ships in the night. Globalization and international relations have met at various points and increasingly there is a recognition of the shared concerns between the two. The democratization discourse appears to occupy a kind of half-way house. It features as international doctrine but its significance in the social context has been largely ignored. This is in line with the continuance of the traditional distinction between the external and the internal, and the long-standing disciplinary neglect of issues of social change.[2]

Questions about positioning discourses raise issues concerning sources. As a general rule, different formations of knowledge draw on different source materials. I think it is true to say that although most contemporary international relations scholars show a new openness to perspectives from outside the discipline, this has not been accompanied by a corresponding preparedness to tap new sources. This is a matter of the first importance since where we look determines what we see. Without some systematic survey work, judgement about which kinds of materials are utilized must be impressionistic, but there are enough indications that the resistance to change is considerable. Despite the much greater recognition now accorded to the role of culture in international relations, the number of studies actually turning the spade in the soil of culture has been modest. That is to say, it is all very well acknowledging that culture must be taken into account but what is needed is enquiry into its content and meaning in particular contexts, in other societies and in different periods of time. Is there not a sense in which culture has served as a new coinage with which to deal with well-recognized problems using more or less familiar material? An example which springs to mind is Samuel Huntington's use of culture to rehearse a new version of the old game of power politics.[3] On a different tack, two of us have suggested elsewhere that the neglect of Edward Said's *Orientalism* in international relations reflects a disciplinary distaste for his sources, which were primarily literary and cultural and drawn from the annals of British and French imperialism.[4] If I am right about this reluctance to seriously engage with sources outside the established tradition – let us say, literary narratives, exercises in postmodernist geography, studies in cultural change – one explanation immediately suggests itself. Many alternative sources delve into the interstices of social life and are directed to the particular and the local. Yet disciplinary international relations retains something of its long-established commitment to a global or systemic frame of reference and continues to shy away from the complications of other levels of enquiry. Despite the gestures, the discipline remains wedded to a view from above and is little inclined to seek out views from below – or, to put it in R. B. J. Walker's terms, it prefers to look from the outside rather than the inside.

Let me relate all this to our present undertaking. Each of the chapters in this book is written in the light of perspectives outside or at the margins of disciplinary international relations. Each is concerned to rethink the nature of the political and to understand it in relation to social change. Most, though not all, take their bearings from new discourses or contemporary reconceptualizations, involving the elevation of the politics of identity and subjectivity, stressing the capacity for 'subaltern' agency and privileging the sphere of the cultural. Throughout, I hope, it is evident that there is an openness to drawing material from as wide a spectrum as possible. Three of the chapters analyse literary narratives. Another two derive their focus from the writing about space and place. One proceeds on the basis of a reading of nineteenth-century medical discourse. Others, in different ways, interrogate dominant discourses through an examination of how they are viewed at the receiving end – from the standpoint of the subject and through the lens of everyday life.

Yet, as I have already indicated, the book is not entirely won over by contemporary reconceptualizations. It reviews the new discourses critically in the light of earlier writing, both in mainstream international relations and in the Marxist/dependency mould. In particular, reservations are expressed about the extraordinary effectivity attributed to the power of representation and to the power of knowledge – often to the eclipse of traditional concerns about economic, military and technological factors and their role in determining the location of power within and between societies. At various points in the book both postcolonial and postmodern approaches are called into question by returning to earlier structuralist analyses emphasizing the limits of agency in time and place. Arguments will be advanced that material interests must be reckoned with in their own right; that culture needs to connect with politics as conventionally understood; that the forms of discourse studied should be extended to cover armies, the commercial sector, non-governmental agencies and the like.

The book is divided into three thematically related parts. The first part examines the three discourses adjacent to international relations which, implicitly or explicitly, challenge the discipline's suzerainty over the domain of world politics. The chapters in this part critically review postcolonialism, globalization and postdependency in turn. They give an account of the genealogy of each discourse and assess its strengths and weaknesses in the light of the concerns of this book with the visibility of the Third World and the possibility of social change. In certain key respects, therefore, the focus of these chapters is similar and they are written to a collective design. Their leitmotif is the way in which the respective discourses approach what we once called the North–South encounter. All three are concerned with global processes and how they impinge on Third World societies. All three reflect on the meaning of the political, the significance of modernity and the scope for Third World agency – though not necessarily in those terms. To further make clear the relationship between the chapters – and the discourses which they interrogate – there are cross-references in the text, and in a few cases the same material is examined from different perspectives. In addition, we have attempted to develop certain themes sequentially – as, for instance, the limits imposed by the material on any imaginative recasting of the global order.

Notwithstanding the shared features of the various chapters, there are also significant differences between them which follow from the distinctive character of the discourses themselves – not to mention the particular standpoints of the contributors. The chapter on postcolonialism recognizes the importance of the conceptual transformation wrought by that discourse, which in large part must be related to its insistence on revisiting the past. It is, however, critical of the reluctance of writers to grapple with the future in other than gestures of hopefulness. The chapter on globalization expresses concern that the present is too easily read off projected futures, to the neglect of issues about place and space in the here and now. What this means very often is that the Third World disappears in the face of the universalization of Western hopes and fears. The chapter on postdependency concedes that dependency theory as it was elaborated in the 1960s and 1970s has had its day – hence the prefix 'post' in the title. It insists, however, that a structural antidote is needed to the free-floating conceptions of interdependence, globalism and postcolonialism which have such influence in contemporary scholarship. To this end, the chapter develops a case for divesting dependency of its economistic predilections and reworking some of its major tenets to take account of processes of global rather than national capitalism, patterns of deterritorialization and changing modes of practice.

The second part consists of examinations of particular episodes and issues in the interaction between North and South, or earlier between colonizer and colonized. The idea here is to focus on specific discursive formations, thus providing studies which are anchored in time and place. The tendency in international relations and globalization – certainly in so far as they bear on the Third World – is to write at a high level of generality, with occasional references to case material by way of illustration. A similar pattern of approach is evident in postcolonial theory and was manifest in the early elaborations of dependency theory also. This part of the book, by concentrating on the particular, provides an opportunity for more grounded judgements and may thus offer a partial corrective to the expansive generality of some of the literature. At the same time, it aims to do more than this in that it is concerned to relate the international to modes of thought and to spheres and contexts which may at first sight seem well removed from global politics. Our purpose here is to show something of the selectivity with which the international is constructed within the discipline and, more generally, to indicate how issues can take on a very different complexion when viewed from perspectives which fall within the purview of other bodies of knowledge. Again, the intention is not to engage in a detailed critique of the international relations material but to suggest the possibilities of alternative approaches.

Susie Prestney recounts the story of a Hottentot woman who was brought to England in the early nineteenth century, and who after her death became the subject of a medical discourse which brought together race, sexuality and the body. The narrative provides an entry into the construction of race as a category of analysis and gives insights into the psychology of domination and subordination at a crucial stage in the development of global cultural relations. Glenn Matthews takes as his subject settler representations of the Mau Mau during the 'emergency' in Kenya between 1952 and 1956. He deconstructs the moral topography which pictured the forests of the Aberdare Mountains as a place of darkness and powerfully reinforced the identification of the 'native' with atavism and evil. Michael Connors directs attention to the democratization discourse which has become a pillar in the structure of Western thinking about Third World change. Examining the case of Thailand, using Thai sources, he shows how different democratization appears when viewed from closer to the ground. He concludes that the rhetoric of democracy is essentially a new form of development thinking which facilitates capitalist penetration. Edgar Ng tackles an associated stream of contemporary theorizing about change in the Third World: the idea of partnership between donor and recipient which has become emblematic of the reformulation of thinking on the part of Western non-governmental aid organizations (NGOs). After reviewing its meaning and genealogy, he raises questions about how far partnership can be implemented in practice and the extent to which it is reflected in NGOs' representations of their role.

The third part of the book explores issues of gender and sexuality which arise in the context of relations between North and South. It does so largely through examining literary narratives, although reliance is also placed on recent theoretical debates in related fields. It is not intended to make direct connections between the issues canvassed here and international relations as it is presently constituted. Rather, our object is to bring to attention other approaches to 'relations international'[5] which might contribute to a rethinking of the limits and possibilities of global change. Literary sources are ideal for this purpose because so often they give expression to cultural and psychological forces which are seldom reckoned with in international relations owing to disciplinary closures and conventions. And of course they themselves are part of the process of international exchange, and the critical debate which they engender represents a new form of enquiry into the relationship between different peoples.

There are three individual contributions to this section. Grant Parsons asks what difference sexuality makes to how the other is seen. His enquiry focuses on British homosexual writing about India and it reflects back on the masculinity of the dominant and the feminization of the other. The second and third chapters address the position of African women, in part from different angles. Pam Stavropoulos takes agency as her theme and traces her analysis from the colonial period. She reviews the different bodies of theoretical writing and raises questions about the relevance of agency to international relations. Sekai Nzenza stays closer to the literary narratives and reads them in the light of her personal experience. She is concerned to negotiate a course between the distinctiveness of the situation of African women and the universalizing claims of Western feminism. *Inter alia*, all three studies reflect on the utility of literary discourses for the study of the international politics of the North–South encounter.

I have emphasized the logic behind the choice of the subject matter of chapters in the second and third parts of the book and the way in which they relate to each other. I would not, however, want to suggest that the composition of the book is purely the outcome of logical selection. Parts II and III could both have been conceived differently. In the second part, other issues could legitimately have been substituted for those we have chosen. With respect to the third part, it would not have been inappropriate to have examined (say) travel writing instead of literary texts. There is no reason to be defensive about the fact that the selection of subject matter covered in part reflects the interests of the people committed to the larger conception of the book and whose work meshes with the collective project. In the various chapters the way that the contributors choose their sources and develop their material speaks of their individual preferences and excitements. To my mind, this is as it should be – a mixture of logical connectedness and personal passion. Surely we are long past the time when anyone should insist (shades of Lord Acton and his editorship of the *Cambridge Modern History* at the end of the nineteenth century) that there is only one story to be told and that it must be told in a particular way. The whole point of being 'at the edge' is to catch something of different currents – and cross-currents – of thought.

An afterword reflects on the burden of argument of the book as a whole. Even there, however, no attempt is made to present a collective overview, an alternative blueprint of Third World futures or an agenda for redefining disciplinary international relations. Each of the chapters represents a contribution in its own terms. Each reflects the political views and theoretical orientations of its writer. None the less, there are thematic connections between the various chapters and a common commitment on the part of all the contributors to the object of the book and to its general design. In editing the book, I have endeavoured to highlight the linkage points and shared suppositions without, I hope, muffling the diversity of opinion.

Notes

1. See for instance George Yudice, 'We are *not* the world', *Social Text* 31/32 (1992), 202–16; Ania Loomba, 'Overworlding the "Third World"', *Oxford Literary Review* 12 (1991), 164–91; and Mark T. Berger, 'The end of the "Third World"?', *Third World Quarterly* 15:2 (1993), 257–75.

2. On the latter point see Jan Aart Scholte, *International Relations of Social Change* (Buckingham, Open University Press, 1993), especially p. 2.

3. Samuel P. Huntington, 'The clash of civilisations?', *Foreign Affairs*, 72:3 (1993), 22–49.

4. Phillip Darby and A. J. Paolini, 'Bridging international relations and postcolonialism', *Alternatives* 19 (1994), 371–97 (p. 381).

5. I borrow the phrase from Christine Sylvester, *Feminist Theory and International Relations* (Cambridge, Cambridge University Press, 1993), p. 219.

— Part I —

Framing Discourse

CHAPTER ONE

Postcolonialism

PHILLIP DARBY

Of the three discourses reviewed in the first part of the book, post-colonialism stands most on its own. It has had practically no engagement with international relations and very little, for that matter, with global-ization or dependency. It has developed its own critical modes and specialized language. It has tended to rely on distinctive source materials. Its politics diverge sharply from those of mainstream international relations and globalization theory, and although it shares similarities with dependency its radicalism is more personalized and less focused. Yet partly because of its very difference, its rejection of established agendas and accustomed ways of seeing, postcolonialism has powerfully influenced the conception of this book. It has encouraged an openness to new approaches while at the same time, and by way of reaction to the extravagance of some of its formulations, it has prompted a re-evaluation of older lines of thinking which had seemed *passé* or plainly mistaken. To varying degrees, the chapters in the second and third parts of the book represent attempts to apply or to appraise postcolonial perspectives in particular contexts and they illustrate, I think, the productive tensions inherent in such an exercise.

In this chapter I propose to outline what I take to be the distinctive features of the postcolonial discourse and to consider its contribution as a way of apprehending the North–South engagement. This involves posi-tioning the discourse relative to contending approaches to the North–South engagement and, at least to some degree, approaching its concerns and configurations from external reference points. I will begin by tracing the evolution of the discourse, paying particular attention to its changing focuses and themes. These, it will be argued, are becoming increasingly removed from some of the key issues facing the Third World. By way of explanation and in an attempt to explore how the discourse could have greater relevance, I will then discuss the nature of postcolonialism's politics and raise the question of its approach to Third World futures.

By way of preliminary, the difficulty of mapping the field of postcolonial studies needs to be acknowledged. Postcolonialism's primary concerns have been understood differently depending on the disciplinary background and political leanings of writers, and in any case they have changed over time. In many respects the source material drawn upon and the issues of contention have been determined in the course of dialogue between the principal participants. As postcolonialism has passed into wider currency, it has drawn expressions of discontent about its fluid expansionism, its lack of clarity about objectives and purposes, and its increasingly self-referential character. The mobile and variegated nature of the discourse stands in substantial contrast with international relations which, until the recent opening up occasioned by the so-called 'third debate' and gender critiques, has had a more or less clear sense of its objectives and a considerable measure of agreement over many years about the areas of internal dispute. In this respect the contrast between international relations and postcolonialism reflects the general situation which exists between established disciplines and the new formations of knowledge.

To better appreciate the nature of the discourse and its relationship with what customarily has been regarded as international politics, it is instructive to review its genealogy briefly and to note some of the inputs which have shaped its development. There is room for argument about the origins of the discourse, and a claim can be made that the writings of Fanon, Foucault and Said provided the basis upon which others built. But such a view involves a very selective reading of the early texts and a good deal of hindsight. A much stronger claim can be mounted that postcolonialism grew out of the study of fiction written in ex-colonial countries and the attempt to discern commonalities in both content and form. In this first phase, the discourse was essentially a comparative study of Commonwealth literature which then broadened out to consider Third World literature as a whole. Even at this stage literary narratives were invested with political significance; they were, after all, the expression of those who had been deprived of their land and liberty, and very often their history and culture as well. Mostly, however, their politics were seen in terms of cultural assertion and they had little resonance with those concerned with the changes in global power. Certainly postcolonialism's concerns and critical practices were far removed from disciplinary international relations; consider writers such as E. K. Brathwaite or Ayi Kwei Armah, a text like *The Empire Writes Back*,[1] or even the earlier work of Edward Said and Benita Parry, which related mainly to metropolitan writing. Such excursions as were made into theory were primarily of a literary bent, for example regarding language, genre and textuality, and addressed the need to assert and to account for difference from European narratives which for so long had carried the stamp of universalism.

Then, in the space of a few years, other accents and focuses broadened the nature of the discourse and shifted its centre of gravity away from literature. Some arose naturally from the concerns of Third World fiction. Such was the case with the role of culture but it was given much greater explanatory significance, partly because it meshed with changing appreciations in other discourses and with the development of cultural theory. So also the concern with place which had its origins in Third World writing about displacement and the more general treatment of landscape.

This has led to the incorporation of some material from postmodernist geography on the part of writers such as Doreen Massey[2] – although there are perhaps fewer such cases than might have been expected. By far the most distinctive development in this area has been the privileging of the margin and the migrant over the centre and the emplaced, which has become a hallmark of the discourse. The historical leaning which character-ized much of African and Asian fiction provided an incentive to tap other ways of approaching the past. The key initiative here was drawing on subaltern studies, a project directed to rewriting Indian history by establishing the strength and ubiquity of resistance to elite domination on the part of the subaltern.

In common with almost all disciplines and new configurations of knowledge, postcolonialism has also been confronted by the profound changes in thinking about gender and about modernity which have taken place over the past decade or so. More than many, it has been responsive to the claims that our received ways of seeing the world are in need of overhaul and it has attempted to marry contemporary revisioning with its established agenda. Feminism entered the discourse mainly by way of literary studies, especially with regard to imperial texts. I would argue that it has gelled with postcolonialism's foundational assumptions – which has certainly not been the case with international relations. In some respects feminism has also been more imaginatively extended, as for example by the writing on the gendering of other peoples and continents.

The rise to prominence of postmodernism has been more challenging and has met with more resistance. In postcolonialism's most recent move-ment, postmodernism has been the dominant influence and it pervades almost all aspects of the discourse. Homi Bhabha and Gayatri Spivak have been seminal figures as carriers, interpreters and adaptors of post-structuralist thought and the practices of deconstruction. Drawing especially on Derrida, Lacan and Foucault, they have been instrumental in turning around the discourse in a number of ways: most importantly, to be on its guard against closures of all kinds and to recognize that identity is constructed, contingent and open to multiple claims. Thus postcolonialism has been given greater theoretical sophistication and brought abreast with thinking in other discourses. Yet all this has had a dual-edged significance for the process of articulating Third World dissatisfaction with its lot and attempting to change it. In some respects the new perspectives and techniques accorded with earlier postcolonial purposes and they have carried them further or given them more bite. This can be said of the emphasis placed on subjectivity, the critique of modernity, the challenge to positivism and the rejection of European universalism, the prising open of the nation-state, and the commitment to the marginal. But in other respects they have been seen as compromising the enunciation of oppositional politics. The established lines of demarcation between North and South, and the issues of engagement have been unsettled by the process of decentring, the rejection of grand narratives, the rupturing of self–other binarisms and all that follows from this, and the neglect of material interest and structural determinants. Such muddying of the waters has been rebuked by critics such as Chinweizu of the so-called Nigerian troika, Edward Said, Aijaz Ahmad, Rosalind O'Hanlon, David Washbrook and Arif Dirlik, and it has opened a deep division within the ranks of postcolonialists.[3]

The foregoing survey has outlined the major influences on postcolonial thought, and we are now in a position to consider the way in which they have shaped the development of the discourse. Bearing in mind the heterogeneity of thinking, what can be said about the changing nature of the themes and approaches which have given the discourse its distinctive currency? Three propositions encapsulate the shifts which have occurred in the discourse's orientation to its subject matter and how it should be tackled. First, there has been a movement from the personal and the particular to increasingly abstract analyses. Second, there has been a movement from resistance and recovery to ambivalence and hybridity. Third, there has been a movement from essentially Third World experiences and concerns to globalized perspectives. I will elaborate on each of these propositions in turn because an appreciation of the pertinence of postcolonialism to international relations requires that attention be directed not only to the general nature of the discourse but also to the characteristics of its various movements and manifestations.

On the first count, the argument is that as the discourse has developed there has been less direct engagement with ordinary people acting in the context of their local cultures; less working out from the personal and the particular to the politics of North and South. This lack of rootedness is partly a consequence of the declining reliance on fictional narratives and of the growing currency of the view that the text is merely a site for theoretical contestation.[4] But it is mainly the result of the elevation of theory signified by the change in nomenclature from postcolonial writing or the post-colonial discourse to postcolonial theory. From its earliest days post-colonialism was concerned to generalize, to identify broad themes and recurrent patterns, but it did so very largely on the basis of specific accounts of personal behaviour, political practice and cultural formations. One thinks of the sociological orientation of African literature or of Mulk Raj Anand's accounts of the life of a coolie, an untouchable, or the pickers on a tea estate in Assam, which ensured that the understanding of the impact of imperialism and of the politics of resistance and collaboration were tied to human experience in the particularity of time and place. Something of the same can be said of studies which if not themselves postcolonial have come to be drawn upon in postcolonial analysis. I have in mind James Scott's account of hidden resistance in Malaysia (foot-dragging, rumour, folk-tales), which he characterizes as 'weapons of the weak',[5] and some of the less personalized but historically and culturally grounded studies undertaken as part of the subaltern studies project. Such integrated analysis is much less evident in recent postcolonial writing, where the tendency has been to pursue issues in a more abstract manner, occasionally introducing illustrative material of a personal or situational nature. Characteristically, individual interventions are positioned by reference to the work of other theorists, and a more or less agreed agenda emerges from the process of dialogic exchange.

This sense of a discourse adrift in a depersonalized and decontextualized world has been greatly accentuated by the ascendancy of postmodernist thought. The death of the author, the insistence on the contingency of identity, and on the provisional, constructed nature of place and culture, the recognition that power is implicated and options are foreclosed in taking a fixed position or telling a story have in practice encouraged a retreat from the personal, the empirical and the historical. The pressure to deconstruct, and especially to bury the idea of the knowing subject, has inhibited attempts to draw on lived experience. For all the insistence on the need for agency, in most contemporary chapters the opening up of possibilities is curiously lacking in flesh and blood. Moreover, agency is a kind of ideal category, not to be problematized by too much enquiry into the bases of action or its longer-term efficacy. In rejecting the grand narratives of the Enlightenment in favour of local initiative and the creativity of the margin, the local and the marginal are often enough given generic form – the uprooted, the diaspora and so on – but seldom are they articulated in such a manner that we are able to determine whether those who comprise the various subsets should be grouped together, how they challenge thinking, or why they might be especially influential.

The way in which postmodernism distances itself from the world as we experience it, and the contingency and indeterminism with which it approaches issues and action, are intrinsic to the disposition of thought itself. There must be a constant mindfulness not to be entrapped by the very things that the discourse rails against: a reality independent of representations and theorizing, fixed and integrated conceptions of identity, culture and place, the closures and binarisms of traditional social analysis. But the theoretical precepts which so effectively disrupt the narratives of modernity by no means dispose of the significance of the material and the social and the question of political action, even in the Western context in which they were developed and with which they remain principally concerned. Take for instance their application to international relations – a discipline customarily placed in the modernist camp, although it seems to me that its situation is decidedly ambiguous given its foundational appeals to human nature and its strictures about the lessons of history from time immemorial. Recent studies written along postmodernist lines have been extremely critical of conventional international relations' failure to acknowledge the social construction of reality and of its universalist pretensions.[6] In these and related respects there is a gulf between the two systems of thought. But in some respects they are not as dissimilar as is usually assumed. Disciplinary international relations shares with postmodernism a sense of remoteness from the phenomena under analysis; both look on an essentially de-peopled landscape where ethics and intentions do not rate highly (admittedly from very different perspectives), and consequences are not much pursued in human terms. Like postmodernism, international relations manifests a profound cynicism about emancipatory possibilities. There is a similar reluctance to address the role of social and economic processes.

What I am suggesting is that even when applied to a deeply Eurocentric discourse, postmodernism's censures and revisions gloss over important spheres of human experience and crucial questions of political debate. When postmodernism is called into service to rejig postcolonialism, its omissions and elusions become the more serious. Given the historical and systemic marginalization of the Third World, postmodernism's problematizations become less productive. I do not want to quibble about phraseology – in all these discourses there are enough words which resonate suggestively but convey very little – but the need is not for space-clearing exercises to allow something to happen or to highlight silences which will in some mysterious way be heard. There have been enough gestures of stripping away: Africa as 'blankness', 'without history'; outside Europe as being 'beyond the comity of the civilized world'. By now we have been told *ad infinitum* that everything is constructed. What is required is 'peopling' discourses about the Third World and providing footholds for action. There is a demonstrable need to go beyond invocations about the contingent and the indeterminate and to face up to the enormity of the problems. In turn, this must involve tackling questions about global structures and entrenched interests which impede social change. In his recent essays, Said has been forthright about the necessity of taking firm positions despite the dehortations of poststructuralism and the risks of political practice going bad.[7] In his review of postmodernist writing in international relations, Sankaran Krishna stresses the requirement for making a space for enabling political action.[8] Many of the luminaries of the postcolonial discourse have argued to similar effect, though often in a guarded and qualified way. But if there is a cautious consensus that something must be done, the chosen instrument – strategic essentialism – lacks a cutting edge. To resort to such a defensive tactic seems an odd way of proceeding; akin to entering by the back door or, to change the metaphor, moving by sleight of hand. Strategic essentialism is a technique which enscribes the secondary status of the Third World in the thinking of the First; it represents an attempt to establish a basis for thinking positively and politically in the crevices and recesses between the forbiddens of postmodernist thought. There is a strong argument to be advanced that the point has been reached where we need to give much more weight to the problems of the Third World, rather than continue down the track of adjusting our approach to the issues in hand to the requirements of an often resistant body of theory. In this respect, Achebe is a better guide than either Derrida or Foucault.

Our second proposition – that there has been a shift from resistance and recovery to ambivalence and hybridity – hinges on the weighting attached to the issues which have given postcolonialism its special character as a discourse. In its first movement, when postcolonialism emerged as a political formation as distinct from a literary enquiry, it flew the flag of resistance not only to imperialism as a political system but to the ideas, values and cultural practices that empowered and sustained it. The rejection of an externally imposed order and way of life went hand in hand with attempts to recover, so far as possible, the indigenous culture and the native voice. The accent was therefore on the difference of the non-West from the West, and in theoretical terms the tendency was to proceed on the basis of antagonistic paradigms. Writers who did not fit the mould – as for example Wole Soyinka and R. K. Narayan – were left out of account, or at least pushed to the sidelines. Resistance theorists such as Abdul Jan-Mohamed and Chinweizu in a sense shared the commitment of the first generation of nationalists; their position was akin to Ali Mazrui's that the Third World was on the side of rights and justice rather than order and stability. But they were convinced that the day of transformation had not yet arrived.

Partly under the influence of postmodernist perspectives, overtly oppositional politics came to be replaced by a more nuanced reading of the colonial encounter and of the postcolonial predicament. Imperialism was not as secure and single-minded as it had earlier been presented. Moreover, its very fascination with the other was shot through with fantasy and desire.[9] The colonized subject was never entirely resistant to the appeals and inducements of the imperial project. Inevitably some of the values from the outside took root within colonial societies. In any case there could be no return to a precolonial order. This had been irretrievably damaged by the violence of external intervention. Even as an ideal, 'nativism' had its shortcomings – patriarchy being an obvious example. It was also too easily manipulated to serve the interests of cultural and racial exclusiveness and dictatorial rule – themes of V. S. Naipaul's *A Bend in the River* and Nuruddin Farah's trilogy *Variations on the Theme of an African Dictatorship*.[10] Bhabha has been the most conceptually innovative of the revisionists of otherness: 'The place of difference and otherness, or the space of the adversarial . . . is never entirely on the outside or implacably oppositional.'[11] In many ways, Said's writings may be taken as a case study of the movement from binaries and boundaries to a recognition of meeting-places and points of congruence. *Orientalism*, although decidedly of the former cast – '[a] line is drawn between two continents'[12] – hints towards the latter: 'The Orient at large . . . vacillates between the West's contempt for what is familiar and its shivers of delight in – or fear of – novelty.'[13]

These lines of thought which unsettle the allegories of otherness have implications for almost every aspect of the North–South encounter. The masculinity of imperialism is to some degree undercut by the homoeroticism which accompanied it. The feminization of other lands and peoples signifies vulnerability as well as empowerment. Modernity is revealed as containing within it elements of the premodern. The language of the centre is a means not simply of extending control but of challenging it. The meaning of place cannot be read directly from geographical location. In his autobiography, John Masters describes his arrival at the mess of the 4th Gurkha Regiment in a long passage which begins: 'The Victorian founders of our regiment had built the mess low, of stone, and set it on the edge of the ridge, its front turned to the Himalaya.' He ends: 'I had come to my home.'[14] More introspective and more anxious versions of the Anglo-Indian journey in reverse are given by Nirad Chaudhuri in *A Passage to England* and V. S. Naipaul in *The Enigma of Arrival*.[15]

I have chosen to illustrate the proposition about place by reference to writers outside the postcolonial discourse to make the point that postcolonialism's recent turn to ambivalence and hybridity breaks less new ground when viewed from outside the discourse than when viewed from within it. In many respects, in fact, the redirection of postcolonial thinking brings the discourse into line with revised readings of literary texts and imperial history which had already been given in other quarters. Think, for example, of the re-evaluation, which dates back at least to the 1960s, of Kipling's approach to the Raj. Then there is a long-established tradition of writing about the dilemmas of imperialism emphasizing the attraction of the pagan and the pull of the premodern. Joyce Cary's African romances are a literary expression of this thinking. In African historiography there is the work by scholars such as Terence Ranger drawing attention to the radical and radicalizing potential of Christianity, evidenced by the rise of the separatist churches. And further back there is Joseph Schumpeter's understanding of imperialism's dual cast of mind – a view which was taken up by Hannah Arendt among others.

Although the reorientation of the discourse away from the enclosures of binarism has enlivened intellectual exchange and opened a space for rethinking the politics of North and South, rather less has emerged than might have been expected. In other words, the possibilities implicit in the recognition of shared moments and interactive aspects of the imperial experience have not yet been much explored. Why should this be? It is, I think, partly a matter of the difficulty of rethinking oppositional politics and partly a function of the increasingly theoretical bent of the discourse. We have discussed both points earlier, but a few additional remarks are necessary to establish their relevance in the present context. Ambivalence and hybridity clearly complicate the articulation of oppositional politics and this appears to have created an understandable uneasiness, an uncertainty about which direction to take. Despite the fact that mimicry, appropriation of the symbols of the centre and various other subversive manoeuvres open up new possibilities of challenge to the inherited and constituted order, there is a sense of having conceded too much. The lack of boldness, the absence of a demonstrable mass element and the very ambivalence inherent in the concepts unsettle and inhibit. As a result there are tendencies to slip back into the old alterities or to reposition them within colonial societies. As examples of the latter, consider the way in which, according to some formulations, the rejection of modernity comes to be located in the sphere of private or domestic life or tied to the activities of 'ordinary' people and the underclasses. Such redrawing of the boundaries between self and other needs to be considered in its historical specificity, but we should certainly be on our guard not to identify the politics of the everyday with the progressive preferences of postcolonialism. And even if some support can be derived from episodes in early colonial history – I am thinking of primary resistance – have not the processes of globalization and the accelerated ease of movement of the modern greatly compromised any notion of secure anchorages of resistance? Here attention needs to be directed to the pull of the city in the countryside, the circulation of feminist thought, and the impact of the Bombay film industry and the Sony Walkman, among other symbols of modernity.

It is issues of this nature which to date have received only a limited airing in the postcolonial discourse because of the reluctance to engage with the day-to-day and the permutations of time, place and culture. Hybridity is too general a category to give much solidity to thinking about the growth and character of postcolonial societies. To extend the chosen metaphor, we need to know more about the process of hybridization and we need to take account of soils, climatic conditions and so on. Thinking historically, for example, the differences between formal and informal empire, between direct and indirect rule, between the nature of the interests pursued and between different processes of value transmission are not incidental to the contemporary inheritance. Perceptions of identity, especially with respect to ethnicity, cultural formations and patterns of violence all have the stamp of particularity alongside the sign of the generic.

This brings us directly to our third proposition, which is that there has been a movement from Third World concerns to globalized perspectives. What began as an enquiry into the problems and position of the non-European world has broadened out to encompass other regions and peoples. The self–other dichotomy, which although always pivotal had been set in the context of relations between colonizer and colonized, has come to be examined as a subject in its own right. What is now at issue is the whole nature of 'othering', meaning the way in which a self comes to understand the relationship between itself and some other. The process of extending the reach of the discourse is illustrated by the way that the logic of 'worlding' leads the authors of *The Empire Writes Back* to make assumptions about the cultural and literary commonality of African and Asian countries, on the one hand, and settler societies such as Australia, Canada and even the United States, on the other.[16] By 1992 a stage had been reached such that the editors of a special issue of *Social Text* were able to suggest that in postcolonialism we are witnessing the emergence of a 'new discourse of global cultural relations'.[17] It is almost as if postcolonialism has caught something of the spirit of globalization theories of which Albert Paolini writes in the next chapter.

What is significant about all this is that the urge to generalize and to take a holistic view impedes recognition of the differences between national and cultural formations and the distinctive claims and interests of particular classes, ethnic movements and other sectional groupings. The tendency is thus to essentialize and to universalize, and it keeps company with the proneness to dehistoricize to which I drew attention before. Postcolonialism's 'globalizing gesture', as one writer put it,[18] has drawn sharp criticisms, especially from those concerned about the declining visibility of material interest. Aijaz Ahmad has rebuked Fredric Jameson for sweeping aside the diversity of Third World experience in his pursuit of supposed patterns of commonality.[19] Arun Mukherjee has drawn attention to the homogenizing functions of postcolonialism's categories and subcategories and to its essentializing terminology and vocabulary.[20] On several occasions it has been suggested that the case of India serves as a model for assertions about non-Europe as a whole. Arif Dirlik has gone so far as to argue that in terms of its discursive thematic, postcolonialism excludes from its scope most of those who inhabit postcolonial societies.[21]

These reprovals of the global reorientation of the postcolonial discourse deserve to be considered very seriously. And associated with them or implied in some of the specific lines of criticism is an even more troubling concern: namely, that in much contemporary writing enquiry has come increasingly to focus on the epistemological basis of Western knowledge. It is not easy to spell this out in a hard-edged way without straining the material, but often the discourse gives the impression that its foremost purpose is to develop a critique of Western formations of knowledge and their claims to universality. In other words, what was once a necessary but essentially subordinate exercise in the assertion of the primacy of Third World experiences and concerns has become the principal object and rationale of the discourse itself. To the extent that this is so, it seems to me a regrettable development – all the more so when it is recalled how often and how in so many different ways the non-European world has served as a testing-ground for the West. To argue thus is not to deny the far-reaching impact of Western constructions of knowledge or to minimize the heavy Western inputs into the processes of hybridization. Nor is it to reject the parallels between First and Third Worlds – as for example Basil Davidson's comparison of the processes of nationalism in Africa and in Eastern and Central Europe.[22] Rather, it is to question the utility of yet another exercise in Western navel-gazing. If one reads recent postcolonial contributions, it sometimes seems as if all roads lead back to the West, but this reflects less on the lie of the land than on the direction that we choose to take. In any case, proceeding along these lines is hardly the most useful way of harnessing emerging sensibilities or of addressing issues such as development or violence outside Europe.

To give a little more body to these contentions, let us consider the celebration of the margin which has emerged as a feature of recent postcolonialism. The enunciation of the margin as the site of creative thinking at first sight appears a salutary corrective, and an empowering one. But when we listen to the voices associated with the margin and reflect on the messages conveyed there is less cause for confidence. Overwhelmingly the voices are those of people now situated within Western universities – Said, Spivak, Bhabha, Appiah, Mbembe, Mazrui and the like – speaking the language of the contemporary academy. Spivak is persuasive on the unspeakability of the subaltern but the margin cannot be identified with the subaltern – in any case an elusive and idealized figure. What have we heard or read in recent times about the intellectual concerns of universities in Asia and Africa which are off the international circuit, so to speak, and have only very limited access to Western journals and monographs? What do we know of the cultural distinctiveness of places such as Dar es Salaam or Calcutta which are backwaters so far as globalization is concerned? What I am suggesting is that the margin is located within the body of the West – in the place of international universities and major Western cities such as London and Los Angeles, and in the configurations of thought which are taken to define the era. Dependency theory reworked in the light of local conditions may not win much space in contemporary journals, yet almost certainly it expresses more of the thrust of thinking outside Europe than does the politics of identity.

To take stock of the position we have reached, postcolonialism's contribution to rethinking a neglected sphere of global politics and culture has been immense. It brought into prominence the position of the non-European world and it established the continuing relevance of the imperial experience. Through its reconceptualizations and its capacity to harness earlier formulations of writers and scholars, it has exposed some of the mechanisms of colonial control and it has celebrated some of the means by which they were subverted or undermined. Central here has been the role of the text as a repository of discursive power. But as postcolonialism has become more wide-ranging and more conceptually sophisticated, it has moved away from its Third World moorings; as it has confirmed its status as an academic discourse, its connection with the interests and aspirations of Third World peoples has been much weakened. Reflecting on the contemporary debates makes it hard to avoid the feeling that the discourse is becoming an end in itself. With some exceptions, as for example the writing on postdevelopment by people like Gustavo Esteva and Arturo Escobar,[23] its concerns cannot readily be translated into action on the ground and its oppositional stance does not have much purchase on the power imbalances between North and South. As I see it, the question becomes: how can the discourse be redirected so that it might have more immediate and practical relevance?

As a first step, we need to look more closely at the politics of the discourse. From its outset, postcolonialism involved a sensibility to the position of those who were the colonized, the exploited, the cast aside. Especially in its early formulations, it was concerned to present their experiences, to see things through their eyes. This often involved considerable presumption. The question of who could speak was less important than what was said. It followed that the act of speaking or writing was not a detached exercise; what was represented was understood and intended as a contribution to change. Hence postcolonialism proceeded on the basis of assumptions diametrically opposed to those which informed traditional international relations and imperial studies. International relations was the expression of those who held power; it began at the centre (in Europe) and was concerned with those states (called 'powers') which managed the system of states (understood as the maintenance of international order). Imperial studies restricted its attention to that part of the system which regulated the relationship between the centre and its margins. It was less prescriptive but its perspective was still from the centre. It told of how power was exercised, not of how it was experienced. Of course in both international relations and imperial studies there were elements of radicalism but the commitment to scholarly objectivity severely limited their expression and impact.

In contrast, postcolonialism, and the sources upon which it draws, have been partisan, and self-consciously so. When Achebe, for example, is cited with approval, what is significant is not simply that he depicted the Ibo experience of the imperial encounter but that he did so in the belief that he had a political contribution to make. As he put it, he was writing as a teacher, but it could equally be said that he was involved in the construction of a different kind of world. A similar point can be made with respect to many of the theorists who came later with their own projects to transform the way the past was told. Dipesh Chakrabarty calls for Third World histories to be written in a way which marginalizes Europe, instead of being simply variants of a master narrative in which Europe remains the subject. His purpose is to expose the collusion between history and the nation-state so that ideas about citizenship can be rethought without the modern having the stamp of normalcy imposed upon it.[24] Writing about the African exhibition at the Royal Ontario Museum in 1989 and 1990, Linda Hutcheon contends that to be designated as postcolonial the exhibition would have had to be overtly oppositional. It was not enough to be deconstructive or ironic; it was necessary to pass a judgement about the evils of imperialism in Africa.[25]

Yet oppositional politics have their limits and dangers. Accepting that there are compelling reasons for Third World studies to challenge the situation as it has developed, it is quite another thing to embrace political struggle from an idealist viewpoint. Regard must be paid to the coercive power of established authority and to the appeals of accommodation and co-option. In any case, radical commitment is too precarious a base from which to order the present or plan the future. Necessarily we cannot be sure what might prove enabling or what might foreclose productive avenues of approach. In the case of postcolonialism, it is now generally conceded that the earlier commitment to resistance was overdone. Resistance, as has been argued, cannot stand alone. Equally, it is clear that conceptions of what is resistance and what is collaboration change over time. For years V. S. Naipaul was left off the postcolonial agenda because of his apparent lack of sympathy for the Third World and his ostensibly reactionary politics.[26] Yet as Sara Suleri has shown,[27] there are other ways of reading Naipaul, and in any case he had a significant contribution to make. Quite apart from its theoretical impossibility, the project of marginalizing Europe runs the risk of failing to recognize how much of what was once European has found a place outside Europe and in a sense has become non-European. In the case of the African exhibition, Hutcheon's insistence on making 'a judgement about the effects of colonization' carries with it a privileging of ethics over processes and might well work to cut short the potentialities of creolization in the pursuit of historical guilt.

Now that postcolonialism, in its contemporary manifestation, has reoriented itself away from binaries to an indeterminate 'in-between', the argument I have been putting needs to be formulated in a somewhat different way. The problem is not an indiscriminate radicalism but that oppositional politics have come to be articulated in a way which misses some of the issues of most salience to Third World change. Challenge tends to be addressed more to earlier modes of scholarly thinking than to practices on the ground. Radicalism resides mostly in identity politics at the expense of material ones (though the two are of course related). Increasingly, the arena of politics has come to be construed as textual rather than empirical. These contentions can best be pursued by looking ahead and considering Third World futures in the light of the leads given in the literature.

To date, the postcolonial discourse has shied away from thinking too much about futures. In this respect, postcolonialism is the obverse of globalization. Considering how much attention has been directed to the past, it is remarkable how little the 'might-have-beens' of historical revisionism have been extended to the 'what-might-yet-be'. Perhaps even more remarkable, given the spate of writing on hybridity, is the fact that this runs dry or is diverted when it comes to considering its implications with regard to the kinds of society that might emerge and how they might relate to the global system. Bhabha is an exception here, although his writing about 'the beyond' has a literary quality which gives it great expressive power but much less political content.[28] Bhabha aside, the reluctance to pursue hybridity's possible trajectories perhaps registers a concern that as of the here and now the influence of the West may weigh too heavily or even that to think in such terms is a form of Eurocentrism. If so, let these things be said and they can be debated. The tenor of the discourse does allow a sense of openness to a range of possibilities to emerge, together with a reluctance to countenance any substantial narrowing of options. This appears to stem from the free-floating nature of the discourse itself and, in its present incarnation, the rejection of fixity and the fascination with the mobile nature of subjectivity.

The notion of the openness of the future calls for interrogation. This is difficult when it is not spelled out, but it can be done. Just as the past is not 'back there' (cut off from the present and from contemporary sensibilities), so the future is not 'beyond here' (without contact with where we are now and our present ways of thinking). What I mean by this is that future possibilities and how we approach them are conditioned by our understanding of the past and the present, and the concepts we employ to this end. It follows that to some degree assumptions and predispositions about Third World futures can be read off the writing about the colonial discourse, ambivalence, hybridity and so on.

For all the regret about the expansion of Europe and notwithstanding the condemnation of the harm done in the name of progress, postcolonialism's reading of the past has a hopeful aspect. Indeed, hope lies at the heart of reconceptualization, in that presenting things differently may provide a basis for making a fresh start, for getting around discursive practices which had blocked challenge or change. With respect to the processes of imperialism and the indigenous response, we are told things were different from how they earlier appeared. And often there is an underlying assumption that they might have been more different still. This is how I interpret the writing on the limits and illusions of dominance, the insecurity and ambivalence of the colonized, the gestures of resistance in unexpected places and taking unlikely forms. Certainly resistance as it is now reread is not as clear-cut as formerly – there were elements of collusion and moments of intimacy – but this also has its hopeful side, namely the possibilities opened up by moving beyond the old binaries of total opposition.

Then two more cards are brought into play: the construction of the past, including such features as tribalism and underdevelopment, and the power of representations. At this point the postcolonial hand seems to offer some promise that the next round will be different from the last. In other words, that which is constructed can be deconstructed; representations can be re-represented. As discursive practices these are admirable moves but do they cancel out what went before, do they erase what has already been inscribed? I do not think so, whether one looks at the Third World as text or as beyond text. In varying degrees, meanings and mythologies have been transfused into the distribution of power within and between societies and into the codes by which people live. Communalism in India, the culture of violence in Somalia or Liberia, access to political influence and material rewards almost everywhere attest to the continuing relevance of earlier representations and constructs. In this sense, the past – both colonial and pre-colonial – is present in so many ways.

To put this in rather different terms, some of the moves made by contemporary theory which seem to lay the ground for a fresh start are more suspect than they appear at first sight. Despite the space-clearing gestures, major impediments to change remain in place; the new formulations resituate but do not resolve many of the older problems. Let me give some illustrations. As we have seen, ambivalence and hybridity have become pillars of recent postcolonial theory. Despite the different meanings that have been given to both terms and the fact that both have been employed to different ends, generally they have been presented in a very positive light as undermining colonial authority and denoting, or creating a space for, new cultural and political forms.[29] Yet when viewed from outside the discourse, it is by no means clear that the internal dialectic is always creative. Can it not also be immobilizing? Naipaul writes of the rejection of and attraction to the United States on the part of Iranians during the Revolution and afterwards. He comments that in that attraction, which was not admitted, there lay disturbance.[30]

The word 'disturbance' fits alongside those other words which Naipaul uses to probe the postcolonial condition: 'uneasiness', 'anxiety', 'panic', 'confusion', which lead to 'hatred', 'rage', 'darkness' and 'nihilism'. The moral that has been drawn from one narrative after another is that imperialism has so dislocated the sense of self, so maimed the spirit, that the future cannot be made; in Ferdinand's words in *A Bend in the River*: 'Nobody's going anywhere.'[31] It is not my purpose here to endorse this reading – and in fact I am strongly drawn by Suleri's argument that Naipaul's writing 'suggests a profound ideological ambivalence' on his own part rather than a pronouncement of authorial authority on the state of the Third World.[32] My point is that Naipaul's approach to the significance of the colonial inheritance is provokingly different from that which has gained acceptance in the discourse and that it needs to be taken seriously, not simply dismissed as outside the postcolonial canon.

Closely related to the inscription of ambivalence and hybridity is the affirmation of multiple identities. The recognition that people have multiple attachments, different affinities depending on context, derives of course from social theory. Increasingly it informs postcolonial theory, but very often it is used in a way which disposes of issues about identity in Africa and Asia before they have even been raised. That is to say, the significance of multiple identities tends to be read off Western critical practices rather than addressed in the light of the experiences of non-European peoples and societies. There is a case to be argued that multiple identities may take different forms in the Third World from in the West and that fluidity and ease of adaption may be confined to small and unrepresentative sectors. In his book on Africa in the philosophy of culture, the Ghanaian scholar Anthony Appiah writes movingly of his and his father's multiple identities, of the lack of conflict between their various affinities and of how natural it seemed to belong to different worlds.[33] Yet without in any way doubting the sincerity of Appiah's conviction, how far can one generalize from this? In some respects Ghana is distinctive in that its colonial experience had little of the violence and extreme racism of other parts of Africa – for example Kenya or Zimbabwe. And Appiah himself is in a special position, belonging to one of the most powerful political families in the country, a nephew of the Asanthene, as a child paying visits to his mother's family in the West Country of England, before attending an English boarding-school and going on to Cambridge.

I am aware that African studies has moved in much the same direction and that it is no longer the practice to write, after the style of Colin Turnbull, of Africans being caught between two worlds. Yet there are enough sociological studies and literary and other narratives to cast doubt on the ease of adjustment to the dislocations of colonialism and modernity. At times the contradictions were so severe as to lead to personal and social disintegration. Consider, for example, the work of Dambudzo Marechera, a Zimbabwean novelist who died in Harare at the age of 35. Marechera writes with vehemence against nearly all the influences which shaped his life: 'the siren's promise of English pleasures';[34] the African image as 'an obscene idol';[35] exile as 'dry and deathlike';[36] the African village 'bask[ing] in the sun, waiting for death';[37] the new towns as 'the new dunghills from which will emerge iron flies in a cloud to scatter all over the hills'.[38]

Another concern relates to the way resistance has been resituated so that it now lies largely outside the arena which we have traditionally regarded as the political and it is mostly distanced from consciously directed political action. In much recent postcolonial writing the emphasis is on subversion, appropriation, ridicule and parody. Resistance is located in gestures, in the symbolic and in the practice of unsettling meaning. Yet it is by no means clear how the existing order is compromised and alternative futures advanced as a result. Reading Bhabha, for example, one is left to wonder how far in fact the 'menace' of mimicry disrupts the exercise of colonial or other power and in what way initiatives are taken up by subjects who (in Bhabha's Lacanian reading) have no subjectivity. There is also a cause for scepticism in the way that attention has shifted from major issues in the public domain to the politics of the everyday. I am not for a moment suggesting that the unselfconscious action of ordinary people is not of political significance. What is of concern, however, is the tendency for the politics of the everyday to displace interest in more conventional politics such as those of dependency. Furthermore, it seems to me that very often too much is taken for granted about both the radicalism and the effectiveness of the politics of the everyday. In a recent essay, three graduate teachers of English at Delhi University lament the response of their students to an orientalizing project calculated to expose the hegemony of the West. The student response is described thus: 'Irresistibly drawn to the electronic and consumer goods made possible by Western technology, avidly reading Western magazines from *Time* and *Newsweek* to women's and fashion magazines, their perception of the West is marked by desire.'[39] Moving further down the social scale to a less privileged everyday, there is Scott's account of peasant resistance in Malaysia to the introduction of double-cropping as part of the 'Green Revolution'. In this case many of the everyday activities challenged the dominant order, often ingeniously, but what emerges is their ineffectiveness. And what are we to make of the claim advanced in an essay on ambiguity in African political and cultural practices that superficiality becomes political protest? According to the authors, the 'average person' in Kinshasa attempts to keep up with the latest Western dress fashions and looks for designer labels.[40] This is described as a 'revolution in the mirror' – which is reminiscent of something out of Lewis Carroll.

My purpose in introducing these lines of thought which cut across the grain of so much postcolonial writing is not to suggest a dark future for Third World societies but to argue that an easy optimism is misplaced. If thinking about the future of the non-European world is to be more than simply wishful, it needs to be less selective about the material it brings to account. Moreover, the assumptions on which it proceeds need to be spelled out and contested much more than is the case with recent interventions. Postcolonialism's cultural radicalism draws its strength from textualizing politics and from looking in new places for initiatives and processes of change. This is well and good, but the position I have advanced here is that on both counts there are limits. On the first, we still have to confront a politics which runs beyond text and is written into the life situation of the poor in Africa or the parties to communal violence in India. On the second, in reaching out to new sources of challenge we nevertheless have to reckon with old barriers to change, both within Third World societies and in the processes of international exchange.

In large measure, the argument of the last few pages can be re-expressed in terms of agency. The crux of the matter, to state the case baldly, is that postcolonialism has had an extraordinarily expansive understanding of the potentialities of agency. Postcolonialism shares this social optimism with other new discourses. In some instances – as for example gender and sexuality in the West – rethinking accords with and has helped generate very substantial changes in political practice. In others, much less has been achieved or is even in sight. Such is the case with the politics of North and South. Earlier and more ends-oriented attempts to rethink some of the problems or to approach issues in a different way at best yielded only modest results. (I have in mind peace research and John Burton's view that conflicts of interest are essentially subjective[41] or the schemes for a new international economic order and a new information order.) Post-colonialism's reconceptualizations go far beyond these and, at least until recently, they have had a much easier scholarly passage. But I do not see how opening up space for agency extends to breaking down the closures of material interest and power politics which characterize the workings of the international system. To face up to the issues involved, it is instructive to change the terms on which so much postcolonial analysis goes forward; to ask about what people can accomplish in particular contexts. Could imperialism or some such system have been averted? Can the villagers of Chad or the shanty-dwellers of Dacca do much to improve their lot? In broader terms, how might the South resist the cultural domination of the North?

The point of asking such questions is to concretize the problems which need to be tackled instead of distancing analysis from them by writing about agency and irony and style. As I see it, while there is much to be said for defamiliarization, we have reached a point where it needs to be supplemented with a measure of refamiliarization. That is to say, it is important not to lose sight of the conditions of international life. In particular, account must be taken of the disparity of power between North and South which is the result of material development and historical processes now written into the international system. I will attempt to highlight some of the issues involved by commenting on James Der Derian's response to Krishna's concern that in some respects postmodernism can all too easily work against the interests of the Third World.

According to Der Derian, the logic of Krishna's argument is that it is up to some other to enable the subject to act. 'This leads to the logic of victimhood – a self-marginalization and self-ghettoization that only augments hegemonic power. Power comes from the taking of it, not by others bestowing it.'[42] As expressed, 'the logic of victimhood' very seriously distorts the situation of much of the Third World. By now I would have thought it well accepted that Asians and Africans acted and continue to act in the pursuit of their own interests; that they were not passive bystanders in either the colonial or postcolonial eras. Further, that their initiatives and responses helped shape outcomes but within limits set by external forces. To cite one case from the library of studies to this effect, Susan Martin has shown how the Ngwa people of the Delta region of Nigeria took it upon themselves to develop a palm-oil industry. For a considerable time they flourished until factors beyond their control eroded the palm-oil economy, chief amongst these being the change in the barter terms of trade during and after the First World War.[43] Even putting aside the historical and empirical studies, there is a conceptual problem with Der Derian's assertion of how power is transferred. The either/or formulation misses the interactive nature of the relationship between taking and bestowing. By his own Foucaultian lights, Der Derian should know better than to resort to such a binarism.

Der Derian also takes Krishna to task for his fetishization of oil, territory and weapons of mass destruction. It is Der Derian's firm belief 'that the Gulf War took place because those who wanted to resolve the disputes through violence won the war of representations before a shot was fired'.[44] Even if we accept the presumption of inevitability that events follow representations, does not Der Derian's formulation set the problem at one remove? Are wars of representation conducted on an equal footing? How might we weight tangible inputs [technology] and intangible ones [style]? Here certainly there is no inevitability, but material resources and access to global telecommunications set up very strong likelihoods. The development of orientalist thought, which we now recognize as such a powerful weapon in the armoury of imperialism, can scarcely be understood except in relation to the rise of industrialism and materialism in eighteenth- and nineteenth-century Europe. For all the changes over the past century – more contestation, more counter-penetration, more awareness of opportunity costs – new forms of orientalism continue to disadvantage the Third World. One has only to read the World Bank on democratization or Western newspaper reports of violence in Africa or Asia to realize this.

The emphasis in this chapter has been on the problems of postcolonial discourse and on the areas it neglects. In arguing thus, I have kept company with the growing body of recent writing of a critical nature.[45] A reminder is therefore appropriate that the chapter proceeds on the premise that postcolonialism has opened up new ways of thinking about what is politics and the nature of the international. Throughout, I have endeavoured to establish that by privileging the non-European world and through imaginative reconceptions, the discourse constitutes a much-needed corrective to the Eurocentrism and conservatism of so much writing about international relations.

However, as is characteristic of many innovative formations of thought which challenge the established scholarly order, postcolonialism has overweighted the explanatory capacity of its own formulations and it has too readily disregarded those of existing bodies of knowledge. The two chapters which follow, although written to more general briefs, help situate postcolonialism in relation to other approaches to international studies. The chapter on globalization makes clear that the claims of this discourse need to be moderated by postcolonial perspectives, and in some respects it gives a more positive reading of postcolonial reorientations than I have done. The chapter on postdependency corroborates the contention of this chapter that structures of material interest matter enormously and need to be addressed in their own right. On the basis of an analysis of contemporary global processes, it rejects the possibility of transforming North–South relations solely through the new politics of difference and agency.

Notes

1. Bill Ashcroft, Gareth Griffiths and Helen Tiffen (eds), *The Empire Writes Back: Theory and Practice in Post-colonial Literatures* (London and New York, Routledge, 1989).

2. See for example Doreen Massey, 'A place called home?', *New Formations*, 17:Summer (1992), 3–15.

3. For representative critiques see Chinweizu, *The West and the Rest of Us: White Predators, Black Slavers and the African Elite* (New York, Random House, 1975); Edward Said, *Culture and Imperialism* (London, Chatto and Windus, 1993), pp. 29–30 and 'Orientalism and after: an interview with Edward Said', *Radical Philosophy*, 63:Spring (1993), 22–32 (pp. 24–6); Aijaz Ahmad, *In Theory: Classes, Nations, Literatures* (London and New York, Verso, 1992); Rosalind O'Hanlon and David Washbrook, 'After Orientalism: culture, criticism and politics in the Third World', *Comparative Studies in History and Society*, 34:1 (1992), 141–66; Arif Dirlik, 'The postcolonial aura: Third World criticism in the age of global capitalism', *Critical Enquiry*, 20:Winter (1994), 328–56.

4. See for example M. Ben T. Marrouchi, 'Literature is dead, long live theory', *Queen's Quarterly*, 98:4 (1991), 775–801.

5. James C. Scott, *Weapons of the Weak: Everyday Forms of Resistance* (New Haven, CT and London, Yale University Press, 1990).

6. See for example James Der Derian and Michael Shapiro (eds), *International/Intertextual Relations: Postmodern Readings of World Politics* (Lexington, MA, Lexington Books, 1989); Michael J. Shapiro, *Reading the Postmodern Polity: Political Theory as Textual Practice* (Minneapolis, University of Minnesota Press, 1992); and R. B. J. Walker, *Inside/Outside: International Relations as Political Theory* (Cambridge, Cambridge University Press, 1993).

7. Said has argued thus in many essays and interviews. For representative statements see Edward Said, 'Intellectuals in the post-colonial world', *Salmagundi*, 70–71 (1986), 44–64 and 'Identity, negation and violence', *New Left Review*, 171 (1988), 46–60.

8. Sankaran Krishna, 'The importance of being ironic: a postcolonial view of critical international relations theory', *Alternatives*, 18 (1993), 385–417.

9. I am here paraphrasing Homi K. Bhabha, 'The other question . . .', *Screen*, 24:November/December (1983), 18–36 (p. 19).

10. V. S. Naipaul, *A Bend in the River* (Harmondsworth, Penguin Books, 1980 – first published 1979); Nuruddin Farah, *Sweet and Sour Milk* (London, Heinemann, 1980), *Sardines* (London, Heinemann, 1982) and *Close Sesame* (London, Allison and Busby, 1983).

11. Homi K. Bhabha, 'Signs taken for wonders: questions of ambivalence and authority under a tree outside Delhi, May 1817', *Critical Enquiry*, 12:Autumn (1985), 144–65 (p. 152).

12. Edward Said, *Orientalism* (London, Routledge and Kegan Paul, 1978), p. 57.

13. Ibid., p. 59.

14. John Masters, *Bugles and a Tiger* (London, Michael Joseph, 1956–Four Square edition 1962), pp. 62–3.

15. Nirad Chaudhuri, *A Passage to England* (London, Macmillan, 1959); V. S. Naipaul, *The Enigma of Arrival* (Harmondsworth, Viking, 1987).

16. Ashcroft, Griffiths and Tiffen (eds), *The Empire Writes Back*, pp. 2 and 133–5.

17. John McClure and Aamir Mufti, 'Introduction', *Social Text*, 31/32 (1992), 3.

18. Ella Shohat, 'Notes on the "post-colonial"', *Social Text*, 31/32 (1992), 99–113 (p. 104).

19. Aijaz Ahmad, 'Jameson's rhetoric of otherness and the national allegory', *Social Text*, 7:Fall (1987), 3–25.

20. Arun P. Mukherjee, 'The exclusion of postcolonial theory and Mulk Raj Anand's *Untouchable*: a case study', *Ariel*, 22:3 (1991), 27–48 (p. 29).

21. Dirlik, 'The postcolonial aura', p. 337.

22. See Basil Davidson, *The Black Man's Burden: Africa and the Curse of the Nation-State* (London, James Curry, 1992), introduction and ch. 9.

23. See by way of illustration Gustavo Esteva, 'Regenerating peoples' space', *Alternatives*, 12:i (1987), 125–52 and Arturo Escobar, 'Imagining a postdevelopment era? Critical thought, development and social movements', *Social Text 31/32*, 16:243 (1992), 20–56. It may well be considered that much postdevelopment thinking raises problems of a different kind because its empirical material so closely conforms with its preconceived moral agenda; it evinces a happy coincidence of ethics and ordinary behaviour. On this point see Chapter 7.

24. Dipesh Chakrabarty, 'Postcoloniality and the artifice of history: who speaks for "Indian" pasts?', *Representations*, 37:Winter (1992), 1–26.

25. Linda Hutcheon, 'The post always rings twice: the postmodern and the postcolonial', *Textual Practice*, 18:2 (1994), 205–38.

26. It is extraordinary that the recently published Routledge postcolonial reader fails to include a contribution from Naipaul among its 86 extracts. See Bill Ashcroft, Gareth Griffiths and Helen Tiffin (eds), *The Post-colonial Studies Reader* (London and New York, Routledge, 1995).

27. Sara Suleri, *The Rhetoric of English India* (Chicago and London, University of Chicago Press, 1992), ch. 7.

28. See Homi K. Bhabha, *The Location of Culture* (London and New York, Routledge, 1994), introduction and ch. 11.

29. But note Robert Young's claim that hybridity as a cultural description will always carry with it an implicit politics of heterosexuality: Robert J. C. Young, *Colonial Desire: Hybridity in Theory, Culture and Race* (London, Routledge, 1995), p. 25.

30. V. S. Naipaul, *Among the Believers: An Islamic Journey* (London, André Deutsch, 1981), p. 17. See also p. 398.

31. Naipaul, *A Bend in the River*, p. 10.

32. Suleri, *The Rhetoric of English India*, p. 150.

33. Kwame Anthony Appiah, *In My Father's House: Africa in the Philosophy of Culture* (London, Methuen, 1992). See especially the preface but also ch. 9 and the epilogue.

34. Dambudzo Marechera, *The Black Insider* (Harare, Baobab Books, 1990), p. 63.

35. Ibid., p. 106.

36. Dambudzo Marechera, *The House of Hunger* (London, Ibadan and Nairobi, Heinemann Educational Books, 1978), p. 129.

37. Marechera, *The Black Insider*, p. 79.

38. Ibid., p. 80.

39. Zakia Pathak, Saswati Sengupta and Sharmila Purkayastha, 'The prisonhouse of orientalism', *Textual Practice*, 5:2 (1991), 195–218 (p. 196).

40. Abdul Maliqalim Simone and David Hecht, 'Masking magic: ambiguity in contemporary African political and cultural practices', *Third Text*, 23:Summer (1993), 107–13 (pp. 111 and 112). A practitioner of no fixed address but who owns a Yves Saint Laurent suit is quoted as saying: 'A true master can stand in his underpants and completely demolish a rival.' In the next chapter, Albert Paolini reviews this and associated material more positively and in some detail.

41. See John Burton, *Conflict and Communication: The Use of Controlled Communication in International Relations* (London, Macmillan, 1969).

42. James Der Derian, 'The pen, the sword, and the smart bomb: criticism in the age of video', *Alternatives*, 19 (1994), 133–40 (p. 135). For our purposes here, it does not matter that Der Derian is in the camp of postmodernist international relations and that Krishna puts himself in the camp of postcolonialism. Der Derian's arguments could well be made by postcolonialists of a strong postmodernist orientation. Krishna positions his postcolonialism in terms similar to Said's recent writings; that is, he acknowledges his debt to poststructural thought but expresses disenchantment with the kind of politics that this disposition sometimes seems to entail. See Krishna, 'The importance of being ironic', p. 389.

43. Susan M. Martin, *Palm Oil and Protest: An Economic History of the Ngwa Region, South-Eastern Nigeria* (Cambridge, Cambridge University Press, 1988).

44. Der Derian, 'The pen, the sword, and the smart bomb', p. 137.

45. In addition to the essays already cited, see Benita Parry, 'Signs of our times. Discussion of Homi Bhabha's *The Location of Culture*', *Third Text*, 28/29:Autumn/Winter (1994), 5–24 and Russell Jacoby, 'Marginal returns. The trouble with post-colonial theory', *Lingua Franca*, September/October (1995), 30–7. Parry's essay, which I read after completing this chapter, is of especial importance. In certain respects, it powerfully extends arguments which I have advanced here.

CHAPTER TWO

Globalization

ALBERT PAOLINI

The Third World, it seems, is condemned to invisibility, particularly at the centre. In international relations, both as practice and as theory, it resides at the edge. In emergent discourses about 'global culture' and globalization, it becomes mostly incorporated, repressed, homogenized. Some critics even find the 'Third World' of decreasing utility as theoretical and descriptive application in the contemporary world.[1] Yet to the extent that the 'Third World' still carries meaning as a shorthand for the multitude of cultures and identities that remain marginalized, dispossessed and increasingly insignificant in the late modern age, it is useful not only as a sign of discomfort for various global scenarios and projections, but also as a key site of the unfolding of intersubjective identities between North and South (however inadequate some find these terms) within the intersecting parameters of (post)modernity, tradition and globalization. In this sense, the rubric of the Third World remains indispensable to any attempt to understand the global nature of modernity in the contemporary period, if only to remind us that the 'global' does not end at the Tropic of Cancer.

One of the central contentions of this book is that by positioning ourselves at the edge, we can glimpse alternative vistas which prompt us to rethink the boundaries and agenda of international relations. It is paradoxical that globalization discourses, directed primarily to an understanding of the First World and so ensconced in a Western epistemology, are evident only at the margins of international relations. This is certainly true of globalization writing which springs from sociology. Yet it is no less true of other discourses which have attempted to embody a global perspective in their revision of traditional international relations, in particular the world-system theory of Immanuel Wallerstein, the World Order Models Project involving Richard Falk and Saul Mendlovitz, and the critical theory of Robert Cox and Andrew Linklater, among others. These discourses, unlike perhaps sociological perspectives, are not unknown to international relations. In fact, writers such as Falk and Linklater explicitly define themselves as international relations scholars. They remain marginal, however, because of their specifically non-state-centric approach and their underlying brief, whether normative or theoretical, that the global rather than the national better frames the contemporary structure of world politics. They challenge international relations to rethink the narrow boundaries of the discipline; the inside/outside logic that R. B. J. Walker views as so constricting and artificial.[2] The pivot of disagreement remains the role of the state and, increasingly, a critical engagement with the question of modernity.[3]

However, there is common ground. It can be argued that both international relations and globalization discourses share a universalist perspective and Eurocentric grounding, and consequently their shared blind spot remains an appreciation of particular identities and cultures in the Third World. The danger of embracing globalization as a means of rereading international relations is that however useful and overdue this critique may be in reconsidering the state's centrality, it results in the reinscription of a marginalized Third World. It is this margin in both international relations and globalization that this chapter addresses, in particular how a focus on the global, while enlarging our field of vision in world politics, simultaneously loses sight of specifics and particularities that may not conform to the overall picture. The aims of this chapter are threefold: to survey various discourses which endeavour to map the nature of globalization; to provide a more precise and critical reading of globalization, in particular postmodern notions of global space; and to locate the place of the Third World in the various accounts of globalization. In doing so, it argues that a focus on the specifics of the Third World unveils the limits of globalization thinking.

There are two key difficulties in attempting to understand the phenomenon of globalization: grasping its precise nature and significance; and determining its relevance for marginalized societies in the Third World. The first difficulty is compounded by the fact that there is little agreement on the meaning of globalization. In many respects, it does not constitute a discrete discourse, except perhaps when it is viewed from the outside. More so than postcolonialism, globalization is an amalgam of different discourses. As an overarching concept, it is deployed in various disciplines in an attempt to make sense of certain processes and movements which seem to stretch across the globe. There appears little disagreement over the existence of these global processes. However, it would be hard to find common ground on how we are to comprehend and interpret them. The second difficulty derives from the evident Western orientation of much globalization theory and writing. We are dealing not only with deeply embedded processes located at the centre, but with conceptual categories and assumptions that proceed from this reference point. The terrain of globalization is surveyed very much from the viewpoint of the Western observer. When we travel to the outer perimeter of the Western reach and vision, in particular to Africa, globalization not only takes on a different character, but also encounters a different set of forces and pressures. One obvious indicator of this is that at the same time that much Western theorizing about globalization spins off into accounts of cyberspace and a 'postnational' world, specifically Third World critiques of globalization emphasize an older paradigm of economic dependency and North–South imbalances. Thus, we not only need to take care with how we define globalization, but require a keen appreciation of its manifestations and implications in particular local contexts.

First, what is the 'global'? What is meant by 'globalization' and what is the genealogy of the term? Broadly speaking, globalization pertains to a set of writings and movements that have responded and sought to characterize the significant transformations of the mid- to late twentieth century, also referred to, particularly in social theory, as the 'late modern age'. These transformations in communications, technologies, capital, labour, markets and trade, the production and distribution of goods and services, and the mass movement of peoples have been seen as embodying a 'global' character; that is, they have tended to transcend the traditional boundaries of the nation-state to initiate a restructuring of relations between cultures, nations and states along more transnational, supranational or even subnational lines. The effect of these transformations, at least in popular parlance, is the rise of ideas about a 'global village', 'one world', 'global civil society' and a 'global culture', particularly evident in the spread of social movements organized along the configuration of global issues such as ecology, gender and peace. Yet we need to distinguish between process and prescription in response to the increased global landscape. Although all globalization discourses attempt to make sense of the global nature of the late modern world and can be seen, consequently, as a direct response to the transformations of the present age, certain discourses attempt to theorize the nature and possibilities of the global processes along normative and even utopian lines, evident particularly in the World Order Models Project and the critical or 'emancipatory' perspective of Cox and Linklater, and, of course, in global ecology movements such as Greenpeace. On the other hand, postmodern approaches celebrate the possibilities unleashed by globalization along less utopian lines and instead point to hybridity, multiple identities and indeterminacy as a condition of living in the late modern age. Further, there is a growing distinction between a materialist or neo-Marxist position and a more culturalist one in theorizing globalization. Thus, whereas sociological perspectives – and even some postcolonial ones such as that of Arjun Appadurai – have tended to highlight the cultural basis of globalization, world-system and critical theorists, postmodern geographers such as David Harvey, as well as postcolonial critics such as Aijaz Ahmad and Arif Dirlik, have insisted on the materialist basis of the new global age. This is an important divide that needs to be addressed, and indeed it is noteworthy that a materialist such as Wallerstein has made an attempt to incorporate a cultural reading into his world-system perspective. Notwithstanding this divide and mindful of the distinction between process and prescription, it is clear that in a wide-ranging body of work from social theory and postmodern geography to certain approaches in international relations itself, there is a sense that the category of the global constitutes something crucial about the contemporary period.

How do we map the global condition, or, more to the point, how is it mapped in the various discourses which have taken on a global perspective? Those writers committed to a global prospectus broadly agree on the existence of the global condition, although they may differ on its parameters and scope. As noted by Featherstone, the idea that we live in one world has become a cliché.[4] There is less agreement, however, on more normative questions of social, economic and political organization, emancipatory value, and questions of gender. The specific concern in this chapter is with the characterization of globalization and its implications for the place of the Third World in the 'world-system'. Although such representations often carry an implicit normative or ideological agenda, this will not be the focus here. The uniting thread of the various global scenarios is, as previously indicated, an attempt to categorize the new and profound institutional and social transformations which are occurring in the world at large. Because of these transformations, it is felt that the world is shrinking, values are becoming more global, cultures more integrated and national boundaries either less significant or irrelevant depending on which global scenario you subscribe to. Underpinning all these developments is modernity, or, to be more precise, the *globalization of modernity* beyond its specifically Western borders to encompass non-Western societies such as Japan, the newly industrialized countries (NICs), Eastern Europe and most of the Third World. The feeling here is that with this spread of modernity we are all tuned into a shared frequency, particularly in an economic sense.

Although this focus on a so-called global condition is relatively recent, there would seem broad agreement across disciplines on the scenario briefly mapped out above. In fact, the emphasis on globality, global culture and globalization would now appear to be ubiquitous in academic discourse. According to one of its central proponents, the sociologist Roland Robertson, 'globality is a virtually unavoidable problem of contemporary life', with even explicitly anti-global movements such as those at the fore of communal and ethnic uprisings being merely a response to globalization.[5] Anthony King, whose world-economy focus on modern cities and the impact of imperialism and colonization has incorporated a more cross-cultural and less Western-centric perspective than that of many other global writers, nevertheless argues that the term 'global' has assumed a new urgency. He views the world, particularly in its built environment, as encompassing 'one large, interdependent city', organized through a single, interacting urban system that is the product of a global system of production and division of labour. Echoing Robertson's famous remark about the world being a 'single place', King points to a greatly increased sense of globalization in the contemporary age.[6] This global sense is seen to condition the very fabric of academic discourse. Frank Lechner contends that sociology is undergoing a profound change in response to an emergent global order so that 'new core problems spring from a basic awareness among contemporary sociologists that we are now living in a truly global society, in a world-system'.[7] Although Lechner hastens to add that this global culture is abstract and open, his insistence on a global focus is mirrored throughout contemporary sociology and social theory, evident particularly in the journal *Theory, Culture and Society* and its recent edited publications. The editor of this journal, Mike Featherstone, while pointing to the diversity of discourses under the global banner, has argued in one of these collections that the globalization process is an extension of global cultural interrelatedness leading to a 'global ecumene'.[8]

The writer most associated with globalization discourses is Robertson. The significant shift in academe toward globalization receives probably its least critical treatment here. Having gone perhaps the furthest in globalizing gestures, Robertson argues that the explosion of the use of the adjective 'global', the higher degree of 'global density' and complexity over the past twenty years and the almost universal reach of modernity mean that there is now no denying his much earlier observation of the world as a 'single place'. Indeed, Robertson maintains that the process of globalization is now so extensive that in sociological-theoretical terms it should be regarded as subsuming the classical concern in sociology with the transformation of societies which centred on industrialization, development and modernization. These are now self-evident features of world society; the task, for Robertson, is to chart and explain their global character. It is no longer a question of establishing the credentials of globalization, it is a given for scholars to incorporate into their work. The condition of globality is seen to encompass even world-system theory. While praising world-system theorists as having accomplished 'something of significance in emphasizing the idea that the world is a systemic phenomenon', he nevertheless admonishes writers such as Wallerstein and Jameson to the extent that they still insist on the primacy of the economic infrastructure in their view of a globalized world rather than 'globality' itself which includes and transcends the global economy. Thus, Robertson is interested in 'explicitly globe-oriented ideologies, doctrines and other bodies of knowledge', which he defines as those which espouse as their central message 'a concern with the patterning of the entire world'.[9] This recognition of a 'global culture' permits Robertson to construct typologies of the contemporary 'global-human condition' and refer to successive phases of globalization. The current phase of globalization, namely the 'uncertainty phase', which began in the 1960s and displays 'crises tendencies' in the 1990s, is outlined as follows: the arrival and inclusion of the Third World; the heightening of 'global consciousness' in the late 1960s; the increase in the number of global institutions and movements; societies increasingly facing problems of multiculturality and polyethnicity; gender, ethnic and racial considerations rendering the conception of the 'individual' more complex; a more fluid, post-bipolar international system; the rise about ideas of humankind as a 'species community'; an interest in concepts of a world civil society and world citizenship; and the rise of the 'global media village'.[10]

Sociology has made the running on globalization discourses. Yet outside this circle, much the same pattern of thinking is evident, albeit at times directed to different conclusions. Fredric Jameson's account of post-modernity or 'late capitalism' refers to the 'new global space' in which 'we can achieve no distance from it', and subsequently resistance to global forces is disarmed and absorbed.[11] It is noteworthy that Robertson claims that Jameson attunes much of his work to Wallerstein's world-system ideas. As indicated above, world-system theory has played a key role in providing the theoretical basis for conceiving the world as globally integrated. While this has mostly constituted a materialist account of the globalization of capitalism and has hence tended to elevate the economic as the key dynamic in the global, of late there has been a significant shift of emphasis, so much so that even Wallerstein now views culture as 'the key ideological battleground' of the opposing interests of the modern world capitalist system. While this does not signify a complete change of heart in terms of how culture is understood, what is fascinating is the manner in which Wallerstein effortlessly weaves 'geoculture' into his previously economic-centric model of 'geopolitics'.[12]

On related terrain but from a critical theory international relations perspective, Robert W. Cox points to a new 'global perestroika' which is fundamentally an extension of the liberal, free-market economic system across the globe. Although it is unstable and lacks an 'explicit political or authority structure' to direct it, there is nevertheless a 'new global political structure emerging' that no longer approximates the old Westphalian concept of a system of sovereign states and is instead characterized by a 'multilevel structure' underpinned by new global social forces (such as those based on issues such as ecology, feminism, peace and democracy), regional groupings, 'world cities', transnational corporations, and multi-lateral institutions providing for both order and functional cooperation. Cox views this world order as vulnerable and thus ripe for an eman-cipatory project revolving around local action. However, this local focus will not be sufficient in itself: 'the counterforce to capitalist globalization will also be global, but it cannot be global all at once.'[13] In another critical international relations piece, Stephen Rosow finds common meanings and a 'common reference world' within a global political space marked by fragmentation and diversity. Although this commonality is based on a narrow Western modernity, the globalizing process nevertheless is one that incorporates identities outside the boundaries of the West into its orbit.[14]

There is an increasing attention to global issues in international relations as a whole. As already mentioned, much of this focus revolves around the question of the state. This is certainly true of mainstream international relations, which has been forced by the global transformations of the past twenty years to address the challenge that globalization poses to traditional conceptions of state sovereignty and the state system. From the rationalist reworking of realism evident in Hedley Bull and Martin Wight to the neo-liberal body of writing evident in the concept of 'interdependency' in world politics (in, for example, Nye and Keohane), mainstream international relations has made some attempt to rethink the parameters of the state system in light of the proliferation of actors and processes which move across national boundaries. However, in the majority of such revisions, the state has remained central to analysis and indeed to future projections of world politics. In this respect, (neo)realist orthodoxy regarding the primacy of the state remains dominant in spite of the increased sophistication and adjustments in perspective. At one level this indicates the adaptive capacity of the realist paradigm and is evident in analyses of the end of the Cold War. Rather than provoke a radical reassessment of assumptions and approaches, in many respects the end of the Cold War and the break-up of the Eastern bloc would seem to have reaffirmed many of the key realist articles of faith concerning the behaviour of states, the cyclical nature of hegemony and the appeal of nationalism.[15]

If we look to the more critical edges of international relations, the global has received a sustained and sympathetic reception. Here, a commitment to a 'global project' is evident in the revisioning of international relations; the state no longer operates as the linchpin in prescriptions of, and analyses of, world politics. Thus in the critical theory perspectives of Cox and Linklater, for example, there is an attempt to reconstruct the ideals of the Enlightenment and modernity within a global, universal framework which places at the forefront ideas about community, autonomy and global citizenship as a way out of the state impasse. A broad emancipatory project is envisaged as the key to 'universal cosmopolitanism' based around social movements and transnational civil societies.[16] The notion of a 'global civil society' is also central to the work of Richard Falk. Working through the World Order Models Project and various other projects of 'global governance', Falk views the 'visible contours of an emergent global civil society' and the decline of the state and the state system.[17] Environmental and economic pressures will lead to a network of institutions and procedures 'cumulatively contributing to a governance structure at the global level'.[18] According to Falk, we are witnessing a 'globalism-from-below' which refers to the 'many facets of transnational democratic initiatives, often given expression by social movements, voluntary associations, and non-governmental organizations and linked in a new configuration identified . . . as the glimmerings of a global civil society'.[19] For Falk, the crucial impetus for this emergent global order is from local sites of political struggle and organization looking beyond state parameters for more universal action and solutions.

Other perspectives follow much the same pattern of thinking. There is a distinct move within postcolonialism to more globalized perspectives, as illustrated by Phillip Darby in the previous chapter. For example, Arjun Appadurai, who has previously cautioned against conflating globalization, which he views as valid enough, with homogenization, writes of a 'global force' which is 'forever slipping in and through the cracks between states and borders'.[20] In a more recent article, he goes further along the global spectrum with his notion of an emergent 'postnational' world. While advancing certain caveats, Appadurai argues that we are in 'the process of moving to a global order in which the nation-state has become obsolete and other formations for allegiance and identity have taken place'. Even the United States, that bastion of patriotism and national allegiance, is 'awash with global diasporas' and is increasingly the exemplification of the postnational world.[21] Doreen Massey's postmodern geography critique develops a similar thesis, although it also highlights certain counter-tendencies and the dangers of universalizing. Although there is no single condition of postmodernity or globality, there has occurred

> a truly major re-shaping of the spatial organization of social relations at every level, from local to global. Each geographical 'place' in the world is being realigned in relation to the new global realities, their roles within the wider whole are being re-assigned, their boundaries dissolve as they are increasingly crossed by everything from investment flows, to cultural influences, to satellite TV networks.[22]

The postcolonial world, no less than the so-called postnational world of the West, is caught up in this new globalized space, no matter how diverse and contradictory it may appear.

Yet immediately we are confronted with a problem. The new global space may be seen to encompass both the postcolonial and 'postnational' worlds; however, in key respects these worlds are far apart. The communal and ethnic upheavals of the past few years in South Asia and Africa, and even in the 'postnational' world itself in the Balkans, suggest that if globalization is to have any purchase for much of the Third World, it cannot be simply on the basis of claims of 'postnationalism' and 'global civil society'. Further, the state is alive and vigorous in many parts of the Third World.[23] When it comes to a consideration of specific places in Africa, we need to proceed with caution when invoking the terms 'modernity' and 'globalization'. As various critics of globalization such as Ahmad, Colin Leys and Dirlik make plain, globalization has fairly obvious and drastic economic consequences for the more marginalized societies of the Third World such as those in Africa. These, in turn, have clear cultural implications. This is not difficult to concede if we keep in mind that an older paradigm concerning the dangers of Western cultural imperialism has advanced much the same argument. The precise relationship between the cultural and material realms of globalization will be explored later. For now, it will suffice to break down globalization into its component strands and then provide a benchmark for understanding modernity in the Third World against which we can range the material on globalization.

Globalization is constantly in danger of becoming a catch-all category that tends to lose any analytical rigour. What is labelled globalization is mostly a series of contemporaneous, not necessarily compatible, processes that have more or less coalesced around the feeling that we have entered a new historical phase. We can break down globalization under the following headings:

- *Economic* – related to the developments of late capitalism in production, distribution, exchange and investment which have increasingly taken on a monopoly, non-state character and are seen as structuring most of the economies of the world. Paul James's second proposition of dependency in the next chapter provides a fuller development of this economic dimension.

- *Governance* – referring to the various mechanisms evident in the UN system and regional integration which increasingly organize governing functions beyond and above the nation-state.

- *Civil Society* – at times running parallel to aspects of global governance and involving the spread of universal values and norms around the concepts of human rights, democracy, ecology, gender and ideas of 'world citizenship' carried forward by a myriad of interlocking, cross-national, non-government organizations and international law. Ideas about a universal process of democratization are relevant here.

- *Knowledge* – proceeding on the basis of the technological developments of late capitalism and referring to the realization of a 'global media village' in which communications and information networks are increasingly integrating the world – at least the Western world – into the same grid.

- *Cultural* – including both older notions of cultural imperialism (cultural transformation as an adjunct to economic globalization) and more contemporary ideas about cultural hybridity and creolization in which a 'world' or 'global culture' is emerging based on interconnected diasporas and increasingly multicultural, cosmopolitan societies. A related factor here – although it obviously feeds off economic globalization – is the rise of a global consumerism revolving around Western commodities.

Most of these dimensions clearly intersect; others, such as the economic and civil society components of globalization, hardly mesh. According to a materialist reading of globalization, all these facets basically proceed from the economic nature of late capitalism. However, outside this materialist perspective, there is much less coherence given to the component processes of globalization. This makes assessment precarious, the more so in the context of most Third World societies where not all of these aspects of globalization are prominent nor indeed evident. Certainly elites in most Third World societies take part in processes of global governance and the globalization of culture, economics, information and civil society: they have delegates and officials in Geneva and New York at the various UN agencies; they have access to the 'information superhighway' and other sources of global communications; they work and sometimes sit on the boards of multinational companies; they are part of the cross-cultural traffic in music, fashion and ideas. Even below the elite level, some Africans, for example, are involved in the global civil society through their activism in human rights, development and ecology movements, whether it be Oxfam, Amnesty International and Greenpeace or the many local affiliates of such groups. Yet one would need to concede that this still constitutes a small minority. In any case, involvement in a social movement and civil society does not mean that you cease to be subject to the perils of the state, or communal division for that matter. In the realm of everyday life that affects the mass of ordinary people, the intensity and reach of the facets of globalization listed above are not always so keenly felt or experienced. Certainly it is difficult to deny the impact of economic forces, from the onset of modernity to late capitalism. Beyond this realm, particularly in most of Africa, globalization tends to have much less purchase.

While one might accept that the category of the global has captured a powerful and indeed symptomatic aspect about modernity, it does so unevenly and selectively. Like most theory of a predominantly Western orientation, it picks up certain processes and developments pertaining to the First World and magnifies them beyond their specifically Western context. Thus, obvious symptoms of globalization such as European unification and multimedia communications (as exemplified by the Internet) are held up as key pointers to a world without borders when in fact they exhibit certain characteristics, such as trading strength or computer technology, not present in many parts of the Third World. A central difficulty lies in how to understand the phenomenon of modernity. Distinctions between modernity and late modernity and, indeed, postmodernity are difficult to delineate, yet they are necessary if we are to avoid a slippage between assumptions relevant to the West and conditions specific to the Third World in all its heterogeneity. If by modernity we are referring to the processes of change and transformation evident from the onset of the Industrial Revolution and the rise of capitalism, then late modernity is marked by the intensification, acceleration and increased reach of capitalist processes of production, distribution and consumption in the transnational era of the late twentieth century, attended by a greater reflexivity regarding the nature of modernity. Postmodernity is most often used to describe conditions of dislocation and flux, an unravelling of time and space brought on by the acceleration of modernity which ushers in an era of uncertainty and contingency. Some prefer to label late modernity or late capitalism *post*modernity; that is, a condition of indeterminacy and contradiction we are living through. In some respects the distinction between late modern and postmodern is one of emphasis and disposition relevant mostly to a Western experience; each refers to the same period and the increased speed and complexity of modernity. However, the postmodern draws certain theoretical conclusions from contemporary developments to characterize political and social relations that more strictly modernist thinkers such as Jürgen Habermas, Marshall Berman and Anthony Giddens would not share.[24] Regardless of such distinctions, it can be argued that understandings and definitions of both late modernity and postmodernity, as the latest stages in the evolution of modernity, display an unmistakably Western texture and proceed from a uniquely Western standpoint.

The implication of this is not that the late modern or postmodern is irrelevant to the Third World. Political space, by which is meant the increasing ability of (predominantly) Western processes to transcend time and distance, has become truly globalized through the intensified spread of capitalism under late modernity. Indeed, it is perhaps not coincidental that the turn to space and spatiality in academic enquiry has arisen at precisely the historical moment that globalization thinking has come to the fore. One could argue that it is precisely the idea of space, in both its material and metaphorical senses, that enables a conception of global politics. Both David Harvey and Fredric Jameson point to this when they argue that the triumph of space over time is particular to postmodernity, by which they mean that space is implicated in the very processes of globalization.[25] To think along global lines is to invoke politics as space, and an understanding of contemporary political space is increasingly the invocation of globalization. It is in this respect that late modern processes cannot help but affect the Third World even if it is not fully plugged into the global 'net'. To the extent that postmodernity tells us about indeterminacy and contingency under (late) modernity it has potentially useful insights for understanding modernity in the Third World, although it is useful to keep in mind Zygmunt Bauman's powerful argument that ambivalence and contingency have always been at the heart of modernity.[26] The argument advanced here is that we need to be careful how we characterize the experience of modernity in the Third World in the contemporary era (even if it does form part of an ill-defined 'global space'), or, more to the point, we need to proceed from a particularly Third World perspective rather than an assumption that what is observable from a Western vantage point is necessarily a *global* phenomenon; that is, a common, homogeneous experience.

We can put forward two working hypotheses on this basis. First, to the extent that one of the central premises of most globalization theories and scenarios is the commonality or homogenization of circumstance – that we are all experiencing global processes in the same manner and indeed at the same time – globalization is profoundly misleading in its characterization of a 'global condition'. To argue that globalization, particularly in its more obvious economic guise, affects the Third World and that we are all part of an interconnected 'global system' is significantly at variance with arguing that it produces the same effects. In this respect, there has been an unfortunate tendency in various global projections to compress the effects of contemporary processes on identity and culture so that both descriptions and prescriptions about developments in the Western world are too easily carried over into the Third World generally, often as an oversight. Second, if our concern is to understand the passage of modernity in the Third World and its effect on various non-Western identities more generally, then we need to acknowledge that for the most part, the modernity we are concerned with in the majority of Third World contexts is of a different order to the modernity theorized in many late modern or postmodern accounts. What is required is a critical *spatialized* account of modernity which takes into consideration uneven development.

As part of this endeavour, postcolonial critics such as Sankaran Krishna and Dirlik insist on a differentiated modernity in their critique of the relevance of the postmodern for the Third World. The idea here is that the currency of postmodernism in the West proceeds from a profound disillusionment with modernity, a disillusionment that is not necessarily present in or appropriate to developing societies which are still coming to terms with the modern and its challenge to the traditional and the premodern. In this reading, modernity in the Third World produces a different set of demands and opportunities, not the least being, as Dirlik points out, 'the attractions of modernization' to vast numbers in Third World populations.[27] Phillip Darby notes a similar tendency in postcolonial accounts which tend to overemphasize the rejection of modernity as part of their oppositional stance towards the West. We need to take into account here a divergent temporal and spatial framework in the experience of modernity in the Third World. Although modernity may truly be a global phenomenon in the sense that it touches all contemporary cultures, there is, as Jean Chesneaux has persuasively argued, a 'modernity differential' between the Third World and the West.[28] We cannot afford to lose sight of this differential when it comes to a consideration of how particular societies experience modern processes.

Consequently, while one can argue that we all manoeuvre within the modern and the global in the accelerated context of late modernity, specific cultures and peoples across both North and South all interact with and make sense of these processes differently. In fact, the transformations and dislocations that affect contemporary identities under the banner of the global are both of a different cast, and more intense and ambiguous, in the various Third World contexts, where we tend to witness what Jonathan Friedman terms a 'consumption of modernity'[29] constituted by interlocking processes of tradition, resistance, difference, hybridity, change and appropriation. In this respect, the global frames identity in the many sites of the Third World, but not necessarily in the way envisaged in globalization discourses operating around an assumption of homogenization. The global is useful in directing our attention towards what is generally distinctive about the late modern age, particularly from a Western angle. However, globalization tends to reinforce the peripheral location of societies such as those in Africa in dominant discourses about the contemporary world and is thus unable to steer us towards a more specific and fundamental understanding of the everyday navigation of modernity there.

Thus, the widespread conviction that we live in an age of globalization is inflated. Too often the various discourses over-globalize a world situation in which certain global processes are of increased significance. The attempt to arrive at a holistic understanding of recent transformations, particularly evident in Robertson's desire to construct typologies and phases of globalization, too often strays into the over-determined. To be fair, other writers advance qualifications in order to mitigate a false universalism. Featherstone, for one, emphasizes diversity and plurality in his account. 'Global culture' is to be understood in a plural sense; there is little prospect of a unified world culture, albeit the import of much of his analysis would seem to suggest otherwise. Appadurai, for instance, reminds us that globalization is constituted around disjuncture as much as homogenization and conjuncture of world cultures and ideologies, although one could reasonably point out that his emphasis on disjuncture has as much to do with his explicitly postmodern reading as with a sense of what is happening on the ground in various parts of the world. Like Cox, Appadurai at least recognizes that the global forces are inherently unstable and hence not necessarily facilitating a smooth passage towards a standardized global (read Western) culture. Even Robertson allows for 'uncertainty' in the current phase of globalization, particularly in light of the 'arrival' and 'inclusion' of the Third World. Yet the broad brush, the sweeping generalization, the creeping ethnocentrism – the latter no more evident than in Robertson's notion of the arrival and inclusion of the Third World into contemporary globalization – too often mark such writing. Allowance is at times made for the local, some space is accorded to the particular, yet the move is more often than not abstract, the reference non-specific. A good example here is Featherstone. He rightly points to the problem of who is defining the local culture, and for what purposes. He goes on to claim that 'We are slowly becoming aware that the West is both a particular in itself and also constitutes the universal point of reference in relation to which others recognize themselves as particularities'.[30] Unfortunately the universal point of reference becomes just that; it subsumes the many particulars. Featherstone admits as much in positing the other as particular only in relation to the universal West. The specific point of reference, the West, becomes universalized.

Particularities are also left out of account in Robertson's schema. Thus, his claim that gender, ethnic and racial considerations are rendering the concept of the individual more complex is made very much from the Western standpoint. Where exactly is the life of the individual complicated? That ethnic and racial expressions are seen as a problem for the ethic of individualism can only proceed from an understanding that the 'concept of the individual' is somehow the universal norm. Yet, if we look to Africa and India for example, one could plausibly argue that individual considerations have rendered older concepts of community, caste and ethnicity more complex. This is the import of much fictional writing from Chinua Achebe to Vikram Seth. If we switch the tables in this fashion, it is difficult to view the current phase of globalization as having the degree of coherence and connectedness that Robertson sees. Indeed, one can legitimately ask, to what extent are racial or ethnic identities in Africa and the Third World a product of contemporary globalization? Robertson is partly correct in suggesting that the dislocations brought about by economic globalization have fuelled ethnic and racial explosions. The tensions that have arisen between the global imperatives of oil exploration and drilling, and local agitation for indigenous rights in southern Nigeria is a case in point. Paul James provides an elaboration of this case study in his chapter. By the same token, one would have to concede that such expressions of indigenous or tribal identity have a dynamic which predates contemporary global processes.

This tendency to view globalization from the vantage point of the West has led critics such as Massey and Stuart Hall to note how 'unglobal' is the perspective from which the nature of globalization has been analysed.[31] How global processes are played out on the ground in a specific locale, be it Lagos, Dar es Salaam and the myriad of villages in sub-Saharan Africa, or in the so-called 'Fourth World' conditions evident in Central and South American cities such as Mexico City and São Paulo, is left out of account despite the implicit assumption in most analyses that the impact is pervasive and homogeneous. No one doubts that globalized modernity is a real phenomenon in these places, even though at times modernity may constitute anything from 'Green Revolution' technology to the humble transistor radio or bicycle rather than CNN, the Internet or the TGV fast train. Although relations of space and time are affected by all these modern innovations, obviously there is a vast difference in degree, not to mention a significant economic differential in terms of access to these technologies. Even so, the mere presence of such tools of modernity does not inevitably result in a uniform reception. Nor, in fact, does the presence of new technologies in Third World locations necessarily affect local populations directly. A good example is the French space base of Kourou in Guyana. Such space technology is often said to bring the world together in making us aware of our common destiny on 'Spaceship Earth', but the simple fact remains that only the rich and powerful can finance and maintain such projects, and they remain outside the reach of the poorer countries, even those that host them. Indeed, as Chesneaux points out, they may work to 'consolidate the international hierarchies of our planet':

> From above the clouds we can observe, with all the detail of a laboratory test, the Amazon on fire, Abyssinia starving, Afghanistan suffering, Armenia struck by an earthquake at the very moment the Mir satellite station was proudly overflying it and sending its triumphal messages to the open-mouthed gapers below. From high in the sky, the wretched of the earth seem far away.[32]

The inability to view globalization from a more grounded, local perspective is a significant oversight by globalization theorists. Ulf Hannerz has highlighted this in a series of critiques which bring to the fore the local. He argues that a central difficulty in assessing the influence and effects of global cultural flows is trying to understand the sense that people in a given place make of these flows. Assumptions are often made without much direct experience. 'The meaning of the transnational cultural flows is thus in the eye of the beholder; what he [*sic*] sees we generally know little about.'[33] The consequences of these processes also need to be understood as they unfold over time. Elsewhere he posits the same problem in broader terms: 'There is surprisingly little of a postcolonial ethnography of how Third World people see themselves and their society, its past, present and future, and its place in the world; a cultural analysis of their fantasies and what they know for a fact.'[34] A global analysis, without a specific and nuanced sense of time and place, merely replicates the Western experience.

Even if we concede the existence of a 'global condition', the key question remains: where exactly does the Third World in general fit into this globalization scenario? There would seem to be three basic representations of the Third World's place in late modernity. It needs to be pointed out from the outset that whole peoples and cultures, particularly those in Africa, are mostly ignored in this literature. Certain references are made to a cross-cultural traffic in music and fashion, but aside from such attempts to suggest an African presence in global space, Africa simply does not figure in accounts of globalization, except as an adjunct to the Third World in general. Even here, the understanding of the Third World tends to be amorphous and poorly informed. It is thus necessary to explore conceptions of the place of the Third World in globalization discourses which by extension include, however tenuously, the African continent.

First, the Third World is mostly either incorporated by default or simply ignored. In this respect it becomes a significant blind spot in global projections, a repository for what Jameson would view as the 'political unconscious' of the global narrative: silences and omissions which act as 'repressions' or 'strategies of containment'.[35] Robertson's 'inclusion' of the Third World in the latest phase of globalization would be one instance of this. Similarly, Cox points to the liberal/*laissez-faire* paradigm, preaching, as it does, the virtues of a global free market and the necessity for various structural adjustment programmes as an instance of incorporating the non-Western world into the global camp. Even where it is incorporated into the new globality on its own terms, there is an insufficient attempt to distinguish the great heterogeneity of the Third World. The result is that the Third World is understood quite selectively and with reference to what are essentially atypical examples such as Brazil, Mexico or the newly industrialized countries. The Third World is thus flattened into a single dimension and read off mostly unrepresentative case studies. What is distinctive about Hong Kong or parts of Brazil does not equate to much of sub-Saharan Africa.

Part of the problem here relates to the inadequacy of the rubric 'Third World',[36] particularly when it comes to a consideration of Africa. Cities across developing countries may appear, as King argues, locked into an interconnecting global space,[37] yet this is not true of all cities or *all parts* of these cities, or of the many villages and towns outside their orbit. There are different modernities operating in these sites which do not yet make for 'one world'. It is only of late that the number of people across the globe who live in the city has exceeded the number who live in the countryside. In fact, if one were to remove the First World from the picture, the countryside would still predominate as the most common form of 'modern' living. In Africa, the move to the cities has been unfolding since colonial times, with the village or rural town still significant. The limits of Western modernity in Africa are evident here, as is the need to temper assumptions about globalization and the importance of cities in societies which have an important rural population.

The second representation of the Third World in globalization discourses is typically postmodern. Here, the significance of the Third World is located in its otherness and its capacity to work as a discursive rupture in the narrative of Western dominance. In this approach, the Third World is seen mostly in terms of a metaphorical, representational space on the outside of, or opposite to, the West. The Third World becomes what Homi Bhabha (borrowing from de Certeau) has referred to in a different context as a 'non-place' in the discourse of modernity. It is not merely *terra nulla*, but a 'time-lag' in the understanding of modernity, 'a lag which all histories must encounter in order to make a beginning'.[38] In this respect, the wish is not to ostensibly deny its place in the modern, but to reinscribe its *otherness* and emphasize its difference. It exists on the outside of globalization/ modernity as an other which forces the global and the modern to encounter itself and interrogate and interrupt its assumptions about the non-European world. The desire behind such a reading, evident in Fredric Jameson and Ashis Nandy, for example (and prevalent across post-colonialism), is actually to empower the Third World and cast it as a subversive place of resistance to Western hegemony. Thus, Santiago Colas argues that part of the Third World's 'paradoxical double function' in Jameson's theory of postmodernism is to exist outside the cultural logic of late capitalism. In this context the Third World is characterized by Jameson as either 'eliminated' by late modernity, or somehow untainted by and oppositional to this same process.[39] The same view is apparent in Featherstone's notion that one possible response to globalization is an immersion in the local: 'remaining undiscovered' and ignoring the outside as strategies open to local cultures in the Third World.[40]

In a similar vein, Ashis Nandy, not himself a theorist of globalization but one who subscribes to the existence of a 'global civilization', has argued that the Third World has become the 'other' of the West and that this otherness opens up, theoretically at least, many possibilities, one of which is that the Third World 'holds in trust the rejected selves of the First and Second Worlds'.[41] Nandy opens his critique with the observation that 'We are living in a global civilization, even if it does not look to us sufficiently global. This civilization has certain features and "ground rules" and those who want to consolidate, transcend or dismantle it, must first identify them.' The first criterion of this global civilization is that 'all surviving civilizations define themselves with reference to it'. For Nandy, 'the recovery of the other selves and cultures and communities, *selves not defined by the dominant consciousness*, may turn out to be the first task of social criticism and political activism and the first responsibility of intellectual stock-taking in the first decades of the coming century'.[42]

Both Nandy and Jameson, in attempting to confront the Third World directly as part of their taking globalization to task, present us with the flip side of the dominant tendency outlined in the first representation, which is to repress or incorporate the Third World into globalization. Yet this flip side is also problematic: by placing the Third World outside modernity in some mystical or pure state of 'non-modernity', they are effectively not only denying its engagement with the modern, but setting up an untenable binarism which effectively marginalizes the Third World. The danger here is that the Third World becomes merely a narrative or representational technique of deconstruction which systematically ignores the key factor of how the many cultures of the Third World *already* navigate the processes of the modern and the global, albeit to differing degrees. It is one thing for the marginalization of the Third World to serve as a discomfort to global-ization; it is quite another to imply for this 'non-place' an existence outside the influence of global processes. At the very least it would seem a peculiar denial of the economic reach of global capitalism. Such representations of the Third World as a 'romanticized location of Otherness' are also at work, as Paul James reminds us in Chapter 3, in Western mass-cultural images, although these have a less explicit postmodern sensibility, and indeed intersect with older European notions of orientalism.

A third approach to the place of the Third World in globalization is propelled by a more traditional concern to expose the inequality and injustice of the contemporary North–South relationship. Not surprisingly, the emphasis here is on the material basis of this relationship and the economic structure of globalization which underpins it. Representations of globalization are on surer ground here. In this account, globalization is accepted as the logic of late modernity, and Western hegemony is seen as driving global processes. However, the Third World is not left out of account as either a 'non-place' or an 'inclusion'. Rather, the marginal and peripheral position of the Third World is directly confronted and held up as indicating the unevenness of globalization's reach. The critique here is not of the existence of globalization *per se* but of the failure to properly address the exploited position of the Third World. Thus Ahmad regarding the Third World in general and Leys focusing on Africa specifically both attempt to temper the celebratory, triumphal tone of global capitalism. Ahmad argues that globalization leads not to homogenization between and within the First and Third Worlds, but to increased differentiation between the haves and the have-nots in the global system with the gaps likely to increase as globalization intensifies.[43] Similarly, Leys's summary of the 'African collapse' paints a bleak portrait of economic weakness and exploitation, with the 'logic of global capitalism' merely reinforcing Africa's decline.[44]

This critical approach to the homogenizing tendency of globalization is in many respects an improvement on the previous two outlined. It at least addresses what Paul James in the next chapter terms the problem of 'structural wretchedness'. Yet the argument can at times lead into certain dead-ends. The very pessimism of the analysis raises important implications for agency which ironically have the effect of underestimating whatever space subjects in the Third World may currently have in mediating and, at times, mitigating the combined effects of modernity and globalization. Part of the difficulty lies precisely in the structural emphasis of the critique; there is a 'logic' to the system which tends to dictate a subordinate function to the Third World. The Marxist influence is obvious here, and while it certainly drives an oppositional sensibility which is directed to resisting global capitalism, it tends by the rationale of its own argument to constrict the space for individual and collective action. This is apparent in the very characterization of globalization in such analyses, which portray the reach of global forces in such a comprehensive and destructive manner that it is difficult to envisage a way out. The effects of globalization on the Third World, in particular on Africa, are represented so pessimistically that despite the calls for resistance it is almost impossible to imagine what space could exist for any effective counter-offensive. The type of reasoning evident here can lead to a view of the Third World as irredeemable.

These three representations of the Third World's place in globalization are only partly useful in giving us an idea of how the various cultures and identities in Africa and beyond confront and make sense of the global forces of modernity in the here and now. Certainly the second and third – the postmodern and the material-economic approaches – contribute to our knowledge of the Third World's position. The radical commitment of the materialist approach is perhaps a necessary initial step in exposing the myth of globalization's homogeneity. Likewise, the postmodern approach reminds us of the complexity and ambiguity of the Third World's place within the modern. However, one could argue that the material account over-emphasizes the very real systemic considerations which need to be addressed in any analysis of the North–South divide. On the other hand, the postmodern reading is perhaps too detached from what is happening on the ground and experiences what one critic has termed a 'distancing effect' from material realities.[45] Both, in their own ways, provide little sense of a way forward out of the respective impasse they each describe. Further, they each strike me as inadequate in themselves in providing a handle with which to understand the reception of the modern and the global in the everyday experience of peoples and cultures in Africa.

I would instead point to an intermediate path that takes into account the material realities of modernity, realities which have long been present on the African continent for instance, while according a prominent place to the subjective and the cultural. In this respect we need to avoid the implicit reductionism of Dirlik, whose statement that postcolonialism has 'rendered into problems of subjectivity and epistemology concrete and material problems of the everyday world' reveals not only a binary understanding of the interconnections between the material and the subjective but a desire to reinscribe the material at the expense of the cultural.[46] 'Concrete problems of the everyday world' involve questions of subjectivity and identity as much as they refer to material considerations. Indeed, I would argue that *each resides in the other*. Subjects in the Third World (or anywhere else for that matter) cannot simply imagine away material barriers of inequality and dependency. On the other hand, such material factors do not deny a space for navigation and innovation on the part of individuals and cultures in marginalized positions of power. Paul James suggests a similar dialectic in his elaboration of dependency as a process of subjection. In this respect, it may well be that the insidious process of globalized modernity and its attendant cultural Westernization can simultaneously produce a situation of economic marginalization and local indigenization and appropriation. The two are by no means mutually exclusive.

In this I can only follow the lead of Michel de Certeau, David Harvey, James Scott and Terence Ranger in pointing towards the spaces of agency which exist within hegemonic conditions of power and direct attention to what is made of modernity rather than simply what modernity does to those who are subject to it. In light of the manner in which both globalization and international relations have tended to gloss over these spaces, it is important to excavate them and establish their importance. Further, pointing to the necessity for resistance and the insidiousness of globalization does not obviate the need to acknowledge the local strategies *already in place* which empower Third World agents not so much to resist modernity outright as to modify, distort or bend it to their particular desires via processes of appropriation, indigenization and creolization. Ranger has long argued for the creative and resilient pluralism of African societies during and after colonial capitalism which have witnessed 'cheerful adaptations to urban life, the innovation of new structures of fraternity and association, the evolution of an urban popular culture', as well as the capacity of religions to transform themselves.[47] Even if Chesneaux is correct in arguing that politics has been reduced to 'navigation by sight' under globalized modernity so that people can only manage or steer global forces rather than reject or resist them,[48] this 'navigation politics' allows for a significant range of possibilities and manoeuvring under globalization, indicating the existence of a space for agency. Finally, 'othering' the Third World merely distances it further from the mediation of modernity that takes place so that concepts of difference, authenticity and essentialism which often lurk beneath constructions of otherness are as misleading as the notion that globalization inevitably leads to a homogenized global culture.

In this context, we can proceed by acknowledging that globalization, particularly in its economic and cultural guises, certainly informs and frames identity and subjectivity in the Third World. To deny this is to further marginalize the place of non-Western cultures; to place them off the map as it were. However, this is by no means a passive process that involves compliance to the external and destruction of the internal. Modernity is 'consumed', not merely as some fetishized commodity, but as an appropriated, hybridized feature of everyday life. In this respect it becomes as much a part of the local and particular as the traditional and 'indigenous'.

The argument to date has revolved around the inability of globalization discourses to see the trees for the wood. In highlighting modernity's expanded reach, the global becomes a blanket thrown over the various cultures of the world in the process of standardization. Certain features and processes of modern life are internationalized from a narrow Western experience and standpoint so that they *seem* to cover all the world. This point of perception is crucial. The undeniable veneer of globalization is mistaken for something more deep-seated and comprehensive. Bryan Turner has made a crucial distinction in this respect between 'thin' and 'thick' globalization in the context of ideas about 'global citizenship'. The world is mostly undergoing 'thin' globalization, which Turner equates to the somewhat rarefied and artificial experience of commuting between transit lounges of modern airports. There is an unmistakable sameness but it is mostly superficial and locked into a particular circuit. Once you step outside this global transit lounge and journey into everyday life, you constantly experience difference.[49] Chesneaux has utilized the same metaphor in his discussion of the 'jet set' of modernity, the privileged, happy few who, from 'up in the altitudes where they spend a good deal of their lives', 'identify totally with the institutions, systems and currents of the wired planet'.[50] The metaphor of the transit lounge is an apt departure point for a consideration of the view from the ground in the Third World. Rather than develop the arguments in favour of the local and the particular at a general level, I will explore two episodes in what de Certeau has called 'the practice of everyday life'.[51] These brief snippets of everyday life will attempt to chart some instances of the consumption of modernity in the Third World. Framed from differing angles – one sociological, one 'postdevelopmental' – they are attuned to some of the possibilities and risks of encountering the modern outside the transit lounge of globalization. They are by no means definitive but they at least serve to indicate the heterogeneity of experience in worlds caught up in, but not totally captured by global, Western processes.

'*La Sape' in Brazzaville, the Congo/Kinshasa, Zaïre.*[52] Brazzaville-Kinshasa, cities that share their respective countries' borders, constitute what materialist critics such as Leys would consider quintessential African terrain: poverty and despair, shanty towns, structural adjustment programmes, political repression, cultural Westernization.[53] Modernity looms large in what Simone and Hecht term this most desperate of African settings. Indeed, looked at from the outside, the Western commodification of these African cities would appear to confirm the globalization of modernity. The most striking aspect of this commodification is the fetish for Western designer labels, predominantly French but also from other parts of Europe. But this fetish is more than mere imitation of Western taste; an indicator of African incorporation into Western modernity. Because it dovetails with traditional BaKongo beliefs concerning wealth, power and outward appearance, this fetish for Western clothes and dress takes on another meaning, one which suggests that the consumption of modernity that takes place evokes a more complex and ambiguous navigation of outside processes which feed into local strategies for self-definition and empowerment.

'La Sape' derives from the French *saper*, which signifies to dress elegantly. During the 1970s, several clubs called *'clubs des jeunes premiers'* sprang up in Brazzaville, principally among lower-class BaKongo. Familiar with the 'outside' world of French modernity, the members of these clubs, the *sapeurs*, expressed a strong desire to consume the fruits of French fashion (St Laurent, Gaultier, Chanel, Esprit). Eventually, these *sapeurs* became so widespread that an institution was coined to describe them: 'La Sape', or Société des Ambianeurs et des Personnes Élégantes. According to Simone and Hecht, 'sape' pervades Congolese society and can be seen at religious services and 'tribal' events, worn by priests and village chiefs as a sign of power. Interestingly, despite the specific class and ethnic origins, La Sape has come to encompass a more widespread self-definition among the Congolese and Zaïreans.

What does the institution of La Sape amount to against the backdrop of modernity and desperation in Brazzaville and Kinshasa? From the outside it would appear a surrender – and a slavish one at that – to Western consumerism. Yet, as both Friedman, and Simone and Hecht point out, there is a more significant redefinition of tradition and identity going on that complicates a straightforward scenario of submission to the West. There is evidence of an underlying historical continuity in the consumption of modernity that takes place by La Sape. The sacred BaKongo concept of Tsala, of looking good as a symbol of 'life force', well-being and hence power ('you are what you wear'), feeds into a tradition, according to Simone and Hecht, which prizes fine clothing, elaborate hairdos, comportment and the general refinement of one's appearance. As Friedman notes, 'power is a "force" that provides both health and wealth and its differential presence is expressed in the hierarchy itself. This is truly the land of "la distinction".'[54] Clothes make the person, and this is perhaps truer in the Congo and Zaïre than elsewhere. Friedman sees this fetish for these trappings of modernity as a cultural strategy of appropriation which expresses not only 'local structures of desire' for the modern, but a reworking of traditional beliefs and practices within which modernity is consumed and contemporary identity is updated. Even if we concede that this transformation of tradition takes place as part of the integration of the Congo and Zaïre 'into the French franc zone of the world economy', the manipulation and usage made of global products of Western origin by the

[handwritten: BUT it is western fashions being interpreted, not the other way around.]

local Congolese and Zaïreans in their everyday lives inscribes a crucial difference and distinctiveness in the passage of modernity. People in Paris, Brazzaville, Hong Kong, São Paulo and Melbourne may all make a fetish of Gaultier and St Laurent, but this global fetish is consumed in particular situations and with reference to distinct reference points and cultural strategies in which the interplay between history, tradition and material position makes for differentiated outcomes. Even Jean-Paul Gaultier himself, stepping outside the global circuit of fashion shows and transit lounges, would encounter difference in the reception of globalized modernity in Brazzaville, beyond the obvious economic disparities between North and South. It is precisely the revitalization of tradition within a broader process of the indigenization of modernity that many globalization discourses tend to ignore or downplay as insignificant. Moreover, such processes are invisible in international relations scholarship.

Women's Cooperatives, Mashonaland, Zimbabwe.[55] In what Christine Sylvester has labelled Zimbabwe's 'terrain of contradictory development', women and cooperatives are perched somewhat precariously between competing pressures of global economic liberalization, 'progress', state socialism, traditional patriarchal values and poverty. This is very much a post-developmental terrain – beyond traditional conceptions of modernization where attempts to tap local traditions and agents create an ambiguous space for 'partnership' within the global economic system. Women's cooperatives occupy what Sylvester notes as 'positions in between and marginal to old and new' which 'struggle for space in Zimbabwe's inherited matrix of identities, as does a state that is itself multicentered and cross-pressured'.[56] The political economy of Zimbabwe provides a backdrop against which it is clear that cooperatives and especially the female workforce are not doing particularly well despite state attempts to promote equal rights and the advancement of both women and cooperatives. According to Sylvester, of the collective cooperatives she studied in 1988, 'not one had successfully done away with inherited practices of sexually divided labour'.[57] In strict economic terms, cooperatives as a whole, and particularly those run by women, are certainly struggling. Yet within such a bleak environment, the traces of agency and the navigation of 'old and new', even from such a marginalized position, are visible.

In a particular study of women-run silk-making cooperatives in Mabvuku, Mashonaland, Sylvester outlines the attempts by Zimbabwean women to advance their cooperatives by applying to the EEC Micro-projects Program for funding. It is in the interaction between women's cooperatives and the wider network of modernity (represented by international agencies such as the EEC[58]) that we witness the mediation of Western ideas about development, progress and even feminism by African women in their everyday practices. The material barriers are immense: the women are economically marginal and the lack of formal education (particularly in English) hinders the effective exploitation of EEC funding procedures. They rely on two Greek women as sponsors to put their case to the EEC investigation group that comes to assess the viability of the project. The EEC is initially reluctant and cynical: it highlights certain 'economic realities' and fears that the cooperative venture is too reliant on the Greek women who have helped set it up. The Zimbabwean government itself is suspicious and has delayed approval of sufficient land to make the cooperative viable. Nevertheless, the Zimbabwean women, through their silk-making cooperatives, 'become entangled in identity-shifting negoti-ations with international donors'[59] in which they learn to speak a different language for the betterment of their local position. Sylvester sees these 'reginas' as involved in a discourse of cooperation which is not only empowering, but as worthy of attention as any macro study of regime cooperation in international relations. Indeed, the international/global and local enter a dialogue in this episode of intersubjective relations. Not only are the local reginas obviously affected by regimes affiliated to the global political economy, but in the instance of the EEC these reginas also manage to influence the policies of this international regime.

Thus, the proper Western patron–client relationship is bypassed; the quite strict, authoritative rules slanted towards serious business enterprises are overcome. This is particularly evident in the fact that the EEC funding programme eventually gives generous funding to the cooperatives despite the fact that they fall outside official notions of sound business practice. Interestingly, the Greek women are able to convince *Greek* EEC delegates to back the Zimbabwean women. Sylvester sees this as another instance of 'family' values cutting across institutional rules (the cooperatives are seen by the participants as 'family enterprises'). For the Zimbabwean women themselves, a process of empowerment takes place. Also, the women have a dual sense of 'cooperation'. They have an instrumental view that allows the Greek women to negotiate on their behalf for EEC funding. This facilitates a more non-instrumental understanding of cooperation in which the women, through their cooperatives, share skills and nourish each other's desire for connection and autonomy. As noted by Sylvester, in the process of the local–global interaction between the EEC and the Zimbabwean women's cooperatives, a 'strange cooperation emerges across differences': 'People who have no canonical right to narrate issues of inter-national cooperation do so anyway. Subjectivities become mobile. Funds are dispensed to the "wrong" identity.'[60] This indicates that the local women, with the help of their sponsors, have managed to mould global economic processes to their ends.

The turn to the global opens up a panorama which invites us to think anew conceptions of self, society and politics. In this respect it opens up on to a greater ontological terrain. It challenges international relations to move out of its traditional bunker and look on a radically transformed world, in both conceptual and actual terms. While it is true that both international relations and globalization discourses tend to share a Western sensibility which presents them with obvious difficulties in coming to terms with the place of the Third World, their differing trajectories (the global as against the state) afford them crucially different vantage points. The focus of this chapter has been to highlight a common margin in both international relations and globalization: the Third World. However, it has also indicated that the global illuminates at least two key edges beyond the field of vision of traditional international relations: that there is life beyond the state and that politics is increasingly seen as the 'invocation of spatiality'.[61] Let me conclude by advancing a few comments on both counts.

In spite of blind spots and repressions regarding the Third World, globalization discourses home in on a landscape where questions of culture, identity and subjectivity are central to social and political analysis. Gathered around the pivot of modernity, such questions attempt to make sense of a world in which it is taken for granted that established boundaries and borders are, if not transformed, then at least in flux. The contrast with mainstream international relations could not be greater.[62] Revolving as it does around the state and associated questions of order and power, international relations has only grudgingly come to acknowledge globalization as a key process in world politics. In fact, it is revealing that when it has attempted to address the global, it has mostly done so from the perspective of the state and the challenges globalization poses it. Even where globalization is taken on board as a significant feature of contemporary world politics, the instinct is to position it in terms of the continued legitimacy or relevance of the state. It is as if international relations continues to be stuck in the groove of the state, even where it is prepared to move towards a more extensive notion of 'international' politics. Reading globalization discourses puts into relief how attached international relations is to the traditional notion of political space as bounded by the state.

Globalization also accentuates the increased significance of 'space' and 'spatiality' in contemporary academic enquiry. By way of social theory and postmodern geography, the 'spatial vogue'[63] has served to renovate the architecture of politics, problematizing the previous ascendancy of historicism and temporality. As already argued, the emphasis on space has gone hand in hand with a rethinking of politics along global lines and an embracing of identity as a relational interaction between global and local processes, as is evidenced in the work of Friedman, Hannerz and Massey. Spatial metaphors have come to dominate the language of analysis: mapping, landscape, place, (subject) position, location, situation or situated, centre/margin, inside/outside. This suggests that traditional questions of political belonging and being have taken on a complexion in which the previously dominant category of the state (as a bounded, territorial entity) has diminished in stature in the face of an array of spatialities wherein cultures and individuals interact with one another.

This idea of space is both real and metaphorical; at once 'located' and contextualized, yet also transgressive. It constitutes both a notion of place and position and a more symbolic or imaginary realm of signification and belonging. It invites us to make sense of social and political life with reference to the simultaneity and complexity of experience, from the local to the global level. The very canvas of globalization, in all its manifestations, allows, indeed encourages in some critical discourses, the charting of multiple spatialities between the local and the global. This canvas includes the state as but one variable and manifestation of spatiality. Against this vastly expanded backdrop of political space, international relations and its traditional agenda can only appear impoverished. Once again, an engagement with globalization unsettles international relations, reinforcing the belief that there is life after the state.

Notes

I am indebted to Phillip Darby, Anthony Elliott and Paul James for reading this chapter and providing useful suggestions, many of which have been incorporated.

1. See Aijaz Ahmad, *In Theory: Classes. Nations. Literature* (London and New York, Verso, 1992), pp. 304–11.

2. R. B. J. Walker, *Inside/Outside: International Relations as Political Theory* (Cambridge, Cambridge University Press, 1993). Richard Devetak also notes in a recent article that both the critical theory and poststructural schools in international relations converge, in their respective revisions of the project of modernity, on the question of the constitution of boundaries and their attempted closure in traditional international relations. See 'The project of modernity and international relations theory', *Millennium*, 24:1 (1995), p. 47.

3. Devetak, 'The project of modernity and international relations theory', pp. 27–8.

4. Mike Featherstone, 'Global and local cultures' in Jon Bird, Barry Curtis, Tim Putnam, George Robertson and Lisa Tickner (eds), *Mapping the Futures: Local Cultures, Global Change* (London and New York, Routledge, 1993), p. 170.

5. Roland Robertson, 'Globality, global culture and images of world order' in Hans Haferkamp and Neil J. Smelser (eds), *Social Change and Modernity* (Berkeley and Los Angeles, University of California Press, 1992), p. 409.

6. Anthony D. King, *Global Cities, Post-Imperialism and the Internationalization of London* (London and New York, Routledge, 1990), p. 4 and *Urbanism, Colonialism, and the World-Economy: Cultural and Spatial Formations of the World Urban System* (London and New York, Routledge, 1990), pp. 2, 100.

7. Frank J. Lechner, 'Cultural aspects of the modern world-system' in William H. Swatos Jr (ed.), *Religious Politics in Global and Comparative Perspective* (Westport, CT, Greenwood Press, 1989), p. 11.

8. Mike Featherstone, 'Global culture: an introduction' in Mike Featherstone (ed.), *Global Culture: Nationalism, Globalization and Modernity* (London, Newbury Park and New Delhi, Sage Publications, 1990), p. 6.

9. Robertson, 'Globality, global culture, and images of world order', pp. 395, 396, 403, 405.

10. Roland Robertson, 'Mapping the global condition: globalization as the central concept' in Featherstone (ed.), *Global Culture,* p. 27. See also his attempt to construct theoretical typologies of images of world order in Robertson, 'Globality, global culture and images of world order', pp. 404–9.

11. Fredric Jameson, *Postmodernism, or, The Cultural Logic of Late Capitalism* (London and New York, Verso, 1991), p. 49.

12. Immanuel Wallerstein, *Geopolitics and Geoculture: Essays on the Changing World-System* (Cambridge and Paris, Cambridge University Press and Éditions de la Maison des Sciences

de l'Homme, 1991), p. 166 and *passim*. For a critique of this conversion to culture, see Roy Boyne, 'Culture and the world-system' in Featherstone (ed.), *Global Culture*. See also Wallerstein's reply in the same volume: 'Culture is the world-system: a reply to Boyne'.

13. Robert W. Cox, 'Global perestroika' in Ralph Miliband and L. Panitch (eds), *The Socialist Register 1992* (London, Merlin Press, 1992), pp. 30, 34–41.

14. Stephen J. Rosow, 'The forms of internationalization: representation of Western culture on a global scale', *Alternatives*, 15:3 (1990), 288–94.

15. See, for instance, John J. Mearsheimer, 'Back to the future: instability in Europe after the cold war', *International Security*, 15:1 (1990), 5–56, who displays an unashamed nostalgia for the certainty of the Cold War and confidently expects a return to power politics after the warm inner glow of the 'new world order'.

16. See Devetak's overview of critical theory perspectives in 'The project of modernity and international relations theory', pp. 35–6.

17. Richard Falk, *Explorations at the Edge of Time: The Prospects for World Order* (Philadelphia, Temple University Press in association with the United Nations University, Tokyo, 1992), p. 103.

18. Ibid., p. 123.

19. Ibid., p. 124.

20. Arjun Appadurai, 'Disjuncture and difference in the global cultural economy' in Featherstone (ed.), *Global Culture*, pp. 307, 366.

21. Arjun Appadurai, 'Patriotism and its futures', *Public Culture*, 5:3 (1993), 421–4.

22. Doreen Massey, 'A place called home?', *New Formations*, 17 (1992), 6.

23. See the chapter by Beverly Blaskett and Loong Wong, 'Manipulating space in a postcolonial state: the case of Malaysia' in Joseph A. Camilleri, Anthony P. Jarvis and Albert J. Paolini (eds), *The State in Transition: Reimagining Political Space* (Boulder, CO and London, Lynne Rienner Publishers, 1995), for an account of how a vigorous postcolonial state such as Malaysia can manipulate political space to suit its own ends. This, at times, entails restricting outside processes or at other times turning them to the state's advantage.

24. See Jürgen Habermas, *The Philosophical Discourse of Modernity* (Cambridge, MA, MIT Press, 1987); Marshall Berman, *All That is Solid Melts into Air: The Experience of Modernity* (New York, Simon and Schuster, 1982); and Anthony Giddens, *The Consequences of Modernity* (Cambridge, UK, Polity, 1990).

25. See Jameson, *Postmodernism* and David Harvey, 'From space to place and back again: reflections on the condition of postmodernity' in Bird *et al.* (eds), *Mapping the Futures*, p. 23.

26. See Zygmunt Bauman, *Modernity and Ambivalence* (Cambridge, UK, Polity Press, 1990).

27. Arif Dirlik, 'The postcolonial aura: Third World criticism in the age of global capitalism', *Critical Inquiry*, 20:Winter (1994), 328–56 (p. 337). See also Sankaran Krishna, 'The importance of being ironic: a postcolonial view on critical international relations', *Alternatives*, 18 (1993), 385–417 (p. 388).

28. Jean Chesneaux, *Brave Modern World: The Prospects for Survival* (London, Thames and Hudson, 1992), p. 57.

29. This notion of modernity being consumed is developed by Jonathan Friedman in 'Being in the world: globalization and localization' in Featherstone (ed.), *Global Culture*, pp. 311–25.

30. Featherstone, 'Global culture: an introduction', p. 12.

31. Massey, 'A place called home?', p. 10 and Stuart Hall, 'The local and the global: globalization and ethnicity' in Anthony D. King (ed.), *Culture, Globalization and the World-System: Contemporary Conditions for the Representation of Identity* (London, Macmillan, 1991), pp. 24–5. It is interesting to note that in an earlier piece, Hall, reflecting somewhat autobiographically, advances the provocative notion that marginality and migranthood become both centred and *the* representative (post)modern experience. What Hall says of blacks and migrants in London may well be true *of London*. Yet to what extent does it capture a more general global condition? In this respect, one needs to critically ask how centred people in various parts of the Third World feel, be they migrants, displaced refugees in border camps, or foreign labour, as for instance the experience of Sri Lankans and other South Asians in Saudi Arabia and the recent controversy over Filipino maids in Singapore. In fairness to Hall, he advances some qualifications of his reflection that more and more people share his experience of being 'recently migrated' by stating that identity is placed and

positioned in specific, particular circumstances and histories. See 'Minimal selves' in *The Real Me: Post-Modernism and the Question of Identity*, ICA Documents 6 (London, Institute of Contemporary Arts, 1987), pp. 44–6.

32. Chesneaux, *Brave Modern World*, p. 88.

33. Ulf Hannerz , 'Notes on the Global Ecumene', *Public Culture*, 1:2 (1989), 72.

34. Ulf Hannerz, 'The world in creolisation', *Africa*, 57:4 (1987), 547.

35. Fredric Jameson, *The Political Unconscious: Narrative as a Socially Symbolic Act* (London, Methuen, 1981), pp. 32, 53–4.

36. This problem of accurately defining the Third World is alluded to in Paul Rabinow's 'modern tour of Brazil'. After his survey of Brazil's almost schizophrenic character (chaos, poverty, shanty towns, the eighth-largest GNP in the world, modern cities, substantial computer, arms and automobile sectors), he muses 'First, Second, Third?' in reference to what 'world' Brazil fits into. See 'A modern tour of Brazil' in Scott Lash and Jonathan Friedman (eds), *Modernity and Identity* (Oxford, UK and Cambridge, MA, Blackwell, 1992), pp. 248–63 (p. 253).

37. King, *Global Cities*, p. 7, and *Urbanism, Colonialism, and the World-Economy*, p. 50.

38. Homi Bhabha, *The Location of Culture* (London and New York, Routledge, 1994), p. 246.

39. See Santiago Colas, 'The "Third World" in Fredric Jameson, *Postmodernism, or the Cultural Logic of Late Capitalism'*, *Social Text*, 31/32 (1992), 258–70.

40. Featherstone, 'Global and local cultures', pp. 181–2.

41. Ashis Nandy, 'Shamans, savages and the wilderness: on the audibility of dissent and the future of civilizations', *Alternatives*, 14 (1989), 273.

42. Nandy, 'Shamans', pp. 263–5; emphasis added.

43. Ahmad, *In Theory*, pp. 313–16.

44. Colin Leys, 'Confronting the African tragedy', *New Left Review*, 204:March/April (1994), 44–7.

45. Ibid., p. 43. Leys juxtaposes his material realism with the hope and commitment of Basil Davidson and the poststructural approach of Jean-François Bayart whom he sees as producing the 'distancing effect' referred to. See pp. 41–4.

46. See Dirlik, 'The postcolonial aura', p. 356.

47. See Terence Ranger, 'Concluding summary: religion, development and identity' in Kirsten Holst Petersen (ed.), *Religion, Development and African Identity: Seminar Proceedings No. 17* (Uppsala, Scandinavian Institute of African Studies, 1987), pp. 150–1.

48. Chesneaux, *Brave Modern World*, p. 117.

49. Bryan Turner, 'Global citizenship', paper presented at the seminar 'Citizenship and Transgression', Centre for Citizenship and Human Rights, Deakin University, 6 April 1995.

50. Chesneaux, *Brave Modern World*, pp. 45–6.

51. Michel de Certeau, *The Practice of Everyday Life*, trans. by Steven Rendall (Berkeley, Los Angeles and London, University of California Press, 1984). De Certeau makes a vital distinction between the production and utilization of a particular commodity or representation suggesting that local, specific consumptions of global processes produce crucial differences and heterogeneity: 'The presence and circulation of a representation . . . tells us nothing about what it is for its users. We must first analyse its manipulation by users who are not its makers. Only then can we gauge the difference or similarity between the production of the image and the secondary production hidden in the process of its utilization' (p. xiii). Foucault draws a similar distinction between the existence of a particular code or system of thought and its varied and particular reception by individuals so that the continuity or otherwise of the code is not as pertinent as the 'practices of self' individuals employ to modify, recast and diversify these codes. See Michel Foucault, *The History of Sexuality*, vol. 2: *The Use of Pleasure*. Trans. Robert Hurley (Harmondsworth, Penguin Books, 1992) (originally published in French, 1984), pp. 31–2. David Harvey advances a similar thesis: 'It is only in the social practices of daily life that the ultimate significance of all forms of activity is registered': 'From space to place and back again' in Bird *et al.* (eds), *Mapping the Futures*, p. 23.

52. This episode is drawn from the following sources: Friedman, 'Being in the world', pp. 314–19 and Friedman, 'Narcissism, roots and postmodernity: the constitution of selfhood in

the global crisis' in Lash and Friedman (eds), *Modernity and Identity*, pp. 348–53; and Abdul Maliqalim Simone and David Hecht, 'Masking magic: ambiguity in contemporary African political and cultural practices', *Third Text*, 23:Summer (1993), 107–13 (pp. 111–12).

53. The official language of both countries and capitals is French, with Christianity the predominant religion in Zaïre (over 70 per cent) and significant in the Congo (40 per cent). Their respective economies are also locked into the French/Western, IMF orbit.

54. Friedman, 'Narcissism, roots and postmodernity', p. 350.

55. This 'postdevelopment' episode is based on the research of Christine Sylvester into Zimbabwe, in particular 'Reginas in international relations: occlusions, cooperations, and Zimbabwean cooperatives' in Stephen J. Rosow, Naeem Inayatullah and Mark Rupert (eds), *The Global Economy as Political Space* (Boulder, CO and London, Lynne Rienner Publishers, 1994); and *Zimbabwe: The Terrain of Contradictory Development* (Boulder, CO, San Francisco and Oxford, Westview Press, 1991). See also 'Urban women cooperatives, "progress", and "African feminism" in Zimbabwe', *Differences*, 3:1 (1991), 29–62.

56. Sylvester, *Zimbabwe*, p. 161.

57. Ibid., p. 127.

58. EEC (European Economic Community) at the time; now EU (European Union).

59. Sylvester, 'Reginas in international relations', p. 117.

60. Ibid.

61. Doreen Massey, 'Politics and space/time' in Michael Keith and Steve Pile (eds), *Place and the Politics of Identity* (London and New York, Routledge, 1993), p. 141.

62. This is not true of postmodern writers such as R. B. J. Walker, Richard Ashley, James Der Derian, Michael Shapiro, V. Spike Petersen, Christine Sylvester and others who make such questions central to their analysis of world politics. One could argue, however, that these writers remain decidedly at the margin of mainstream international relations. Also, at least according to Krishna, writers such as Der Derian exhibit all too familiar problems to traditional international relations with their tendency to marginalize the Third World. See Krishna, 'The importance of being ironic'.

63. See Michael Keith and Steve Pile, 'Introduction Part 1: The politics of place' in Keith and Pile (eds), *Place and the Politics of Identity*, p. 2.

CHAPTER THREE

Postdependency?

PAUL JAMES

> Many governments fail today to enable people to meet even their most basic
> needs. Over 1.3 billion lack access to safe drinking water; 880 million adults
> cannot read or write; 770 million have insufficient food for an active working
> life; and 800 million live in 'absolute poverty', lacking even rudimentary
> necessities. Each year 14 million children – about 10 per cent of the number born
> annually – die of hunger.[1]

Despite an increasing global division of wealth and poverty, dependency
theory, with its thesis about the structural domination of the Third World by
the capitalist West, is all but dead. Its passing has been slow and faltering,
but inexorable. In both mainstream and avant-garde international relations
writing it is now commonly reduced to a theoretical-political memory,
mentioned only as part of an interesting historical lineage. At best, and this
is still not very helpful, it is treated as a once-relevant attempt to understand
a long-gone era (that is, prior to the 1970s) when nation-states were supposed to have acted as unitary agents within a grand international system
called economic imperialism. Avant-garde theory is now consumed by poststructural questions about globalism as a chaotic process and neo-colonial
identity as an ambivalent subject position. Mainstream theory in its various
guises – conservative, liberal and radical – now takes for granted the very
structures of global capitalism that dependency theory in all its faltering
over-confident dogmatism tried to criticize. In general, as the earlier
chapters by Phillip Darby and Albert Paolini indicate, amorphous conceptions of interdependency, globalism and postcolonialism have tended to
replace the hard-edged connotations of imperialism, dependency,
underdevelopment and structural wretchedness.[2]

This twofold softening of the theories of structural wretchedness is
mirrored darkly by Western mass-cultural representations of the Third
World.[3] The images take two major forms: first, as an aestheticized theatre
of horror in which only a few can be rescued from amongst the mass of
unredeemable; and second, as a romanticized location of otherness. The
global electronic media has enhanced the possibility of our witnessing
famines and floods on the other side of the world, but in one of those tragic
contradictions of globalism, the images of Third World poverty and
exploitation are far more likely to be aestheticized in the form of

advertisements for World Vision, the Body Shop or the Italian clothes manufacturer Benetton[4] than they are to be systematically examined on the evening television news. It is not that we are unconcerned. Michael Jackson's 1995 world-release single 'Earth Song' speaks to this political concern, and as a nigger–Jew–Christ figure he takes on the voice of the Third World. Unfortunately in the process of repeating the song's refrain 'What about us? What about us?', Jackson claims for himself (and therefore for all of us in the West) an easy messianic reversal of the plight of the Third World, its people and their forests. It is all a matter of running the film images backwards.

The second form taken by popular images, romanticization, can be found everywhere: from the ridiculous – for example, IBM's current postmodern advertising campaign, 'Solutions for a small planet™', depicts Buddhist monks in saffron robes meditating on the side of a mountain and telepathically anticipating the joy of being able to communicate globally – to the commodified sublime, including the marketing of world music and the conferencing of novels by Salman Rushdie. The latest issue of *Studio Bambini*, 'Out of Africa', features '102 pages of vibrant winter fashion photographed in Zambia and the *new* South Africa'. Its front-cover image brings black and white together, as an African boy dressed in safari leather gear protectively embraces a European girl wearing a delicate turtle-neck knit.[5] Recent advertisements for the Australian–American cable network Foxtel depict three tribal African women, one balancing a television on her head. The accompanying blurb reads: 'On the Discovery Channel you'll meet an African tribe, explore the Simpson Desert and float down the Amazon in your lounge chair. . . . Naturally the jungle drums are beating out the message "I want my Foxtel".'[6]

With the problems of the dispossessed of the Third World anaesthetized in our short-term memory, the virtues of the poorer regions of the world as sources of interesting anguished literature, as producers of rain forest timber, and as tourist destinations (that is, at least the unspoilt, unlogged bits) can be presented without fear of too much guilt. Commentators such as Peter Bauer no longer write tomes of expiation 'on Western guilt and Third World Poverty'.[7] Instead, in the late twentieth century a conservative liberal, Francis Fukuyama, comfortably pronounces the victory of market-oriented liberal democracy and writes a book entitled *Trust: The Social Virtues and the Creation of Prosperity*. Why are significant parts of the Third World poverty-stricken? Implicitly in Fukuyama's account it is because they have low levels of trust in strangers, the '*spontaneous sociability*, which constitutes a subset of social capital'.[8] It is no wonder we feel that the plight of the Third World is all too complicated. And it is not surprising that dependency theory has passed into history: it has no purchase in the West any more, either as explanation or as political sensibility.

Dependency theory has also lost favour among its early proponents. The once strong advocate of dependency theory, André Gunder Frank, rationalizes his decampment with a self-serving valediction:

The evidence is accumulating that 'dependence' has ended or is completing the cycle of its natural life, at least in the Latin America that gave it birth. The reason is the newly changing world economic and political reality that in a word may be summarized as the crisis of the 1970s.[9]

The most resounding death-knell of all comes from Susan Strange, herself a radical commentator on international development issues:

It is no accident that the 'dependency school' of writers of the 1970s have lost so much of their audience. In Latin America (where most of this writing was focused), politicians and professors were almost unanimous in the 1970s in castigating the multinationals as agents of American imperialism, but now they acknowledge them as potential allies in earning the foreign exchange badly needed for further development.[10]

Susan Strange, like so many commentators, implicitly equates capital investment with development. Following similar assumptions about how the world goes round, the Jamaican economist Nassau Adams mentions dependency theory only once in a book which begins and ends by highlighting the increasing economic division between the two major geopolitical 'regions' of humanity, North and South. His passing comment on dependency theory has peculiar parallels with the politics of blaming-the-victim: he criticizes the theory for contributing to a psychology of dependency, thus serving 'to inhibit the realization of full development potential'.[11] The *coup de grâce* is struck: dependency theory is now the cause of that which it was trying to criticize.

Echoing Antony's funeral oration from Shakespeare's *Julius Caesar*, I want to make it clear that this chapter is intended to bury dependency theory, not to praise it. The problem is that the usual mortal critiques, too-easy dismissals and avant-garde inattentions are part of a more general trend taking international relations away from the difficult task of theorizing the *structures* and *determinations* of inequality in global politics. My argument is very simple. Dependency theory was not a very good theory, but it brought themes into focus to which contemporary international relations has still to attend adequately: structures of power; systematic patterns of inequality; practices and ontologies of dependence. There is no point in attempting to give new life to dependency theory itself, but it is the argument of this chapter that in the age of globalism the concept of 'dependency' itself deserves renewed attention.

In order to revivify the concept of 'dependency' we have to divest it thoroughly of its economistic and mechanistic heritage. First we shall work through the major problems associated with the theory in which it was embedded; then the second half of the chapter goes on to set up an argument for the importance of the concept of 'structural dependency'. Wretched poverty is no accident even if it is not the intended consequence of the willed actions of key international 'actors' – nation-states and their agencies, transnational corporations and global institutions such as the World Bank and the International Monetary Fund (IMF). The central argument involves the following steps: first, broadening the emphasis that dependency theory places on state-to-state exchange relations by relating the concept of dependency to processes of global capitalism; second, qualifying the neo-imperialist argument about the relation between territorial imperialism and capitalism, and arguing that modern imperialism is now framed by the structures of globalism; third, reasserting the importance of seeing globalism in structural rather than anarchic terms, drawing implications from this structural perspective about the patterns of global integration; fourth, stressing the self-active nature of subjectification; fifth, broadening out the mode-of-production debate to discuss the intersection of a manifold of modes of practice: modes of production, exchange, communication, organization and enquiry. (It is not very hard to show how the Third World is thoroughly integrated into, and dependent upon, the dominant modes of practice. The usual counter-position that a number of erstwhile Third World countries are undergoing hyperdevelopment is only an argument against a position that suggests that dependent development is not possible. My argument, to the contrary, is that the current form of global capitalism substantially undermines attempts at independent, or even semi-autarchic, development – and that is not only because of economic processes.) Last, but not least, the sixth step involves relating the 'modes of practice' argument to more abstract-cultural questions about categorical formations: for example, to how ontological categories such as time, space and embodiment are lived in this changing world. This move is intended to provide a more theoretical point of reference for the emphasis in the third part of the book on sexuality and gender.

Our discussion of dependency theory begins by briefly introducing and contextualizing the approach as a counter to the dominant Western paradigm of development in the post-war period: modernization theory. Looking back from the end of the twentieth century it is hard to appreciate the emotional and theoretical hold and emancipatory excitement that dependency theory once generated amongst a range of people, from Third World policy-makers and academics to Western commentators and students of international relations. Certainly it always remained at the edge of Western academic respectability; for example, one well-known theorist of socialist economics once wrote that he would have failed the tracts of André Gunder Frank if they had been submitted as university essays. However, the strength of the theory was that it challenged prevailing mainstream assumptions about development; in particular, the neo-classical liberal view that capitalism and economic growth were inextricably linked. Writers as diverse as Frank, Fernando Cardoso, Theotonio Dos Santos, Colin Leys and Samir Amin were early contributors to the dependency approach,[12] and while they diverged in how they presented the problems faced by the Third World, they were critics-in-common of the ethnocentric tendency to assume that the Third World would simply follow the fivefold path taken by the West.

According to mainstream development theory in the 1960s, for the Third World to reach the stage exemplified by the United States – the splendorous age of 'high mass consumption' – there was entailed a movement through a number of prior stages. Leaving behind the limitations of technological backwardness, a developing country moved through (1) a pre-take-off stage creating the prerequisites for (2) 'take-off', where the last limiting vestiges of tradition were removed and people learn to 'enjoy the blessings and choices opened up by the march of compound interest'. This generated the possibility of (3) travelling down the 'road to maturity', and on to (4) the penultimate stage of high mass consumption. Beyond that, signalling what Francis Fukuyama and his cronies now call 'the end of history', it was envisaged that we would desire to live postmaterial lives based on simple though (naturally) class-divided aesthetics.[13]

Mainstream development theory of that time can be criticized for universalizing history as a process of teleological and unilinear evolutionary development, evolution along a pathway already travelled by the West. This charge of ethnocentrism cuts deep. The theory sets up a dichotomy between different forms of society, and notwithstanding the positing of intermediary take-off stages, it implicitly divided societies into traditional and modern, simple and complex, backward and developed. It posited a simplistic dualism and separation between the traditional and modern sector as if there were no determining relationship between them. Influence was said to work by a process of diffusion from the modern to the traditional, from the city to the countryside. The limitations on development were all internal (or endogenous) to the essential characteristics of traditional society. Change would come only from the outside through the diffusion of capital and technology (Rostow), through transforming cultural-psychological values (D. McClelland), or instituting Western rational administrative practices and techniques (Samuel P. Huntington). Whatever ideological assumptions we can now see to be blatantly permeating modernization theory, at the time it was invested with a common-sense validity that a few maverick critics from Latin America were not going to dislodge easily. It had an internal logic that explained everything, even its own failure. The transitional stages between tradition and modernity were periods of upheaval: other nasty outside pressures were just as likely to be taken up as were democracy, development and the American way. In this sense, communism was the 'disease of transition'. Hence, despite the impression that modernization theory had an ivory-tower benevolence, we find development theorists caught up in advocating active military intervention in the Third World. Walt Rostow features in several memoranda in the *Pentagon Papers* as a proponent of Operation Rolling Thunder and arguing for the extension of bombing in Vietnam. 'Gentleman' Sam Huntington became one of the most important theorists of cold war counter-insurgency techniques.

The strengths (and weaknesses) of dependency theory come to the fore as a critique of these prevailing theories of development. The classic definition of dependency is given by Theotonio Dos Santos:

> By dependence we mean a situation in which the economy of certain countries is conditioned by the development and expansion of another economy to which the former is subjected. The relation of interdependence between two or more economies, and between these and world trade, assumes the form of dependence when some countries (the dominant ones) can expand and be self-sustaining, while other countries (the dependent ones) can do this only as a reflection of that expansion, which can have either a positive or a negative effect on their immediate development.[14]

Where the mainstream development theorists posited a linear notion of development from a primeval condition of predevelopment, the dependency theorists countered that underdevelopment was not an original condition but one which represented a relationship beginning in the sixteenth century and culminating in the consolidation of twentieth-century capitalism. The postcolonial condition was not necessarily one of expanding economic possibilities. Rather, the legacy of the nineteenth-century second expansion of Europe, coupled with the continuing penetration of Western capital into the Third World, served to bind those countries into a nexus of exploitation and underdevelopment or, at the very best, dependent or distorted development. To use Samir Amin's later term, regions such as Africa experienced 'maldevelopment'. In this view, underdevelopment was not due to endogenous factors such as the persistence of traditional institutions or the lack of a Protestant work ethic, insufficient capital or inadequate resources. It was due to the under-developed country's long-term external relationship to world capital. By the same argument the emphasis placed by mainstream development theory upon the hopes that diffusion of techniques, technologies and capital from the West would bring about development was criticized as an ideology which served the interests of First World capital.

Dependency theory tended to speak from the edge of the Third World, while technocratic theories of development and their more benign-sounding alternatives, liberal reformism and interdependence theory,[15] spoke from the centre of the West. Nevertheless, this should not qualify our criticizing of dependency theory for its numerous deficiencies. The purpose of the following critique is not to dig over the *dependentistas'* burial ground, but to establish some guidelines for an alternative method, a broader framework which nevertheless is intended to be in keeping with the radical spirit of the original theory.[16]

At the risk of over-generalizing amongst a diverse range of writers, dependency theory vastly overstated its conclusions. It turned mainstream development theory on its head, up-ending its suppositions rather than rethinking a comprehensive alternative approach. Instead of development theory's assumption about the evolution of the Third World towards a desired end, dependency theory argued that the development pathway was blocked for underdeveloped countries – that is, unless there was either a crisis of capitalism or a delinking of those countries from the global economy. Instead of a dichotomy between modern and traditional, they posited a dichotomy between developed and underdeveloped, centre and periphery. (The later move by world-system theorists to interpose the category of 'the semi-periphery' was of the same order as Walt Rostow's theory of stages: a makeshift revision.) Instead of a dualism between the modernizing and traditional sectors of a country, the constitutive power of capitalist penetration was overstated, particularly in relation to the first half of the twentieth century and earlier. The contradictory, uneven nature of the process of commodification was treated as a blanket layer of market relations imposed from the outside. And instead of development theory's over-emphasis upon the endogenous limitations to development, dependency theory over-emphasized external (exogenously generated) pressures. Further to these problems we should also note the tendency of dependency theory, particularly in its early stages when talking in the language of metropole–satellite relations, to rely implicitly upon a state-to-state theory of international relations, even as it argued that states were subordinate actors within the overbracing world system. All too often the United States, through its agencies and multinational corporations, was placed as actor-in-control of the chain of exploitative exchange relations. Moreover, the theory tended to over-emphasize the importance of the mode of exchange while downplaying other modes of practice that also structure the relationship between the First and Third Worlds. This has parallels with the critiques levelled at world-system theory. Certainly, later Third World theorists such as Armand Mattelart,[17] influenced by neo-Marxism, came to write on the mode of communications, but their writings were bound by many of the orthodox assumptions of theories of neo-imperialism.

It seems, then, that there is little point in bringing dependency theory itself back from the edge. When in the opening paragraph I suggested that dependency theory was all but dead, I refrained from making the statement conclusive because there are perhaps three senses in which ghosts of the *dependentistas* are still walking around today. A recent international relations reader, *Development and Underdevelopment*, links the dependency approach to a more recent theoretical approach, world-system theory, devoting a major section of the book to documenting the lineages of each.[18] It is significant, however, that rather than commissioning new work for the contributions on dependency theory the editors of that volume chose to reprint articles from the 1970s, including a classic essay by Dos Santos cited above. This is the first sense of the ghost that walks; dependency theory as part of the history of social thought. It is useful as far as it goes. It helps us to contextualize, and therefore to denaturalize, the theoretical fashions that in the present are assumed to be unassailably correct-line.

A second sense in which we can still see the ghosts of dependency theory is evidenced in the publication of an anthology called *Dependency Theory and the Return of High Politics*.[19] It is a strange book for many reasons – reasons that there is not the space to explore here (including a chapter explaining how dependency theory is only partially helpful in understanding the UN treaty governing the 'Activities of the States on the Moon and Other Celestial Bodies') – but it is relevant here because its editors, Mary Ann Tétreault and Rick Abel, attempt to reclaim dependency theory by damning it with faint praise. Moreover, they provide an unintentional lesson on how not to bring the strengths of dependency theory 'back in'. They begin their introduction with a superficial but unproblematic passage: 'There are two realities in modern international political economy. One is material and the other is ideological. Both are absolutely real and they occupy the same space at the same time.' However, they then go on to ignore this premise in relation to foreign policy. Ideology is given the constitutive edge: 'it is ideology that makes policy, and policy has the power to constrain the normal interplay of material forces.' Hence, in a leap of logic, dependency theory is said to be better than the liberal and rationalist models because it is an ideologically derived theory:

> Because of nationalism, the fusion of situation and framework that leads to an us-versus-them approach, and the search for a rigged game, we believe that the rationalist approach or the liberal model of the relationship between the United States and the Third World, or more generally, between a core power and peripheral countries, is not adequate either to describe such relationships or to serve as the basis for American foreign policy, in spite of its normative attractiveness. Either the realist 'high politics' approach or the dependency approach fits this relationship better because they are themselves expressions of nationalism and a search for a rigged game.[20]

This is an inadequate (some might say, bizarre) rendition of an important insight into the recursive relationship between theory and practice: that is, the recognition that theories are no more, and no less than, abstractions from practice. As such they are influenced by, and in turn act back upon, their ideological-material context. If we are to draw any lesson from the series of gauche methodological moves made in *Dependency Theory and the Return of High Politics*, it is that any attempt to incorporate some of the strengths of dependency theory needs first to clarify the outlines of the alternative framework into which the concepts of 'dependency' are being incorporated. Analytical terms like 'dependency' float freely along with various popularized versions.[21]

The third sense in which the spectre of dependency theory lives on involves this very process of incorporation that I wish to defend. For all the powerful criticisms levelled at world-system theory, it has to its credit taken up some of the analytic categories used by dependency theory, such as the core–periphery distinction, and made systematic use of them within a developed alternative.[22] However, despite recent attempts to respond to their critics, the proponents of world-system theory have still a very long way to go to redress the problems of economism and structural reductionism.[23]

The present chapter parts company with world-system theory on this and many other points. However, it continues to work from a premise close to the hearts of the writers under critique. Although 'dependency' and 'globalism' are treated as socially contingent, historically specific and analytically limited concepts, the chapter suggests that they can be usefully interlinked within a framework which continues to take seriously the Marxist notion that people make history but not under conditions of their own choosing. Global capitalism is the dominant condition of our time. If 'structural dependency' is a relational term, defined as a condition of subjection (often actively embraced) within a dominant pattern of social practices or institutional framework(s), then it is my argument that in the late twentieth century we are seeing an increasing dependency of locales, regions and states upon processes of global capitalism. Paradoxically, delinking from the global economy and culture has become less possible at the very time (and partly for the reason) that most people, including policy-makers in the Third World, have no way of thinking outside the terms of the global condition.

The structures of globalism involve both constantly reproduced material constraints and actively lived sensibilities. In this sense the term 'structure' is used to indicate a pattern of lived (instantiated) practices, not a thing 'out there'. The argument can be presented as a series of interlocking propositions.

Proposition 1. Dependency operates differently across various levels of social extension: local, regional, nation-state and global relations. Over the past couple of decades a framework of globalizing connections has emerged as the dominant form of extension (dominant especially in terms of the way in which power is exercised).

To say that we have seen the emerging dominance and increasing penetration of various modes of practice including production and communication conducted across a global reach is not to imply that the immediacy and efficacy of other levels of extension are simply dissipated into what some theorists have homogenized as 'the global flow'. (Albert Paolini's chapter, Chapter 2, expands upon this point.) Dependency theory attempted to have it both ways by statistically documenting dependency in terms of state-bounded development, and simultaneously treating the world-system as the primary object of enquiry. The emphasis placed by early dependency theorists such as Gunder Frank upon state-bounded pathways of exchange within a totalizing world-system needs to be doubly qualified, but not by dismissing the continuing importance of questions of nation-state sovereignty even under contemporary conditions of globalizing (postmodern) capitalism, nor by totalizing those structures of capitalism. At least one world-system theorist has responded to this problem by designating 'the region' as the primary subunit of 'the world-economy',[24] but this overly restricts the analysis while at the same time problematically leaving the category 'world-economy' as a definitional totality characterized by a single mode of production.

The geopolitical designations – locale, region, nation-state and global setting – can usefully be deployed as descriptive of various overlaying levels of social extension. This kind of argument (which we will complicate more as we proceed) allows us to show how cultural contradictions and tensions of interest emerge in the overlaying of levels.[25] The corporate and communications culture of globalism is the most obvious area where we can see the levels of extension being collapsed into each other. Transnational corporations increasingly present themselves as bridging the local and the global. An advertisement for the Japanese car manufacturer Toyota run in the *Cambodian Daily* depicts a satellite photograph of our planet and plays across the shifting reference points of place:

> *This is our town.* It's the global village. We live here. You do too. We're neighbours. And since we're neighbours, we should be friends . . . for the first half century we thought of ourselves as a Japanese company. But we don't think that way any more.[26]

Proposition 2. The changing structures of capitalism, a racing globalization and an enhanced sense of comparative place and comparative identity have both subjectively and objectively reframed (though not necessarily replaced) the old imperial connections. Dependency is no longer predominantly based upon the old lines of imperial exploitation and subjection.

Global capitalism, not classical imperialism, I suggest, now frames the various forms of dependency and exploitation. However, in making this argument the concept of 'framing' is intended to emphasize the reconstitutive and delimiting processes of social reproduction, not to suggest that historically long-term institutions such as colonialism or imperialism are magically irrelevant to the picture of the present. It is certainly not to agree with the poststructuralist Gianni Vattimo that we have seen 'the end of colonialism and imperialism'.[27] Within this emerging global (postmodern) setting of the late twentieth century, acts of imperially driven (modernizing) activity continue to occur with unfortunate regularity. One of the predominant determinations of the United States' precipitous involvement in the 1991 Gulf War – with a heavier bombing of Iraq in 43 days than of Vietnam in eight years – was the anticipated destabilizing of the world's oil production. The resumption of nuclear testing by France at Mururoa Atoll indicates that a European power can still treat its old colonies as part of its sovereign territory. Nevertheless, despite the regularity of such acts, they no longer constitute a way of life. They no longer dominate the structures of world politics. They have to be rationalized and defended against ever more acerbic scrutiny. And increasingly, they have become ethically ambiguous and half-thought-through reactionary attempts to ameliorate problems exacerbated by earlier activities of imperialism. Take the following examples: the Falklands/Malvinas war (1982) was defended by the British establishment as necessary to uphold old imperial obligations. No sense of irony was involved and no moral ambiguity could be

move e.g.s - note down

admitted. However, it was no longer upheld as simple common sense that this would always be a good thing to do. The US invasion of Panama, the defensively named 'Operation Just Cause' involving the fatal bombing of an estimated 2000 civilians in 1989, was justified as delivering the people from an evil drug-lord general. However, it was more than a quaint embarrassment that General Manuel Noriega had previously been supported by the United States as a client dictator to aid the US covert war against the Nicaraguan Sandinistas. The intervention of the United Nations peacekeeping force in Rwanda in 1994 was defended (I think quite rightly) as attempting to stem the genocide of the Tutsi people. However, even though few commentators noted that this intertribal war has its roots in a long history of imperial interventions – German and then Belgian colonialism and, more recently, support by the French, and also by the Belgians and US-backed Zaïrean troops for the repressive Habyarimana regime – there was no automatic sanctioning of Western involvement in Africa. We had just witnessed the complications of Western intervention in Somalia. The world's media were already on the beaches waiting for the marines to arrive – and some of us had cringed; first, because the United States was being so self-sanctifying about sending in the troops, and second, because acts of this kind were now being framed as global media spectacles.

Classical imperialism, from the ancient and traditional empires to early-twentieth-century colonialism and mid-century neo-colonialism, was based largely upon a control of territory (however uneven that might have been) and the relatively direct exploitation of the production and trading of material commodities. It entailed forms of agency extension; that is, the presence on the ground of agents of the empire. With the development of electronic trading, computerized storage of information and an exponentially increasing movement of capital, there has been an abstraction of the possibilities of control and exploitation, an abstraction of the relationship between territory and power, and an abstraction of the dominant level of integration. Susan Strange's term 'casino capitalism' partly captures this process, but together with terms such as 'fictitious capital formation' – that is, capital produced without a growth in production of material objects – it gives the misleading impression that this abstraction is less real than gunboat diplomacy, more ethereal than factory production. To the contrary, when for example global electronic markets sell futures options on agricultural goods not yet produced and transnational corporations speculate on the basis of satellite weather-forecasting, the effects are very real. Production choices are being framed by interests other than the feeding of people. When economically viable agricultural production in the post-Green Revolution stage is increasingly bound up with a mode of enquiry which accentuates genetically engineered plant hybrids, farmers are seemingly caught between two choices – independent but marginal productivity or enhanced but ecologically vulnerable production with increasing dependence on Western biotech corporations.[28]

Proposition 3. The processes of globalism are structured in various ways across different levels of integration. Globalism is not simply a process of disorder, fragmentation or rupture. (Nor on the other hand is it simply a force of homogenization.)

The argument that the postmodern world has become increasingly fragmented is found in writers as sophisticated and concerned about the structures of the 'social whole' as Fredric Jameson and David Harvey.[29] World capitalism has not recently become disorganized: it was never very organized in the first place, and certainly not when Rudolf Hilferding first coined the term at the beginning of the twentieth century.[30] It is true that the pace of change has accelerated and the life-world is experienced as increasingly in flux, but this does not mean that generalizable patterns cannot be ascertained. The critics of postmodernity are right to point to the subjective experience of fragmentation, but they have done very little to theorize the relationship between the more abstract integration and interconnection of social relations (able to be generalized when viewed from afar) and the confusing, variable pastiche of fragmented practices and counter-practices (apparent when viewed at close hand). By explicitly recognizing how the nature of our analysis depends upon the place from which we begin the analysis (in other words, the level of abstraction taken by the theory), we can usefully move across a manifold of theoretical levels from on-the-ground detailed description to generalizations about modes of practice and forms of social being without privileging any one level. (See the Appendix below.) In doing so, it becomes possible to say that the world is becoming increasingly interconnected at the most abstract level of integration – for example, by the disembodying networks of electronic mass communication – even as social difference and social disruption at the level of the face-to-face is accented in and through that same process.

Proposition 4. Dependency is a process of subjection, but that does not mean that it is a passive process.

There was a tendency in dependency theory to treat subjection as a one-sided activity – as something done to the Third World by the West and supported by local *compradors*. The concept of 'subjection' is used here with an imbrication of meanings, analytically separable, but in practice bound up with each other. First, it is used in the old-fashioned political sense of being subordinate rather than independent, 'a subject of the realm', whatever that realm might be: state, corporation, peace-keeping force or the world economy. It is important that we do not lose sight of this crude sense of 'the power of the realm'. People living in Rwanda, Eritrea, Tahiti and Burma, as well as in Europe and North America, are regularly confronted by it in their everyday lives. Second, it is used in the current theoretical sense of the 'subject as agent', with a nod to the way in which Homi Bhabha uses the concept as emphasizing the contingency of outside inscription and the temporary closure involved in self-active enunciation, but much closer to writers such as Raymond Williams and Aijaz Ahmad, who talk of persons being self-active in their own constitution as subjects with the self-activity itself being framed by intersubjective structures.[31] To paraphrase the classic Marxist premise to which I referred earlier: people make themselves but not as monads and not under conditions of their own choosing.

Subjection within global capitalism is a thoroughly double-sided and self-active process. Recent controversies in Papua New Guinea, Zambia and Nigeria indicate how the economic-cultural terms of the global market are actively embraced by Third World policy-makers. In Papua New Guinea, the government is solidly behind its Australian mining partner BHP and legally defending a class action brought against it by its own people of the Fly River region. The dispute is over the environmental effects of tailings waste from the Ok Tedi mine. During 1995 and 1996 BHP has been conducting an advertising campaign in Australia to counter adverse publicity, and it has been hinting that Slater and Gordon, the Australian law firm acting for the Fly River people, is only in it for the money. To state the obvious – they all are. In particular, the Papua New Guinean economy is overwhelmingly dependent upon companies such as BHP and CRA for generating export income.

In Zambia, now 25 years after the post-independence nationalization of Zambia's copper mines, the government of Frederick Chiluba has entered into negotiations with the Anglo American Corporation to place Zambia Consolidated Copper Mines (ZCCM) under the control of boardrooms in Johannesburg and London again. According to Western newspaper reports, the sell-off to global capital of the state-run enterprise which accounts for more than 90 per cent of Zambia's export earnings is economically rational because of the cumulative effects of the declining reserves, undercapitalization and inadequate skills and management. It simply 'makes sense'.

In Nigeria, the November 1995 execution by General Sani Abacha's military regime of the novelist Ken Saro-Wiwa and eight other Ogoni environmental activists evidences the same point but with a couple of moral twists. The Anglo-Dutch oil company, Royal Dutch Shell, which has operated in Nigeria for almost 40 years and owns about 30 per cent of the state oil company, is involved in a public relations attempt to distance itself from the 'judicial killings' as international accusations of moral complicity circulate throughout the global media. Ken Saro-Wiwa was a leader of the Movement for the Survival of the Ogoni People (MOSOP), a group that five years ago began campaigning against Shell's role in environmentally degrading its region. In 1990 the Etche people demonstrated peaceably against Shell. The company responded by asking for military protection. The Mobile Police Force was sent in: it massacred 80 people and destroyed 495 homes. Against its critics, Shell can claim that it halted its operations in Ogoniland three years later in 1993 (though it continued as the largest oil producer in Nigeria), and since the execution of the novelist it has delayed its decision about whether to proceed with a $5.3 billion natural gas plant.

Similarly, the Commonwealth countries which responded ineffectively to the oilfields killings in the early 1990s can claim to have symbolically censured Abacha, finally suspending Nigeria from the Commonwealth forum. Be that as it may, through all this the ruling junta clearly want Shell to continue operations. They do not understand that the executives of Shell have to leave a decent amount of time before they return to the task of making profits. On the world stage, killing novelists (or women and children) gets a very bad reception: much worse than executing dissidents.

How does state–corporate dependency work? In this case, and many others, it is through Third World regimes binding themselves to the global market nexus both economically and culturally, thus confirming a historical condition which makes the nexus tighter. Through all but ten of Nigeria's 35 years of independence the country has been under repressive military rule with the bulk of its income coming from oil export revenue. Such regimes need the corporations, just as the corporations are constantly searching out new markets and sites of production, but it is not so clear that the state–corporate interdependence is benignly balanced.

Proposition 5. The various forms of dependency are structured by the dominant modes of practice operating across various levels of spatial extension.

In over-accentuating the capitalist mode of production or exchange as the basic determinant of contemporary international relations, dependency theory, world-system theory and some of their recent variants present us with a thoroughly reductive account of social practice.[32] One problem, as I began to discuss earlier, is that capitalism is treated as a system of economics which reconfigures and replaces everything that came before it. Dependency theory gave market capitalism the upper hand centuries before it came to be the predominant formation of practice, but even in the present period it is important not to turn late capitalism into a one-dimensional system. Fredric Jameson is a brilliant exponent of this ultimately problematic position. He says that with late or consumer capitalism of the post-war period has come

> the purest form of capitalism yet to have emerged, a prodigious expansion of capital into hitherto uncommodified areas. This purer capitalism of our own time thus eliminates the enclaves of precapitalist organization it had hitherto tolerated and exploited in a tributary way. One is tempted to speak in this connection of a new and original penetration of Nature and the Unconscious: that is, the destruction of precapitalist Third World agriculture by the Green Revolution, and the rise of the media and the advertising industry.[33]

It seems churlish to take issue with Jameson on methodological grounds when I so thoroughly agree with him about the expansion and changing nature of capital over the past couple of decades, but the points of contention have important political consequences. If we accept that late capitalism has completely replaced prior modes of production then we have no way of understanding why practices of resistance keep occurring in the Third World, or why the penetration of capitalism, as extensive and intensive as it is, has not produced a homogenization of cultures and economies. In the same way that 'Proposition 1' put forward an alternative analytic scheme based on the metaphor of overlaying (or imbricating) levels of extension, here I am suggesting that modes of production should be treated in the same way as overlaying modes with the dominant mode setting the framing conditions for other modes of production.

I need to complicate this even further in order to broaden out the concentration on modes of production and exchange to examination of other modes of practice: particularly the modes of communication, organization and enquiry. The Appendix on pp. 78–80 attempts to schematize this. The dominant mode of communication in the age of globalism is the electronic, allowing the disembodiment and abstraction of interaction across time and space. This mode extends upon rather than replaces the less abstract modes of voice and print: one of the most strikingly recurrent media images of recent times has been of apparently isolated traditional people using cellular mobile phones. The dominant mode of organization is the technical-rational bureaucratic. What we have seen is not the replacement of prior forms but their subversion, so that a more 'personal' form of organization (for example, chiefdom or patrimony) becomes the source of corruption as relations of kinship or ethnicity form a distorted part of the basis of policy-making on issues from sporadic familial favouritism to systematic ethnic genocide. Rwanda is the latest horrific example. The dominant mode of enquiry in the late twentieth century is the techno-scientific. It is impossible to understand the reconstitutive capacities of contemporary capitalism without placing science right at the centre of any analysis. Jameson implicitly recognizes this in the passage just cited, but the recognition fails to dislodge the primacy of the mode of production.

Proposition 6. Dependency, defined earlier as a condition of subjection to a dominant pattern of social practices and institutions, has an ontological dimension.

This dimension is usually badly handled by contemporary theory, so in making this point let me begin with an initially obtuse methodological premise. The most complex and politically useful accounts of social life are conducted across the full range of theoretical abstraction from the most 'concrete' kinds of analysis involving empirical generalization to the most 'abstract' explorations of categories of existence such as time, space, embodiment, desire, ambivalence and so on. (For a suggested way of setting out a manifold of four such levels of theoretical abstraction see the Appendix.) Dependency theorists and orthodox Marxist scholars have tended to concentrate on two levels of analysis: conjunctural studies of particular developments, and social formational studies of systemic structures. However, as Theda Skocpol writes of one important theorist in this tradition:

> Wallerstein creates an opposition between a formalistic theoretical model of universal reference, on the one hand, and the particularities and 'accidents' of history on the other hand – an opposition that uncannily resembles the relationship between theory and history in the ideal type method of the modernization approach.[34]

The problem here lies not in making an analytic distinction between empirical description and social formational analysis, or between theory and history, but in setting them up as two sides of a great divide. Attempting to get around this problem, poststructuralists writing from the standpoints of postcolonialism or subaltern studies problematically head off in the opposite direction, tending to collapse theory and practice into each other. They start from the most abstract level of analysis, deconstructing categories of ontology such as identity and difference, and draw back to the particularities of history without the use of any middle-order structural concepts such as 'social formation' or 'mode of practice'. Moreover, as Phillip Darby argues, the most excessively abstract postcolonial tracts reduce social life to a textual landscape of ambivalences and hybridities – ontologies without a living subject. The practices of actual people become allegories of this and that.

There is a further methodological point. The concept 'ontology' is intended to refer the most basic framing categories of existence, but we have to be careful to distinguish the use of the concept from the psychologistic tendency to attribute dependent personalities to the dispossessed of the world: the passage from Nassau Adams on psychological dependency quoted earlier in the chapter is a case in point, but it is found in the most unlikely places from the travelogues of the poststructuralist Jean Baudrillard to occasional moments in the revolutionary writings of Frantz Fanon. Baudrillard writes that the weak are imbued with a 'contempt for themselves by a sort of capillary action from the superior race'; and on Africa we are told that 'the West will be hard-pressed to rid itself of this generation of simiesque and prosaic despots born of the monstrous crossing of the jungle with the shining values of ideology'.[35] Fanon writes 'The colonized man is an envious man. . . . It is true, for there is no native who does not dream at least once of setting himself up in the settler's place.'[36] I am not objecting here to Fanon's use of psychoanalysis or to Baudrillard's implicit point about the intersection of the values of tradition and modernity (that is, leaving aside Baudrillard's appalling expressions of racism). Rather, I am questioning the way in which, as subjectivity is totalized and the layers of categorical meaning are read off in terms of the dominant level, the ontological complexity of peoples and individuals is reduced to a psychology of common personality traits.

Wary of such tendencies, some writers have shied away from delving into the depths of social existence. However, as the chapters in the rest of the book go on to discuss, questions of ontology – questions about how people live as embodied persons, how they understand the nature of identity, how they exist in overlaying senses of place and space – are crucial to understanding the settings across which the so-designated major actors of international relations strut their stuff.

As the political arguments, theoretical moves and questions of method compound upon each other it is, in conclusion, worth returning to the underlying political concern of the chapter. One of its key premises has been that major discrepancies of power operate across the supposedly open flow of global exchange and interdependence. Global capitalism may have brought varying degrees of 'development' to Third World countries such as Brazil and Thailand, but it has brought a certain kind of development, and with enormous social costs. Sixty per cent of the people of Brazil now live below a harsh poverty line, but without the old means of agricultural subsistence. Its tourist mecca of Rio has been through a stage of poverty cleansing – including the murder and clearing out of its street children – but over a million people cling to its outskirts, living in shanty towns with nowhere else to go. Thailand's capital, Bangkok, is one of the most polluted cities in the world, with people commuting five hours a day along the congested freeways. One of its major industries is tourism. The Tourism Authority of Thailand advertises itself in the West as 'An exotic mixture of floating markets, street stalls and designer boutiques. . . . Have a stopover in Thailand and you'll soon see why they call it the land of smiles.'[37] No mention is made of the largest component of Thai tourism, the sex industry, including the burgeoning use of an estimated 200,000 young teenage and child prostitutes (brought in because they have not yet contracted AIDS). Global capitalism in conjunction with the expansion of consumerism and travel has revived the body as a form of traded commodity in ways which, unlike eighteenth-century slavery, have subverted local village and family life. As the rural north-east becomes more impoverished, families sell their children into sex slavery for lonely Western *fahrangs*. Thus a country that remained relatively independent during the colonial era, is now thoroughly bound into the global economy from its growing development-based debt to its increasing incidence of child indenture. In short, even in the 'economic miracles' of the Third World, development is associated with costs: being bound within the fluctuations of global capital, going through an uprooting of rural populations; and living with metropolitan overcrowding, ecological degradation and an increased domestic division between rich and poor:

> If one defines dependence as a conditioning factor that profoundly affects the development strategies of developing economies, then the fact of dependency can hardly be denied. Every less developed economy is certainly dependent upon fluctuating world market conditions; each must import capital, technology, and industrial know-how. . . . A continuum exists in which every country is more or less dependent than others, and some are certainly more dependent than others. If, however, one employs this condition of dependence

as an explanation of underdevelopment, the argument loses much of its force. There is a tendency, unfortunately, to confuse these two meanings of dependence and to assume that the *fact* of dependence provides the *explanation* of economic underdevelopment.[38]

In other words, let us not lose sight of the issue that the developing countries are bound tightly into the global economy and culture, and that even if the dependency theorists were wrong about the causes of underdevelopment, they pointed with passion to structures of inequality, exploitation and subjection that continue unabated. Occasional newspaper reports acknowledge the facts: 'Every night 800 million people around the world go to bed hungry'; 'Next year, the world's stocks of grain will become critical, plunging to their lowest level in human history with just 53 days' supply, more than a week short of the amount that prompted warnings of a global food crisis in the 1960s.'[39] But these get lost in the complex glut of half-connected discussions about the world's population explosion, the need for new technological breakthroughs to solve the social problems of the previous technological breakthrough, as well as a plethora of miscellaneous human-interest stories such as the report that the Kingdom of Tonga is going on a national diet.[40] Inured to the hype and sensationalism, we read the warnings that the world is becoming increasingly unequal, and except at the margins we seem to carry on regardless.

Appendix: Levels of theoretical abstraction

The overall argument is that a comprehensive theory of social relations and subjectivities has to work across a manifold of levels of theoretical abstraction. Below is set out one possible way of conceiving such a manifold.

I. *Empirical Generalization*

(a) In particular:

- Conventional biographies written as time-line accounts of a particular person's life: 'letting the facts speak for themselves';

- Histories of particular polities such as post-independence Rwanda or the post-cold war United States;

- Descriptions of particular institutions, fields of activity and discourses: for example, a descriptive account of Rudyard Kipling's discourse of 'empire loyalty' which does not attempt to do much more than document and trace its development.

(b) In general:
Drawing on particular accounts and studies, analysis at this level attempts to be more comparative and to survey the longer-term processes, for example:

- Histories of the practices of 'personhood', gender relations, class-based life-worlds;
- Comparative histories of a political form such as 'the nation-state';
- Descriptions of an institution-in-general such as 'bureaucracy', fields such as 'the law', or discourses such as 'empire loyalty'.

At this level, analysis which emphasizes the particular, and does not reach for more abstract ways of understanding, runs the risk, however detailed its description, of superficiality or empiricism. Nevertheless, empirical generalization remains a basic level of analysis necessary to any approach in order to avoid abstract theoreticism.

II. *Social Formational Analysis*
(a) In particular:
Analysis at this level of theoretical abstraction proceeds by resolution of particular *modes of practice*. The present approach complicates 'classical historical materialism' by analytically distinguishing:

1. modes of production;

2. modes of exchange;

3. modes of communication;

4. modes of organization;

5. modes of enquiry.

In practice, no mode of practice exists as a separate, autonomous form. The rationale for this five-fold classification is that it avoids some of the reductionism of a classical 'mode of production' approach without becoming too unwieldy.

(b) In general:
Drawing on analyses of particular modes of practice, analysis at this level attempts to describe conjunctures between such modes. Generalizations are made about the structural connections between dominant modes of practice, thus allowing for the shorthand designation of actually existing formations of practice, for example:

(reciprocal) tribalism
(absolutist) feudalism
(industrial) capitalism

These designations, as with all concepts of all classifying schemes, can be used only as working appellations, not reified entities. In practice, social formations tend to be defined in terms of the dominant *formation of practice*, but this is not to rule out subordinate formations.

III. *Social Integration Analysis*

(a) In particular:
Analysis proceeds by resolution of *levels* of social integration (and

differentiation). While in theory one could distinguish any number of levels of integration, the present approach sets out three such levels:

1. face-to-face integration (the dominant level in tribal societies);

2. agency-extended integration (the dominant level in traditional and early modern societies);

3. disembodied integration (the dominant level in modern into postmodern societies).

In practice, no level of integration exists as a separate, autonomous form. Levels of integration are lived in contradictory intersection.

(b) In general:
Drawing on analyses of levels of integration, generalizations can be made, first, about the *intersections* between these (ontological) levels – for example, charting the emergence of ontological contradictions – and, second, about the complexities of social life as summarized at less and more abstract (epistemological) *levels* of theoretical abstraction. Following the second path, generalizations can be made which further enrich and contextualize our understanding of particular life histories, fields and discourses (Level I), modes and formations of practice (II), and the ontological categories and formations of social life (IV).

IV. *Categorical Analysis*
At this level, analysis works by reflexively 'deconstructing' categories of social ontology. It attempts to take nothing for granted, including the epistemological and ontological assumptions of its own approach (especially the tendency of some deconstructive projects to give priority to the so-argued 'liberatory' potentialities of practices of deconstruction).

(a) In particular:
Structural genealogies (as distinct from 'classical' histories or descriptions – see I(a) above) of particular categories of existence such as:
time and space, culture and nature, gender, embodiment, knowledge, language, theory, and the unconscious.

(b) In general:
Drawing on discussions of particular ontological categories, general-izations can be made about different forms of ontological formation (and different epistemes), for example: traditionalism, modernity, post-modernity, phallocentrism.

As with all other concepts in the present approach to 'levels of theoretical abstraction' they remain provisional concepts, provisional as tested against the criterion 'Are they useful for understanding the complexities of social life?' At this level, analysis which is not tied back into more concrete political-ethical considerations is in danger of abstracted irrelevance, utopianism without a subject, or empty spiritualism.

Notes

With thanks to Phillip Darby, David Goldsworthy, Gyorgy Scrinis, Richard Higgott, Alison Tait and Peter Christoff for reading the manuscript or suggesting readings.

1. MacNeill *et al.*, cited in Stephen Gill, 'Theorizing the interregnum: the double movement and global politics in the 1990s' in Björn Hettne (ed.), *International Political Economy: Understanding Global Disorder* (London, Zed Books, 1995), p. 74.

2. See for example Robert Keohane's highly regarded text *After Hegemony: Co-operation and Discord in the World Economy* (Princeton, NJ, Princeton University Press, 1984). He devotes a grand total of two paragraphs to what he calls 'negative reciprocity'; that is, 'attempts to maximize utility at the expense of others' (p. 128). There are of course exceptions. See for example Samir Amin, *Maldevelopment: Anatomy of a Global Failure* (London, Zed Books, 1990) or, from a quite different perspective, Andrew Linklater, *Beyond Realism and Marxism* (London, Macmillan, 1990); also Jeremy Seabrook, *Victims of Development* (London, Verso, 1993); however, the strength of the book is as eloquent, passionate description, not as theory. In addition, it is worth returning to Samir Amin's *Accumulation on a World Scale* (New York, Monthly Review Press, 1974).

3. As Phillip Darby and Albert Paolini point out, it is no longer *de rigueur* among the avant-garde to use the term 'the Third World' (see particularly Darby's introduction). Reading Aijaz Ahmad's chapter 'Three worlds theory' is instructive on the contradictory political layers of meaning in the term – from *In Theory: Classes, Nations, Literatures* (London, Verso, 1992) – but I use it here nevertheless as a collective noun naming the very diverse regions and nation-states that were historically not included in the industrial capitalist and industrial (post)communist 'worlds'. Its use here presumes no homogeneity, no hierarchy of centrality, no sense of a continuing political bloc.

4. Benetton, with 6500 shops in 100 countries, a turnover of $US2.3bn and an advertising budget of $US80m, uses images of South American toddlers working as slave labourers in a brickyard to promote Luciano Benetton's concept 'of a world without borders'. The aid agency World Vision advertises its project by asking Westerners to sponsor individual Third World children. In November 1995 it incorporated its message into an episode of the Australian soap opera *Neighbours*. This takes us another step beyond the usual mediation of African famines: television celebrities cuddling hungry children and hosting tours of the trouble spots.

5. Emphasis added; *Studio Bambini*, 10:19 (1995). The latest *Studio for Men*, 7:14 (1995), includes an article on Buenos Aires which turns the shanty town of La Boca into an off-Broadway stage setting: 'I left the theatre in a state of mild intoxication and wandered Avenida 9 de Julio in my dinner suit and stiff collar. I asked my companion what a threadbare Louis XVI chair was doing on the sidewalk. "It has been left here by someone for the homeless," she said. Let them eat cake, I thought' (p. 145). No irony was intended by the author.

6. *Sunday Age*, 19 November 1995.

7. The title of ch. 4 from P. T. Bauer, *Equality, the Third World and Economic Delusion* (London, Weidenfeld and Nicolson, 1981).

8. Francis Fukuyama, *Trust* (London, Hamish Hamilton, 1995), p. 27 (emphasis in original). He writes 'one of the most important lessons we can learn from an examination of economic life is that a nation's well-being, as well as its ability to compete, is conditioned by a single, pervasive cultural characteristic: the level of trust inherent in a society' (p. 7). See also Fukuyama's *The End of History and the Last Man* (New York, Free Press, 1992).

9. Cited in Magnus Blomström and Björn Hettne, *Development Theory in Transition: The Dependency Debate and Beyond* (London, Zed Books, 1984), p. 184.

10. Susan Strange, 'Rethinking structural change in the international political economy' in Richard Stubbs and Geoffrey Underhill (eds), *Political Economy and the Changing Global Order* (London, Macmillan, 1994), p. 106. It is indicative that the dependency theorist Fernando Cardoso is now a prominent politician and avowed economic rationalist.

11. Nassau Adams, *Worlds Apart: The North–South Divide and the International System* (London, Zed Books, 1993), p. 91.

12. The most influential and most criticized book of the formative years was André Gunder Frank's *Capitalism and Underdevelopment in Latin America* (New York, Monthly Review Press,

1967). Samir Amin's *Accumulation on a World Scale* (New York, Monthly Review Press, in translation 1974), like the work of Dos Santos and Cardoso, was much more heavily influenced by Marxism than was Frank's. Blomström and Hettne, *Development Theory in Transition* and Ian Roxborough, *Theories of Underdevelopment* (London, Macmillan, 1979) provide very helpful descriptions of the various strands of dependency theory and their historical twists and turns.

13. This was the doctrine of Walt Rostow in *The Stages of Economic Growth: A Non-Communist Manifesto* (Cambridge, Cambridge University Press, 1960). To this day there are transcontinental research teams doing very dubious empirical surveys showing the maturing of people in the West from hyperconsumption to 'postmaterialism' (Inglehart's term). On the background to development theory and its critics see Roxborough, *Theories of Underdevelopment*.

14. Theotonio Dos Santos, 'The structure of dependence' in Mitchell Seligson and John Passé-Smith (eds), *Development and Underdevelopment: The Political Economy of Inequality* (Boulder, CO, Lynne Rienner Publishers, 1993), p. 194.

15. Mainstream development theory remade itself in the 1970s and 1980s. Although very different from postcolonial theory, it similarly attempted to shed itself of any vestiges of 'Grand Theory'. Development theory re-formed itself as the narrow public policy approach and fragmented economic studies: it became incrementalist, technocratic and instrumental, rationalizing the status quo.

16. Among the sympathetic but still damning critiques see Peter Limqueco and Bruce McFarlane (eds), *Neo-Marxist Theories of Development* (London, Croom Helm, 1983). Colin Leys's classic article 'Underdevelopment and dependency: critical notes', reproduced there from the *Journal of Contemporary Asia* (1977), is significant because it is written by a person who for a decade had worked within the dependency paradigm.

17. Armand Mattelart, *Multinational Corporations and the Control of Culture* (Sussex, Harvester Press, 1979).

18. Seligson and Passé-Smith, *Development and Underdevelopment*, p. 194.

19. Mary Ann Tétreault and Charles Frederick Abel (eds), *Dependency Theory and the Return of High Politics* (New York, Greenwood Press, 1986).

20. Ibid. The quotations are from pp. 3, 4 and 13–14 respectively. To make matters more confusing, the paragraph quoted from p. 14 concludes 'However, this is not to say that any one of these models is adequate, by itself, either to inform or to interpret American foreign policy or to suggest what might be the best international economic order from the standpoint of raising total productivity and wealth. Their strong nationalist biases militate against their usefulness as theories in this sense.'

21. See Nancy Fraser and Linda Gordon, 'A genealogy of "dependency"' in P. James (ed.), *Critical Politics: From the Personal to the Global* (Melbourne, Arena Publications, 1994).

22. For me at least, more impressive than the writings of the best-known theorist in the world-system literature, Immanuel Wallerstein, is a volume by Christopher Chase-Dunn, *Global Formation: Structures of World-Economy* (Oxford, Blackwell, 1991). Alternatively, Linklater, *Beyond Realism and Marxism*, sets up a 'critical theory' framework for rethinking questions of imperialism, class structure and the system of states.

23. Compare the different styles of approach of Etienne Balibar and Immanuel Wallerstein in their jointly authored compilation, *Race, Nation, Class: Ambiguous Identities* (London, Verso, 1991).

24. Chase-Dunn, *Global Formation*, pp. 207–10.

25. For a discussion of levels of extension in relation to the changing form of the economy see John Hinkson, 'Postmodern economy: value, self-formation and intellectual practice', *Arena Journal*, new series 1 (1993), 23–44.

26. *Cambodian Daily* (13 July 1994), with thanks to Peta Arbuckle for sending me this reference. The newspaper itself is constructed around this layering of geopolitical reference points. The news is first presented in the global language English; then extracts are given in Khmer; finally news of one of Cambodia's most economically important neighbours, Japan, is printed in Japanese.

27. Gianni Vattimo, *The Transparent Society* (Cambridge, Polity, 1992), p. 4.

28. Gyorgy Scrinis, *Colonizing the Seed: Genetic Engineering and Techno-Industrial Agriculture* (Melbourne, Friends of the Earth, 1995); and Seabrook, *Victims of Development*, ch. 7 'Replacing the biosphere'. See also Seabrook's chapter 'Regenerating the countryside' on the thriving cooperative economy of the Indian village of Ralegan Siddhi.

29. The classic early statement on the fragmentations of postmodernity by a structuralist is Fredric Jameson's 'Postmodernism, or the cultural logic of late capitalism' (1984), republished as ch. 1 of *Postmodernism, or, The Cultural Logic of Late Capitalism* (London, Verso, 1991). Similarly, David Harvey's *The Condition of Postmodernity* (Oxford, Blackwell, 1989) is a brilliant attempt to theorize the structures of the changing world, but he still falls back upon the postmodernist language of fragmentation without providing us with an account of the levels at which it occurs. Joseph Camilleri and Jim Falk's *The End of Sovereignty: The Politics of a Shrinking and Fragmenting World* (Aldershot, Edward Elgar, 1992) distinguishes between international integration and domestic fragmentation (p. 250), but, as their title suggests, this distinction does not sit very easily with the rest of the book.

30. Scott Lash and John Urry, *The End of Organized Capitalism* (Cambridge, Polity, 1987); Claus Offe, *Disorganized Capitalism* (Cambridge, Polity, 1985).

31. Homi Bhabha, *The Location of Culture* (London, Routledge, 1994), ch. 9; Raymond Williams, *Marxism and Literature* (Oxford, Oxford University Press, 1977); Ahmad, *In Theory*, pp. 128–9.

32. For a useful discussion of the relevance of a non-reductive 'modes of production' approach to the study of international relations see Robert Cox, *Production, Power and World Order: Social Forces in the Making of History* (New York, Columbia University Press, 1987). Though he starts off strangely by saying that 'Specific modes of social relations of production are treated as Leibnizian monads, as self-contained structures each with its own developmental potential and its own distinct perspective on the world' (p. ix), it soon becomes clear that the notion of 'self-containment' is meant only in terms of being separable for analytical purposes, not as separable in lived circumstances (p. 15).

33. Jameson, 'Postmodernism, or the cultural logic of late capitalism', p. 36.

34. Theda Skocpol, 'Wallerstein's world capitalist system: a theoretical and historical critique' in Seligson and Passé-Smith, *Development and Underdevelopment*, p. 236.

35. Jean Baudrillard, from *Cool Memories*, cited in David Slater, 'Exploring other zones of the postmodern' in Ali Rattansi and Sallie Westwood (eds), *Racism, Modernity and Identity on the Western Front* (Cambridge, Polity, 1994), p. 95.

36. Frantz Fanon, *The Wretched of the Earth* (Harmondsworth, Penguin Books, 1961, 1977), p. 30. See also Albert Memmi, *The Colonizer and the Colonized* (London, Souvenir Press, 1965, 1974); Octave Mannoni, *Prospero and Caliban* (New York, Frederick Praeger, 1964); and the commentary of Jock McCulloch, *Black Soul, White Artifact* (Cambridge, Cambridge University Press, 1983).

37. *Australian Magazine*, 16 December 1995.

38. Robert Gilpin, *The Political Economy of International Relations* (Princeton, NJ, Princeton University Press, 1987), pp. 303–4.

39. *Australian* (1 July 1995).

40. '[A]larmed by the growing incidence of obesity and its associated health problems, the country's government has introduced the world's first national slimming contest. UNICEF donated nine sets of scales . . . ', reported in the international fashion magazine *Marie Claire* (November 1995), 12–18.

Part II

Placing the International

CHAPTER FOUR

Inscribing the Hottentot Venus: generating data for difference

SUSIE PRESTNEY

It is a presupposition of this book that international relations, like imperial relations before, proceeds on the basis of hierarchy. The principle of hierarchy has been intrinsic not only to how we think about the system 'out there', but to the formulation of knowledge itself. This chapter explores the significance of hierarchy at one remove from disciplinary constructs: with respect to race and sexuality. It follows the case history of a remarkable black African woman, the Hottentot Venus, whose body, according to nineteenth-century medical discourse, confirmed the hierarchy of peoples. The narrative, which was stamped with the authority of science, provides a point of entry into the Victorian era's psychology of domination and subordination. More than this, it offers insights into the role that culture has played in the historical construction of the Self in relation to its Other by the appropriation of 'difference' in all its guises: social, racial and sexual.

The specific episode explored in this chapter might at first glance appear well removed from the province of international relations. Yet, in its uncovering of relations of dominance and power with respect to the body and race, and of the intimacy between conceptions of self and other, us and them, we can observe the very terrain of North–South relations. In particular, this chapter substantiates the argument that culture, in the guise of knowledge, has played a crucial role in discursively mapping international relations as hierarchical and binaristic. The relevance of narrating the story of the Hottentot Venus to a contemporary understanding of the historical construction of international relations is twofold. Her story not only exposes an uncritical acceptance of knowledge or 'reality' as often merely a belief in a cultural vestige of a bygone era, but also enables us to trace the history of marking encounters between the Western and non-Western worlds with the stamp of difference. What is more, the particular significance of the tale of the Hottentot Venus is reinforced by the contemporary campaign to have her remains returned from Europe to Africa. The postscript of her story is thus a case study in the way in which a cultural fragment can become a political issue of immediate relevance.

Nineteenth-century Europe, in particular Victorian England, fostered a keen interest in the notion of 'normality' and a penchant for the 'perverse' both in the realm of science and with respect to culture at large. Within scientific circles, conceptions of normality spawned the highly contentious notion of a standard human type or 'medical norm' against which people the world over could be measured. Essentially, this development succeeded in arming science with the power to define what would henceforth be considered as both physically and psychologically 'normal'. As such, it also invested nineteenth-century Europe's medical community with the authority to classify those seen to stray from the perceived pattern of normality as 'abnormal' or 'pathological'. Persons deemed to have been tarred with the brush of abnormality were subsequently dealt with by that century's concomitant development to the medical norm, which Foucault has referred to as the 'medicine of perversions'.[1] In effect, the medicine of perversions provided a space in which to house medical 'misfits' which was located at the very periphery of social approval and acceptance within the cultural framework of the age. Yet this new domain into which medical 'anomalies', 'perversions' and 'curiosities' were shunted, although partitioned from mainstream culture, was not invisible. Such people were not simply hidden away. In fact, they were highlighted by being put on display in the exhibitions or *expositions* and 'freak shows' which flourished in the Victorian age. During this era, popular interest in the 'curious' or *le spectacle* reached a high point in both Europe and North America, where millions flocked to see displays such as those made famous by P. T. Barnum with his 'Gallery of Wonders', 'Congress of Curious People' and 'Greatest Show on Earth' in which dozens of 'freaks', 'curiosities', 'monstrosities' or 'prodigies' were paraded before awe-struck audiences. In effect, this public display of medical 'curiosities' allowed for the cultural and aesthetic portrayal of what medicine enunciated scientifically.

The 'freak show' portrayed observable difference within a framework of familiar categories. The freak was depicted as a fixed reality that was at once 'different', and yet essentially knowable and visible. Implicitly, 'freaks', 'curiosities' or 'monstrosities', being *ab*-normal, had strayed from the medical norm. The fact, however, that they were regarded as ab-*normal* implies that such people had not been led so far from the path originally set by nature as to be mutually exclusive of the norm, yet were still far enough to be considered merely *versions* of it. In this way, the production of meaning through the notion of the 'freak' belongs to the process of apprehending knowledge that Said has identified as that by which 'something patently foreign and distant acquires . . . a status more rather than less familiar . . . a new median category emerges, a category that allows one to see new things, things seen for the first time, as versions of a previously known thing'.[2] The outcome of this process of measuring the unfamiliar against what is held in place as the 'norm' is not to come to a better understanding of it, but merely to turn all hitherto unknown phenomena into versions of what is seen as the original. 'Freaks', however, were not only versions of the known medical norm, but bad versions of it, hence *per*-versions. In fact, the very word 'freak' is an abbreviation for 'freak of nature', which is a translation of the Latin expression *lusus naturae*, implying that a person deemed to be a freak is not only anomalous, but ludicrous as well.[3] Thus, the freak is a grotesque, absurd or even comical version of nature. By extension, it is also a substandard, perhaps defective, and certainly an unnatural one. As *perversions* of the original human type, freaks or curiosities of medicine assumed the character of a failed copy of the norm and, as such, the freak personified not only abnormality, but inferiority as well.

Developing alongside the cultural and scientific interest in the 'perverse' was a curiosity about the idea of eugenics, which is concerned with the production of fine human offspring by the improvement of inherited qualities. This interest in the fortification of life saw a centralization of issues concerning the body in the social discourses and practices inscribed by the time. From the end of the eighteenth century, the human body was seen as reflecting a person's social position as well as characterizing the individual. At the higher echelons of the social system were said to be found those people who embodied the characteristics of human perfection, and anyone who did not conform to this mould was seen as destined to occupy a subordinate social status. The fact that physiology or biology was regarded as the epistemic foundation for prescriptive claims about the social order meant that the human body came to be placed at the very heart of social, political and cultural signification. Moreover, as sex was essentially held to be 'a means of access both to the life of the body and the life of the species',[4] this centrality of concern with the human body compelled the advancement of a 'politics of sex' – a new medico-political thematic concerned primarily with the management of the species and its collective welfare and descent. Foucault has argued that at this time, both politically and socially, sex was effectively 'put forward as the index of a society's strength, revealing of both its political energy and biological vigor'.[5] As such, it came to be placed in a position of obligation or 'biological responsibility' with regard to the species. The outcome of this new disciplinary focus on sex and heredity was that power was now located at the level of human life and aimed at the body, the population and the race. Indeed, as Foucault has highlighted, while Victorians, for instance, managed to win for themselves the reputation of the most sexually repressed society in history, nineteenth-century Britain and Europe were, in fact, fixated with sex. By bringing the body ever more fully into politics, discourses on sexuality actually flourished in the nineteenth century as never before.

At the level of medicine, Foucault has observed that 'there was scarcely a malady or physical disturbance to which the nineteenth century did not impute at least some degree of sexual etiology . . . the medicine of that era wove an entire network of sexual causality to explain them'. The idea of the 'perverse' that began to emerge in the field of sexuality and medicine thus commenced its task of setting apart the sexually 'unnatural'.[6] In particular, attention turned increasingly to the reproductive organs.[7]

Because perceived genital abnormalities were believed to be the work of

Providence, not only were they considered to be endowed with an aura of apparent factualness, but the semantic signification attached to them was such that physical aberrations which affected the sexual organs were said to evoke some larger truth about the nature of those they marked. In this way, Sander Gilman has argued that 'the very term *semiotics* which today rings with the claim of literary scholarship, is inherently and historically a term describing medical interpretation'. The body or the 'flesh', as the essential component of this interpretive system, is always part of a process that generates meaning. It is, therefore, never neutral nor meaningless.[8]

Although the cultural and the biological have traditionally been separated into the respective realms of the subjective and the objective, in fact the thematic principles of both these worlds have been woven from the same socio-historical imagination. Science and, more specifically, medical research and discovery, are as much at the mercy of the ideology and needs of the age in which they function as any other system which plays a role in organizing our perceptions of the world. Taking this idea one step further, Donna Haraway has contended that 'scientific practice is above all a story-telling process in the sense of historically specific practices of interpretation and testimony . . . Biology is inherently narrative.'[9]

In this chapter, I am concerned to establish that while conclusions reached in nineteenth-century medicine were expressed in terms of the concrete 'realities' of the human body, they were more deeply grounded in assumptions about normality and the perverse which were peculiar to the era. To do this, I have based my enquiry on three nineteenth-century anatomists' analyses of the bodies of South African Bushwomen. Foremost among these is the first discussion in medicine of the 'Hottentot Venus', perhaps the most famous of all Africans who exemplified the long-held association of physical eccentricity with exotic origin, and participated in engendering an enthusiasm for the spectacle. The question which will be pursued is what broader significance cultural norms attributed to the physiology of the Hottentot Venus and, by extension, the black 'race' as a whole. As such, the reasons as to why this woman was found so freakishly fascinating, even as a corpse, will be addressed.

A popular song of the time, 'The Humours of Bartlemy Fair', contains the following verse:

Here, here, the only booth in the fair,
for the greatest curiosity in all the world –
the Vonderful and surprising Hottentot Wenus is here,
who measures three yards and three quarters round.[10]

Saartje Baartman, Sartje Bartmann, Saartjie Baartman, Saat-je or Sarah Bartman, popularly known in England and France as the 'Hottentot Venus', is said to have been the first imported 'savage' to win publicity in the new century. She was either taken or lured from the Cape of Good Hope in Southern Africa, where the Khoi or the Khoisan, known as the Hottentots, a small-statured nation held up to be a racial 'type' which included the Bushman (or Bosjesman) people, are said to have originated. The Hottentot Venus was a Bushwoman whose reign as a popular attraction commenced some time in the early part of 1810 when she began to be exhibited daily to the English public in Piccadilly. As an exhibit, she was displayed on a small stage with a cage at the end of it, and clothed in a tight-fitting dress of a colour as nearly resembling her skin as possible so that the exact form of her body could be seen by the viewing public. When ordered to do so, it is said that she would come out of the cage and parade herself before the audience, who became fascinated with what they saw as her most intriguing feature: her possession of steatopygia or protruding buttocks. It is speculated that from Piccadilly, the exhibition of the Hottentot Venus then toured the English provinces until September 1814, when she began to be shown in Paris. The Hottentot Venus was displayed here daily for fifteen months, and during this time she managed to make her mark on the popular imagination of the French as she had done across the Channel, becoming the subject of satirical cartoons and popular songs, and even being incorporated into Parisian theatre in a one-act vaudeville. In March 1815, the eminent French naturalist, Georges Cuvier, arranged for the Hottentot Venus to be examined in the Jardin du Roi by zoologists and physiologists, and even persuaded her to disrobe so that a nude portrait of her could be effected.

The Hottentot Venus died towards the end of the following year, of either smallpox or syphilis. Cuvier now sought and acquired official permission to dissect her. During his examination, he made several plaster moulds of her body, including separate replicas of her skeleton and brain, along with a waxen mould of her genitalia. His findings were subsequently published in 1817.[11] In the fifty years after Cuvier subjected the renowned Hottentot Venus to the probing gaze of nineteenth-century medicine, further dissections of Bushwomen were conducted by European medical practitioners. In 1864, Cuvier's infamous autopsy was followed up directly by the English doctors William H. Flower and James Murie, who dissected a young Bushwoman who had also been exhibited in Britain. Flower and Murie believed that the physiology of the subject of their examination corresponded to that of the Hottentot Venus as described by Cuvier, and their findings were later included in the opening volume of the *Journal of Anatomy and Physiology* (1867).[12] A review of this discussion, including extracts of the dissection reprinted for a lay audience, was published in the same year in the *Anthropological Review*.

In an obscure article in which he narrates the tale of how Saartje Baartman came to be such a freakish attraction both while she was alive and after her death, Percival Kirby argues that 'it is neither necessary nor desirable to follow Cuvier in his elaborate anatomical analysis of this unhappy woman. Let it suffice for me to say that a cast of her body was made, and her skeleton prepared and mounted.'[13] Such a demonstrably concluding statement to the life story of the Hottentot Venus, however, is not at all a sufficient ending to her colourful existence and omits a large part of her saga. Indeed, many questions are left completely unanswered. No account is given as to why this remarkable African stirred European medical circles to the extent that a renowned French doctor chose not only to rigorously examine the Hottentot Venus even as a cadaver, but also made a cast of her body and preserved her skeleton for posterity's sake. In addition, no attention is given to the extraordinary fact that fifty years later, two English doctors elected to follow in Cuvier's footsteps. There is, therefore, a lacuna in the biography of the Hottentot Venus and a gap in our understanding of the construction of race. It is thus necessary to follow the anatomists in their analyses of this Bushwoman.

Cuvier's fascination with the Hottentot Venus lay in his contempt for her outward appearance. The most striking aspect of his analysis of this African woman is his graphic examination of her buttocks and detailed commentary on the nature of her genitalia.[14] Cuvier even went so far as to measure the distance that the buttocks of the Hottentot Venus protruded from the line of her back, and to examine their physical make-up. He concluded that they jutted out more than half a foot, and that their consistency was 'elastic' and 'jelly-like'. What is more intriguing is the fact that Cuvier's finishing touch to his dissection of the Hottentot Venus was to present her actual anus and genitalia to the French Academy of Medicine. Similar attention to describing in detail the buttocks and, especially, the genitalia of the Bushwoman is also found in Flower and Murie's work. An entire section of their essay is headed 'Generative organs'. They remark that the nature of the buttocks and sexual organs of this Bushwoman corresponds in the main with the description of Cuvier. Like Cuvier, they too were intrigued by the physical make-up of her steatopygia, and argued that it was entirely attributable to the accumu-lation of fat. This curiosity with the mass of her buttocks is also evident in Dr Paul Topinard's *Anthropology* (1878), the first volume of the popular 'Library of Contemporary Science'. Interestingly, his discussion of steato-pygia is found under the general heading 'External genital organs'. In the same way, Flower and Murie included their description of steatopygia in the Bushwoman under the subheading 'Generative organs', and Cuvier, in his examination of the Hottentot Venus, refers collectively to both her buttocks and her actual sexual organs as her 'genitalia'.

Evidently these doctors saw the buttocks, a secondary sexual character, as possessing as profound a sexual nature as the primary sexual organs themselves. Havelock Ellis, in his *Studies in the Psychology of Sex*, which he began to write in the last decades of the nineteenth century, explained why this was so. In his account, the buttocks were far more aesthetically pleasing than the naked sexual organs, and for this reason they had come to displace genitalia as the ultimate sign of sexuality.[15] The scientific and popular curiosity about the Bushwoman's buttocks, therefore, followed essentially from a fascination with the nature of her genitalia or sexuality.

Yet the protruding buttocks of the Hottentot Venus were not the only aspect of her genitalia that brought fame to her and notoriety to the

Bushman people as a whole. Nor were they the only feature of her anatomy
which intrigued medical practitioners. Cuvier himself believed that the
most remarkable particularity of the Hottentot Venus's anatomy was her
tablier or 'apron'; that is, her elongated labia minora or nymphae, so named
because of the way they were said to hang down between her thighs.[16]
Cuvier contended that this development of the nymphae was 'not a
product of art', and concluded that the *tablier* was, in fact, part of the
Bushwoman's anatomy which 'nature has made . . . a special attribute of
her race'.[17] Similarly, Flower and Murie, when commenting on the Bushwoman's 'remarkable development of the labia', asserted that this
anatomical 'organization' 'was not produced, as had been supposed, by the
degraded and filthy habits of the tribe', but was 'so general a characteristic
of the Hottentot and Bushman race' as to be 'natural and congenital'.[18]

   Medical interest in the nature of the Bushwoman's genitalia was directly
related to the belief propounded by pseudo-scientific race theories that
genitalia provided the all-important clue that would solve the riddle of
human evolution. What was seen as the differing nature of the genitalia of
the world's peoples was regarded as the determining factor that would
remove the obscurity clouding the question of whether all human groups
were of the same 'species'. But it was the female generative organs which
were singled out as crucial: 'the uterus is to the Race what the heart is to the
individual.'[19] The reproductive biology of woman was seen as the key to
nature. As life itself takes form in woman, so she was seen as being
responsible for the safeguarding of society, and her obligations were thus
primarily conjugal and parental. If science could prove that the genitalia of
the Bushwoman were unlike the genitalia of the white woman, then herein
lay proof that the black race itself was atypical. Along these lines, Topinard
argued that 'the external genital organs present very marked differences in
different races. In the male these are but slight. In the female the differences
are very considerable.'[20]

   Regarding the Bushwoman's buttocks, Topinard contended that 'nothing
in the European has any resemblance in the slightest degree to steatopygia',
and that 'it is more than an hypertrophy of the adipose tissue, it is almost a
supplementary organ . . . the particular use of which is not known'.[21] In
sum, he argued that steatopygia in a human was equivalent to the fact that
a bison has an extra pair of ribs. Just as the ribs of the bison distinguished it
at once from all other animals, so too the Bushwoman's exaggerated
buttocks set her apart from all other humans. The Bushwoman's buttocks
were believed to signify that blacks were anatomically aberrant in relation
to the white race. Essentially, the attribution of a sexual nature to the
buttocks coupled with the steatopygia of the Bushwoman meant that what
Europeans saw represented by her buttocks was actually the notion that
she had enlarged genitalia. Moreover, in that her steatopygia was said to
signify that she possessed what was close to being an extra organ, the
Bushwoman was held to be atypical because this presumed super-
numerary organ was, in essence, a genital one. Even more substantive

evidence which pointed to the abnormality of the Bushwoman's genitalia, and thereby, that of the black race, was said to be her elongated labia minora. For Georges Cuvier, the Bushwoman's *tablier* was an extraordinary appendage of the design of Providence.

Fifty years later, Flower and Murie took Cuvier's conviction one step further, proclaiming that the elongated labia minora of the Bushwoman were 'sufficiently well marked to distinguish these parts at once from any of the *ordinary* varieties of the human species'.[22] In the period between the examinations of the Bushwomen performed by Cuvier, then Flower and Murie, Josiah Nott MD of the United States professed his views regarding the outward appearance of the Bushwoman's labia and buttocks in a book he co-wrote which was entitled *Indigenous Races of the Earth* (1857). He stated: 'I assert that these peculiarities . . . incontestably prove the Hottentots to be a distinct "species".'[23] Furthermore, towards the end of the century, Topinard concluded that 'hitherto we have met with many opposite characters in the human groups, but few so remarkable as these . . . the line of separation between the European and the Bosjesman as regards these two characters is . . . still wider'.[24]

Thus, when Cuvier presented the anus and genitalia of the Hottentot Venus to the French Academy of Medicine, he was effectively offering up, in the name of science, what was held to be anatomical evidence which established both the inherent abnormality and the inferiority of the black race. Given the significance attributed to the sexual organs of woman at this time, Cuvier was also presenting the European medical community with proof of the validity of the polygenetic view of humankind which began to gain in credibility at this time. Polygenism holds that blacks and whites did not evolve in varying degrees from the same point in history but had, in fact, descended from two separate pairs of Adams and Eves. Its supporters argued that because the races were separate, they had evolved major inherited differences in talent and intelligence.

Nineteenth-century biology constantly needed to deal with the poly-genetic argument, and to meet the scientific standards which the age demanded, a paradigm was needed which would technically place the black in a position antithetical to that seen as being occupied by the white race. Such a paradigm needed to be rooted in some type of unique and observable physical difference. The Bushwoman, not only in her skin colour, but above all else, in the form of her genitalia, was seen as providing scientists with proof that the black and white races were not of the same 'species', and hence furnished the scientists with the perfect basis for polygenism. Proof of the validity of polygeny sanctioned the idea that the blood of blacks and whites, by nature, was not meant to be mixed – whence the coining of the term 'miscegenation'. Apart from being a word which developed out of the nineteenth century, miscegenation was also an emerging phobia of this era. What was feared most about it was the 'unknown' element it entailed, the inherent fear being what might be discovered as a result of interracial breeding.

While polygenists argued that a study of genitalia was able to uncover the mystery of whether the world was populated by a plurality of human creations, monogenists propounded the theory that variations in genitalia were, in fact, vestiges of the white race's evolutionary past. Monogenism was based on the idea that there existed an evolutionary scale which ranked all beings by virtue of their supposed physical, moral and mental development. It was believed that the white race had managed to ascend the ladder of evolution, leaving the black race behind in a stationary position somewhere in a historical stage of development through which the white race had already passed. Accordingly, so-called primitive societies were seen as possessing, in their very nature, the key that would unlock the mystery of human evolution. Yet while the white race was celebrated for having climbed the evolutionary ladder, it was argued that along its upward journey it had not been able fully to rid itself of all traces of 'primitivism' or 'savagery'. It was felt that within the white race, signs of its evolutionary past were evident, indicating a direct link between the black and white races. Genitalia were viewed as the most aesthetically crude aspect of the human body. Indeed, the expression of any kind of emotion and sexuality was seen as indicative of a 'primitive' mind-set. Genitalia and sexuality were seen as confirming the validity of the notion of the 'savage within', and hence were propounded as a 'missing link' with the evolutionary past of the white race. As Sander Gilman has poignantly observed, 'no Victorian scientist made this claim about the nature of the brain'.[25]

In the case of the Hottentot Venus, as with other nineteenth-century Bushwomen, interest in the nature of her genitalia transcended mere titillation, for scientists had long regarded the Bushman nation itself as the *true* 'missing link'. The very anatomical structure of the Bushwoman's sexual organs and buttocks was seen as placing her at a level of development closest to the earliest stages of human evolution. Her genitalia themselves were seen as immanently 'primitive': 'from a primitive point of view', Havelock Ellis argued, 'a sexually desirable and attractive person is one whose sexual characters are either naturally prominent or artificially rendered so . . . "with buttocks brode and brestes rounde and hye . . ."'.[26] The fact that the labia and buttocks of the Bushwoman were considered to be unusually large gave currency to the belief that she had a comparably crude and oversized sexual appetite.

Seen as a sign of the 'swamp', the earliest stage of human history, sexual lasciviousness was regarded as characteristic of humans' evolutionary past, which was understood as an era marked by unbridled sexuality. Dr Charles Letourneau in *Sociology* (1881), another volume of 'The Library of Contemporary Science', encapsulated this belief. He argued that 'as a matter of course, the more inferior the race is . . . the nearer it approaches to animal existence, [and] the more the question of generation becomes unlimited'.[27] Consequently, he contended that 'the life of the Australian woman [was] but a long state of prostitution',[28] as was the fate of the female population of the Bushman people, whom he saw as being 'not more developed than the Australians'.[29] The realm of the 'primitive' was thus seen as inherently sexualized. Moreover, it is still evident within Western culture, as Marianna Torgovnick has argued, that 'the idiom "going primitive" is in fact congruent in many ways to the idiom "getting physical" '.[30]

The superiority of whites was seen in part as having been achieved by their ability to exert control over themselves and their world by developing moral values. Freud argued that civilization arose to protect humans from the uncontrolled imperatives of aggression, and in return it exacted the repression and control of aggressive impulses, including sexuality. Primitive societies, however, were seen to be exempt from such repression and control. In this way, Letourneau claimed that

> the white race, like all other races, most probably began by living promiscuously, of which practice they have slowly corrected themselves . . . [thus] it is to this total absence of control that we must lay the charge of coarseness in all primitive morality.[31]

In nineteenth-century Europe, to lose control was seen to descend the evolutionary ladder, to degenerate into the unfettered or primitive expression of emotions. To lose control over one's sexuality was therefore to risk absorption into 'otherness', which itself was seen as lurking beneath the façade of civilization, capable of being released at any moment. It was thus believed that at the very heart of European civilization lay the expression of bad instincts or the 'dormant savage being'. This conceptualization of the 'savage within' was captured in the popular fiction of Rider Haggard in his novel *Allan Quartermain* (1888). Quartermain, explaining his own psychology, reflects that 'civilization is only silver-gilt . . .':

> This being so, supposing for the sake of argument we divide our-selves into twenty parts, nineteen savage and one civilised, we must look to the nineteen savage portions of our nature if we would really understand ourselves, and not to the twentieth, which, though so significant in reality, is spread all over the other nineteen, making them appear quite different from what they really are, as the blacking does a boot, or the veneer a table.[32]

Yet while 'civilization' essentially masked inherent elements of savagery, what differentiated the European from the actual primitive being was the fact that Europeans had (mostly) been able to restrain their savage ego. On the other hand, it was argued that the black did not have the capacity to do this and was thus steeped in savagery. In *Sociology* (1881), Charles Letourneau encapsulated this notion of the 'savage within' that begs restraint in a voice typical of the time. 'Often enough in our law-courts', he argued, 'we are reminded that under the polish of our modern society – proud as it is of the advance of every kind – there is always remaining an old remnant of savagery which is still our duty to abolish. *Memento quia animal es*' (p. 73).

Essentially, the application to the Bushwoman of the age-old view that the body was the externalization of the soul meant that her perceived biological variations were taken to be an indication of an anomalous black essence. While the notion of the immoral, lascivious world of the primitive was sometimes seen as epitomizing the idea that this world was actually a lost paradise or Eden, it more often represented a degraded state of human nature and living that was closer to the conditions of Original Sin. The apparent exaggerated genitalia of the Bushwoman were seen as providing proof of the fact that in her physiology, the Bushwoman both defied nineteenth-century notions of beauty and represented the antithesis of European sexual mores. As Frantz Fanon was to observe much later, 'In relation to the Negro, everything takes place on the genital level. . . . The Negro is the incarnation of a genital potency beyond all moralities and prohibitions.'[33]

What was extrapolated from the nature of the Bushwoman's buttocks and labia was the belief that non-white races lived in the harsh conditions of Adam after his expulsion from the Garden of Eden or were the descendants of Canaan, the son of Ham who was accursed by Noah. Thus, sexuality and civilization were coupled: unbridled sexuality and primitivism were not coincidental. It was felt that this observation discredited the notion that moral worth was innate to all human groups. Indeed, it was commonly held that morality, one of the greatest virtues of the Christian religion, was a quality which was exclusively white. The ethereal quality of whiteness, associated as it was with the light of God, His goodness and purity, had not yet reached, and perhaps could never reach, the African continent – the very Heart of Darkness – where even the people were black, the colour of Satan and his devils. Hence, whereas the white race had managed to ascend the evolutionary ladder, it appeared either that the development of the black race had stagnated somewhere along the line, or that the black race had, in fact, sunk deeper into the dark depths of the white race's evolutionary past.

In essence, monogenetic evolutionary theory gave 'civilization' a 'savage' past. Letourneau offered a pithy summary of the meaning of this fact for the Victorian European:

> man [sic] has long enough deceived himself with the idea that he was made in the image of Divinity. It is now more than time to say and to repeat to this poor creature that he is animal in every fibre and in every particle of his existence.[34]

However, in that monogenism graded races according to their perceived level of progression on the Great Chain of Being, it was held that those races deemed to occupy a place at the bottom end of the scale were inherently more 'animal' than those at the top. The evolutionary debate between polygenists and monogenists was now resolved by a comprehensive evolutionism which was at once racist and monogenist. Its appeal lay in the fact that even as it affirmed human unity, it relegated the black savage to a status very near that of the ape. By situating more 'poorly evolved' races closer to a state of animality, it created a kind of buffer zone that effectively separated whites from their anthropoid ancestors. The Bushman people, it was argued, could be found clinging to the very bottom rung of the evolutionary ladder.

In their mid-nineteenth-century text *Indigenous Races of the Earth* (1857), Dr J. C. Nott and the geologist R. Gliddon included a map of the world on to which is superimposed what is referred to as a 'chart illustrative of the geographical distribution of monkeys in their relation to that of some inferior types of men [*sic*]' (p. 640). This chart represents both the Hottentot 'type' and all members of the anthropoid ape family as co-habitators of the southern region of Africa. Furthermore, in the 'explanation of the tableau', Nott himself declared this human 'type' to 'differ as much from anything human I ever saw'.[35] Evidently, European fear and contempt for the unknown had led to a judgement which confused the apes in the jungle with those who lived near them so that the savage seemed at once a person, a locale, and a determining influence on human beings. As a locale, the savage state was believed to be a level of human evolution that was situated just above the stage of development occupied by humans' anthropoid relatives. Those people perceived to be mired in this ancestral stage of superior groups not only were regarded as situated in close proximity to apes on the Great Chain of Being, but also were seen to live in those areas where such animals could be found. As such, the savage being was considered to share many characteristics with its anthropoid kin. These shared qualities were said to be dictated by nature and both determined social ranking and reflected innate mental worth.

In the case of the Hottentot Venus, Letourneau wrongly believed that 'the fact [had] escaped Cuvier that this type is the most animal known'.[36] At the outset, what is as remarkable about Cuvier's discussion of the cadaver of this Bushwoman as his detailed examination of her genitalia is his commentary on what he perceived to be '*the savage appearance of her form*'.[37] In the opening paragraphs of his dissertation, Cuvier remembered this African woman as he had seen her in the flesh, noting that her mannerisms were 'brusque' and 'capricious', and that her facial expressions conjured images of the pouting lips of the orang-utan. To this last remark, Topinard added 'to anyone who has seen these anthropoids, the simile is very expressive'.[38] Dotted throughout Cuvier's medical enquiry are also frequent comparisons made between the physical make-up of the Hottentot Venus and the appearance of apes, monkeys, and even dogs and other carnivores. Even the ears of the Hottentot Venus were said to have resembled those of monkeys, and commenting on her 'snout' (*le museau*), Cuvier found that in this last regard he had 'never seen a human head look more like a monkey's than that of this woman'.[39] After having described the bones of the skeleton, he then concluded that contained therein were 'all the characteristics of animality'.[40] The apparent simian likeness of the Bushwoman did not escape the gaze of Flower and Murie either. They often referred to the Bushwoman as a member of one of 'the inferior races of the human species', and made comparisons between the Bushwoman and 'inferior primates', in particular the chimpanzee. Furthermore, the author(s) reviewing their work for the *Anthropological Review* stated that the bone structure of the Bushwoman had 'an obvious simious character . . . suggestive of the pithecoid outline'.[41]

In particular, and perhaps not surprisingly, the Bushwoman's genitalia were seen as exhibiting the greatest signs of apish morphology and thereby as confirming the primitive nature of her anatomical structure, and the inferior status of her race. Her buttocks were believed to look like an ape's or monkey's. In fact, Cuvier felt that they 'offer[ed] a striking resemblance to those which appear in the female mandrills, baboons, etc., and which assume at certain epochs of their life, a truly monstrous development',[42] and Topinard argued that steatopygia 'correspond[ed] . . . with the callosities of apes'.[43] However, it was largely the structure of the Bush-woman's pelvis which was held up as specific evidence on which to base arguments indicating her race's proximity to savagery. In nineteenth-century Europe, a woman's pelvis came to be placed in an intermediary role as a secondary as well as a primary sexual sign. This was due to the fact that it houses the very place where life takes form, and whence it is brought into the world. The nature of the female's pelvis was seen as being as important to the race as her actual genitalia because its breadth was said to be commensurate with the size of the heads her race had been blessed with. According to nineteenth-century craniologists who measured the skull and its contents, the results gathered from the measurement of heads were capable of ranking human groups on a linear scale of mental worth. It was said that the bigger the size of the skull, the greater the volume of brain matter and hence the higher the level of intelligence. It was thus held that those endowed with the largest heads and, coincidentally, a high intellect had, as a rule, been born from women with large pelvises. In this way, Havelock Ellis argued that 'broad hips, which involve a large pelvis, are necessarily a characteristic of the highest human races, because the races with the largest heads must be endowed with the largest pelves to enable their large heads to enter the world'.[44] Furthermore, he contended that the white woman has the broadest pelvis and that black women possess the least developed, the narrowest and the flattest pelvis.

Although Cuvier, in his extracts on the Hottentot Venus, remarks on the enormous size of her hips, it is not to point out that her pelvis was anatomically broad, and therefore similar to the pelvises of white women. In fact, the large size of her hips was seen merely as having resulted from her steatopygia, and not the actual bone structure of her pelvis, which apparently was narrow. Essentially, to argue that the black woman's pelvis was the narrowest of all human groups was to argue that the black woman produced offspring with smaller heads and, by extension, a lower level of intelligence. The very nature of the Bushwoman's pelvis was, therefore, seen as verifying the arguments of craniometry, which merely confirmed the common prejudice that the black race occupied its subordinate position in society by the harsh dictates of nature, and that 'sexual selection [was] thus working in a line with natural selection'.[45]

The level of intelligence of the adult black, as indicated by the size of the head, was said to be comparable to that of the white child. In its own development, it was believed that an individual passed through a series of phases which represented adult ancestral forms in their correct order. This idea, known as the theory of recapitulation, or what Stephen J. Gould refers to as the notion of 'the ape in all of us',[46] held that intelligence steadily increased with the passing of time. In this way, the child was regarded as representing a primitive adult ancestor in the form of the savage being. Likewise, adults of inferior groups were perceived as akin to children of superior groups.[47] Aside from her pelvis which signified the head size and thus the level of intelligence of her offspring, other aspects of the Bushwoman's corporeality were seen as supportive of the validity of recapitulation, which was, in essence, merely another way of expressing the common prejudice that blacks' development had been arrested at a lower stage of evolution. The *Anthropological Review* concluded that 'in their very *deviations* these races [read: Hottentot and Bushman people] exemplify the infantile characters of the higher types'.[48]

Even the stature of the Bushman people and certain sociological aspects of Bushman society were seen as endorsing the validity of the notion that the Bushwoman's 'abnormal' anatomy had culminated in the birth of an entire race of degenerates. Topinard argued that the Bushman people were the smallest in the world, and that the Hottentot Venus, whom Cuvier noted to be 4 ft 1 in tall (or 124.5 cm), was considered tall by her own people. Similarly, Drs Flower and Murie contended that the Bushwoman appeared to have permanently maintained the proportions of a European child of between 4 and 6 years old. The apparent immorality of the Bushman people was also said to prove their childlike disposition. For instance, Letourneau argued that their 'predominance of amorous desire, and the total absence of any scruple of shame . . . coincide[d] with an infantine nature'.[49] In addition, the Bushman language was highlighted as indicative of the black race's innate mental inferiority. As the Bushman people were considered to be anchored in a stage of development comparable to that of childhood in the white adult, their language was believed to be akin to the unintelligible gabble of young children just learning to talk. Letourneau even argued that 'the language of the Bushmen [was] so poor that they [had] constantly to make gestures one to the other; they [could] not therefore talk in the dark'.[50]

Ranking among the most influential ideas of the nineteenth century, recapitulation enjoyed the respectability of mainstream scientific theory. It provided the perfect basis for scientists wanting to hierarchize the world's peoples, and became a general focus for the theory of biological determinism. In essence, this theory was an approbation of the Enlightenment idea that societies progress in stages from infancy to maturity. As Europe's origins or childhood were seen as being embodied by the societies of the black African savage, it was clear that the 'civilized' European would be their most appropriate guardian. Approximate in nature to the European child, the black race was considered to be unable to develop its own society, or the land on which it eked out an existence. It thus followed that the onus was on the white race to endeavour to yank the black primitive, described by Kipling as 'half devil and half child',[51] out of its quagmire of savagery – hence the ameliorating ideology of the 'civilizing mission' which accompanied British imperialism.

Myriad discourses which both shaped and were shaped by nineteenth-century cultural assumptions about normality, race and sexuality echo through medical depictions of the Bushwoman. However, the ideology they absorbed had been critically sifted, for the picture they present is a selective one which conjures some of the most remarkable differences between the European and the Bushman people – or at least how Europeans perceived themselves. Particular attention is focused on those parts of the Bushwoman's anatomy that were politically significant. A powerful assumption which underlined much thinking of the time was the notion that physical evidence or 'nature' provided a point of certainty from which issues concerning human nature and development could depart. Consequently, biology was regarded as the epistemic foundation for prescriptive claims about the social order, and science was increasingly held up as an arbiter on social questions. However, when it was employed as a guide in the task of ranking human groups on a scale said to reflect their innate differences in physiology, customs and mentality, it is clear that the decision to place the white race at the top of the global hierarchy and the black race at its very bottom was not dictated solely by the facts of human biology. Even so, in that the persuasiveness of science is based on the assumption that what it discovers is 'real', and that what it expresses is 'natural', the pronouncements made by these scientists were implicitly conceptualized as immutably fixed, and they themselves were regarded as mere humble observers who provided a gateway to an already established truth, or in other words, a transparent window on reality. The assumptions they made about the nature of the Bushwoman and the black race, however, far from being original, irreducible nodes from which a reliable understanding of the world could be constructed, were actually powerful metaphors that endowed what may well have been quite transient affairs with an air of finality and eternity. Essentially, these examples of medical discourse lent their authority to racist characterization. As such, they should be seen as part of yet another system of representation which constantly reinforces the binary divisions of normal/abnormal, healthy/ diseased, us/them to which every individual is subjected.

Inherently, 'otherness' is a site of knowledge that is thoroughly imbued with a distinct power relation. Foucault has argued that 'it is the peculiarity of the nineteenth century that it applied to the space of exclusion of which the leper is the symbolic inhabitant . . . the technique of power proper to disciplinary partitioning'.[52] Medical curiosities, 'freaks' or the 'perverse' essentially functioned to remind Europeans what they were not, and to exemplify what they did not want to be, but could turn into if the categories normal/abnormal, 'us' and 'them', became blurred. Fundamental to ensuring that this composition remained intact was the notion of discipline, of which the architectural figure is Bentham's Panopticon – the author of the Foucaultian concept of a disciplinary society. The Victorian era's medicine of perversions and freak shows were appurtenances of a disciplinary mechanism which employed a technique comparable to that of the Panopticon, where power was dispersed and decentralized. Like the Panopticon, these two peculiarly nineteenth-century icons were controlling devices. In effect, they arranged 'spatial unities that [made] it possible to see constantly and to recognize immediately'.[53] For both the prisoner isolated in the Panopticon and the freak, set apart from mainstream society and/or as a display in an exhibition, 'visibility was a trap'.[54] Like the confined prisoner, the freak was ensnared in a sticky web of surveillance and discipline. This is evident in the fact that both the Panopticon and the medicine of perversions enframed their subjects – the former in a prison cell, the latter by means of representation. Like any modality of social restraint, the medicine of perversions evolved to control the abnormal and, once it was established, continued to revolve around it. In the same manner as modes of social control, the distinguishing feature of the medicine of perversions was that it was a social arbiter of what was 'normal' and 'abnormal', and thereby a defining force behind the construction of the binarism 'us' and 'them' or the Self and the Other. The creation of this social order should be seen as a means of social control: once this division is set up, its components are then distanced from each other for the sole purpose of maintaining social disunity.

The deployment of this type of social ordering, of which the eventual outcome is the privileging of one group and the repression of another, has to be seen, as Foucault has noted, as 'the self-affirmation of one class rather than the enslavement of another: a defence, a protection, a strengthening and an exaltation that were eventually extended to others . . . as a means of social control and political subjugation'.[55] While the medical depictions of the Hottentot Venus and other Bushwomen essentially constructed her as the quintessential black other, both in the verbal sense of 'thinking' her and in the nominal sense of 'building' her, these medical texts also constructed the identity of the Self. The picture of the Bushwoman they present us with is one that is counterposed to how the white race perceived itself. Antithetical comparisons are constantly made between what were seen as her essential characteristics and what were said to be the main attributes of the nineteenth-century European. In this way, it was argued that whereas the European was 'normal', the Bushwoman was 'abnormal'. While the corporeality of the white epitomized that of God's original human type, she herself was nothing but a perversion. Whereas the morality of the white race remained unblemished, her moral countenance was immanently diseased. The Bushwoman possessed neither the refined anatomical structure, nor the superior intellect of the white race. In every way, the European was perfection and the black race was degenerate. In relation to such series of antinomies, Jacques Derrida has argued that:

> All metaphysicians have proceeded thus, from Plato to Rousseau, from Descartes to Husserl: good before evil, the positive before the negative, the pure before the impure, the simple before the complex, the essential before the accidental, the imitated before the imitation, etc. This is not just *one* metaphysical gesture among others; it is the metaphysical exigency, the most constant, profound and potent procedure.[56]

Furthermore, he contends that historically, one has always conceived, firstly, of the normal, the pure, the original, in order *then* to be able to conceive of its derivation, its deterioration, its perversion. It is not only inevitable, but also imperative that the second part of this logocentrism be constructed, in order more clearly to define the original, the pure, or the 'normal'. Yet by setting up the subject to be defined in opposition to what it is not, or, in other words, by defining the Self in relation to its Other, the essence of the Other, or how it is perceived at a given moment, is also given shape. It is, therefore, not by accident that the picture of the Bushwoman that was presented by Drs Cuvier, Flower and Murie reveals far more about nineteenth-century European culture and the Victorian psyche than it does about the Hottentot Venus and other South African Bushwomen. As Edward Said has argued in relation to Orientalism, these medical texts are essentially an episode in modern political culture, and as such have less to do with the Other than they do with 'our' world.[57]

Until the mid-1970s, the genitalia of the Hottentot Venus continued to be paraded before the gaze of Europe. Over 150 years after her death, Saartjie Baartman's genitalia still floated in formalin in a bell-jar on a shelf in the Musée de l'Homme in Paris among a ghoulish pot-pourri of exhibits accumulated in the course of the nineteenth century. Although the remains of the Hottentot Venus are no longer on public display, they are still housed in the Musée de l'Homme albeit in a locked back room somewhere in the building. In one reading, their continued existence serves as a permanent reminder of nineteenth-century Europe's fixation with issues concerning notions of normality, race and sexuality. In a more profound sense, they constitute a case of frozen imperialism; a contemporary reiteration of nineteenth-century ideas about racial and cultural hierarchies. In 1995, a campaign was launched in South Africa to close this final chapter in the colourful biography of the Hottentot Venus by having her remains released by the Musée de l'Homme and returned for burial in her native South Africa.[58] In sum, this latest addition to the story of the Hottentot Venus provides us with one more illustration of the linkage between nineteenth-century imperialism and contemporary international relations, and reminds us of the way in which culture can resurface as politics.

Notes

1. Michel Foucault, *The History of Sexuality*, vol. 1 (Ringwood, Australia, Penguin Books, 1978), p. 118.

2. Edward Said, *Orientalism* (Ringwood, Australia, Penguin Books, 1978), p. 58.

3. See Leslie Fiedler, *Freaks: Myths and Images of the Secret Self* (Ringwood, Australia, Penguin Books, 1981), p. 19.

4. Foucault, *The History of Sexuality*, vol. 1, p. 146.

5. Ibid.

6. Ibid., p. 65.

7. In the late nineteenth century, one of the most popular books in both Europe and the United States was *Anomalies and Curiosities of Medicine* (1896). Written by doctors, George M. Gould and Walter L. Pyle, it is described as being 'an encyclopaedic collection of rare and extraordinary cases, and of the most striking instances of abnormality in all branches of medicine and surgery'. On the very first page of this best-seller, the authors contend that it is in cases where 'perversions' or 'monstrosities' are apparent that 'we seem to catch forbidden sight of the secret work-room of Nature, and drag out into the light the evidences of her clumsiness, and proof of her lapses in skill': George M. Gould and Walter L. Pyle, *Anomalies and Curiosities of Medicine* (New York, The Julian Press, 1896), p. 1. Moreover, in relation to sexuality, Drs Gould and Pyle argued that it was in the 'aberrations of form or function of the generative organs' that the imperfections woven by the 'artisan of Life . . . upon the mysterious garment of corporeality' are most clearly revealed.

8. Sander L. Gilman, *Sexuality: An Illustrated History* (New York, John Wiley 1989), p. 1; emphasis in the original. See also Sander L. Gilman, 'Black bodies, white bodies: toward an iconography of female sexuality in late nineteenth-century art, medicine and literature', *Critical Inquiry*, 12 (1985), 204–42; this fascinating article, in which Gilman discusses the meaning of the sexualized body in diverse examples of late nineteenth-century popular culture and medicine, provided me with the impetus for conducting further research on the Hottentot Venus.

9. Donna Haraway, *Primate Visions: Gender, Race, and Nature in the World of Modern Science* (London, Routledge, 1989), p. 4.

10. From the song 'The Humours of Bartlemy Fair', quoted in P. R. Kirby, 'More about the Hottentot Venus', *Africana Notes and News*, 10 (1953), 127.

11. Georges Cuvier, 'Extraits d'observations Faites sur le Cadavre d'une femme connue à Paris et à Londres sous le nom de Vénus Hottentote', *Mémoires du Muséum d'Histoire Naturelle*, 3 (1817), 259–74; my translation.

12. W. H. Flower and J. Murie, 'Account of the dissection of a Bushwoman', *Journal of Anatomy and Physiology*, 1 (1867), 189–208.

13. Percival R. Kirby, 'The Hottentot Venus', *Africana Notes and News*, 6 (1949), 61.

14. Yet in comparison, when one turns to examine the descriptions of autopsies conducted on black males in approximately the same period, such as the three dissections of African-American males carried out by William Turner in 1878, 1879 and 1896, what is remarkable about them is the absence of any discussion of the male genitalia whatsoever. See William Turner, 'Notes on the dissection of a Negro', *Journal of Anatomy and Physiology*, 13 (1878), 382–6; 'Notes on the dissection of a second Negro', *Journal of Anatomy and Physiology*, 14 (1879), 244–8; 'Notes on the dissection of a third Negro', *Journal of Anatomy and Physiology*, 31 (1896), 624–6.

15. See Havelock Ellis, *Studies in the Psychology of Sex*, vol. 4: *Sexual Selection in Man* (Philadelphia, F. A. Davis, 1905), pp. 161–3.

16. However, it was not until the Hottentot Venus died that knowledge of this aspect of her genitalia was procured: 'she kept her "apron" carefully hidden', Cuvier argued, 'either between her thighs, or more profoundly, and it was not until after her death that we came to know that she had it'. See Cuvier, 'Extraits d'observations', p. 265.

17. Ibid., pp. 265 and 268.

18. Flower and Murie, 'Account of the dissection of a Bushwoman', p. 208.

19. C. Gallagher and T. Laqueur (eds), *The Making of the Modern Body: Sexuality and Society in the Nineteenth Century* (Berkeley, University of California Press, 1987), p. x.

20. Paul Topinard, *Anthropology* (The Library of Contemporary Science), trans. R. T. H. Bartley (London, Chapman and Hall, 1878), p. 362.

21. Ibid.

22. Flower and Murie, 'Account of the dissection of a Bushwoman', p. 208; emphasis added.

23. J. C. Nott and R. Gliddon, *Indigenous Races of the Earth* (Philadelphia, Lippincott, 1857), p. 628.

24. Topinard, *Anthropology*, p. 363. Incidentally, these are not the only examples of medicine where the genitalia of the black woman have been held up as proof of the non-unity of the races. In 1868 Dr Edward B. Turnipseed of South Carolina in an article entitled 'Some facts in regard to the anatomical differences between the white and negro races', which was published in 1877 in vol. 10 of the *American Journal of Obstetrics and Diseases of Women and Children* (pp. 32–3), argued that 'the hymen of the negro woman is not at the entrance of the vagina, as in the white woman, but from one and a half to two inches from its entrance in the interior' (p. 32). From this, he concluded that 'the knowledge of the position of this membrane in the negro race is of vital importance to the [medical] profession . . . as one of the anatomical indications Providence has given us of the non-unity of the races' (p. 33). Turnipseed's views were supported by Dr C. H. Fort of Tennessee in the same volume of this journal in his article 'Some corroborative facts in regard to the anatomical differences between the negro and white races' (pp. 258–9). Presenting another six cases of this apparent anomaly, he thus concluded: 'I sincerely believe that this peculiarity . . . would enable any practiced physician to distinguish the negro from the white race, even in the dark, by the aid of touch alone' (p. 259).

25. Gilman, *Sexuality*, p. 2.

26. Ellis, *Studies in the Psychology of Sex*, vol. 4, p. 156.

27. Charles Letourneau, *Sociology* (The Library of Contemporary Science), trans. H. M. Trollope (London, Chapman and Hall, 1881), p. 60.

28. Ibid., p. 60.

29. Ibid., p. 554.

30. Marianna Torgovnick, *Gone Primitive: Savage Intellects, Modern Lives* (University of Chicago Press, Chicago, 1992), p. 228.

31. Letourneau, *Sociology*, p. 69.

32. Henry Rider Haggard, *Allan Quartermain* (London, Longmans, Green and Co., 1888), pp. 4–6.

33. Frantz Fanon, *Black Skin, White Masks* (London, Pluto Press, 1986), pp. 157, 177.

34. Letourneau, *Sociology*, p. 450.

35. Nott and Gliddon, *Indigenous Races of the Earth*, p. 628.

36. Letourneau, *Sociology*, p. 494.

37. Cuvier, 'Extraits d'observations', p. 264; emphasis added.

38. Topinard, *Anthropology*, p. 493.

39. Cuvier, 'Extraits d'observations', p. 269.

40. Ibid.

41. *Anthropological Review*, 'Flower and Murie on the dissection of a Bushwoman', 5: July (1867), 319–34 (p. 332).

42. Cuvier, 'Extraits d'observations', p. 268.

43. Topinard, *Anthropology*, p. 508.

44. Ellis, *Studies in the Psychology of Sex*, vol. 4, p. 165.

45. Ibid., p. 164.

46. Stephen J. Gould, *The Mismeasure of Man* (Ringwood, Australia, Penguin Books, 1981), p. 113.

47. Interestingly, in *The Mismeasure of Man* Stephen J. Gould argues that 'many primary school curriculums of the late nineteenth century were reconstructed in the light of recapitulation. Several school boards prescribed the Song of Hiawatha in early grades,

reasoning that children, passing through the savage state of their ancestral past, would identify with it' (p. 114).

48. *Anthropological Review*, 'Flower and Murie on the dissection of a Bushwoman', p. 322; emphasis added.

49. Letourneau, *Sociology*, p. 64.

50. Ibid., p. 578.

51. From the poem 'Take up the white man's burden', quoted in Gould, *The Mismeasure of Man*, p. 119.

52. Michel Foucault, *Discipline and Punish: The Birth of the Prison*, trans. Alan Sheridan (New York, Pantheon Books, 1977), p. 199.

53. Ibid., p. 200.

54. Ibid.

55. Foucault, *The History of Sexuality*, p. 123.

56. Jacques Derrida, *Limited Inc.* (Baltimore, Johns Hopkins University Press, 1977), quoted in J. Culler, note 1, *On Deconstruction: Theory and Criticism after Structuralism* (Ithaca, NY, Cornell University Press, 1982). (Emphasis is Derrida's.)

57. Said, *Orientalism*, p. 12.

58. See Esmare Weidman, 'New drama as the pickled remains of the Hottentot Venus become the centre of a dramatic tug of war between the French and her angry descendants', *Drum* (Cape Town, February 1996), 100–1.

CHAPTER FIVE

Forests of the night: the moralized topography of Mau Mau

GLENN MATTHEWS

> . . . the forest, in whose depths wild beasts
> and wilder men might lurk.
>
> C. T. Stoneham, *Mau Mau*, 1953[1]

Darkness, violence and landscape intersect in unforeseen ways. These diffuse elements dynamically combined in the mountainous forests of the Aberdare ranges to substantially influence events in the Mau Mau revolt in Kenya in the 1950s. In this strange landscape the colonials and the British security forces found themselves operating in a realm of uncertainty where the normal rules of conflict, even of reality, were severely strained. Exploring the way in which the forest was perceived by the security forces indicates the profound significance of the role of space and place in violent action. In this context, space and place are relational terms. The former invokes a symbolic, metaphorical realm of signification and belonging which is geographically mobile and transgressive; the latter refers to more grounded processes and specific sites of action in which space is vivified.[2] A knowledge of the way that the place of the forest was seen by colonials and combatants challenges assumptions that Mau Mau can be understood solely in terms of formal political rationalities.

For the security forces that engaged with the Mau Mau in the Aberdare ranges, combat constituted an excursion into dark landscapes of memory and culture, of peculiar violence and distorted realities. More generally, the moralized topography of colonial Kenya formed part of a military and ideological battle between the colonials and their security forces, and the Mau Mau. In the conscious and unconscious constructions of the space of the forest, the whites in Kenya operated in a field of perception in which their violence could be legitimated. Yet this space, inhabited by symbols of ancient magical evil let loose in the modern world, seriously disturbed them. The ultimate source of this evil was seen as being the landscape of Africa itself, in the residue of the old 'dark Africa', found in this instance in the uncleared and untamed forests of Kenya.

The object of this chapter is to examine the way in which the colonial response to Mau Mau was partly driven by a particular perception of space. The focus lies in the place of the Aberdare ranges in Kenya, where much of the fighting occurred. When D. H. Rawcliffe, a relatively liberal colonial, commented that 'Mau Mau is a barbaric terror, that only Africa itself could have produced',[3] he implicitly raised questions which went to the heart of the colonial understanding of the 'other'.

How was colonial space formed in the imagination? What historical process lay behind the way that the colonials and the security forces saw these towering, dark and threatening forests? The argument is that ideas of the 'wild man' of ancient legends and the 'darkness' of Africa, incorporated into colonial fantasy and imperial history, interacted with the forest landscape to give the violence of the security forces a viciousness that cannot be accounted for in conventional terms. This is combined with an analysis of colonial culture that draws out the white attraction to forests as places of freedom where colonial masculine fantasies form part of a highly authoritarian ideology.

Strategic studies, as a subdiscipline of traditional international relations, contains an implicit theory of spatiality. Territory, speed and communication form an integral part of any military campaign. The tactical analysis of troops and their units is a measure of how territory and space are assessed. To a large extent, the type of terrain in which troops move determines their reach and influence. Deserts can be controlled far more easily than forests, where the trees and valleys serve to conceal and protect. Military influence can be mapped according to the ability of modern equipment to detect the presence of hostile forces, to traverse space and to establish domination.

The level of morale of the troops also plays a significant part in the success or failure of a campaign. It seems axiomatic to say that tightly disciplined and well-motivated troops are more effective than disenchanted troops in gaining and holding territory. Morale is conventionally treated as a monolithic concept working independently of the place of military engagement. What is understood as morale may be an umbrella concept covering a cultural baggage of fears and fantasies that are activated by the place of encounter to powerfully affect the performance of a military unit. This is not to say that the state of mind normally analysed in terms of good or bad morale is necessarily an indicator of military effectiveness. The disquieting sense of dislocation felt by the security forces in the Aberdares manifested itself in the adoption of a brutality which may well have led to the campaign's being concluded more quickly than if the constraints of civilized mores had prevailed. The fact that these constraints did not prevail indicates that an analysis of the way in which the colonists and the security forces encountered the forest of the Aberdare ranges has value. The actions and reactions of the security forces provides a fund of material that draws out and informs the spatial assumptions of strategic analysis and, ultimately, international relations.

An examination of the significance of place and space is a journey below the surfaces of colonial history. What emerges is a different angle which brings into view the topographic, the tactical and the ideological. The telling of a different story simultaneously hints towards an international relations that takes account of notions of spatiality. Investigating place and space is an excursion into an area of silence that lies behind the disciplinary view that states are the only significant actors in world politics and that their behaviour can be understood in terms of high-level power equations and rational processes.

The narrowness of focus which subordinates the Mau Mau revolt to an internal dispute within the British Empire is part of an international relations that distances itself from the Third World. Traditionally, power is seen as the property of states and policy-makers. This way of seeing becomes uncertain in the face of the realization that power comes from below as well as above. Power is understood here to exist in highly complex micro-relations which disrupt the apparent line of continuity between the authorizing institution of Whitehall and action as it was played out in the forests of Kenya. Settler culture influences metropolitan culture and directs us to the way in which the particular and local interact with the systemic and the international. Armies, strategies and political economies are not displaced in this schema but are seen as instruments of explanation that leave substantial gaps. The questions and issues that emerge in these gaps between the larger categories of analysis lead towards seemingly peripheral yet important episodes in international relations such as the Mau Mau revolt. In the process of understanding the linkages between space, violence and perception, we are able to glimpse another international relations.

This chapter is in five sections. First, an outline of the historical events of Mau Mau is given. This leads to the second section for a consideration of the way that landscape, history and modernity combined to create a moralized topography of the forest. The third section then considers the cultural formation of the tropes of African darkness and their connection with the 'wild man' of medieval legends. The fourth section examines the way in which these tropes infiltrated the colonials' representations of Mau Mau. Finally, analysis concentrates on the way that such representations combined with masculine fantasies to materially affect violence in the forest.

A conventional version of the events of the Mau Mau rebellion would hold that an armed peasants' revolt took place in Kenya, precipitating the Declaration of Emergency in October 1952. The participants attempted to build a resistance movement through the swearing of an 'oath of unity'. The leaders defined the movement politically by using the term 'Land and Freedom Party'. Much of the fighting took place in the dense forests of the Aberdare ranges. The revolt was ultimately put down by the security forces with heavy casualties among the Kikuyu, the 'tribe' predominant in the rebellion. Despite the absence of external support, it took 21,000 paramilitary police, many thousands of armed 'loyalist' Africans, plus the equivalent of a full division of British troops supported by the Royal Air Force, equipped with Vampire jets and heavy bombers, more than four years to destroy the Mau Mau as a military threat. The last prisoners were not released from the detention camps until 1959, in the wake of the killing of eleven men at Hola detention centre.

The 'reality' of Mau Mau remains, however, contentious. It has been argued that Mau Mau, with its associations with atavism, bestiality, witchcraft and cannibalism in the forest, was constituted by and existed only in colonial discourse.[4] One can certainly concede that in the colonial representations of 'Mau Mau', fiction and non-fiction were virtually indistinguishable. Yet it is a very limited view of Mau Mau that would confine its existence as manifest horror purely to colonial discourse. While the extent to which this discourse increases our understanding of colonial ideology should be acknowledged, separating the Land and Freedom Army from Mau Mau seems a spurious and misguided exercise which acts to reinscribe the categories of international relations against which we seek to establish a critical perspective.

Mau Mau was in fact a terrible reality to the white Kenyans and to thousands of Kikuyu. Although only 32 civilian Europeans were killed, the horror produced by the deaths was immense. Whites may have exaggerated the lurid nature of the oathing ceremony but there is no doubt that tribal witchcraft was a crucial element in the oathing ritual, and that this in turn spurred on the killing. Mau Mau constituted itself as a terror to the colonials and the Kikuyu through ghastly murders. The imagined military value of the image of wildness was not missed by the rebel leaders, such as Dedan Kimathi, who, reportedly, ordered dismembered bodies to be placed at the edge of the forest.

The tactical gains produced by terror were more than offset by the blows this image delivered to the movement in terms of international propaganda. The cause was not aided by the name Mau Mau. This was a colonial invention to signify primitivism and had no origin in Kikuyu or Swahili. It was eventually, and perhaps misguidedly, 'used with pride by participants in the struggle'.[5] This greatly assisted those who sought to portray the revolt as pathological rather than political. The acceptance of the image of wildness by both sides to the conflict calls into question the idea that either Mau Mau or the security forces were simply rational organizations acting in pursuit of clear goals. Any such view is challenged by a deconstruction of the perception and representation of the place of violent encounters – the forests of the Aberdares.

A moralized topography was created out of the fusion of landscape and history. Novelist Robert Ruark encapsulated this in the introduction to *Something of Value* when he emphasized that the African landscape was imbued with evil, such that 'in order to understand Mau Mau it is first necessary to understand Africa . . . to understand Africa you must understand a basic impulsive savagery that is greater than anything we civilized people have encountered in two centuries'.[6] Writing such as this formed part of an ideological process where the landscape of Kenya was created by social as much as by natural forces. Historical and pseudo-historical narratives overlap. These narratives then act as potentials for the stimulation of memory and action.

The symbols that the colonials encountered in a particular place meant that the past took an objectified form in the immediacy of spatial cognition. In this sense the forest cannot be reduced to its topography, flora and fauna; nor the Mau Mau to simple combatants. How things are perceived is related to the context of perception, and the process of recognition that the site activates. The landscape of the Aberdares generated more in the colonial mind than any array of objective phenomena. In 'Geography, experience and imagination', D. Lowenthal argues that 'every image is a product of personal experience, learning, imagination and memory. Each is shaped by the refraction through cultural and personal lenses of custom and fancy.'[7]

The idea of landscape as a social phenomenon is part of the notion that landscape does not exist without an observer. In this sense, although the *land* exists, the *scape* is understood as a projection of human consciousness, an image received. Mentally or physically, we frame the view and our appreciation depends on our frame of mind. This approach emphasizes the view that it is the geography within the minds of people that is the most fascinating geography of all, even more so than the geography of the earth.[8]

The geography of the colonial imagination of Mau Mau can be read off the historical structures of space formed by the colonists in the nineteenth century. These provided a place for those who sought to settle and 'improve' the land and for those who sought conquest and adventure. The initial taming of the landscape was an important part of the formation of space and the creation of the settlers' topographic origin myths. These familiar myths of *terra nullius* inscribed the space as empty and waiting, an untamed wilderness with inconvenient tribes fleeing before the settlers' advance, and portrayed as retreating to the tribes' natural surroundings. In the case of the Kikuyu the forest was represented as their favoured haven. The Kikuyu had traditionally retreated to the forests in the face of Masai attacks, but only for reasons of immediate survival. Their use of the forest in this way led to claims being made about their possessing a 'psychology' of the forest. This contributed to the myth that the lands desired by the whites were free for the taking because the Aberdares were where the Kikuyu really belonged.

The origin myths of colonialism were founded in a way of seeing that demanded that space be unbounded in its reality; at once empty and waiting for inevitable development. This was coincident with the emergence of imperialist discourse, which Homi Bhabha sees as a non-dialogic, unitary enunciation that is unmarked by difference.[9] This discourse was characteristic of the political ideology of the colonists, many of whom displayed highly authoritarian tendencies. For highly author-itarian people, simple, firm, often stereotypical cognitive structures are required. There is no place for ambivalence or ambiguities, and this is reflected in unitary colonial constructions of space as ready to be tamed or beyond control. This led the early colonials to understand the incompre-hensible as latently evil. These spaces, when revisited in the 1950s, became sites for the re-enactment of early conquests and for the simulation of power; for making power tangible as material force.

The structure of memory that space evoked for the colonial was a part of the mental mapping of the structure of the colonial state. The claims and practices of white power are inscribed in the command and naming of space. The explorer Barry Lopez writes 'It is easy to underestimate the power of association with the land, with the span of it in memory and imagination'.[10] The formation of historiographic surfaces occurred within a continuum of spaces: the colonial state of Kenya, the ordered farmlands of the White Highlands and the forests of the Aberdares. This process divided territory into zones of controlled and uncontrolled space in which wild places like the forest were 'created' as the other to the civilized places. Notions of magical and savage killing were compressed into imaginings of the dark forest where a wild history threatened to erupt into rebellion, messianically led by prominent Mau Mau such as Dedan Kimathi.

Historically, the forest has been seen as a primordial element, a landscape of fear that gives the house and garden meaning as sanctuary spaces. At best forests are ambivalent, brooding, grim places, as in Teutonic fairy-tales; full of unknown dangers.[11] The Kenyan colonial author C. T. Stoneham felt this so strongly that he wrote: 'The "Power of Darkness" has frightened every people, especially those who lived among dense, gloomy forests, where darkness was a tangible evil, and the unruly imagination could produce all manner of hideous images.'[12] These fears combined with the harshness of the conditions of the forest to produce the effect of convincing many in the security forces that the space in which they operated was not simply strange, but actively malevolent.

The command of space involves the reorganization of codifying appar-atuses such as mental maps. Colonial mapping of the boundaries of the safe and the dangerous resonated with traditional metaphysical structures of paradise, purgatory and hell. This general trope can be witnessed, for example, in the naming of a large-scale military foray into the Aberdares as 'Operation Dante'. In this mental framework the security forces moved from sanctuary, through a neutral zone thence to a hellish realm of uncontrollable danger and back again. The political codification of space fuelled the ideological perceptions of the security forces. This directly mobilized and channelled action. In *The Divine Comedy* Dante journeyed to the depths of hell and discovered his only escape route lay in clambering over Satan's great shaggy body.[13] The gigantic wild man in the last circle of hell was appalling to civilized sensibilities, but he could be of service. In the depths of the Aberdare forests the bush skills of the 'wild men' who were no longer Mau Mau could aid those in the security forces, such as Captains Kitson and Henderson, to hunt and kill the wild men who remained their enemies.

Modernity at best provided an unstable bulwark against the forest. The British had advanced technology at their disposal, materially affecting their comprehension of space by militarizing the landscape. Yet they were unable fully to assert domination over areas of operations where primitive rites were still powerful forces. Writing 60 years earlier, Joseph Conrad pointed out that the move from magic to the machine was part of a shift from the fabulous geography of the Middle Ages to the militant geography of modern times.[14] There were in some senses two competing geographies that the British were trying to master. To obliterate the primitive/magical and establish the modern/military they deployed all the technology at their disposal. With their radio communications the security forces could coordinate their efforts relatively easily. This contrasted with the Mau Mau, who were basically isolated from each other's groups, and found it difficult to act in a unified way. Where the security forces could use four-wheel drives, or call on Vampire jets, the Mau Mau were confined to the speed of their feet.

Aircraft technology, so defining of modernity, was nevertheless a weapons system that worked only in daylight hours and in good weather. It was ineffective in destroying Mau Mau as a guerrilla force. This failure of the modern, which frustrated the air force while confirming the prejudices of the army, was disturbing to the colonials, who sought a quick, 'surgical' response to the 'disease' of Mau Mau. Modernity had not triumphed over the primitive. The dark, magical powers of the Mau Mau proved to be far more resilient than anticipated.

When the security forces proved unable to provide the much-desired quick victory, one solution was to pen the Mau Mau in the forest. As commander-in-chief, General Erskine was intent on forming space and changing the topography. He conceived the idea of cutting off the Mau Mau supply line from the Kikuyu Reserves through the construction of a gigantic ditch. It was 50 miles long, and 12 feet deep and 20 feet wide. It was filled with impenetrable mazes of booby-trapped barbed wire and sharpened bamboo stakes. This project was a sustained atrocity of forced labour.[15] Behind it were the imagined sanctuary spaces of the reserves, the farmlands, the cities where white futures stretched hopefully to utopian horizons. Beyond this moat of militant modern geography was the forest, redolent of primitivism.

The British were forced to move from the realm of a technologically advanced way of seeing space, from above and at speed, to seeing it physically in the same terms as the Mau Mau, on the ground with restricted movement. This departure from the modern produced a perception of space which was heightened by the appearance of the Mau Mau. It has been contended that, in general, the British soldier treats well enemies he respects, but the functional efficiency of animal fur clothing for warmth and hair-plaiting for lice-catching among the Mau Mau were alien to the security forces. The Mau Mau appearance served further to justify prejudices of racial superiority and placed discipline under strain, leading to particularly violent action.[16]

When William Baldwin of the colonial security forces tracked down a Mau Mau gang, he found them dressed in rags and covered with sweat and blood. To him, they looked like wild beasts of the forest.[17] In the course of attempts by the security forces to 'truthfully' depict Mau Mau, and legitimize action against them, a subtle but profound distortion of perception had to take place, precipitated by the fact that stereotypical categorizations can never do justice to all aspects of reality. This distortion of perception manifested itself in the elevation of the idea of African landscapes of darkness inhabited by 'wild men' conducting evil ceremonies. The sense of threat that was felt as a consequence of this distortion meant that many of the colonials were under great strain.

The years of the emergency have been seen as a time when Kenya's settlers lived in a pathological atmosphere. Every Kikuyu was possibly a Mau Mau. Visiting British critics could be agents of the Kremlin. The atmosphere of fear and loathing was so powerful, so laden with tension, that Graham Greene, then a visiting correspondent, wrote of how the Mau Mau conflict, although much smaller than the Malaya conflict, preyed much worse on his nerves.[18] Even the Colonial Secretary, Sir Oliver Lyttleton, safe in London, could recall no instance when he felt the forces of evil so strongly: 'As I wrote memoranda or instructions, I would suddenly see a shadow fall across the page – the horned shadow of the Devil himself.'[19]

The anxiety produced by the abuse of power is revealed in the demented obsessions and terrors contained in the imaginings of oathing ceremonies and 'wild men'. Sir Oliver Lyttleton's thinking is indicative of the broad base of colonial belief which saw fighting Mau Mau in terms of the defence of civilization. This is important in terms of the way in which colonial policy was actualized in the field. Serious doubt is cast on the notion that policy was exclusively driven by concerns of strategy in light of imperial contingencies. In the image of the colonial secretary being troubled by the Devil we can see the periphery producing unpredictable elements that may then influence decisions in the metropole. While official discourse may have concentrated on divisions, tactics and practical military policy, beneath this veneer of calculating efficiency there clearly lay a perception of the conflict in Kenya profoundly influenced by cultural factors. In this sense, understanding policy formulation demands the inclusion of much that lies outside of traditional imperial interests.

The central element that drew together the fears and fantasies of the colonial and the imperial policy-makers was the Mau Mau oathing ceremony. The possibility of political or social reasons for the revolt was denied. The cause of Kikuyu unrest was located in a primitive evil that formed the inspiration for psychotic behaviour. The armed resistance movement of the 1950s could then be comprehended as an ancient scourge erupting from the wild. The oath was understood to be a process which escalated in violence. This view was legitimized by the Nairobi psychiatrist Dr J. C. Carothers. In his 'psychological study' he made a connection between Mau Mau and resurgent medieval evil:

> At the midnight assemblies, homage was paid to the Devil . . . dances followed, a meal was taken which sometimes included human blood and urine and the flesh of infants who had been exhumed or murdered . . . as in Europe until the end of the sixteenth century.[20]

Colonial imaginings of the depravity of the oathing ritual and the idealized place of its enactment were drawn out by Carothers when he claimed that orgiastic ceremonies took place in deep forest clearings by the light of bonfires.[21] Reportage and fantasy mingled in the mythologizing of Mau Mau. Yet these stories were not trivial just because they were extraordinary. Colonial myths combined with the landscape to create a realm of terror that allowed the whites to wantonly kill Kikuyu people 'othered' into Mau Mau.

The joining of a transcended European past with the idea of Africa as a dark continent, as a repository for generations of fantasies of 'wild men', comes from a Western tradition associating place and evil. The Bible, the works of Homer, Virgil, Dante, Hieronymus Bosch, Brueghel and Rimbaud, and Conrad's *Heart of Darkness* all contributed to the trope of darkness. The nexus between darkness, the supernatural, tribal custom and menacing landscapes was given a sharp edge by legends of the 'wild man'.

Margaret Hodgen, in *Early Anthropology in the Sixteenth and Seventeenth Centuries*, states that Leo Africanus declared that not only did Negroes lead a beastly life, but they were 'utterly destitute of reason'. For Hodgen this is an important declaration because she sees it in the great chain of ideas of Europeans that the pagan inhabited a zone somewhere between animal and human.[22] The essentialized figure of the 'wild man' is the final result of this reductive process of discourse that began with a host of extraordinary creatures and monsters that existed in European imaginings of the East: Ethiopia, India, the periphery of the Old World. The 'wild man' was originally a hairy, cruel beast, usually deformed in body to reflect the savagery of his mind. He was physically superior and mentally inferior. The trope is reflected in works such as Pierre D'Ailly's *Imago Mundi*, Sir John Mandeville's *Travels* or Pope Pius II's *Historia Rerum*. These writings were part of the dissemination of a set of images that in popular, as well as scholarly, form made a deep impression on large numbers of people.[23]

The literary tradition of darkness helped form a site of social imagination populated by metamorphosing images of evil and the underworld. This formed part of an iconographic development that parallels the development of European imperialism. Modernity, travelling in the coach of Imperialism, crystallized the racism of the West through the tropes of wildness and darkness. The argument here is not that there was a unilinear development of a consciousness of Africa as a location of the savagery of the wild man; rather that, from a number of different ideas constituting Africa, the notion of wild savagery became the dominant paradigm.

The notion of Africa as a place of wild darkness was an idea especially prevalent in the Victorian era, the moment of origin for the colony of Kenya. The notion was associated with political and economic pressures with a strong psychology of blaming the victim through which Europeans projected their darkest impulses on to Africans. The taint of slavery and the displacement of blame on to Africans, when coupled with the sensational reports of cannibalism, witchcraft and apparently shameless sexual customs, led to a cloak of darkness descending on the Victorian perception of Africa. Patrick Brantlinger in his genealogy of the myth of 'the dark continent' argues that this perception was generally accepted as reality.[24] The cultural residue of these distortions was African images of backward-ness, childishness, superstition, great physical prowess and a genetic pre-disposition to run amok. When this image fused with the political economy of colonialism, it meant that native resistance to colonial rule could be characterized as the forces of an ancient evil made manifest by 'wild men' in the forest. Into this psychic and actual landscape entered the Mau Mau of Kenya.

Literary representations played a pivotal role in the imaginary landscape of Mau Mau. Most societies probably take their fictions as real. The distinguishing feature of the culture of terror is that fields of knowledge are encased in a framework of ideology. The representations produced within this structure reflect the problem of distinguishing reality and illusion. Separating the one from the other becomes infinitely more than a merely philosophical problem of interpreting knowledge and its sources. Ideological representations form part of a high-powered medium of domination and epistemic and ontological distortion. The importance of the colonial work of fantasy extends beyond the nightmarish quality of the contents of the oath. Its fundamental aspect was the way in which a tenuous reality was created out of a fiction. The unstable interplay of truth and illusion becomes a phantasmic social force. This discourse of facts and fantasies tenuously secured the settlers in their ideological positions. It could also work to bring those outside the conflict into the values of the colonial world.

In considering the way that the colonial world created its own reality for the newcomer, it is instructive to consider the background information supplied to Captain Frank Kitson as part of his briefing to his post as an intelligence officer in Kenya. He was issued with the standard pamphlet on the Mau Mau supplied by the British Army, accompanied by Elspeth Huxley's books depicting settler life. This reading appears to have both resonated with his own values and drawn him towards Kenyan colonial culture. On his arrival in Nairobi he went for a walk. One of the first sights he encountered in Kenya was three blacks sitting around a fire: 'This brought back to my mind stories of age old magic rites, of bestiality, obscenity and the power of unseen forces.'[25]

What were these stories that came back to his mind? Were they legends of 'wild men' such as the cannibals on the beach in Daniel Defoe's *Robinson Crusoe*, or the timeless evil of Rider Haggard's *She*? Or perhaps Kitson was reminded of John Buchan's *Prester John*, in which the narrator David Crawfurd and two friends come across a black man walking around a fire on a beach. They instantly know what he is doing: '"It's magic," said Archie. "He's going to raise Satan."'[26] Kitson's act of cognition in the streets of Nairobi is also an act of recognition and transference in which the idea of the fire-lit oathing ceremony is incorporated from the fictional world of the past and the primitive into the 'civilized' present.

The significance of the fire-lit dance of the Devil receives its most forceful expression in Ian Henderson's account, *The Hunt for Kimathi*. Dedan Kimathi was the last Mau Mau mountain leader to be captured. Henderson describes following a Mau Mau gang, with their stolen cattle, into the forest at night:

> The glow of the fire became brighter and brighter as they crept nearer. Before them was an oval shaped clearing covered with a low grass. In the middle of this arena a large fire was burning furiously, throwing up a spray of bright red sparks . . . . All around this area were groups of terrorists, some skinning dead cattle, some keeping live beasts at bay, others slaughtering the animals. The scene was a whirl of moving figures. One of the terrorists would hold a cow by the tail while the others hacked at its legs with their simis until all four legs were cut off or were hanging by no more than a shred of skin. There the cow would be left, struggling hopelessly, unable to move except by rolling from side to side.[27]

This Brueghel landscape of nocturnal hell draws together the anxieties and fantasies of the colonial. Enormously strong terrorists immersed in blood and bathed in firelight, legless rolling cows – these tropes of horror manifested in the forest powerfully evoke cultural memories of magical evil. This imagined remembering legitimizes Henderson's description of the attack he claimed to launch and in which he claimed to have taken no prisoners.

Was this bizarre scene something that really happened? It is presented as a factual account. Probably there was an ambush, but a simple description of the ambush would not have conveyed 'the truth' to an eager colonial population. His attempt to demonstrate the 'darkness' of the Mau Mau in the forest suggests a belief that the 'truth' was unavailable in straightforward military terms.

The mixture of apprehension and hatred behind the ferocity of the events described by Henderson was powered by the nature of the physical landscape. He depicted the forests of the Aberdares as an extremely difficult and dangerous place in which to operate. The book includes details of many of the more trying elements of the region. The steepness of the rise from the plains of the Central Province and the crudeness of the topography at 11,000 ft, where the mountains looked as though they had been cut away with a saw, are dwelt on extensively. The inhospitable climate and terrain were part of an 80 mile field of operations made arduous by cutting winds and mists, in which swamps oozed and bubbled underfoot. The catalogue of trials altered at lower altitudes in the bamboo belt, an area of 4000 square miles. Old bamboo formed a thick mat on the ground and new shoots grew up so thickly that only a glimmer of light could be seen when the sun was directly overhead. This tangled inter-woven mass, with stands 25 ft high, made an ideal hiding-place for the 'terrorists'. The 'treacherous' nature of the bamboo, its sharp cutting leaves and its fine hair that caused great itchiness, the sharp-pointed shoots and sticks, were a constant menace and reminder of the hideous nature of the place. Below the bamboo there was deciduous black forest. This was extremely thick in parts, making it difficult to see more than three or four feet ahead.[28]

The security forces found the forest an ambivalent place, where a valley or alpine meadow could be a space of death in the form of a perfect ambush site.[29] This was especially so at night, when less sense can be made of objects and the imagination becomes more active. The distortions and strains which darkness can evoke were widely represented in popular culture. This *Boy's Own Paper* world of imperial fiction was reduced to its essence in the series of adventures by Captain W. E. Johns. In *Biggles and the Leopards of Zinn* he felt it necessary to dwell on the effects of darkness on night actions, for these are

> always a period of strain . . . perhaps this fear of what darkness may hold is something we have inherited from our remote ancestors . . . sounds take on a sinister quality. Inanimate objects have a strange way of moving, of altering their shape, of appearing and disappearing.[30]

The sensory difficulties of operating at night combined with the strange-ness of the forest to separate Captain Frank Kitson from his reality. He reflected extensively on this oddness that made it a place 'unlike that of the outside world'. He was disturbed by a skyline that was no more than a few feet away, with light being reflected from all angles. All his senses were on edge. The background noise of the forest 'adds up to little less than a din . . . it is not easy to register the unusual'. In this place the sense of smell becomes heightened to the extent that 'I soon learned to distinguish my men in the dark by their smell'.[31]

Kitson states that the security forces rapidly learned that the smell which they exuded was important as well. Initially they polished their boots, washed with soap, smoked cigarettes, wore laundered clothing, shaved and cleaned their teeth. These scents were an olfactory intrusion to the animals in the forest. The security forces were a disturbing presence which set off warning calls which caused, in many cases, frequently injurious and sometimes lethal charges by rhinos, elephants and buffaloes. The Mau Mau quickly learned to interpret the reactions of the forest animals, particularly the *ndete* bird and the deer and monkeys, which were especially sensitive to the presence of the security forces. Laws were made by the Mau Mau which forbade the killing of many of their forest 'allies', 'who had kindly welcomed us into their home'. The exception was the rhino, which they called the 'home guard' because of its brutality and willingness to destroy human life. However, once the rhino became accustomed to the Mau Mau, they treated them 'like any other beast'.[32] The behaviour of the animals, and their apparent alliance with the Mau Mau, deepened the sense of the security forces that the forest was actively hostile.

This belief was reinforced by the climate, which formed yet another disturbing aspect of the forest. Torrential rain made life uncomfortable while adding substantially to the weight of heavy packs. There was also the problem of sometimes severe heat, which combined with the altitude to induce a very strong urge to sleep. This would have made the security forces very vulnerable, yet the nights were often tense and sleepless. Forest patrols worked virtually blind as map coordination in the Aberdares was at best 'mere guesswork'.[33] Henderson found that among his unit 'some people suffered hallucinations', and 'almost all were extremely jumpy and short tempered'.[34] Much earlier, the explorer E. A. T. Dutton had written about being apprehensive in the Aberdares; he felt 'the tremendous presence of the unseen . . . a feeling of littleness among vast, silent, incalculable surroundings that steals from you confidence and even peace of mind'.[35] The security forces were hampered by the Mau Mau's ability to lay false trails and place false clues as to their presence by leaving food scraps and strategically placed blood spots. These tricks compounded the security forces's sense of uncertainty and increased their antipathy to their foes. The Mau Mau were deeply resented by the security forces for their reluctance to come out and fight 'fair'. There is a considerable body of evidence to suggest that 'what we see' is partially independent of 'what there is to see'.[36] On this basis it can be argued that members of the security forces were not passive receptors of visual stimulation but participated actively in the structuring of their own percepts. Thus the trees themselves were fetishized with the menace that they might conceal to become agents of terror. What, in other circumstances and to other eyes, was a podocarpus fig becomes an apparition of shadows that might hide an enemy. It ceases to be significant in itself but becomes important for what it may conceal. From there it was a simple step to see a tree and its potential threat as a single entity in a landscape of unreality and danger. Unconsciously animated trees were part of the combination of the Mau Mau, the forest animals and the landscape, which became fused together in a milieu of malevolence.

The construction of the 'wild man' also fed into certain masculinist fantasies. There existed in Kenya a cultural connection with pastoral, romantic traditions. Its open spaces and dense forests offered to the

European the hope of finding a less tainted, Arcadian world of the land where a man could find spiritual fulfilment previously denied him by metropolitan restrictions. The genealogy of this common fantasy throughout the European world included the writings of Rousseau, Coleridge, Browning and Blake. There was a link between the authoritarianism of the early colonists and the notion of the pastoral space as the ideal site to actualize masculine identity. This ideological hybrid was an early manifestation of a trope that operated as a legitimizing force for violence against the Mau Mau.

The campaign in the forests was an opportunity for some in the security forces to indulge themselves in roles in which the savage was permissible because of the civilized purposes of the Colonial Office. Weapons and regular lines of supply, in tandem with imperial purpose, furnished the counter-insurgents with a sometimes exhilarating sense of freedom and personal power. The combatants' shared experiences and common feelings of empowerment made the forest a place where 'true' male friendships, including interracial relationships, became possible. This was a radical development for people like Kitson. In some ways he assumed a dual identity.

The first step in changing who he was occurred when he put on the special disguise he wore in the forest to make himself look like a Mau Mau. This meant blackening his face and putting on skins and a big wig. This was a counter-insurgency tactic in which security forces formed pseudo-Mau Mau gangs. The change in appearance seems to have had a significance to Kitson beyond that of mere camouflage. While he felt in some ways defiled by the 'ritual' of making himself look like a Mau Mau, it enabled him to enter the forest safely. On the first occasion that Kitson crossed into the forest disguised as a Mau Mau he felt something strange occur. After walking with his gang throughout the night, he noticed in the morning that 'I was not walking along with Eric and Matenjagua and Kihara but with a Mau Mau gang. I began to think like a Mau Mau – or so I thought.'[37] Shared experiences in combat brought Kitson closer to his black troops than he had imagined possible. In the forest he established friendships that were proscribed in his outside world. Years later he often wished that he could return to the camp-fires he enjoyed with those comrades in arms, lamenting that 'I often felt far closer to these people . . . than I do to more normal acquaintances'.[38]

Kitson's experiences were by no means unique. Henderson, along with the settler novelists, wrote of the bonds between men of action. For writers such as Robert Ruark, the forest became a place where masculine fantasies of wildness could be lived. This mimicry of the imagined 'wild man' was drawn out most clearly in Robert Ruark's *Uhuru*. The militant settlers called themselves '*Shenzis* – wild men, a force composed of hunters'.[39] Armed and independent, they are presented as men in their element. More sinisterly, they could hunt and kill Mau Mau without compunction.

Yet for all its appeal and fascination, this exploration of masculinity beyond the frontier cast doubt on the merits of the civilization which the security forces sought to defend. To allay these doubts, rituals had to be undertaken which allowed for re-entry into the colonial world. When Kitson left the forest there was a process of washing and resuming of colonial identity. On Sunday he entered the sacred space of the church where he would be spiritually cleansed. Then he would go out on patrol again, mentally and physically refreshed. Henderson broke off his hunt for Kimathi at one point in order to 'scrub up' and meet a visiting royal in Nairobi. Cleanliness and the approbation of moral authorities secured the counter-insurgents in the justness of their cause and the legitimacy of their methods. A complete knowledge and comfort with the rules of metropolitan society were part of an ability to be alternately a 'wild man' and a gentleman. This ability was seen in colonial culture as completing the masculine persona.

When the settlers evoked myths of action and place they turned to the previous century and people like Richard Meinertzhagen, a young Harrow-educated army captain. Despite his German name, Meinertzhagen was from a wealthy and respectable upper-middle-class British family. For later colonials his social position was important because it heightened their sense of contrast with the Africans and seemed to increase the legitimacy of his actions. Meinertzhagen's notional role was that of protector to the white farmers. In the 1890s settlers dispossessed the Kikuyu of their land. This led to increased tensions. After the brutal murder of a white settler, Meinertzhagen led the massacre of an entire village. By 1901 'the British regularly sent out military expeditions, typically killing ten or twenty Kikuyu'.[40] The expressed wishes of the Colonial Office that African interests be protected did not impede the actions of those in Kenya who sought to secure white domination.[41] The limited ability of the Colonial Office to restrain settlers meant that a culture was set in place at the turn of the century which made possible the massacres of Kikuyu in the 1950s.

The deeds of the 'founding fathers', such as Meinertzhagen, were admired and imitated. The tradition of freedom of action worked to liberate settlers and security forces from the rule of law as they hunted the Mau Mau. The cult of action and violence, combined with the priority of instinct over reason and discussion, made the values of the lynch mob inevitable. At weekly meetings in Nairobi settlers urged the most violent methods possible for dealing with the Mau Mau. These ranged from the summary hanging of all suspects to, in one instance, the extermination of most of the Kikuyu tribe, 'like the American Indians or the Maoris of New Zealand'.[42] These demands were expressive of settler and security force dissatisfaction with due processes of law. They saw such institutions as hindering them from achieving victory against Mau Mau; as stopping, in the words of General Erskine, 'brave and gallant men like Frank Kitson from getting on with the job'.[43]

The colonial images of brave young men were contrasted with depictions of cowardly, cunning and animal-like Kikuyu leading a verminous existence. Bravery acted as a force of ideological legitimation. In an environment where authoritarian masculinity was dominant and the lines between the primitive and the modern could be so easily drawn, virtually any action by the settlers became acceptable. Thus they began to operate in death squads.[44] John Wainright, a young settler in 1952, recalled: 'We set up private armies, mounted cavalry. For us it was a bit like being cowboys – *Boy's Own* stuff. . . . We found three people asleep and one of them was the gang leader we'd been looking for, Brigadier Kago. We shot them.'[45] This was the modern re-enactment of the origin myth, the spatial performance of violence which flows from a moment of recognition where the settlers and the security forces of the 1950s replay the slaughter and the conquests of people like Meinertzhagen. This process, where the whites themselves become wild men, gives power to the way that place evokes myths. These myths in turn operate as a mnemonic device to legitimate action.

When the whites became 'wild men', the Mau Mau were forced into an even more extreme position. Henderson reached the common conclusion that 'They lived like animals. They survived because of their animal skills, and when caught they reacted like trapped animals.'[46] General Erskine had given orders to his soldiers emphasizing that 'the qualities which must be developed in troops engaged against the Mau Mau are those required to track down and shoot shy game'.[47] The reification of the forest fighter into forest animal by the settlers and the acquiescence of their superiors led to their body parts becoming trophies. Andrew Clayton notes that there was a furore over the way that the hands of killed forest fighters were being cut off rather than the whole body being taken down for the purpose of identification.[48] At this point the forest fighters became little more than big game, with the Kikuyu merely a particularly clever species. Scoreboards of kills were kept by British units, as reported in the *East African Standard*: 'The total bag of the four day operation is 25. . . . Several of these had been run to earth as the Masai *morani* do with game in their native plains.'[49] Operation names such as 'Longstop' (a cricket term) indicate the pervasiveness of the sporting imagery. Frank Kitson and his troops revelled in the opportunities for action: 'There is no doubt at all that one cannot savour the full thrill of the chase until one hunts something which is capable of retaliation.'[50]

The reordering of topography in moral terms manifests itself in violence. Violence colonizes and reinscribes anomalous space with codes of domination. Thus topography ceases to function as an object. The place of action becomes more than a neutral site for the inscription of violence or something to be manipulated in order to create political representations: it affects the enactment of power. The security forces operated in the forest to create sites of power, but it was a power operating in a space of distortions.

The security forces' perception of the Mau Mau, as with the general colonial perception, was powerfully driven by the significance of the place of encounter. Their actions and ideas were materially affected by cultural memories of darkness and magical evil, and structured by white colonial history. The particular way of seeing of the whites drew all these elements together and led to the peculiar way in which they understood the Mau Mau in the Kenyan forests of the night.

Seldom has the material explored here been brought to bear in mainstream analyses in international relations. The reality that the discipline constructs is altogether too orderly. The tendency is for space to be depoliticized and for the local to be derived from a reading of the global. This desire for an objective framework within which to establish meaning incorporates the traditional dichotomy of subject and object, which supposes that there is a world 'out there'; an object which is independent of us, the subject. In this chapter I have contended that the counter-insurgency against Mau Mau can be more fully understood by an analysis of the interaction between the landscape of the Aberdare forests and the perception of darkness in imperial history by the colonial settler. The joining of these elements challenges the idea that there exists an objective geography independent of the historically formed subject. Topography and its cultural formations is a territory which opens virtually limitless avenues of exploration.

Understanding the meaning and significance of the forest for the settler community and for people like Kitson and Henderson offers the possibility of uncovering important but hitherto hidden elements of the counter-insurgency against the Mau Mau. Understanding the importance of the Mau Mau revolt is not simply an exercise in colonial African history. Mau Mau reinscribed the traditional tropes of Africa as the last repository of darkness and 'wild men'; as a place of danger and irredeemable backwardness. These tropes still assume relevance to world affairs in contemporary images of African catastrophes in Rwanda, Somalia and Liberia. The openings found in the convergence of place, perception and action indicate the value of exposing an all too cohesive international relations to perspectives that take greater account of history, culture and geography. This avoids the reductionism that consigned Mau Mau to a domestic dispute of the British Empire. It also suggests a way to explore other conflicts in other spaces.

Notes

1. Charles Stoneham, *Mau Mau* (London, Museum Press, 1953), p. 70.

2. See Michael Keith and Steve Pile (eds), *Place and the Politics of Identity* (London and New York, Routledge, 1993), especially Introduction Part 1 and 2, and David Harvey, 'From space to place and back again: reflections of the condition of postmodernity' in John Bird, Barry Curtis, Tim Putnam, George Robertson and Lisa Tickner (eds), *Mapping the Futures: Local Cultures, Global Change* (London and New York, Routledge, 1993).

3. Derek Rawcliffe, *The Struggle for Kenya* (London, Gollancz, 1954), p. 187.

4. David Maughan-Brown, *Land, Freedom and Fiction: History and Ideology in Kenya* (London, Zed Books, 1985), p. 260.

5. Kofi Buenor Hadjor, *The Penguin Dictionary of Third World Terms* (London, Penguin, 1994), p. 193.

6. Robert Ruark, *Something of Value* (New York, Doubleday, 1975), p. 209.

7. David Lowenthal, 'Geography, experience, and imagination: towards a geographic epistemology', *Annals of the Association of American Geographers*, 51 (1961), 245.

8. John Wright, '*Terrae incognitae*: the place of the imagination in geography', *Annals of the Association of American Geographers*, 37 (1947), 1.

9. Homi K. Bhabha, 'Signs taken for wonders', *Critical Inquiry*, 12 (1985), 157.

10. Barry Lopez, cited in J. D. Porteous, *Landscapes of the Mind* (Toronto, University of Toronto Press, 1990), p. 3.

11. Porteous, *Landscapes of the Mind*, p. 98.

12. Charles Stoneham, *Mau Mau*, p. 142.

13. Dante Alighieri, *The Divine Comedy*, 1: *Hell*, trans. Dorothy L. Sayers (London, Penguin, 1976), p. 287.

14. Joseph Conrad, 'Geography and some explorers' in *Last Essays* (London, Books for Libraries Press, 1970), p. 19.

15. Robert Edgerton, *Mau Mau: An African Crucible* (New York, Free Press, 1989), p. 92.

16. Andrew Clayton, *Counter Insurgency in Kenya: 1952–1960* (Nairobi, Transafrica, 1975), p. 41.

17. William Baldwin, *Mau Mau Manhunt: The Adventures of the Only American Who Fought the Terrorists in Kenya* (New York, E. P. Dutton, 1957), p. 17.

18. Graham Greene, *Ways of Escape* (London, Bodley Head, 1980), p. 190.

19. Brian Lapping, *End of Empire* (London, Granada, 1986), p. 420.

20. Ibid., p. 421.

21. Ibid., p. 422.

22. Margaret Hodgen, *Early Anthropology in the Sixteenth and Seventeenth Centuries* (Philadelphia, University of Pennsylvania Press, 1964), pp. 412–13.

23. Rudolph Wittkower, cited in Michael Taussig, *Shamanism, Colonialism and the Wild Man: A Study in Terror and Healing* (Chicago, University of Chicago Press, 1986), p. 212.

24. Patrick Brantlinger, 'Victorians and Africans: the genealogy of the myth of the Dark Continent', *Critical Inquiry*, 12 (1985), 198.

25. Frank F. Kitson, *Gangs and Counter Gangs* (London, Barrie and Rockcliff, 1960), p. 6.

26. John Buchan, *Prester John* (Harmondsworth, Penguin, 1960), p. 18.

27. Ian Henderson, *The Hunt for Kimathi* (London, Hamish Hamilton, 1958), p. 180.

28. Ibid., pp. 46–7.

29. Explorers' images of the Aberdares emphasized descriptions of the forest such as 'mysterious' and 'uncanny'. E. A. T. Dutton found the forest intensely disturbing, such that 'you move along with an undefined sense of insecurity'. He felt on the precipice of some indefinite catastrophe, while constantly oppressed by his surroundings: 'You become as one in a dream, who traverses a nightmare forest, waking and falling asleep by turns, a prey to unimaginable fears.' E. A. T. Dutton, as quoted in Elspeth Huxley, *Nine Faces of Kenya* (London, Collins Harvill, London, 1990), p. 194.

30. W. E. Johns, *Biggles and the Leopards of Zinn* (Leicester, Brockhampton Press, 1960), p. 96.

31. Kitson, *Gangs and Counter Gangs*, p. 178.

32. David Barnett and Kariuki Njama, *Mau Mau from Within: Autobiography and Analysis of Kenya's Peasant Revolt* (New York, Monthly Review Press, 1966), p. 168.

33. Edgerton, *Mau Mau*, p. 171.

34. Henderson, *The Hunt for Kimathi*, p. 115.

35. E. A. T. Dutton, as quoted in Elspeth Huxley, *Nine Faces of Kenya*, p. 194.

36. Paul Davies, 'Changes arising from movement of the observer in relation to the previously afterimaged scene', *Perception*, 2 (1973), 156.

37. Kitson, *Gangs and Counter Gangs*, p. 177.

38. Ibid., p. 132.

39. Robert Ruark, *Uhuru*, p. 39.

40. Edgerton, *Mau Mau*, p. 5.

41. In 1908 Winston Churchill, then Under-Secretary of the Colonies, wrote of expeditions such as these: 'It looks like butchery, and if the House of Commons gets hold of it all our plans in the East Africa Protectorate will be under a cloud. Surely it cannot be necessary to go on killing these defenceless people on such an enormous scale.' Winston Churchill, as cited in Lapping, *End of Empire*, p. 396.

42. Rawcliffe, *The Struggle for Kenya*, p. 111.

43. George Erskine, introduction to Kitson, *Gangs and Counter Gangs*.

44. Edgerton, *Mau Mau*, p. ix.

45. As cited in Lapping, *End of Empire*, p. 427.

46. Henderson, *The Hunt for Kimathi*, p.166.

47. George Erskine, *A Handbook on Anti-Mau Mau Operations* (Nairobi, Government Printer, 1954), p. 11.

48. Clayton, *Counter Insurgency in Kenya*, p. 25.

49. Maughan-Brown, *Land, Freedom and Fiction*, p. 40.

50. Kitson, *Gangs and Counter Gangs*, p. 90.

CHAPTER SIX

When the dogs howl: Thailand and the politics of democratization

MICHAEL K. CONNORS

Several years before he was overthrown in 1932, King Rama VII, absolute monarch of Thailand, noted:

> Perhaps some countries have adopted democracy merely as a necessity, knowing full well that it does not suit the character of the people. That is why there are countries who *play* at having parliaments. It seems to me that it is quite on the cards that we shall have to play that sort of game in Siam sometime. It is with these considerations in view that I am now considering certain reforms.[1]

History records that the King's intended reforms were overtaken by a bureaucratic and middle-class elite, which had emerged via the monarchy's modernization of the state. Nevertheless, the game of democracy has never ceased being played. Over 60 years since its advent, Thai democracy has been wrapped in numerous abolished constitutions, frequently suspended in the rhetoric of Thai-style democracy, reanimated in popular struggles for 'edible' democracy and more lately commodified by intensive vote-buying. Despite apparent flaws, for many commentators it appears that Thailand's grim history of *coups* and abolished constitutions is finally giving way to a new game of democracy, one more in accord with Western democratic forms. Notwithstanding the fact that pre-election night in Thailand is colloquially known as 'the night dogs howl' – so called because last-minute vote-canvassing and -buying keeps the canines awake all night – the national election in 1995 yet again reinforced the fact that electoral succession of government is becoming institutionalized. Although government placards and advertisements had proclaimed 'selling your vote is like selling your rights and nation', over US$½bn was spent winning parliamentary seats. Such expenditure bought to power a coalition of parties closely tied to veteran authoritarians and new capitalist elites. Whatever the obvious limitations of this crony capitalism, it is the apparent institutionalization of democracy that has led some commentators to identify Thailand as a partner in a larger global transition to democracy.

Indeed, so rapid has the turn to democracy been across the globe that Samuel Huntington suggests we are living through the third wave of democratization, with more than a ripple effect on international politics.[2] Huntington, following a Kantian strain in international relations theory, suggests that the possibility of global peace is enhanced because democratic countries do not fight each other. Also, a global environment which nurtures democracy is an environment that bolsters US identity and that, he claims, is inseparable from 'its commitment to liberal and democratic values'.[3] This articulation of democratization with international themes increasingly commands serious policy considerations and academic treatment.[4]

The projection of democratization as a universal phenomenon raises several issues of crucial significance to this book. There is the relationship between the global and the local. There is the ethnocentrism which lurks behind the allegedly international. There is the connection between material interest and contemporary doctrinal orthodoxy. And there is the question of disciplinary paradigms and biases. Let me elaborate.

Caught in the study-maze of state power politics, international relations scholars have not previously dedicated much analytical rigour to the domestic politics of regimes. Those states considered to be allies against communism were traditionally left alone to their own political development. Whatever the nature of their regimes, they were part of the rhetorical 'free world'. This cold war condition accounts very much for the development of the subdiscipline of political development studies, a field which focused on the tasks of ordering and stabilizing modernization. The domestic–international split worked to interiorize problematic questions of democracy and authoritarianism in a bid to sever these issues from the calculus of power operative in the international field. But now democratization and political development studies have re-entered mainstream discussion in international relations, most dramatically reflected in Francis Fukayuma's work and the resulting fracas.

As the end of the cold war promises to accelerate global integration, the rigid disciplines that buffered cold war knowledge disintegrate, reformulate and appropriate new conditions for knowledge production. If international relations has proved mostly impregnable against postmodern and postcolonial renovation, it seems possible that a more open posture may be taken *vis-à-vis* political development studies; international relations' concern for order and balance, condensed as power, is exactly what political development studies seeks to install domestically.

The historical circumstances of the cold war and the conditions of nationally organized monopoly capitalism largely dictated a division of labour between the international relations and political development studies, expressive of the rationally, or nationally, bounded anarchic international system idealized by realist theorists. Contemporary capitalism, partially deterritorialized and in global pursuit of accumulation, has cannibalized its previous conditions of existence, unravelling borders and disturbing the domestic and international axis. Democratization, once the preserve of a subdiscipline, now becomes an issue of global politics because, conceived as the promotion of efficient decision-making unencumbered by the weight of patronage and corruption, it promises to facilitate global capitalism. It promotes state efficiency through accountability, allowing a flexible response to the changing fancies of internationally mobile capital. And if democratization entails a clearing of the stables, it can equip trim, clean governments with the new-blood technocratic know-how necessary for domestic capital to enter the global market-place.

If this explains the capital imperative behind a shift towards democratic sentiment, there is also another level of interest at work, indicated by Huntington's ruminations on US identity. Operative in the bulk of liberal democratization literature is the intention to produce ordered knowledge of historical processes corresponding with and expressing the interests of an ideologically conceived Western capitalist democracy. Historical processes in the Third World are being appropriated in an attempt to verify the supremacy of the 'Western' democratic form and the market. In this secular eschatology, emerging Third World democracies are represented as delinquent offspring undergoing rehabilitation. This chapter explores the elaboration of interest embedded in this knowledge complex. The efficacy of this interest articulation is then explored through an examination of the evolution of Thai democracy. This entails some accounting of democratic discourse in Thailand and close scrutiny of recent developments considered to have brought Thailand into step with rational political forms.

In democratization literature, the reasons for democracy's emergence and its political form are linked to imagined Western patterns. Larry Diamond, a chief contributor to democratic transition literature and presently editor of the *Journal of Democracy*, has boldly written of the 'globalization of democracy'. Borrowing from modernization theory, he traces the origins of democratization to developing countries' readiness for diffusion, to adapt democratic forms of governments from the West. On the preconditions for democracy, Diamond writes, 'the higher the level of socioeconomic development, the larger the middle class, the more educated the population, the more organized and informed the society, the riper it will be for diffusion'.[5] The idea that some countries have matured is explicit:

> it is in this secular increase in independent organizational capacity and density that represents the real indigenous origins of the democratic trend. . . . And this is not a new development, it was a crucial dimension in the spread and invigoration of democracy in the United States almost two centuries ago.[6]

Diamond's work represents a major trend that seeks out and analyses conditions seemingly conducive to democratization.

For Giuseppe Di Palma, veteran democracy-watcher, democratization reflects the maturing of historical consciousness, which 'consists in the emergence among political practitioners of a more realistic assessment, already gleaned in postwar Europe, but clearer and more global today, of what makes democracy's performance as a concrete system of government attractive'. Against myriad forms of failed undemocratic regimes, democracy is the ascendant angel, finally in flight. Pushing aside the iron law of numerous preconditions, Di Palma argues that democracy arises from the prudent choice of elite actors who recognize democracy's 'pristine and unique virtue as protection against the oppression of arbitrary and undivided rule'.[7] In an idiosyncratic twist on Marx's theory of commodity fetishism, he writes of Third World elites encountering Western styles of democracy as consumers: 'democracy's attractiveness may stir the "prospective consumer" to become worthy of the product.'[8] Yet Di Palma fails to consider the critical element of alienation implied in his formulation.

Inclined towards structuralist and voluntarist perspectives respectively, though not exclusively, the two authors none the less agree on matters of democratic inspiration: the modular democracy of the West. Their problematic is also shared: how can democratic values be implanted – *as they exist in the West*? What is the basis of institutional endurance – *as it exists in the West*? How can a dynamic capitalist economy that attends to economic well-being be sponsored – *as it exists in the West*?

The notion of diffusion of Western-inspired democratization is prevalent in much work on transition. It teleologizes democracy as an inherent purpose in the development of political form. The terminal point is the construction of a rational mechanism for conflict resolution defined by adherence to procedural norms engendering free electoral contest in the selection of leaders. Reading democracy as diffusion entails a fanciful termination of history in existing forms of democracy, while sanctifying bourgeois civil society as destiny. It is not difficult to detect the workings of a narcissistic transition narrative[9] in 'diffusion', whereby the trajectory of the Third World has already been traversed by the First. If a defining feature of narcissism is ignorance of flaws – indeed flaws presented as virtues – it may be asked, what has been obfuscated in this narcissistic fury to adjudicate on democratic progress?

While popular understandings of democracy generally incorporate some notion of people's sovereignty, the hardened realists of post-war political science, following Schumpeter's lead, argue that the functioning of existing democracies diverges greatly from the ideal. Considering 'classical democracy' as too optimistic about people's rationality and their participatory capacities, Schumpeter, writing in the 1930s, redefined democracy. Rather than wanting to know if a regime served and expressed the sovereign will of the people – considered too intangible to deliberate on – Schumpeter delimits the role of people to that of choosing a government. A country is considered democratic to the extent it has democratic methods: 'that institutional arrangement for arriving at political decisions in which individuals acquire the power to decide by means of a competitive struggle for the people's vote'.[10]

For Schumpeter, rationality is an attribute of elites for whom playing politics comes naturally. There exists a division of labour between the masses, who are lured into supporting particular policies, and strategic elites, who articulate such policies and implement them. Thus 'democracy does not mean and cannot mean that the people actually rule in any obvious sense of the terms "people" and "rule". Democracy means only that the people have the opportunity of accepting or refusing the men who rule them.'[11]

A variant of Schumpeter's notion of democracy entered studies of political development primarily through Dahl's standard work on democratic transitions, *Polyarchy*. Dahl's work, still the main touchstone for many works on democratization, argued for a differentiation between democracy as an ideal and as a method relating to actual institutional arrangement, terming the latter 'polyarchy'.[12] One exhaustive review of transition work notes that polyarchy remains the assumed goal of democratic transition in many studies.[13] In transition literature, developing countries are considered democratic to the extent that they match the procedural/method definition. Democracy defined by form allows the illusion of a third wave of democratization, which, by processes ill defined, will allow for greater individual liberties and freedoms.

The conception of democracy as mere form is a strikingly negligent one, banishing distributive questions from the arena of formal politics. Unfortunately, it is as popular as it is negligent. Unfortunate because democratic theories which took questions of sovereignty seriously at least opened a theoretical space to explore the contradictions of representation, rights and sovereignty. Most studies of democratic transition engage in a deliberate transposition of the democratic ideal into institutional norms that facilitate the competitive circulation of elites. In doing so, the fault lines of democratic rhetoric are overlain by the firmer ground of institutions, the existence of which seemingly testifies to a healthy democracy. This regression reflects a disenchantment, a banal exercise in making democracy matter only to those who seemingly matter. Schumpeterian realism, democracy with(out) ideology (sovereignty), engenders a reduction of democracy to narrowly defined form. In wishing away sovereignty, realism neutralizes its ideological aporia and that aporia's potential disruption of the hard empirical science of investigating democratization. Such are the 'flaws' willed away in the transition narrative. This is no slip of the unconscious, but an explicit manoeuvre. The procedural approach to democracy allows empirical work mapping democratic progress to proceed untroubled by what Huntington terms the 'fuzzy norms' of true democracy. He recognizes that 'serious problems of ambiguity arise when democracy is defined in terms of either source of authority or purposes'.[14] Having propagated minimal notions of democracy, democratization theorists see compliance to democratic norms among elites as the central task of democratization. The task is to engender an attitude among competing elites that democracy can replace zero-sum struggles for power with, as Di Palma puts it, 'a competitive political market giving contestants fairly equal chances to affect and share in outcomes'.[15]

Democracy so narrowly defined compels no theorist to consider the obviously undemocratic and arbitrary control of wealth by minorities that is left untouched by procedural democracy. Indeed, wealth is idolized as the outcome of the liberal market-place, buffered by democracy. Within the framework of procedural democracy, in which elites are the inspired players and market economies go unquestioned, the functioning of elite interests can actually be legitimized through electoral sanction. With the end of the cold war the democratic rhetoric issuing from the United States finally has influential proponents. Most famously, former US secretary of state James Baker in 1990 defined the post-cold war mission as the 'promotion and consolidation of democracy'. One-time patrons of author-itarianism now regularly espouse a desire for democratic governance across the globe: marines into Haiti, sanctions here, stern words there. One-time dictators stand aside and submit to electoral wish, allowing the new regime to implement IMF structural adjustment programmes.

This new international sensibility on the feasibility and desirability of democracy does not protect would-be democratizers from the principled expediency that forms modern statecraft. Democracy can just as easily be forsaken according to circumstance and place. But for now, as an array of literature suggests, democratic prospects have never been so good.

The new optimism is reminiscent of the initial expectations for demo-cracy after the Second World War. When many postcolonial states failed to democratize, however, some theorists settled comfortably into integrating authoritarian regimes into patterns of modernization. Huntington's *Political Order in Changing Societies*[16] did most to codify this new attitude, arguing that authoritarianism was a transitional stage on the road to modernity. A growing body of literature assumed the incongruity of demo-cratic forms in developing countries and worked towards naturalizing authoritarianism. Yet what this literature signally failed to recognize was the existence of discourses on democracy which drew on the very notions of sovereignty that many theorists of democracy in the West were rapidly junking. It is only now, with the emergence of democratic forms that resemble the West's, that political development theorists can contemplate democratization. Thailand's own democratic development, seemingly part of the third wave of democratization, in fact reflects a complex use of democracy as a legitimizing symbol dating back at least sixty years. Thai democratic discourse has shifted from state-centred notions of sovereign democracy towards notions of democracy preferred by transition theorists.

In the immediate period after the overthrow of the absolute monarchy in 1932 the new rulers, influenced by Western liberalism, justified their rule in democratic terms. They implemented universal suffrage and promulgated a constitution, while ensuring strong executive control. In the period of Thai constitutionalism (1932 till the late 1930s) there was a struggle to establish political legitimacy and stability on the basis of constitutionalism. However, as a result of internal clashes between reformers and between reformers and royalists, the military emerged as the arbiter of political power. Increasingly interventionist and abhorring the disorder of putatively parliamentary politics, military leaders embraced statism and nationalism as ideological substitutes. The constitutional foundations of the state were overshadowed by an orgy of xenophobic nationalism, disciplinarianism and a cult of military leadership.

Following the end of the Second World War, democratic discourse again emerged. A liberal democratic constitution was promulgated in 1946 and a relatively free political atmosphere prevailed. However, splits within the civilian regime, economic deterioration and resentment within the military of the civilian government's appointments paved the way for another military take-over of power.

Although following the Second World War developmentalism was the legitimating ideology of the various regimes, there was frequent recourse to democracy as that ideology which symbolized rule in the interests of the people. Until the late 1950s political elites saw Thai democracy as a Western inheritance. When free from military dominance, the early constitutional regimes functioned under nominally democratic conditions, civil rights discourse developed and arguments about the separation of power ensued – all referenced to the imagined condition of democracy in the West.

When Field Marshal Sarit came to power in the late 1950s he rehabilitated traditional institutions marginalized after the 1932 revolution, particularly the monarchy. It is in this context that notions of guided democracy, or Thai-style democracy (hereafter, following the Thai language, *prachathipatai baep Thai*), emerged as a basic component of Thai military and bureaucratic ideology.[17] Under Sarit a deliberate shift away from Western ideology of democratic government occurred. Such ideology, when let loose in an authoritarian context, subversively undermined the regime's legitimacy. Sarit's international spokesperson explained:

> the fundamental cause of our political instability in the past lies in the sudden transplantation of alien institutions on to our soil without careful preparation and if we look at our national history, we can very well see that this country works better and prospers under an authority, not a tyrannical authority, but a unifying authority.[18]

Ideologically enmeshed in a history of benevolent monarchy, and the supposed familial relationship between the governors and the governed, Sarit pronounced on the limits of Western-style democracy in Thailand. According to him, 'The people should accept their status as being under the government, because they are not yet able to govern themselves well and they should not get involved in government which is the work of the "big people"'.[19] It was with this thinking in mind that Sarit's government, having overthrown an elected government in 1958, announced 'The Revolutionary Council wishes to make the country a democracy . . . [which] . . . would be appropriate to the special characteristics and realities of the Thai. It will build a democracy, a Thai way of democracy.'[20] For many years *prachathipatai baep Thai* meant that Parliament counted for little; it involved a deep blurring of executive and legislative power, and the dominance of a ruling council. When elections were allowed, a stacked upper house closely connected with the military and bureaucracy ensured that the situation was tightly controlled. And the *coup* was always available if the situation became unwieldy. Though frustrated, business and commercial sectors worked within its limits. Economically, from the 1950s onwards, a pattern of mutual alliance between the state and capital had developed. State-led accumulation policies were geared towards enhancing private-sector capitalism. Capitalists reciprocated state support through complex mechanisms of patronage and reward; the formal political realm was left to the bureaucratic state, which itself was made up of various cliques.[21] However, all were bound up as pretenders to the people's sovereignty.

In 1973 a student uprising overthrew the military regime, opening up the possibility of developing liberal democracy. The successful diversification of the economy and the rise of an educated population from the 1960s onwards, among other factors, provided the sources for a new phase of democratization. Rising political participation certainly belied the cultural strait-jackets of passivity and obedience that elites had placed on the Thai masses. Business also became more active, supporting political parties and leading individuals. But the open period lasted only three years, truncated by a particularly vicious military *coup* in 1976. By the time of the *coup*, prospects for liberal democracy had once again diminished, dwarfed by an intense ideological and real warfare between communist insurgents and the state. Rising internal class struggle and the triumph of communism in Indo-China raised the very real spectre of communism in Thailand.[22] Reaction set in, business acquiesced and strong military leadership in politics again became the norm.

Prachathipatai baep Thai again resurfaced, receiving its latest exposition in the context of a rising communist threat. A year of severe dictatorship under a civilian prime minister, however, served only to polarize social forces, making plausible the Communist Party of Thailand's claim that only armed insurgency could bring democracy. Faced with this explosive situation, the military launched a *coup* against the very prime minister it had installed a year earlier. The *coup* signalled a liberalization of Thai politics; political dissent could be aired and press censorship was eased. Faced with an increasingly combative and confident Communist Party, whose ranks had been swollen by thousands of students, academics and activists fleeing to the jungle after the 1976 crackdown, military leaders rearticulated the role of the military as guiding Thailand towards a democracy answerable to people's economic, social and political needs. Democratization was seen as the only means of combating the communist threat. While previously communists had been characterized as 'un-Thai' and as having only external support, it was now recognized that they gained support because of economic, social and political injustices.[23]

The Constitution of 1978, characterized as establishing 'semi-democracy', defined the boundaries of a dual power system that recognized the emergence of extra-bureaucratic players, excluding the left, and yet entrenched bureaucratic power in the upper house. So formulated, it laid the basis for political competition into the next decade.

By the mid-1980s the Communist Party of Thailand was a spent force, owing to the combined impact of internal division, military losses and political liberalization. Under conditions of amnesty thousands of Communist Party members defected. The Thai military claimed victory. But the process of liberalization also set in motion new social dynamics which placed the military on the defensive. Politically this was registered when liberal forces, principally major political parties, defeated pro-military amendments to extend by four more years a provisional clause in the 1978 Constitution allowing serving officers in the military and bureaucracy to sit in Cabinet until 1983. Furthermore, against the military's own preference for an appointed prime minister, in 1988 an elected MP, the retired General Chatichai Choonhaven, took office.

Although the basis of this new politics was competing factions of the bourgeoisie in alliance with reformist sectors in the state, other groups took advantage of the open political atmosphere. Non-government organizations contested local inequalities and issues – sometimes succeeding in changing policy. Open debate in the press and universities on political reform burgeoned, mostly along the lines of liberal democracy. Of course, the elected Chatichai government was no reforming regime; its epithet 'the buffet cabinet' sums up its aggrandizing ambitions. Nevertheless, a booming economy, a revitalized Parliament and Chatichai's own conflicts with the military created a space for political transformation that severely curtailed military political ambitions. In 1991 the military resorted to a *coup d'état* in a bid to restore order. The rationale for the *coup* was the corruption of the so-called 'parliamentary dictatorship' of the government, a term which hinted at the power-drift away from the military.[24]

There was little outcry against the *coup's* apparent affront to Thailand's democratic transition. Indeed, big business was compliant, and a leading representative, Anand Panchayun, head of a peak Thai business association, accepted appointment as interim prime minister. The military leadership, it seemed, was attempting to relegitimate its political leadership while also drawing big business into a governing alliance. Not unwilling to consider the proposition, the newly appointed business government legislated prodigiously, enacting pro-market reforms that several years earlier they could only dream about. But while Anand may have been handed the reins of government by the military, it became clear that he had a different destination in mind.

Anand, a liberalizer, used his position to forge a new national consciousness on the nature of post-cold war security which brought into question the prominence of the military in Thai politics.[25] Anand's government was also strengthened by support from reformist wings in the state bureaucracy, technocrats keenly aware of the need to restructure the state in response to economic globalization.[26] The relative and sometimes vacillating independence of the Anand regime and its intention to ensure that the logic of military and bureaucratic imperatives would not govern the post-*coup* state soon led the military to forge an electoral alliance with the politicians it had displaced in the 1991 *coup*.

Having framed a controversial constitution that restored certain features of *prachathipatai baep Thai*, including a military-appointed upper house granted substantial powers, and provision for an appointed prime minister, the military allowed an election to be called for March 1992. Pro-military parties, composed of many corrupt politicians from the Chatichai regime, won the election.

Having previously promised not to take office, General Suchinda Krapayoon, military strongman, became prime minister in early April 1992. Immediately, thousands of protesters rallied. Fearing economic consequences, business representatives eagerly promoted an image of business as usual. The vice-chairperson of Thailand's stock exchange argued publicly that 'Foreign investors understand that our democracy is a mixture of politicians and military personnel. They must go together in order to have stability.'[27] Deaf to such rationalizations, in late April over 50,000 people attended a rally calling for Suchinda's resignation.

In early May, Major-General Chamlong Srimuang announced a fast till death unless Suchinda resigned. Chamlong, an enormously popular politician owing to his reputation as the incorruptible Bangkok mayor, had raised the stakes. Daily rallies of over 100,000 protesters ensued. The opposition was unprecedented, forcing conciliatory gestures on the government. On 9 May, the opposing sides agreed to talk on constitutional amendments. Chamlong ended his hunger strike.

The following week, hopes of compromise faded as various statements issuing from the government suggested hard-liners were ascendant. In mid-May pro-democracy rallies again drew hundreds of thousands of protesters on to the streets. The events following, now known as Black May, are well documented.[28] On the night of the rally crowds estimated at between 150,000 and 250,000 marched towards Government House. Early next morning troops fired on them. In the following days the killings continued. Approximately 100 people were killed, although no definitive figure has been established.

Defying repression, protests broke out across the country. In the midst of this national crisis universities and businesses closed. On 20 May, ostensibly to end the bloodshed, the King, in a dramatic move, met with Suchinda and Chamlong to call for a compromise. Despite the King's intervention, Suchinda remained in power, but when government parties supported constitutional amendments, including the requirement of an elected prime minister, he resigned. Before his resignation, Suchinda was able to secure an amnesty from the King for those involved in the massacre.

Parliament was dissolved on 10 June and Anand was reappointed as interim prime minister. A new election was scheduled for September.

During his second tenure Anand's political position had crystallized. He declared himself supportive of democracy and moved to liberalize the press. When Supreme Commander Kaset Rojananil threatened military intervention if the people elected 'lousy' politicians, Anand publicly stated that all *coups* were treason. Facing concerted pressure from pro-democracy groups Anand removed top military figures in late August.

The central theme of the September election was the May massacre. Bloody images of the events were screened on television. Although the election was close, the pro-democratic parties won.

With business and reformist sections of the state now on the political offensive against Suchinda's anachronistic intimation of *prachathipatai baep Thai*, the entrenchment of procedural democracy seemed possible. Ideally, with a disengagement of capital from the tutelage of state, procedural democracy promised a clean start, a level playing field of honest tender and contract, against the monopolistic and corrupt practices of the past – democracy as best practice.

Theorists typically present a series of factors as the catalyst behind democratization. As discussed earlier, such factors are invariably matched to the conditions of democracy in the West. Democracy is seen as emerging from Western attitudinal diffusion on the basis of economic dynamism. And though most are not so crass as to sloganize *come the American way*, the frenzy of public policy on democratic consolidation is a veritable industry of universalistic back-slapping, intoning: *the West has something*. Of course the image is a willed one, glossing over the class tensions that are constitutive of democracy in the West. One problem is inescapable, though: democratization is an uncertain process. It is not an ossified democratic form. Precisely because democratization is a fragile contemporary process it is vulnerable to a critique which exposes the raw power politics that go into its making. By historicizing its conditions of existence such a critique enables the relativizing of democracy as a rational form. If democratization theorists prioritize the West and attempt to impose a silence on the ideological underpinning of democracy, the following discussion of Thai democratization aims precisely at undoing the ideological sediments that present democracy as an aspect of modernity's rationalization. Some account of the class forces behind Thailand's shift towards procedural democracy must now be given.

By the 1980s big business, overshadowed by the bureaucracy, was increasingly driven to renegotiate aspects of economic policy in order to respond to the challenges of globalization. Having failed to claim the mantle of hegemony in the 1973–76 period, business struggled to edge out a realm of autonomy where it could pursue its imperatives, while leaving the state in the hands of the bureaucracy and military. This new relationship was politically expressed through representative associations and their work within the Joint Public Private Sector Consultative Committee (JPPCC), which directly influenced government economic policy, appeasing business interests. The new dynamics in this relationship differed from the bureaucratic hegemony of the past. Anek Laothamatas has described the relationship as a system of liberal corporatism.[29] But it was a corporatism of limited partnership, excluding emergent capitalist forces in the provinces. Bangkok-based business seemed content with this arrangement throughout the 1980s.

Liberal corporatism – in which business was the only recognized corporation *vis-à-vis* the state – seemed sufficient to capital interests. Even the events of the early 1990s did not shake this attachment. Business found itself promoting both the Anand and Suchinda governments. The voice of big business in Thailand, *The Manager*, in its post-massacre editorial, while declaring the inevitability of democratic forms of government, bemoaned the loss of autocracy. Conceding that democratic government in Thailand was necessary, the editorial read:

> Do not expect a democratic government to perform better than the super efficient non democratic one that ruled for a year after the 1991 coup, . . . [but recognizing the growth of economic diversity] . . . we now urgently need a mechanism by which the transfer of power, and the process of economic and political debate and its resolution, can be accomplished peacefully through the rules of democracy.[30]

Profoundly ambivalent in its political position, big business felt compelled by the instability of the Thai polity to throw its weight behind more democratic forms of government. Before the May crisis few in business dissented from Anand's minimalist position that trade liberalization was 'the essence of democracy'.[31] One of the purportedly pro-democratic business groupings, lauded by Anek, displayed a fundamental ambivalence towards democracy. Nominally democratic, the Business Management Services Company (BMS) actively legitimized the unelected Anand regime.[32]

The BMS is a loose grouping comprising many members of the elite of financial capital in Thailand. It includes chief executives of the Bank of Thailand, Siam Commercial, the Thai Military Bank and board members of the SET. After the 1991 *coup* BMS members set themselves the task of restoring international confidence. Suchinda found willing allies in BMS members, particularly Dr Amnuay Viravan, whom he appointed to the military's Economic Authority Board. Amnuay said 'The military has provided an opportunity for the country to restructure its decision making mechanism for implementing economic policies in the future without political influence'.[33] Amnuay's acceptance of the opportunities offered by the military *coup* reflected that of big capital generally, with Anand's government its concrete manifestation. But faced with certain international sanctions and domestic crisis should Suchinda remain in power, peak business bodies joined the chorus of condemnation in the wake of the massacre.

Another compromised democratic player was a section of the provincial bourgeoisie known as *jao poh*.[34] Clusters of these entrepreneurs organized politically and succeeded in gaining enough parliamentary seats to help bring General Chatichai to power in 1988. The *jao poh* had been excluded from the post-1976 alliance of business and state, and resented the closed shop that made up the Bangkok elite. Their emergence was a significant pressure on the 'semi-democracy' compromise of the 1978 constitution. Rather than parliament merely rubber stamping Cabinet decisions and policies devised in the theatre of real power, Parliament was used aggressively to pursue particular interests, often in conflict with established elites. The initial power of the *jao poh* derived from the substantial financial resources with which they were able to bribe local officials. Such resources were built up from local entrepreneurial activities – legitimate and illegitimate. As business concerns grew, local power and influence was insufficient to meet *jao poh* needs and many turned to winning seats in Parliament, or having supporters elected. Through patronage of village leaders and local officials, or as village or local leaders themselves, they possessed the necessary resources to succeed in winning seats. This enabled them to press their demands in a national arena and gain access to the powerful Bangkok bureaucracy. The *jao poh* did not envisage Parliament as a means of 'democratic' politics. Rather, Parliament was an additional way 'of doing business'.[35] Since the 1980s the Thai party system has been dominated by fluctuating networks of *jao poh*.

The increasing importance of Parliament throughout the 1980s was, then, a reflection of the growth of the *jao poh* as a political and economic force, a result of Thailand's growing economy and the geographic spread of capitalist production.

In the context of business's compromised position, some theorists have focused on the middle class as the catalyst for democratization in Thailand. Certainly, during the democracy protests the media seized on the fact that many protesters were in possession of mobile phones and dubbed the crowds the mobile telephone mob (*mop mu thu*). A survey by the Social Science Association of Thailand seemingly confirms middle-class dominance in the events. The survey found that close to 50 per cent of participants received lower- to higher-middle-class incomes and over 60 per cent of participants had university degrees.[36] Economic factors are paramount in explaining the participation of these protesters in the democracy movement.

The growth of the middle class in commercial and industrial sectors is a product of Thailand's quest to become a 'newly industrializing country'. Collectively, the middle class have formed the managerial legions of Thailand's uneven economic development and are among its principal beneficiaries.

Foreign investment in Thailand, which grew to extraordinary heights in the late 1980s, is credited with increasing the political confidence of the middle class.[37] The significance of global capitalism in Thailand's economic boom has led a number of commentators to contend that the Thai middle class are internationally conscious in the extreme.[38] Their location as individuals in multinational companies and exporting companies makes them aware of the need for political stability as a precondition for economic growth. As Voravidh Charoenlert argues, among the middle class there is a desire for 'peaceful politics' in which political succession is orderly and policy formation is open and accountable.[39] Having believed that the military provided political stability in a climate of global conflict and internal class rivalry, some sections of the middle class realized that even with the retreat of superpower conflict, the army was rearticulating its role as national leader and threatening the 'open politics' thought necessary for economic growth.[40]

Following the *coup* in February, academics petitioned the King, arguing that democratic forms of government were more suitable to Thailand. The petition epitomizes liberal logic regarding democracy:

> In recent years Thailand's economy has . . . [become] more complex . . . [and] more closely linked to the world economy. Such an economic system can progress further only within a liberal economic and political framework, which permits everyone the freedom to participate and organize to claim their economic rights. . . . In today's world situation it is vital for Thailand to maintain a good standing as a democratic country in order . . . to further Thailand's trading position.[41]

The new period promised to provide exponents of liberal democracy with an enlarged constituency. But rather than ideals, it was the contingent demands of the early 1990s that sustained middle-class commitment to democracy. Quite simply, the majority of the middle class, as Voravidh noted, collectively saw 'democracy as a condition of economic development that would be the prime basis for future stability'.[42]

If we have seen the bathos of democracy's assumed connection with rational forms of rule, it is time now to reflect on those aspirations for democracy that express a concern for the needs and sovereignty of the very people often denigrated as irrational by supporters of procedural democracy; in short, with radicalizing democracy.

Labour organizations played an important, if secondary role, in the events of 1991–92. Somsak Kosaisuk, president of the Railway Workers' Association of Thailand and executive member of the Confederation of Democracy (Confederation), has observed: 'History is never about the working class, you will never see the working class in history.'[43] Certainly, mainstream accounts of 1991–92 testify to this. However, despite low levels of unionization there was, as Somsak argues, an organizational presence of workers at the democracy rallies.[44] There was also the struggle to maintain organizational forms conducive to working-class demands, a struggle that is integral to any democracy accountable to people's needs.

In a post-*coup* rationalization Suchinda made it clear that outlawing state enterprise unions was one of the prime reasons for the *coup*. Under the new legislation old unions could register as associations but were barred from striking and sitting on various labour bodies. Despite the attacks on working-class organizations, unionists quickly regrouped. Unions registered as associations and by the end of the year many had reached respectable membership levels.

Somsak and other union leaders were also intimately involved in the struggle for democracy. Somsak became an executive member of the broadly based Confederation for Democracy after being prominent in coordinating the Labour Committee for Democracy.

Union leaders' objectives in fighting for democracy reflected a consciousness of how democracy could be strategically used to advance the interests of workers: 'In the past struggles for democracy around the world, the labour movement has joined those struggles bravely. An increase in the bargaining power of unions depends on workers being under a democratic form of government.'[45]

A series of democratic labour groups, though small, were also established during 1991–92. One such group issued a statement attacking the Suchinda regime for treating the people 'like vegetables and fish'. They went on to call on all Thais to vote in the upcoming election in order to 'use our rights to rehabilitate democracy so that it is a genuine democracy of the people, by the people and for the people'.[46] The appeal to the universal rights of sovereignty, the idea that it is the people who rule, clearly upsets the realist disenchantment with democracy, where sovereignty exists more as a rhetorical apparatus to lure votes than as anything substantive.

During the May events union leaders met to organize a strike but the intervention of the King defused the May crisis. Nevertheless, the ports and railways authorities felt it necessary to declare a public holiday for workers following the massacre rather than face the prospect of strikes or political meetings.

The notions of democracy issuing from labour groups contrast starkly with the rationalistic and economically laden arguments emanating from middle-class intellectuals, business and political scientists. They demonstrate that democracy itself was a contested class concept.

Another force for radicalizing democracy was the non-government organizations. Made up of over fifty different non-government organizations, the Campaign for Popular Democracy (known as Campaign) was the prime force behind the pro-democracy movement, having staged, in alliance with the Student Federation of Thailand, numerous protests well before the crisis of May. Both these organizations sought to expand the democratic arena – to build a participatory democracy which could effectively redress economic and political inequalities. While political parties and business groups were silent in the early months of martial law, these two groups organized public demonstrations and publicly criticized the military. Rural offshoots of Campaign were able to connect local issues, such as the environmental crisis in the north-east and the lack of government assistance, with the problems of authoritarian government. A popular demand was the call for 'eatable democracy', one which could attend to the local developmental issues of the people and concretely improve their well-being. Such a call was a direct challenge to the monolithic state bureaucracies that daily maladjudicate on developmental matters.[47]

However, non-government organization demands for political decentralization, participatory democracy and sustainable development were sidelined in the wider democracy movement. Parinya Thanwanarumitkun, secretary-general of the Student Federation of Thailand, notes:

> We did not hope for this result [middle-class dominance] in the May Event, but when the middle class are the main force of the struggle, that is the result. The issue that concerns the middle class was just the military and the dictatorship, it wasn't the economic issue of equitable distribution in the rural areas. It was just a question of the military: 'Get them out!'[48]

Chamlong brought to the forefront the single issue of an elected prime minister. The final blow to aspirations occurred when Campaign was usurped by Confederation, led by Chamlong. Much criticism had surrounded Campaign's alleged inability to organize the mass demonstrations because of its collective decision-making structures. According to Parinya, the emergence of the Confederation marked a crucial turning-point in cementing Chamlong's leadership of the democracy movement and represented a shift to the narrow focus of fighting only for an elected prime minister. Campaign's eclipse was the eclipse of any hope of radicalizing the democracy movement.

The emergence of non-government organizations as key political actors reflects to some extent the involvement of radicals in new forms of political contestation. Furthermore, the conceptualization of the struggle as one of civil society versus the state, popularized by former student leader Thiriyut Bunmi, reflects an attempt to find a middle road to social change.[49]

Thiriyut's discussion of the events of 1992 is especially significant because he was an adviser to Campaign and student groups.[50] Thiriyut characterizes the 1992 democratic opposition as a diffuse grouping from every class and sector engaged in a struggle against an authoritarian state.[51] By transcending class differences and typifying all organizations as part of an emergent civil society, Thiriyut points to the strictly political nature of the democratic movement. Parinya also sees this as an important aspect in the struggle against authoritarianism. The struggle is no longer class-based but a struggle of the people against the state:

> The problem is not capitalism or socialism but, we conclude from the Tienanmen events, power. In capitalism or socialism state power is held by a few people who can destroy democracy. That is why the struggle in Thailand is . . . for democracy, not just elections but participatory democracy.[52]

Thiriyut has invoked 'civil society' as both an analytical category and a normative ideal through which democracy could become the dominant form of political organization. In appropriating civil society as a theoretical tool for conceptualizing and effecting social change, Thiriyut rides the boundaries between bourgeois fetishing of the non-state sphere and the attempt to democratize that sphere. His work marks the potentially dangerous slide between democracy as a liberating ideology and as an enclosure of people in new forms of political regulation. Profoundly aware of this, he argues that it is necessary to buffer bourgeois individualism with some form of collective consciousness that enables social responsibility to be a mark of the new democratic citizen.[53] The theoretical problems with which he engages are precisely those of how to constitute, practically, a genuine social democracy – the very issue that confronts non-government organizations. It is the issue of radicalizing democracy against regressive procedural democracy. It should be noted that to democratization theorists bent on installing procedural democracy, it is non-government organization activists and intellectuals such as Thiriyut who represent the major threat to the consolidation of democracy. This is so because they bring into the struggle for democracy the expelled issue of sovereignty, raising questions about the particular interests that democracy might serve.

When, in 1995, events of the early 1990s had turned full circle with the election of a coalition government composed of *jao poh* political parties and politicians who had backed the Suchinda regime, some commentators despaired of Thailand's ever becoming truly democratic; for others it reflected the tolerable idiosyncrasies of the evolution of Thai democracy. Whatever one's position, it is evident that a hyperdemocracy, an imagined condition of democracy, haunts much contemporary commentary on Thai politics. Inasmuch as transition theorists package Western democracy as an institutional mechanism and present it to the Third World as a dependable product, many Thai political practitioners and commentators, wanting to move away from *prachathipatai baep Thai*, are not unwilling consumers. Procedural democracy offers the prospect of shifting away from the vulgar state of an earlier developmental period towards a democratic form supportive of bourgeois civil society. Nevertheless, for such theorists, the cynical playing of democracy by elites is considered more a consequence of the lack of a democratic populace than the founding cause of authoritarianism.[54] It is the people who are not yet worthy of the product. Anand echoes this theme:

> Democracy is a reflection of the level of the people who vote . . . if they vote for bad persons, democracy will deteriorate. If people still vote as if they were 2000 year-old turtles who then should take the blame except the people themselves?[55]

Similarly Anek, a consumer and exponent of political development theory, analyses the failure of Thai democracy in relation to idealized images of the progressive realization of democratic polities in the West. His comments are representative of a wide section of liberal opinion in Thailand. His basic point is that Western democracy arose gradually as the franchise widened to assimilate lower classes who had been appropriately educated to perform their democratic responsibilities.[56] According to Anek, the Westernized revolutionaries who came to power in 1932 'gave' democracy to all people instantaneously. This premature designation of the democratic franchise, he argues, has been the root problem facing Thailand ever since: democracy has been taken like technology, 'before the order of our historical development'.[57] The premature embracing of democracy leads, according to Anek, to the prevalent practice of vote-buying, the poor quality of politicians and the strength of the military.

Both Anek and Anand are now in some ways giving voice to the themes of procedural democracy. While others before them have bemoaned the inadequacies of Thai democracy and called for greater adherence to Western forms, such claims have been buried by the weight of state development in Thailand. Many Thai commentators on democracy have adhered patiently to ideas of *prachathipatai baep Thai*, although in varying forms. The prevailing ethos is the idea of a culturally and historically attuned democracy, but more often than not the arguments of cultural specificity and historical circumstance mask the less noble claims of power and interest. Some theorists have hoped that as the achievements of modernity registered in Thailand, as an educated electorate emerged and as genuine interest-representing parties formed, *prachathipatai baep Thai* would be superseded by 'Western-style' democracy. It would appear that this horizon of promise is in sight. But, habitually cautious, few Thai theorists are yet ready to embrace it. It is too fogged by uncertainties.

Democratic discourse, now caught at the intersection of global and domestic changes, is being reshaped to reflect the hybridity of circumstance. While procedural democracy presently appears emergent, it will none the less reflect domestic determinants of class and state as they negotiate their way through globalization. Thus, while democratization theorists generalize on democratic progress, adherents of procedural democracy in Thailand procrastinate.

Given this condition, reflections on how to entrench democratic forms in Thailand have engaged with the problematic of constituting a democratic citizenry. The question of an educated electorate is crucial for big business, and on this issue liberal democratic theory and business interests ideally cross paths. The uncertain and non-institutional nature of present parliamentary politics in Thailand, and the failure of parties to form along broad lines of social interests, makes parliamentary democracy potentially an unstable system as it remains merely a realm of direct competition for political power by fractions of capital and state. Provincial capitalists, with access to the majority of the electorate in the provinces, can succeed in winning government all too easily. Thus, for big Bangkok-based capital, the executive power of the bureaucracy remains a necessary counterbalance to any potential 'democratic' assault on the state by other sections of capital. Such connections are not merely pragmatic but deeply entrenched. Bangkok capital's statist attitude rests in its history of cultural and economic dependence on ruling elites. Having failed to entrench its own ideological codes, the bourgeoisie has a 'thin' hold on society based on money and power.[58] The bourgeoisie cannot claim natural leadership and regulate society according to its own ideals, and so seeks alliance with state-based groups and monarchical institutions. This cultural dependency on tradition inhibits the development of democratic consciousness.

Pre-democratic modes of interpellation in Thailand were framed around Thai national identity and subservience to nation, monarch and religion.[59] Their effect was to exclude from official political processes non-elites, who were to entrust power to benevolent despots. Development paternalism was its legitimating ideology. However, we are now witnessing, in the face of challenges to that old order, some in business setting long-term goals in 'democratic education', against 'money politics'. The seemingly neutral inculcation of democratic values – an outcome of business's tentative shift towards democratic forms and middle-class propagation – is an ideological project, challenged in practice by the social tensions that engulf the Thai social formation. The extent of democratization in Thailand will not reflect the accumulation of modernity but rather the particular nature of the political and economic conjuncture. There is no end-point to modernity whereby democracy greets those fortunate enough to arrive. Rather we may speak, following Bob Jessop, of the indeterminacy of democracy; that is, to recognize our inability to predict a neat fit between capitalism and democracy or, to use the preferred neo-Weberian phraseology of political development studies, modernity and political rationality (democracy).[60] The generalizations made about the globalization of democracy seem nothing more than a painful howling for order. It is with this in mind, perhaps, that Thai cultural critic Kasian Tejapira has adamantly refused to consider that democratization in Thailand involves the globalization of any Western political form.[61]

When the dogs howl on pre-election night in Thailand, it is a reminder of the underhanded ways that democratic power is bought. Such idioms – and there are many derogatory ones surrounding democracy in Thailand – poke fun at the haughty pretence of rationality. This chapter has sought to highlight the historical class and state tensions that have fuelled Thailand's democracy, suggesting that the supposedly subjectless 'rationality' of modernity is, in the context of democratization, stamped with the power and interest of its enclassed historical time.

In pursuit of order, international relations and political development studies have common cause. With order now increasingly realized through the rhetoric of procedural democracy, it would not be surprising if stronger links were drawn between the two disciplines, particularly as their objects of knowledge become entangled. The nexus may well be liberal demo-cratization theory. But getting on with the pragmatic accumulation of power and capital, elite actors – in Thailand and elsewhere – have little regard for academic models of democratization. Simultaneously, those excluded from elite political processes are also making their claims, confounding attempts to rule distributive issues as out of order. General patterns of democratization are perjured. While the narcissistic image of procedural democracy may pass selective examination in the sanitized, media-ized democracies of the West, the untamed emergence of democracy in the Third World portends an unsightly tale to those who imagine in democratization the end of history.

Notes

I am grateful to a number of people who in various ways assisted me with this chapter: Asvin Phorugngam for Thai language assistance and inspiration; Noel Battye for sharing his scholarly understanding of Thai history and guiding my research; and Lucy Chessar, Graham Willet, Donna Buttigieg, Grant Parsons, Albert Paolini, Harold Crouch and John Dryzek for reading this work in various stages of draft. Finally, I owe much to the editor of this book who, during his period of editorial bondage, made countless suggestions and offered friendly support.

1. Cited in Sanit Dachanan (ed.), *Phaen Phatana Kanmuang Paisuu Kanpokkhrong Rabop Prachathipatai Damnaew Phrarachadamrichawngphrabatsomdat Phrapokkaewjaoyuuhua* (Political Development Plan towards Democracy of King Rama the VII) (Bangkok, 1975), p. 164.

2. Samuel Huntington, *The Third Wave: Democratization in the Late Twentieth Century* (Norman, University of Okalahoma Press, 1991). The first and second wave occurred between 1828 and 1926, and 1943 and 1962 respectively. The third wave Huntington dates from the overthrow of Marcello Caetano's dictatorial regime in Portugal in 1974.

3. Ibid., pp. 29–30.

4. See especially M. Doyle, 'Liberalism and world politics', *American Political Science Review*, 80:4 (1986), 1151–69. For an opposing view that considers 'democratic peace theory' damaging to the hard-core realist mind-set necessary for the conduct of international relations see C. Layne, 'Kant or cant: the myth of democratic peace', *International Security*, 19:2 (1994), 5–49. See F. Fukuyama, *The End of History and the Last Man* (London, Penguin Books, 1992) for an extended, if idiosyncratic, treament of this issue.

5. L. Diamond, 'The globalization of democracy' in Robert O. Slater, Barry M. Schutz and Steven R. Dorr (eds), *Global Transformation and the Third World* (London and Boulder, CO, Lynne Rienner Publishers, 1993), pp. 31–69 (p. 58).

6. Ibid., p. 48.

7. Giuseppe Di Palma, *To Craft Democracies: An Essay on Democratic Transitions* (Berkeley, University of California Press, 1990), p. 19.

8. Ibid, p. 21.

9. On the idea of transition narrative see D. Chakrabarty, 'Postcoloniality and the artifice of history: who speaks for "Indian" pasts?', *Representations*, 37: Winter (1992), 1–23.

10. J. A. Schumpeter, *Capitalism, Socialism and Democracy*, 6th edn (London, Unwin Paperbacks, 1987), p. 269.

11. Ibid., pp. 284–5.

12. R. A. Dahl, *Polyarchy: Participation and Opposition* (New Haven, CT, Yale University Press, 1971), p. 9, note 4.

13. D. Ethier, 'Processes of transition and democratic consolidation: theoretical indicators' in D. Ethier (ed.), *Democratic Transition and Consolidation in Southern Europe, Latin America and Southeast Asia* (London, Macmillan, 1990), p. 11.

14. Huntington, *The Third Wave*, p. 6.

15. Di Palma, *To Craft Democracies*, p. 41.

16. Samuel Huntington, *Political Order in Changing Societies* (New Haven, CT, Yale University Press, 1968).

17. Chanwut Witaraphuk, 'Wiwatanakan laksana khong prachathipatai baep Thai' (Evolving characteristics of Thai-style democracy) in Kongbanathikan Warasan Setasatkanmuang (Editorial Office of The Journal of Political Economy), *Bonsenthang Prachathipatai 2475–2525* (Towards Democracy 1932–1982) (Bangkok, Sathaban Wichai Sangkom, Maha. Chulalongkon, 1983), p. 31. *Prachathipatai* is a compound word that loosely means 'people's sovereignty'.

18. Cited in Thak Chaloemtiarana, 'The Sarit regime 1957–1963: the formative years of modern Thai politics', unpublished PhD thesis (Cornell University, 1974), pp. 206–7.

19. Cited in Chalimkian Phiwanuan, *Khwamkhit Thangkanmuang khong Thahan Thai 2519–2533* (Political Thought of the Thai Military 1976–1992) (Bangkok, Samnakphim Phucakkan, 1992), p. 47.

20. Cited in Thak, 'The Sarit regime', p. 208.

21. See K. Hewison, *Bankers and Bureaucrats: Capital and the Role of the State in Thailand* (Monograph Series, Yale University Southeast Asia Studies, Yale Center for International and Area Studies, No. 34, 1989).

22. See D. Morell and Chai-anan Samudavanija, *Political Conflict in Thailand: Reform, Reaction, Revolution* (Cambridge, Oelgeschlager, Gunn and Hain, 1981).

23. See Chai-anan Samudavanija, Khusam Snitwongse and Suchit Bunbongkarn, *From Armed Suppression to Political Offensive* (Bangkok, Institute of Security and International Relations, Chulalongkon University, 1990).

24. See K. Hewison, 'Of regimes, state and pluralities: Thai politics enters the 1990s' in K. Hewison, R. Robison and C. Rodan (eds), *Southeast Asia in the 1990s: Authoritarianism, Democracy and Capitalism* (Melbourne, Allen and Unwin, 1993), pp. 161–89.

25. In a widely reported speech Anand argued that the military should seek funding through normal mechanisms, acknowledging that in the past, 'historically, they [the military] have always been an important element in decision making process . . . they have to adjust themselves to the new political circumstances'. *Bangkok Post*, 5 September 1991, pp. 1–2.

26. See Surin Maisrikrod, 'Emerging patterns of leadership in Thailand', *Contemporary Southeast Asia*, 15:1 (1993), 80–97.

27. Cited in *Business in Thailand*, April 1992, p. 24.

28. See Coordinating Committee of Human Rights Organisations in Thailand, *Crisis in Democracy 17th–20th May 1992, Thailand* (Hong Kong, Coordinating Committee of Human Rights Organisations in Thailand, 1992).

29. See Anek Laothamatas, *Business Associations and the New Political Economy of Thailand: From Bureaucratic Polity to Liberal Corporatism* (Singapore, West View Press, 1992).

30. *The Manager*, June 1992, p. 8.

31. *Bangkok Post*, 2 June 1992, p. 5.

32. Formed in 1981 by businessmen who, in the open period of 1973–76, had established the centrist New Force Party, the BMS was fairly quiet during the 1980s, serving more as a networking organization than any kind of political grouping. See *The Manager*, August 1992, pp. 18–23.

33. *The Manager*, August 1992, p. 21.

34. The term *jao poh* has been translated in the English-language press as 'Godfather'. The term became increasingly common from the 1970s onwards after the screening in Thailand of the 1970s classic, *The Godfather*. The term is not so inappropriate, as many *jao poh* are renowned for illegal activities and assassinations. Pasuk Phongpaichit and C. Baker, 'Jao Sua, Joa Poh, Jao Tii: lords of Thailand's transition', paper presented at the Fifth International Conference in Thai Studies, School of Oriental and African Studies, London, 1993, p. 17. My discussion of the *jao poh* follows Pasuk and Baker.

35. Ibid., p. 18.

36. Cited in Samaphan Prachathipatai, *Saisan Prachachon* (Lines of People) (Bangkok, Samaphan Prachathipatai, 1992), p. 33. Interestingly, the same composition is not reflected in information gathered on 38 people who were killed between 17 and 20 May. It was found that 37 were male, 1 was female; 25 were aged between 20 and 29; 17 were workers and 10 students. See Voravidh Charoenlert, 'Chonchan klang kap hetkan phreusaphakhom' ('The middle class and the May events') in Sungsidh Piriyarangsan and Pasuk Phongpaichit (eds), *Chonchan Klang Bon Krasae Prachathipatai Thai* (The Middle Class and Thai Democracy) (Bangkok, Political Economy Centre, Faculty of Economics, Chulalongkorn University and Friedrich Ebert Stiftung, 1993), pp. 125–7. This volume is cited hereafter as *Chonchan Klang*. Somsak Kosaisuk, a trade union leader, claims that the surveys overestimated the middle-class presence because workers were not keen to fill in the forms and shied away from the interviewers. Interview with Somsak Kosaisuk, by the author, Bangkok, 2 February 1994. Other figures also indicate that middle-class presence was overestimated. The International

Fact-Finding Mission found that of 696 documented cases of medical treatment of wounded protesters, labourers made up 42 per cent, unknown 16 per cent, businesspersons 14 per cent, students 12 per cent, lawyers 8 per cent, government officials 4 per cent, taxi drivers 3 per cent, and the police and military 1 per cent. See Coordinating Committee of Human Rights Organisations in Thailand, *Crisis in Democracy 17th–20th May 1992, Thailand*.

37. Between 1986 and 1988 foreign investment increased from 2.1 thousand million baht to 16.4 thousand million baht and investment in the form of fixed property rose from 3.1 thousand million baht in 1986 to 49 thousand million baht in 1989 (25 baht approximates US$1). Figures cited in Anek Laothamatas, 'Thurakit bonsen thang prachathipatai: threusadi kap khwampenching' (Business on the road to democracy: theory and reality) in Sungsidh and Pasuk (eds), *Chonchan Klang*, p. 181.

38. Pasuk Phongpaichit, 'Botbat chonchan klang nai setakit lae kanmuang prathet Asien Nik lae Thai' (The role of the middle class in the economies and politics of the Asian NICs and Thailand') in Sungsidh and Pasuk (eds), *Chonchan Klang*, p. 95.

39. Voravidh Charoenlert, 'Chonchan klang kap hetkan phreusaphakhom' (The middle class and the May events') in Sungsidh and Pasuk (eds), *Chonchan Klang*, p. 138.

40. Pasuk in Sungsidh and Pasuk (eds), *Chonchan Klang*, p. 106.

41. Anonymous, 'Open statement from academics concerning the recent coup in Thailand', *Journal of Contemporary Asia*, 21:4 (1991), 563–4. The group of academics go on to request that the military curb its power and suggest that a parliamentary democracy under a constitutional monarchy is the best system for Thailand in the present period.

42. Voravidh in Sungsidh and Pasuk (eds), *Chonchan Klang*, p. 140.

43. Interview with Somsak Kosaisuk, by the author, Bangkok, 7 February 1994. Since 1991, state enterprise unions have been registered as associations.

44. Somsak Kosaisuk, 'Khabuankan raengngan Thai kap hetkan phrutsaphatmin' (The Thai labour movement and the bloody May event), *Raengngan Parithat* (Labour Review), 6 and 7 July 1992, p. 5.

45. Somsak, 'Khabuankan raengngan Thai', p. 7.

46. Somuttharasakon and Nakon Pathom Labour Group. 'Thalaengkan prachathipatai' (Democratic declaration) in Somsak Kosaisuk, *Labour against Dictatorship*, trans. Andrew Brown (Bangkok, Friedrich Ebert Stiftung, 1993), p. 191. The main text of this book is in English and Thai but it also has a collection of over twenty Thai-language documents from labour organizations.

47. Niran Kultanan, 'NGOs, movements and democratic transitions: a view from the northeast', paper presented to the International Conference on Thai Studies, London, 5–9 July 1993, p. 7.

48. Interview with Parinya Thanwanarumitkun by the author, Bangkok, 25 January 1994.

49. Thiriyut was a student leader at the time of the 1976 coup and subsequently fled to the jungle, joining the Communist Party of Thailand. He defected in 1980 and both he and a growing band of intellectuals have theorized a space for social democracy in Thailand. His discussion of 1992 is in part a critique of what he considers to be the radical excesses of 1973–76.

50. Parinya notes that Thiriyut's notion of civil society was well understood by key activists and that the SFT was in frequent contact with Thiriyut. Interview with Parinya Thanwanarumitkun, by the author, Bangkok, 25 January 1994.

51. Thiriyut Bunmi, *Sangkhom Khemkaeng* (Civil Society) (Bangkok, Samnakphim Mingmit, 1993), p. 189.

52. Interview with Parinya Thanwanarumitkun, by the author, Bangkok, 25 January 1994.

53. Thiriyut, *Sangkhom Khemkaeng* (Civil Society), pp. 191–6.

54. See Pricha Hongskrailers, 'Thai political culture', *Sangkhomsat* (Social Science), 25:1 (1988), 28–49. Pricha concludes his discussion of Thai political culture thus: 'Thai political culture supports the existence of an oligarchic bureaucratic group. Most socialising agents in Thailand . . . do not encourage a democratic orientation but rather support the bureaucracy by legitimating those who can control power' (p. 49). These sentiments pretty much sum up volumes of work on Thai political culture.

55. *Bangkok Post*, 16 December 1991, p. 4.

56. Anek Laothamatas, *Mop Mu Thu Chonchan Klang lae Nakthurakit kap Phathanakan Prachathipatai* (The Mobile Telephone Mob: The Middle Class and Business and the Development of Democracy) (Bangkok, Samnakphim Matichon, 1993), p. 17.

57. Ibid., p. 18.

58. See Nithi Aewsriwong, 'Watanatham khong chonchan klang Thai' (Culture of the Thai middle class) in Sungsidh and Pasuk (eds), *Chonchan Klang*, pp. 62, 64.

59. See P. Vandergest, 'Constructing Thailand: regulation, everyday resistance and citizenship', *Comparative Studies in History and Society*, 35:1 (1993), 133–55.

60. Bob Jessop, 'The political indeterminacy of democracy' in A. Hunt (ed.), *Marxism and Democracy* (London, Lawrence and Wishart, 1980).

61. Kasian Tejapira, 'Prachathipatai mai lokanuwat' (Non-global democracy), *Phucakkan Raiwan* (The Manager Daily), 3 July 1995, p. 10. See also Kasian Tejapira, 'Kanmuangwatthanatham waduay prachathipatai' (Political culture and democracy), *Ratasatsan* (Political Science Journal), 19:1 (1994), 6–23, where Kasian discusses democracy as a 'free-floating signifier' resisting any single reading.

CHAPTER SEVEN

When ordinary people gather: the concept of partnership in development

EDGAR NG

Bessie Head's novel *When Rain Clouds Gather* has had little or no impact on the writing about development. Written nearly three decades ago, the story is about an agricultural development project in a village in Botswana. Although much of its treatment of political and economic issues is not directly relevant to recent debates about foreign aid, the novel celebrates what development theorists and practitioners today take to be the essence of the concept of partnership. The reader would have to be impressed with the extraordinary relationship between Gilbert, the English agricultural scientist, and the villagers. It is built on trust, respect, and commitment – the very adjectives used to describe the nature of development partnerships. The novel also resonates with contemporary thinking because it ends with ordinary people taking control of and improving their own lives. As the narrator observes, 'People were being drawn closer and closer to each other as brothers, and once you looked on the other man as your brother, you could not bear that he should want for anything or live in darkness'.[1]

In recent years the idea of partnership in development has gained widespread support in aid circles and, at least in terms of doctrine, it has come to represent the new orthodoxy. Yet it seems that the idea has taken hold through an exuberance about a fresh start generated more by disenchantment with past strategies than critical appraisal of contemporary prospects. As a student from Asia committed to Third World development, I shared something of this exuberance and saw partnership as the way forward. However, elements of scepticism have crept in. This chapter, therefore, grew out of a personal sense of bewilderment. How, I want to ask, is the concept of partnership different from what went before? Can it assist the parties in the development process to break through the enclosures of donor and recipient, actor and object, which have been so counter-productive in the past? Does it offer a guide to action on the ground? These questions are explored with reference to the implementation of partnership by international non-governmental organizations (INGOs)[2] in their aid programmes. The dilemmas and difficulties faced by these organizations, it is argued, provide a window on to the meaning and utility of the concept of partnership itself.

The idea of partnership became politically significant in the West in the late 1980s because of economic pressures and a shift in public sentiment. As the economies of major Western countries entered recession, there was increasing public pressure to give priority to domestic welfare. The West thus tried to curtail its bilateral and multilateral development commitments. In order to ease the burden on resources as well as to ensure that whatever funds were appropriated would be spent efficiently and effectively, it was seen as vital that Third World governments had greater involvement in development efforts. This mood was reflected in a substantial decrease in the foreign aid budgets of Western governments. In aggregate terms, the amount of overseas aid for the five-year period 1985–89 was only US$184bn, as compared to US$208bn in the previous five-year period. The magnitude of the reduction was particularly noticeable in the case of major donors such as the United States, Britain and France.[3]

Yet at the same time as government aid budgets were shrinking, the non-government aid sector was growing at an unprecedented rate. In the decade 1978–88, official grants to INGOs rose from US$876.9m to US$2.13bn; private donations more than doubled from US$1.7bn to US$4.2bn.[4] The movement is thus towards what I might call the privatization of the aid venture. This has significant implications for disciplinary international relations. Whereas before the provision of aid fell largely in the official domain, it is now increasingly located at the margins of state politics and even in the community at large. Traditionally, the issue of aid projects and the accompanying debate about development had a somewhat ambiguous status in the discipline; it was *in* international relations but it was not *of* its essence. Only at select points did it figure seriously – as for example when it was used as a weapon in the cold war. Now, with the links between the development project and state action much looser than before, the disciplinary status of development is even more ambiguous – and less to the taste of the discipline because it involves reaching further into the fabric of societies. It is the presupposition of this chapter that the development debate directly affects international relationships and is itself an important issue of international exchange. Hence in substantive terms international relations can hardly afford to remain disengaged – and engagement will carry the added benefit of drawing the discipline away from its state-centric inheritance.

The shift in the location of development projects means that debates over official aid policies and proper management of programmes are no longer confined to the aid community. This heightened interest in development assistance on the part of the general public has resulted in magazines and newspapers being more willing to give exposure to issues of Third World poverty. A study of the *New York Times*'s coverage of Africa, for example, showed that the average length of stories about Africa almost doubled between 1976 and 1990. More importantly, there were clear signs that the newspaper was placing more emphasis on non-crisis themes, such as politics, economics and environment, than on sensational topics such as war and disaster.[5]

Clearly INGOs have been one of the main beneficiaries of this change in public sentiment in the West; people's interest and confidence in INGOs and their programmes has increased markedly. A survey commissioned by World Vision Australia in 1993 showed that, among those interviewees who could name an overseas aid agency, 87 per cent said that they would trust INGOs and 62 per cent believed that INGOs used their funds effectively.[6] In many ways, of course, INGOs have played a central role in heightening public consciousness. Development issues have been brought into the home, and development work represented as a personal responsibility. The INGOs have promoted the message that everyone can be involved and make a direct contribution, as for example by buying designated products in supermarkets, part of the proceeds from which go to supporting development activities abroad. In the survey by World Vision Australia mentioned above, 75 per cent of respondents said that INGOs provided an opportunity for them to be involved in worthwhile causes.[7]

Before we examine partnership as doctrine, it is necessary to have some sense of what went before, particularly with respect to two key aspects: the role of the state and the influence of ordinary people. In traditional development thinking, aid was a strictly state-to-state business. The state was simultaneously the instigator and driving force of development programmes. This emphasis on the role of the state was foundational in the colonial era when development was a matter to be determined by the imperial and colonial governments. In the British case, although the colonial state was responsible for the formulation and implementation of development schemes, all projects had to be assessed and approved by the imperial government. This arrangement was institutionalized with the establishment of the Colonial Development Advisory Committee after the passage of the Colonial Development Act 1929. Under this legislation, the Committee could only consider proposals coming from colonial states. Even though there was some feeling within the Committee that the colonial governments had neither the time nor the capacity to determine what was needed, and the Committee was prepared to go out of its way to initiate plans, the Colonial Office insisted that the Committee adhere to a more passive role.[8]

The belief in the state as the fulcrum of development passed from imperial policy-makers to their nationalist successors. Once independence had been secured, there was optimism that the new state would be able to generate economic development. Kwame Nkrumah, as early as 1949, made the statement 'if we get self-government, we'll transform the Gold Coast into a paradise in ten years'.[9] Although seldom quite so optimistic, scholarly analyses also emphasized the importance of a democratic state in promoting development plans. Much later, David Fieldhouse, for example, suggested that the primary reason independent African states failed to improve their citizens' living standards was their inability to translate development into terms which would elicit a response from local groups.[10] The problem, as he saw it, was not the state as such, but the mis-management of the state. What was required was reform of the state, not removing development from its agenda.

After the Second World War, development thinking in the West placed a similar premium on the role of the state. Most of the official development models relied heavily on an active state for policy implementation. Both the Basic Needs Approach and the Human Development Model, for example, required states to adopt an interventionist position to ensure that aid was directed to providing basic necessities and improving general education and skill levels. Even in the case of the Structural Adjustment Programmes, which take a relatively pro-market stance, the state is still seen as crucial in creating a congenial environment for market operations. Many critics of Structural Adjustment Programmes in fact demand that the state take on a proactive role to ensure that disadvantaged groups do not suffer from extreme hardships as a result of implementing adjustment programmes.

For many years, there has thus been little space for ordinary people either in the West or in the Third World to influence policies. Certainly from time to time commercial interests have had an impact – as for instance on the British government's decision to commit 3.5 million pounds to improve transport infrastructure in Kenya and Uganda in the early 1920s.[11] It is also true that the modified development models of the 1970s made allowance for local consultation. Fundamentally, however, it was believed that decisions about development had to be taken by those who had the knowledge (understood in Western terms) and access to specialized expertise. Such thinking lay behind the doctrines of imperial trusteeship. Later the same idea was enshrined in Article 22 of the Covenant of the League of Nations: civilization had 'a sacred trust' for 'peoples not yet able to stand by themselves in the strenuous conditions of the modern world'. Even when the idea of partnership was flagged by the British Government in the 1940s, it was largely a window-dressing strategy to ward off US criticism of colonialism and a tool to appease emerging local elites. The 'parent–child' nature of the relationship was never questioned.

The trusteeship principle lived on in later understandings of relation-ships between donors and recipients. It was taken for granted that the West had the answers to Third World problems. Led by development economics, various academic disciplines in the West collaborated and competed with each other over how the Third World could be released from its backwardness. Development projects invariably came in packages with a set of instructions. There was also a heavy emphasis on the importance of expert advice from expatriates and on the enabling possibilities of Western technologies. President Truman's address in launching the Point Four

Program in 1949 sums up the essence of the development philosophy for the next four decades: 'We must embark on a bold new program for making the benefits of our scientific and industrial progress available for the improvement and growth of underdeveloped areas.'[12] This faith in scientific knowledge and the role of technology came to be supplemented by a reliance on sociological insights and administrative skills. The optimism about what could be accomplished with comparatively modest inputs was thus more a product of the West's belief in its own empowerment than a result of any sustained analysis of the problems faced. A contemporary illustration is provided by the advocacy of a wider distribution of condoms as the solution to controlling the spread of AIDS/HIV in Africa. The construction of the disease as a medical problem, namely the transmission of the HIV virus through unprotected sexual intercourse, fails to take account of the relevance of social and cultural factors. At issue here is not whether condoms can protect people from contracting HIV, but whether people will actually use them. Yoweri Museveni, President of Uganda, has cautioned that: 'AIDS cannot be understood in biological terms alone. Sex is not a simple manifestation of a biological drive; it is socially dictated.'[13]

At this point, I need to spell out more clearly what I mean by the idea of partnership, how it developed, the conceptual influence behind its emergence, and how it relates to the development principles promulgated by INGOs. The idea of partnership emphasizes a collaborative and non-coercive relationship between donors and recipients. The possession of financial and technical resources cannot be taken as an entitlement to impose blueprints on Third World societies or even to assert exactly how aid dollars are spent. There must be more give and take between the parties; a more interactive relationship. As the International Council of Voluntary Agencies put it, equitable and genuine partnerships should proceed on 'an equality of commitment and involvement . . . [and] the programmes should reflect a spirit of co-ownership'.[14] However, a non-paternalistic relationship between donors and recipients does not necessarily imply that the latter's opinions will always be followed. Partnership should not be interpreted as simply a reversal of traditional donor–recipient relationship with the recipients taking complete control of the design and implementation of projects and the donors being relegated to the role of providing resources. Instead, there is a certain logic to the understanding of the idea of partnership to mean that at times the donors will restrain the recipients. Thus, for example, while there is now considerable emphasis on maximizing the use of local resources instead of importing material and machines from overseas, it might be argued that there is no reason why the adoption of local cultural practices will work to satisfy people's needs. After all, local people and practices can also be exploitative and unproductive.

To ensure that there is adequate exchange of information and experience between aid workers and local people, it is mandatory to establish mechanisms to ensure that local needs can be expressed. Many Western aid organizations have indeed acknowledged the potential benefits of working collaboratively with local groups. The World Bank is a prominent example. From 1973 to 1988, 60 per cent of its projects were undertaken in cooperation with indigenous NGOs, but by 1991 the proportion had risen to 86 per cent.[15] It is also very common for INGOs to set up branch offices in various Third World countries to handle development projects. These local offices mainly employ local people as their staff and often they have a high degree of autonomy in terms of funding and monitoring projects. Oxfam, for instance, has 34 field offices in the developing world which are responsible for programmes within individual countries.

A greater emphasis on partnership between civilian groups has also led to a rethinking of the relationship between the state and local people. In the past, it was invariably central government authorities who dictated the development process – as instanced by the Botswana Government's decision to commercialize communal grazing land in the 1970s. In spite of vehement objections from local authorities and small graziers, the Ministry of Finance and Development Planning was committed to commercialization and was not prepared to make any compromise. A memorandum issued in 1975 declared: 'it should be clear that the public discussion is not being undertaken in order to debate the land development policy per se. Rather, the position is that we have the policy and a proposition to implement it.'[16] It is not possible to maintain this kind of authoritarian relationship once local people and INGOs become more assertive in expressing their opinions. Either acting individually or through alliances, they attempt to influence government policies, insisting that aid programmes bring tangible benefits to local people. Accepting, however, that the state no longer has a monopoly of development, and that at times it may need to make compromises with respect to the objectives and content of programmes, most advocates of the concept of partnership do not subscribe to the idea that people outside official channels should take over the responsibility of development administration from the state. What they suggest can be more appropriately described as a symbiotic relationship whereby both the state and people's organizations can draw on the other's strengths and complement the other's weaknesses. For instance, civilian groups can often be more effective than government authorities in delivering services to remote areas, and the state is often better placed to provide material support.

The appeal of partnership must to some degree be related to changing scholarly thinking about the North–South relationship and of what stands in the way of change. Fundamental here has been recognition of the power of the discursive. Development has increasingly come to be seen not as some expression of the natural aspirations of people everywhere, but as a construct created and sustained by Western discourse and related to Western interests. What needs to be done is to present the problem in a different way. The hope is that by reconceptualizing the idea of development so that it is no longer presumed that all societies will follow the path of the West, new resources can be mobilized and old obstacles bypassed. One form taken by such rethinking has been labelled 'postdevelopmentalism', which, in many aspects, involves a rejection of the postulates of development as derived from classical political economy. Proceeding along these lines, poverty tends to be represented as predominantly a result of representation rather than an outcome of material conditions. Arturo Escobar has stressed that the analysis of political economy 'has to be accompanied by a strategic repositioning in the domain of representation'.[17] His argument is that until we can dismantle the dominating discursive structure, 'development' will never eventuate. The key to achieving social change therefore does not lie solely in receiving foreign aid but also in mobilizing local resources. Gustavo Esteva, in a much-quoted essay, describes an instance of this approach where local people in a Mexico City suburb organized themselves collectively to pursue their own development goals and to fight against encroachments from the West and local elites.[18]

If one follows the arguments of Escobar and Esteva, partnership can be viewed as little more than another attempt by the West to maintain its domination over the Third World. According to their schema, Western governments and aid agencies have no part to play in the development process. Obviously this is rejected by the international aid community. Moreover, it can be safely said that no INGO would identify itself with the kind of model proposed by Escobar and Esteva. Although there is inevitably some variation among INGOs, basically they believe that both the state and international aid agencies can make valuable contributions to improving the living standards of local people. What is significant, however, is that advocates of partnership, including INGOs, have been influenced by key elements of such approaches: by the emphasis placed on the discursive; by the need for development objectives to accord with cultural patterns; and by the need to mobilize indigenous resources.

It can thus be argued that the idea of partnership has drawn sustenance simultaneously from two different kinds of discourse, often with very little dialogue between them. On the one hand, there are traditional discourses – the province of which is economic improvement and project management – directed to the betterment of material conditions. On the other hand, there are new discourses fundamentally concerned with identity politics and subaltern agency. In many respects, proponents of partnership have to attempt to achieve some kind of accommodation between the two. In the case of INGOs, the difficulty of doing so is manifested by the tensions which sometimes arise between their philosophical suppositions and their operational guidelines. I now propose to illustrate some of the dilemmas involved by discussing three problem areas which affect most INGOs: their representations of the development process; the role of both the domestic and recipient state; and the involvement of local people.

Ideally, if INGOs' representations are to conform to the idea of partnership, they should depict the development process as a collaborative exercise between donors and local people. In fact, often the message conveyed by contemporary representations is not so very different from that of the past. The problem is at root financial. Although the level of official aid to INGOs has increased dramatically in the past fifteen years, public donations still remain the major source of income for most INGOs. They therefore need to run successful funding appeals in order to survive, and there is little doubt that sensational images and slogans are very useful in prompting people to become involved.

Victimhood is a constant theme in most INGOs' fund-raising materials. In many cases, the representations are a contemporary reworking of imperial stereotypes: darkness, disease and disaster on the one side; a shaft of light, the possibility of material transformation on the other. Very often, local people are portrayed as helpless, as struck down and dependent. Many of the images used in media campaigns are of distressed women and starving or diseased children. Action is vested in the giver; the key verbs are 'helping', 'giving' and 'averting'. Donors are encouraged to feel sympathy, compassion, responsibility, even guilt. But there is little which is calculated to bring out a sense of working together with local people, of a collaborative venture. Such representations are characteristic of disaster appeals, but they are also adopted in the promotion of long-term development programmes. Promotional material put out by an INGO on the establishment of a health clinic in Sudan, for instance, contrasts indigenous superstition with external enlightenment.[19] Two photographs accompany the text. One shows a pregnant woman looking very stressed, clearly unsure of her baby's future. The other shows the same woman chatting happily with two local health workers. The 'before' and 'after' message is obvious. The woman is pictured simply as a beneficiary and there is no indication that she has contributed in any way to her changed circumstances.

Another common feature of INGOs' publications is the use of personal stories told by aid workers, celebrities, journalists or local people themselves. In many ways, the use of a narrator is crucial in creating a bonding between donor and recipient. The development process is given a human touch by the narrator serving as an intermediary through whom personal feelings, such as sympathy and gratitude, are expressed. It is also significant that donors are often provided with individual details of aid recipients such as their names. This gives the public the impression that their money does not disappear anonymously, but goes to a particular person, or family, or village; in short, their 'partners'. This sense of personal bonding between donors and recipients is fundamental, of course, to the concept of partnership. On the surface, the personalized approach does have the effect of reversing the previous 'dehumanizing' approach of depicting Third World people as faceless aid recipients. Yet the approach is not as unproblematic as it may seem to be.

While a personalized approach makes it much easier to strike a chord of compassion in donors, it also tends to simplify the actual problems. Sometimes situations are trivialized and the impression is given that only a small amount of additional resources will transform the situation of local people. Donors therefore feel that the scale of the problem is not beyond their reach and that their donations will make a difference. An advertisement of the child sponsorship programme of PLAN International says 'Third World child poverty can be solved with PLAN child sponsorship'. This reduction of complex development problems to the provision of resources and its abstraction from the wider social, political and economic contexts mean that the relationship between donors and recipients is not really based on mutual understanding; that the representations do not accord with the concept of partnership. The primary consideration is not so much conveying the actual circumstances, but telling donors what they want to hear. Local people are therefore deprived of the right to represent themselves. They have little control over either the content or the way their story is told.

Recently, INGOs have started to investigate the possibility of collaborating with business corporations to conduct fund-raising campaigns. Some people are already wary that this may tarnish the public image of INGOs as non-profit organizations. A consultant to US non-profit organizations lamented 'Businesses are exploiting [non-profit organizations'] reputations and constituencies as marketing tools. In isolated instances, this trend may seem to be creating win–win relationships. . . . But the trend as a whole may be stealing our soul.'[20] Although there is still no concrete evidence to prove that a company's involvement in the fund-raising activities of charity organizations will contribute to an increase in its market share,[21] there is no doubt that an INGO has to convince a company that such a joint marketing scheme can bring direct or indirect commercial benefits to the company. In a proposal to a local communications company, Oxfam New Zealand emphasized that 'we believe we can bring real marketing benefits to such partnerships'.[22] As the business sector currently accounts for only a small portion of INGO funding, INGOs so far have been able to stand firm. John Healey, executive director of Amnesty International USA, has been adamant that 'Amnesty is particular about not besmirching its stellar reputation with crass commercialism'.[23] The question is whether INGOs will still have the same independence and integrity when they become more dependent on the corporate sector for funding. More importantly, if business interests become increasingly involved, will local people be left with even less space to represent themselves and to act in their own right?

At the moment development partnerships are still largely represented in terms of material endowments. Programmes may be packaged in different ways but materials sent out to constituents mainly emphasize the importance of financial contributions. AWARE, a programme by an Australian INGO Community Aid Abroad (CAA), carries the slogan 'people-to-people projects that tackle the causes of poverty'. It is obvious, however, that people are being asked to give money. One might understandably question whether it is possible to present partnerships in other ways without jeopardizing INGOs' income. Yet at the very least, INGOs could provide more coverage of local people's involvement in projects instead of dwelling on 'feel-good' stories and expressions of gratitude and praise. Surely this would contribute to a more fruitful dialogue on policy issues within the aid sector as well as the wider community.

State controls, whether from donor or recipient governments, constitute another important factor affecting the realization of the idea of partnership. How much freedom INGOs have in forming partnerships with local people usually depends on the responses of both domestic and recipient governments. Significantly, however, states are kept out of INGOs' publications as far as possible. When domestic governments are mentioned, their role in the development process is usually restricted to that of providing finance, leaving the impression that real decision-making is in the hands of INGOs and local people. Seldom is reference made to local authorities such as agriculture and health departments. Because it is partnership with local people that matters, all such bureaucratic structures and intermediary bodies are given as low a profile as possible.

So far as domestic governments are concerned, INGOs need to comply with a range of procedural requirements attaching to state grants, such as the format of funding submissions and progress reports. These requirements may well affect the choice of projects undertaken and they will certainly affect the design and implementation of programmes supported by state grants. For example, as INGOs are required to supply quantitative evidence of project results, they may be reluctant to take up local initiatives which are difficult to quantify or will not show tangible and measurable results within a relatively short period of time. In addition, the need to produce progress reports means that INGOs at times may need to force the pace of implementation against the wishes of local people. It is pertinent to note that some INGOs have been advocating tighter controls on overseas aid organizations, with domestic governments assuming more regulatory powers in monitoring INGO activities. The rationale behind this is the belief that it will make them appear more professional, and hence donors will be more confident that their money will be well spent.

Government aid is hence a double-edged sword for INGOs. While it enables INGOs to carry out programmes that would not otherwise have been possible, it also limits their autonomy over the control of projects. Of course, in some cases, if an INGO can mount enough public pressure, it is possible that the domestic government may make changes to its policy. During the Ethiopian civil war, for example, CAA successfully persuaded the Australian government to reallocate one-third of its Ethiopian food aid to the rebel areas of Eritrea and Tigray. However, the Australian government made it very clear that this did not mean that it would change its foreign policy towards Ethiopia.[24] By and large, it seems that there are strict limits to the influence that INGOs can bring to bear on domestic governments.

The often delicate relationship between donor governments and INGOs is demonstrated by the British Charity Commissioners' inquiry into Oxfam UK in 1990. The inquiry was sparked by the government's concern over Oxfam's campaign strategies, particularly about its stance towards sanctions against the South African government. One of the main reasons Oxfam decided to take a strong stand on the issue was because it felt obliged to show solidarity with its local partners. If Oxfam was found to have breached the laws affecting charities, its trustees might be required to repay all the tax benefits associated with that particular campaign. Because of the potentially disastrous financial implications, Oxfam quickly decided to offer all the relevant promotional materials for scrutiny by the Commissioner before release. Eventually Oxfam was given a severe reprimand and no heavy penalty was imposed. It was widely agreed within the aid community that one of the major motives behind the inquiry was to attempt to 'inhibit [overseas aid agencies] from becoming an alternative voice in foreign policy on issues beyond those reasonably closely related to aid and humanitarian activity'.[25] This view was confirmed in the Commissioners' report, which was released in May 1991. The report concluded that in some cases Oxfam's campaigns had 'overstepped the line in style, content, and degree', and that 'the unacceptable political activities of the charity must cease'.[26] Whether a line can ever be drawn between promoting the welfare of Third World people and engaging in overt political activities is highly arguable, but the episode suggests that state authorities are unlikely to be too interested in debating the issue. The chances are that donor governments will not hesitate to intervene if they consider that the actions of an INGO contradict official policy or compromise their political standing.

The activities of INGOs tend to be even more closely regulated by recipient governments. Most obviously, INGOs must work within national political parameters if they are to undertake any development work within a country at all. In 1978, the socialist Frelimo government of Mozambique told Oxfam UK that its aid was no longer welcomed because of its linkage with projects run by Rhodesian and South African whites.[27] At about the same time, CAA had to terminate its work in Indonesia because of its strong position on the East Timor issue. It was reported that the Indonesian government was unhappy with CAA carrying out development projects in the country and planned to suspend them for twelve months pending further review in the future.[28] Even more telling, one of the reasons why CAA was allowed to return to Indonesia in the late 1980s was that its staff were no longer perceived as displaying the same level of antipathy towards the Suharto government as previously.[29]

However, most recipient governments prefer more subtle forms of monitoring, usually by regulating the operations of indigenous groups. In

Nepal, before the constitutional change in 1990, all NGOs, local and international, working within the country had to register with the Social Service National Coordination Council in order to gain official recognition. As all the six committees of the council were controlled by elites loyal to the government, this measure effectively placed all NGO activities under tight supervision. Indeed, because of the political restriction and patronage associated with development work, several major INGOs refused to become affiliated. These included the Save the Children Fund and CARE/Nepal. Even after 1990, when most of the powers of the council had been stripped, the government still required all NGOs subsidized by official grants or foreign institutions to register with the council. The following year, the Minister of Finance decreed that permission from the government was necessary before any local NGO could receive financial aid from foreign donors.[30]

Even when Third World governments openly endorse the work of local NGOs, there is no guarantee that they are willing to loosen their grip on development policies. In Zimbabwe, President Mugabe has praised NGOs openly for their valuable role in improving the lives of many citizens.[31] However, on another occasion, S. Muzenda, the vice-president, warned that: '[the] Government would not hesitate to intervene whenever it felt that the activities of persons employed by Non-Governmental Organizations or persons who came in the name of the church are working contrary to the aspirations of our people and our national sovereignty.'[32] This speaking with two voices catches something of the ambivalence of many Third World governments towards NGOs. On the one hand, they see the material benefits with respect to national development; on the other, they are worried that, if people identify too much with NGOs, their authority may be challenged.

I am not suggesting that governments, domestic and recipient, always try to manipulate INGOs and local organizations for their own political benefits. But the fact that most of them have installed mechanisms to enable them to intervene when they deem it necessary cannot be denied. Moreover, the very possibility of government intervention in the operation of INGOs highlights important barriers to local empowerment. Often INGOs' use of the term 'empowerment' in their literature connotes only some vague notion about people shaping their own future or transforming their own world. Couched in such abstract terms and devoid of references to specific strategies, the word functions more as a slogan and has the unfortunate effect of raising unfulfillable expectations among donors.[33] It is all very well for proponents of the idea of partnership to wish away existing adversary political structures. As things are, the ability of INGOs to circumvent local authorities and elites is very limited. Even the World Bank, with the backing from Western governments and the availability of huge amount of resources desperately needed by many Third World countries, at times finds it difficult to minimize the role of national governments. This is illustrated by the history of its Women In

Development project in Gambia. The policy guideline stipulated explicitly the requirement to involve local NGOs as partners. In the end, the state managed to control every aspect of the project from the selection of participating groups to the devising of project regulations.[34] INGOs, with fewer financial and political resources, are even less likely to be able to force recipient governments to make compromises.

Behind the rhetoric, of course, INGOs acknowledge that they must develop a working relationship with recipient states and that real benefits can flow from certain kinds of collaborative venture. As INGOs seldom have the resources to support long-term programmes, it often makes sense to attempt to involve official bodies in follow-up programmes. A recent survey of nineteen INGO seed provision schemes showed that most were not sustainable because of lack of staff and funds.[35] As a consequence, the projects could not offer a realistic alternative to government and commercial operations. Even when INGOs have adequate resources, strengthening the capacity of local authorities may be more efficacious than acting independently. In Mozambique in the late 1980s, INGOs were so active and powerful in the country that they tended to erect parallel structures rather than rely on available government bodies to carry out and coordinate their programmes. It is said that the authority of the government and its capacity to manage development were thus under-mined. In one case, donors appropriated US$16m for programmes not requested by the government, while ignoring its plea for emergency health projects. The result was that at least six teams of expatriate doctors flew in to help the same group of people. The cost of the operation was immense and the money could have been better used to train government health workers. It is also alleged that government health policies were jeopardized by the disregard INGOs showed for officialdom. Apparently, the list of nationally restricted drugs was not followed and the results of nutrition surveys were not passed on to the appropriate authorities.[36]

The relationship between INGOs and local groups can also be uneasy, even difficult. In most cases, tensions arise not through philosophical disagreement – INGOs are generally committed to the notion that local people be given as much power as possible – but because INGOs are subject to operational constraints, particularly relating to the monitoring and control of resources. Local groups are often highly critical of what they see as tedious administrative requirements. For example, applications can be presented only in a particular format, internal auditing needs to be carried out at constant intervals, and progress reports have to be compiled and submitted regularly. There have been complaints that the need to satisfy these laborious procedures constitutes a heavy drain on meagre resources and interferes with the work of consciousness-raising. There are often elements of tension between the understanding of partnership based on trust, openness and flexibility and the increasing bureaucratization of the development process.

Yet it is inconceivable that INGOs should not have monitoring and review procedures. While local groups may claim that they are accountable first and foremost to the communities with which they work, INGOs are responsible to their own domestic constituents and governments. In order to maintain the confidence of the public and the government, as well as to satisfy official funding requirements, INGOs need to minimize as much as possible any inappropriate use of funds, and this in turn necessitates putting in place systems of project selection, monitoring and evaluation. Another reason for introducing administrative procedures is that INGOs themselves have certain preferences regarding the kinds of project they want to support, countries in which they feel comfortable working and local agencies whose philosophy accords with their own.[37] They argue that these measures can facilitate the management of their programmes and so the aid dollars will be spent more effectively – a point in fact shared by many local groups. The Organization of Rural Associations in Zimbabwe, for instance, has emphasized the use of internal auditing to improve its operations.[38]

INGOs face a similar dilemma over the issue of foreign technology. For many INGOs, the underwriting of indigenous practices carries a greater meaning than practical considerations such as a reduction of maintenance costs for equipment: it signals a respect for local cultures and represents a reversal of earlier top-down methodologies. A comment by Philip Hunt, chief executive of World Vision Australia, characterizes the thinking of many INGOs: '[local people] have lots to teach us. Many a so-called expert has discovered that university learning is not always as useful as the local knowledge of farmers.'[39]

But for all their commitment to preserving local culture, there is, of course, a realization that there may be certain indigenous practices which are actually detrimental to people's welfare. The celebration of local culture therefore has its limits; at times it may be necessary to work within the local culture precisely to change it; there are occasions when INGOs need to override indigenous opinion, thus putting themselves in an awkward position. If they take a more assertive stance, they may be accused of dominating local people and risk losing local goodwill; alternatively they may accommodate themselves to local preferences, even at the cost of longer-term benefits. In some cases differences can be resolved by negotiation and a compromise reached, as was the case with respect to land-clearing practices in north-eastern Brazil.[40] According to a study by a local NGO, the traditional method of indiscriminate slashing and burning used by local farmers to clear land for cultivation had serious long-term consequences. These included a reduction in the organic content and general fertility of the soil, plus the more rapid growth of native plants, which then required more maintenance work. In consultation with local people, the local NGO then developed a three-year programme to demonstrate the viability of alternative methods of land-clearing, which successfully convinced many local farmers that they should abandon traditional practices. In other cases, however, the introduction of foreign technology may create such political tensions or economic imbalances that a compromise may not be possible. What is certain is that issues about foreign technology invariably raise questions about unequal economic and political benefit which can seldom be resolved simply by references to local culture as a touchstone of equity in the longer term.

To take stock of the position that I have reached, the idea of partnership has reinvigorated development thinking and injected a new optimism into the provision of aid programmes. The 1980s had come to be characterized as the lost decade, but now a set of keywords holds the promise of releasing the creative energy that had hitherto been locked up: people's power, collaboration and cooperation, and the role of the discursive. It is not, however, that straightforward. Keywords conceal as well as reveal. Some of the long-standing problems in development relationships have not so much been resolved as pushed out of sight.

This chapter has shown that partnership cannot somehow be imagined as a natural condition, but needs to be a managed relationship. There are problems that flow from this. For instance, the stress on agency is not necessarily a sound fund-raising strategy. Moreover, some of the objectives which are seen as ethically desirable in the North may not correspond with local cultural patterns in the South. Nation-states, no longer central to the new design, still manage to pull some of the strings. For these reasons and others, there are gaps between the theory and practice of partnership which introduce elements of strain and disquiet. A certain ironing out of such tensions is required. There is, however, another view, which is that practical politics may require elements of disjunction. That is to say, in certain circumstances we may have to accept that there will be a gap between philosophical principles and practice, so that the requirements of political mobilization overseas may run counter to the requirements of fund-raising at home. The burden of argument here has been that INGOs should tackle these problems more seriously than they appear to have done to date.

The significance of the material considered in this chapter is that the traditional categories of reference in international relations have in fact less relevance to contemporary development issues than they had to those of, say, the cold war period. It follows, therefore, that international relations needs to broaden its horizons and pay more attention than it has to the role of aid organizations and their relationships with people both at home and overseas. Certainly the state remains of great importance in the implementation of ideas about partnership. But it cannot be considered in isolation from ordinary people and local politics which are not visible from the lofty purview of international relations. Unless international relations as a discipline moves closer to the ground, it might as well abandon any pretensions it has to addressing issues of global social change.

Notes

1. Bessie Head, *When Rain Clouds Gather* (London, Heinemann Educational, 1987 – first published 1969), p. 181.

2. In the analysis which follows, attention is restricted to INGOs based in the West, and primarily concerned with the provision of aid to the Third World.

3. David Lumsdaine, *Moral Vision in International Politics: The Foreign Aid Regime 1949–1989* (Princeton, NJ, Princeton University Press, 1992), p. 35, Table 2.1.

4. Alan Fowler, 'Distant obligations: speculations on NGO funding and the global market', *Review of African Political Economy*, 55 (1992), 9–29.

5. Hassan El Zein and Anne Cooper, 'New York Times' coverage of Africa, 1976–1990' in Beverly Hawk (ed.), *Africa's Media Image* (Westport, Praeger, 1992), pp. 133–48.

6. Pilgrim International Limited, *Consumer Awareness and Attitude Survey*, Sydney, March 1994, unpublished report, p. 8.

7. Ibid.

8. Stephen Constantine, *The Making of British Colonial Development Policy 1914–1940* (London, Frank Cass, 1984), ch. 8.

9. Quoted in David Fieldhouse, *Black Africa 1945–1980: Economics. Decolonization and Arrested Development* (London, Allen and Unwin, 1986), pp. 89–90.

10. Ibid., p. 132.

11. Constantine, *The Making of British Colonial Development Policy*, pp. 129–38.

12. Quoted in Walt Rostow, *Eisenhower, Kennedy, and Foreign Aid* (Austin, University of Texas Press, 1985), p. 78.

13. Yoweri Museveni, *What Is Africa's Problem?* (Kampala, NRM Publications, 1992), p. 273.

14. International Council of Voluntary Agencies, *Relations between Southern and Northern NGOs: Policy Guidelines* (Geneva, n.d.).

15. Quoted in Mark Denham, 'The World Bank and NGOs' in Larry Swatuk and Timothy Shaw (eds), *The South at the End of the Twentieth Century* (London, St Martin's Press, 1994), p. 105.

16. Louis Picard, *The Politics of Development in Botswana: A Model for Success?* (Boulder, CO, Lynne Rienner Publishers, 1987), p. 247.

17. Arturo Escobar, *Encountering Development* (Princeton, NJ, Princeton University Press, 1995), p. 100.

18. Gustavo Esteva, 'Regenerating people's space', *Alternatives*, 12 (1987), 125–52.

19. World Vision Australia, *News Line* (March 1995), 1–2.

20. David Masons, 'Invasion of the soul snatchers: aliens in our midst', *Nonprofit World*, 10:6 (1992), 27–30.

21. For some preliminary evidence see Colin McDonald, 'Sponsorship and the image of the sponsor', *European Journal of Marketing*, 25:11 (1991), 31–8.

22. Oxfam New Zealand, *A Marketing Proposal to Clear Communications* (June 1993), p. 2.

23. Cyndee Miller, 'Amnesty Intl injects pizzazz into its marketing approach', *Marketing News*, 26:4 (1992), 9.

24. Susan Blackburn, *Practical Visionaries: A Study of Community Aid Abroad* (Melbourne, Melbourne University Press, 1993), pp. 325–34.

25. Ibid., p. 284.

26. Maggie Black, *A Cause for Our Time: Oxfam, the First 50 Years* (London, Oxfam and Oxford University Press, 1992), p. 283.

27. Ibid., p. 245.

28. Blackburn, *Practical Visionaries*, pp. 91–114.

29. Ibid.

30. Narayan Shrestha and John Farrington, 'NGO–government interaction in Nepal: Introduction' in John Farrington, David Farrington, David Lewis, S. Satish and Andrea Mielat-Teves (eds), *NGOs and the State in Asia* (London and New York, Routledge, 1993), p. x.

31. Quoted in Dennis Mungate, 'Government experience of collaboration with NGOs in agricultural research and extension' in Kate Wellard and James Copestake, *Non-governmental Organizations and the State in Africa* (London and New York, Routledge, 1993), p. 27.

32. Quoted ibid.

33. Michael Bratton, 'Non-governmental organisations in Africa: can they influence public policy?' in Eve Sandberg (ed.), *The Changing Politics of Non-Governmental Organisations and African States* (Westport, Praeger, 1994), p. 40.

34. Deborah Brautigam, 'State, NGOs and international aid in Gambia', ibid., p. 79.

35. Steve Wiggins and Elizabeth Cromwell, 'NGOs and seed provision to smallholders in developing countries', *World Development*, 23:3 (1995), 413–22.

36. Joseph Hanlon, *Mozambique: Who Calls the Shots?* (Bloomington and Indianapolis, Indiana University Press, 1991), pp. 216–17.

37. For example, CAA has the following guidelines with respect to assessment of project applications: 'Requests from countries where Community Aid Abroad is not working are automatically declined. For a number of years now the agency has had in place program strategies for each of the countries in which it is working. These may identify a region of the country or a particular sector … in which the agency has chosen to work. Any proposal will be examined to see if it is compatible with this strategy. If so, the feasibility of the project will be examined for technical, social, environmental and economic soundness. There is also the question of whether or not those seeking assistance are known to Community Aid Abroad, and what their capacity for implementation may be. A particular style of work is also favoured by the agency.' *Annual Program Review*, 1 October 1994–30 September 1995), p. 47.

38. Sjef Theunis (ed.), *Non-governmental Development Organizations of Developing Countries* (Dordrecht, Martinus Nijhoff Publishers, 1992), p. 269.

39. Philip Hunt, *World Vision News* (Melbourne, Australia, May 1992), p. 2.

40. 'No more slashing and burning in northeastern Brazil', *DEEP*, July 1994 (Rome, FAO), p. 15.

Part III

Narrating Gender and Sexuality

CHAPTER EIGHT

Another India: imagining escape from the masculine self

GRANT PARSONS

An overarching theme of this book is that the colonial experience has insufficiently informed the perspectives of students of contemporary international politics. The conceptual revolutions current within both fields, leading to the emergence of a fledgling critical international relations and a no less marginalized colonial cultural studies, make the case for a dialogue or for cross-fertilization particularly timely. This chapter takes as its subject one area in which critical international relations is increasingly interested: the feminist deconstruction of foundational precepts such as power, dominance and control as masculinist. Without explicitly drawing parallels between work proceeding in the two fields, I argue that an examination of colonial culture illuminates the theoretical issues involved and brings to the attention of international relations scholars historical material too long neglected and in the context of which more recent experience might be situated. In the narratives to be read in this chapter the connections between gender construct – masculinity in this instance – power and dominance are drawn in suggestive ways, and their significance extends well beyond the particular politics of the Indian Raj, which is their subject.

In his study of the Romantic evocation of India, John Drew has reminded us that Europeans have tended to idealize the sub-continent.[1] This is often overlooked by postcolonial critics, who are understandably more concerned with Western dominance of the Third World than with any deeper appreciation of non-Western culture to be found in Western discourse. Most analyses of gender and imperialism concerned with masculinity have, for example, argued that debasement, negation or denigration were the dominant rhetorical figures found in colonial representation. These recent interventions indeed conform to our intuitive apprehension that the masculine response to India was conceived in terms not of romantic yearning but rather the opposite: as flowing from the idealization of action, control and order. A number of recent contributions have pursued these themes in the light of feminist theoretical arguments about the pervasiveness of gender categorization in established thinking and of gender as a structure of power. A common account has it that India tended to be feminized in British imaginative fiction, historical studies and official policy; meaning that commonly accepted tropes of the passivity or even the corrupting potential of the feminine were extended to non-Western societies and cultures. India was thus available for Western control and, represented as intrinsically corrupt or fallen, was seen as being urgently in need of Western masculine mastery. Only thus could she be reformed and revitalized, it being the West's moral duty to effect change in this direction. The West was thus represented as metaphorically masculine and the Orient as feminine. Like actual women in sexist representation, in the fiction of empire India frequently appears as an object to be conquered or man-handled. Like real women, however, she also had the potential to take control; to throw men off their course.[2]

Yet if idealization is an inappropriate term to describe conventional Western representation of India during the period of empire, normative representation often did hold India up as a place where men could achieve. In the fictional narratives fantasies abound about the availability of the landscape to mastery or control. It is certainly arguable that the dominant men of the Raj, in actuality as well as in fictional narratives, were often driven from society at home by such compulsions, their decision to pursue a career in the Empire being invested with fantasies about leaving their mark on the frontiers of civilization. Such was the mythology surrounding the Punjabi style of administration in the Raj, immortalized in the fiction of Kipling and Maud Diver.[3] The characters who populate the genre of action fiction set in the colonies, generally taken as the subject of most studies of masculinity and imperialism, are commonly drawn as men who act in ways no longer possible in industrial Britain. Self-sufficiency and resourcefulness, freedom from domestic constraint, a radical independence of action, emotional denial; these are the values valorized in this fiction. A common feature of the genre is its emphasis on the marking out of boundaries: between the self and its others, and between the white community and the 'native'. The denial or rejection of cultural difference is a persistent theme: natives are inferior and white British masculinity placed centre-stage as mankind's crowning glory. Anglo-Indian fiction celebrated and agitated for a hypermasculinity of this type. It proposed, for example, that the Raj was a site in which boundaries could and should be scrutinized, hostile experiences repudiated and the phenomenal world reduced to domination – themes pursued, if with some ambivalence, in many of Kipling's Indian short stories. The organizational imperatives of imperial administration were, furthermore, understood as the domain in which this masculinity and political necessity came together, the one being indispensable to the other.

This chapter is not concerned with the fiction of hypermasculinity. It is interested in men whose attachment to India was of the romantic kind; in men who saw India in terms very different from the Anglo-Indian community or the mainstream novelists of empire. It is especially interested in the seduction which India represented to men who sought escape from the strictures of the conventional construction of masculinity in Britain from the turn of the century onwards and who were predominantly homosexual. Escape as transgressive opportunity, rather than as freedom from the feminizing influences of the hearth, is the central concern here. Its principal subject is those literary representations of India which idealize aspects of that culture, written by men who were drawn to India because for them it represented an 'otherness' which contrasted sharply with the familiarity of Western life and which was often inseparably associated with the predominant gender constructions by which they were oppressed. The question which I want to pursue is the extent to which this 'other India' determined broader attitudes towards cultural difference and towards imperialism or Western dominance in particular. I am therefore interested in reflecting critically upon the current gay studies elevation of marginal masculinities as subversive of conventional gender constructs and of the will to power. What is the significance of this material for students of colonial culture and imperialism, and for those interested in gender and international relations? What are its implications for our understanding of the linkage points between gender and the appropriation of difference? Are marginal or marginalized men more likely to empathize with, or even to embrace, cultural difference in contrast to the hypermasculinist rejection or denial of this? This inquiry will be pursued through a reading of the Indian writings of Edward Carpenter and E. M. Forster, two homosexual men who travelled to and wrote about India during the period of empire.[4]

Paul Fussell has observed that during the interwar years the British literary conception of the foreign, and the imaginative significance with which travel abroad was invested, underwent something of a transformation.[5] If the British writer had for centuries been an inveterate traveller, particularly 'south', and especially to the Mediterranean, after the First World War the affectionate yearning for warmer climes developed as its correlate something sharper-edged: a contempt for home. Britain was seen as uninhabitable: 'stuffy, complacent, cruel, bullying, and small-minded'.[6] War-time economic and political restrictions, the greyness and drudgery of daily life with its shortages and the profound disillusion experienced especially by those who had been in the trenches soured the imaginative capacity as far as home was concerned. Fussell no doubt overplays the significance of the war in this; a romantic rejection of the industrialized mass society of modernity was also clearly significant, and in relation to which memories of the war, however powerful, may to some degree have been symptomatic. More significant for our purposes is his failure to develop to any degree the vital experience of the homosexual during this period. Many of the writers with whom he deals were either homosexuals by self-definition, or sexually adventurous with other men. To the British homosexual, particularly in the decades following the 1895 Wilde trials, Britain could not but be conceived of as a hostile place. Indeed, it would not be fanciful to assert that the modern definition of British homosexuality, forged during this time, was largely structured around a foreign–domestic binary in which the foreign was figured as a place of opportunity and of light, in relation to which the domestic was opposed and from which the homosexual man would take flight – in his imagination and, if he could afford it, through foreign travel. Jonathan Dollimore has recently made a similar point:

> For homosexuals more than most, the search for sexual freedom in the realm of the foreign has been inseparable from a repudiation of the 'Western' culture responsible for their repression and oppression. For some, as for T. E. Lawrence, this entailed not just the rejection of a repressive social order, but a disidentification from it requiring nothing less than the relinquishment of the self hitherto constituted and inhabited by that order. In other words, precisely because of the Western integration of subjectivity and sexuality, deviant desire becomes also a refusal of certain kinds of subjectivity.[7]

We will be particularly interested in this 'repudiation' of Western culture, and any disidentification from it. Dollimore's reference to T. E. Lawrence is pertinent in this connection, and many of the contours of the analysis to be presented here have been mapped out in recent discussions of the 'blond bedouin'.[8] One such contribution reads *The Seven Pillars of Wisdom* and the later *The Mint* as central to the location and recovery of subordinate masculinity.[9] That is, feminist and gay theorists have sought to identify a position that might be termed subordinate masculinity which stands, potentially, in opposition to the conventional, hegemonic or normative mode of masculinity which was, at times, fiercely propagated by society and in relation to which men's behaviours and desires were policed. Subordinate men reject, or fail to meet, the expectations of this model and in consequence tend to experience repression, most commonly expressed through the vehicle of homophobia. Lawrence is seen as an example of a man who, driven by homosexual desire, came romantically to idealize the non-Western other to the point where this was turned inward on to the self, in the development of a critique of conventional masculinity and the values of British society. Lawrence may not have suffered homosexual oppression (he did not identify with the position), but he did struggle to relinquish his personal investment in a subjectivity conforming with the idealized model, ironic in view of the fact that his example was used by the post-1918 ideologues of masculinity.[10] It is therefore argued that Lawrence travelled to the Orient not just as an escape from the restrictions of home, nor to pursue adventures conventionally conceived, but that he sought – or came to seek – in Arabia the loss of a particular masculine identity implicated in gender and imperial power. His 'journey', so it is claimed, is profoundly significant for what it reveals about conventional masculinity and its alternatives.

Kaja Silverman develops this argument in the most sophisticated way.[11] Drawing upon feminist rereadings of Lacan, she argues that conventional masculinity is grounded in a denial of the lack which is foundational to all subjectivity. If the infant's appreciation of itself as whole and complete in the mirror stage soon proves to be illusory, masculine subjectivities are conventionally built upon the rejection of the chimeral nature of unity. Phallic masculinity papers over its cracks, denying its alterity, specularity and castration, and projects on to 'others' its doubts and hostilities in an aggressively driven project to build an illusory self as hard and as self-contained as the imaginary phallus in its full plenitude. What is so significant about Lawrence from this perspective is that he sought in the other not the elevation of self, but its very relinquishment. As Lawrence was famously to remark in *Seven Pillars*, identification with the Arabs 'quitted me of my English self and let me look at the West and its conventions with new eyes: they destroyed it all for me'.[12]

Silverman is attentive to Lawrence's position as an agent of imperialism, and is therefore suspicious of his motives in claiming to identify completely with the Arabs, whose cause he championed. Lawrence's assumption of Arab dress and identification with Arab aspirations – certainly unconventional practice for a Western man in the service of an imperial power – does, she argues, enhance rather than detract from his virility to the extent to which these fantasies figure him as a leader of men committed to national formation. The 'rape at Dera'a' at the hands of Turkish soldiers, however, in which Lawrence was apparently beaten and sexually molested, and which he experienced masochistically with pleasure and self-revulsion, led him to take a quite different psychic direction. This precipitated Lawrence's personal fragmentation, leading ultimately to his repudiation of leadership and to his enlistment as an ordinary airman and escape into barracks life, signalling his final repudiation of the powerful self. These moves, Silverman argues, indicate Lawrence's rejection of the phallic masculine subject position and his embrace of the castration which dominant masculinity denies. As he wrote to a friend concerning his decision to enlist in the RAF:

> Henceforth my life will lie with these fellows here degrading myself . . . in the hope that some day I will really feel degraded, be degraded to their level. I long for people to look down upon me and despise me . . . I want to dirty myself outwardly, so that my person may properly reflect the dirtiness which it conceals.[13]

Feminine masochism provides the psychic agency whereby Lawrence effects a retreat from the heroic masculinity characteristic of his self-representation as leader of Arab nationalism, and characteristic of his domestic public persona, to the collective enslavement and anonymity of life as an airman (albeit underwritten, as the above extract reveals, by class snobbery).

This approach to the study of masculinity, and this particular reading of the experience of T. E. Lawrence, does, however, present a number of problems. The valorization of the experience of a man whose disidenti-fication with mainstream masculine subjectivity led ultimately to his

probable suicide is clearly problematical. An argument which in effe
would require the subject to lose all sense of coherent selfhood to be
considered radically transgressive of the culturally idealized gendered
position is clearly not satisfactory. Even if theorists do not quite suggest
that this is a prerequisite for subordinate masculinity, the attraction to
Lawrence's experience might still be somewhat misplaced. Rather than
seriously unsettle the binarisms upon which gender and sexual difference
are built in patriarchal heterosexist society, Lawrence's 'passage' conforms
somewhat with the position of the abjected feminine, rather than offering a
space beyond current categories. Lawrence's assumption of feminine
masochism – if this be what it is – is interesting, but surely cannot be
considered to be an essential, or even a desirable, psychic condition for the
transgression of conventional masculinity.

It might also be questioned how radical Lawrence's experience in fact
was. Insufficient attention is paid by Silverman to his appropriation of the
non-Western other in his self-fashioning. A postcolonial reading of
Lawrence's experience will be less impressed by the 'ruination' of his
masculinity than with the implication of this with respect to cultural and
racial difference. If Lawrence's disidentification with British masculinity is
bought at the cost of an appropriation of the non-Western other, then from
this perspective his experience is no less problematical than the conventional orientalist construction of otherness in service of the elevation of
self. Salutary here is David Spurr's argument that idealization and
eroticization of the non-Western other is no less an aspect of colonial
discourse than the perhaps more usual debasement or negation found, for
example, in imperial fiction.[14] As Rana Kabbani has put the point,

> The Orient becomes a pretext for self-dramatization and differentness; it is the
> malleable theatrical space in which can be played out the egocentric fantasies of
> Romanticism. It affords endless material for the imagination, and endless
> potential for the Occidental self.[15]

Similarly, as Judith Butler has reminded us, there is no utopia beyond
power.[16] The search for 'men who say no to power' might therefore be a
vain one. If, following Foucault, power produces its own positivities, and
as Bhabha has argued, there was an ambivalence at the heart of colonial
discourse,[17] we ought also be on the alert for the investments in power of
those subjects who profess a rejection of power conventionally understood.
Let us consider the issue of Lawrence's practice of dressing like an Arab. It
is certainly arguable that Lawrence's critical cross-dressing, his taking on
Arab dress as a release from his English self, destroying the West and its
conventions for him, was from the perspective of his English masculinity
an instance of what Butler would describe as a radical 'subversive
repetition' of gender subjectivity. It is conceivable, that is, that the cross-
dressing can fruitfully be read in relation to prescribed white middle-class
manliness as an instance of 'the mobilisation, subversive confusion, and
proliferation of precisely those constitutive categories that seek to keep

gender in its place by posturing as the foundational illusions of identity'.[18] With respect to colonial discourse, however, this might be far from radical practice, being an instance of the long-standing tradition of a Western subject visiting his fantasies upon the non-West. Thus, Lawrence's radicalism with respect to his masculine identity is undercut by his appropriation of non-Western otherness – actually in his relations with the Arabs whom he 'led', and at the level of fantasy. Loss of power at one level (gender/sexuality) is thus partly compensated for by gains at another (race). There is something analogous here to Aldrich's worry that homosexual tourists to the Mediterranean, while engaging in a practice potentially transgressive from the perspective of hegemonic masculinity, must be seen as far less subversive of power relations when viewed from the standpoint of the boy who is cajoled, bought or simply 'amused' by his (relatively) wealthy admirer.[19] If that man is also of the colonizing culture from the imperial metropole, then his position of power *vis-à-vis* the object of desire is even more pronounced.

We also need to be highly suspicious of any claim that would exaggerate the difference that homosexuality makes to mainstream representation. Many theorists, some homophobic[20] and others gay affirmative,[21] would want to argue that homosexuality, presumably as a set of experiences, enables in the subject an understanding of, or empathy towards, otherness not readily available to heterosexual men whose investments in power are more marked. This must surely be seriously questioned. There are many instances in the history of imperialism, as the domain of principal interest here, of men who might well be described as homosexual but whose sensibilities and commitments were far from subversive of the logic of imperialism, or indeed of hypermasculinity.[22] It would be too wild to claim that homosexuality as such was a ready guarantor of a particular (hostile) perspective on imperialism, any more than it is necessarily a solvent of many of the more problematical features of conventional masculinity, such as misogyny. Ideological position as much as sexual preference, or even the times during which the author was writing, might have as large a role to play here. Indeed, much contemporary queer theory either assumes a neat homology between sexuality and political commitment or reserves the affirmative designation 'queer' to men and women whose transgression of conventional politics or morality cannot be doubted. A more cautious line will be pursued here. We will interrogate the writings under examination for what they reveal about how each of the men deployed their consciousness of their outsider status with respect to their domestic societies and how this led them to understand the fictions of masculinity. From this insight we will see how the connections between masculinity and imperial dominance were examined, and these insights incorporated into a broader critique of the British Raj. It is this which will be highlighted as the particular contribution of this body of writing. Homosexuality in these instances does, it will be argued, make a difference, but only because these men consciously disidentified with the metropole and found in the other a means of articulating a powerful critique of the self. Self, in these examples, meant British society and the core values around which the late Victorian and Edwardian nation was imagined.

Edward Carpenter and E. M. Forster wrote about India in terms quite at odds with the predominant pattern to be found in Anglo-Indian fiction or the masculinist narrative of colonial travel. Although each of the narratives produced by these men relies to some extent on the standard tropes of Indian backwardness and the essential inferiority of its culture, in significant contrast to established representation, India was constructed as an idyll in which 'deviant' or illicit desire could find an outlet and in which spiritual enrichment could be sought. Significantly, India also provided confirmation to them of the relativity of those Western values which they rejected, especially those related to friendship, gender and sexuality and which were at the basis of their marginality in British society. While the perspectives of these writers share much with the familiar orientalist denigration and idealization of the other (the two strands often appearing uneasily side by side in the narratives), each was also explicitly drawn to India in order to escape from, or to find some alternative to, the repressive social order in Britain. Unlike Lawrence, however, in Carpenter and Forster we do not quite find the problematical appropriation of the Oriental space in service of self-relinquishment, and unlike Lawrence we also find at the centre of the significant narratives a considered critique of imperialism. Carpenter and Forster were explicitly hostile to conventional masculinity and argued that the masculine approach to the world was grounded in the will to dominate and to objectify. This led them, in somewhat different ways, to develop a critique of imperialism as based upon distorted human relations; as a quintessential case of the will to dominate, which they associated with the hegemonic masculinity from which they felt alienated and which they opposed. That neither of these men, unlike Lawrence, was a cultural hero who became an icon of post-1918 masculinity is clearly significant, as is the fact that their homosexuality was openly acknowledged and was articulated as social and political critique. Disidentification with 'home' therefore led beyond the self into the realm of the overtly political, in this case to a critique of imperial domination. What is argued is that consciousness of outsider status within domestic society and the appropriation of India as an escape valve from the strictures at home led to an apprehension of India in terms quite different from those of conventional men or imperial ideology. Carpenter and Forster were hostile towards the British purpose in India and, moreover, used Indian experience as a lens through which the West could be criticized. This suggests a position, I would argue, which gestures some distance beyond the Orientalist 'invention' of the East in service of self-constitution.

Our discussion of Carpenter and Forster must commence by taking note of the English reception (one might almost say appropriation) of Walt Whitman.[23] What attracted the English reader was Whitman's open celebration of manly love, his advocacy of a masculinity which turned its back on instrumental or pragmatic interests to face the spiritual or transcendental, and, perhaps above all, what was perceived as his equalitarian democratic commitment through his lauding of the working class. A unified vision, based on these themes, was to help variously to define the ideological positions of figures such as Edward Carpenter, and was to have enormous influence in Cambridge, eventually influencing E. M. Forster and other men, such as Joe Ackerley. Sedgwick has noted that *Leaves of Grass*, Whitman's major work, 'operated most characteristically as a conduit from one man to another of feelings that had, in many cases, been private or inchoate'.[24] Whitman was thus of unrivalled significance in the definition of British homosexuality, as its positive pole, as it were, in a field whose negative pole was represented by the Wilde trials.

Whitmanesque manly love in the service of democratic ideals provided a major source of inspiration to Edward Carpenter. Carpenter was to note of Whitman's poems that 'thousands date from their first reading . . . a new inspiration and an extraordinary access of vitality carrying their activities and energies into new channels'.[25] First published in 1883, Carpenter's collection *Towards Democracy* contains two poems which are central to our purposes. In one, entitled 'India, the Wisdom-Land', echoes of Whitman's 'Passage to India' are to be found: a similar appeal to the East as exotic frames the poem; a common seductive imagining of a realm beyond the ordinary or pedestrian; above all, the construction of India as divine or spiritual and as in essence timeless:

> Here also in India – wonderful, hidden – over thousands of miles,
> Through thousands of miles of coco-nut groves . . .
> Behind the interminable close-fitting layers of caste and custom,
> Here also, hidden away, the secret, the divine knowledge.
> Ages back, thousands of years lost in the dim past,
> A race of seers . . . Into India, the Wisdom-Land, descended . . .
> Dissolving in its own good time all bonds, all creeds,
> The soul's true being – the cosmic vast emancipated life
> – Freedom, Equality –
> The precious semen of Democracy.[26]

Carpenter was a sharp critic of the Empire. In a poem of that name published first in 1902, he explored the idea that Britain had been corrupted by cynicism and was hostage to the narrow self-interests of a mediocre bourgeoisie who derived benefit from the colonies. Britain's working-class and Empire subjects were together victims of this 'process of decay'. Britain itself was moribund; the call for Empire to Carpenter's mind was rank hypocrisy. Carpenter's poem was predicting the fall of Empire when his contemporaries were prophesying its immortality:

> The brotherhood of nations and of men
> Comes on apace. New dreams of youth bestir
> The ancient heart of the earth – fair dream of love

And equal freedom for all folk and races.
The day is past for idle talk of Empire;
And who would glory in dominating others –
Be it man or nation – he already has writ
His condemnation clear in all men's hearts.
'Tis better he should die.[27]

The central stanza is the one which argues for the connection between the will to dominance over others, 'Be it man or nation', empire and moral degeneration. The critique of empire is thus inseparable on this account from that of distorted personal relations and the wider case against a form of masculinity which overvalued instrumental reason or material achievement, which encouraged emotional detachment, and which made men competitors rather than brothers.

Love and brotherhood are the features of Indian village life which enframe the 1899 short story 'Narayan'.[28] In this narrative about Narayan, 'A well-made youth of about twenty, bright eyed, with something in his face of the . . . decision of the Mahratta', and Ganesh, 'rather darker in complexion and milder, more meditative' (p. 49), the fast friendship of the two, their easy physicality and their emotional responsiveness is celebrated. In this they merge completely with the 'wonderful scene' (p. 50) of the Indian landscape, and are inseparable from the cultural traditions of their village, the latter based on 'simple habits of friendliness and help-fulness among neighbours, a dreamy apathy which dulled the edge of misfortunes when they came, and an unswerving belief in the gods' (p. 51). The opening lines establish the binary opposites around which the narrative is to be structured. The image of the smoke pall of Bombay on the horizon signals the allure and the threat of modernity:

> The beauty of youth was in their faces and dark eyes – the beauty which everywhere, and in all ages and places, marks the completed appearance of the human soul in the world, before it is tied and taken captive by the things which do not belong to it. (p. 55)

'Narayan' is a story about the temptation, and partial corruption, of innocence. The boys' innocence, established through the simplicity and complete naturalness of their religious beliefs, and the leisured certainty of their community life, is dichotomously contrasted to the hard brittleness of the English sahibs and to the corruptions of industrial life. Just as the whites 'come and tax the very necessities of life, and break up the old customs . . . all to no purpose, since they make everybody miserable and never looked happy themselves' (p. 51), so the smoke from Bombay's industrial quarter 'looked . . . detestable . . . like some devil-stain on the shining garment of a god' (p. 53). Ganesh and Narayan, at the latter's instigation, are pulled to the city. The city has power, yet

> standing there in the shadow of a factory on the verge of the native town, between a fringe of coco-nut palms and the cloud of smoke which was blighting

their great fronds, they felt like hybrids, hardly knowing to what world they belonged. (p. 68)

They find employment as coolies in a cotton mill for miserable money. This provides the text with the opportunity to rail against the industrial system and colonial exploitation. It is through Ganesh that the major point of the story is established. Ganesh is in possession of a 'sensitive clinging nature' (p. 66) and is therefore representative of a wisdom which comes from love as the central attribute of character. Ganesh does not quite share Narayan's need to explore the wider world beyond the village, and from the start sees through British values as narrowly materialist. Western people, he says,

> must ever be killing something. These fighting ships they build in order to kill people, and what animal sacred to what god do they not slay, if only to fill their bellies? And as to that dragon cloud which hangs over the city, a poison-dew they say falls from it, and those who live in its shadow die. (p. 55)

Ganesh is killed in an industrial accident and Narayan is sickened by the offer by the factory management of (meagre) financial compensation. He returns to the village. Remembering the 'piercing beauty' of the eyes of a priest, he seeks out his temple: 'Perhaps he would feel more at home there than anywhere else. At any rate he would go and see' (p. 85).

India's salvation required the overthrow of imperialism. The text argues, in this respect, for the termination not only of British overlordship, but of Westernization as such. That Oriental wisdom was superior to Western materialism made preposterous the notion that Britain could offer moral guidance to India.[29] In this text the critique of masculinity and of imperialism, and of the industrialism which undergirded the latter, therefore flows from the advocacy of a refurbishment of emotional life along feminine lines. The close, richly emotional and 'natural' lives of Ganesh and Narayan represent an ideal which the West had lost and which further Westernization would only imperil in India itself. The relativism of 'Narayan' was not, however, to characterize the point of view of Carpenter's reflective travelogue, perhaps his most considered thinking about the subcontinent.

Carpenter had travelled to Ceylon and India in 1890 and as a result published *From Adam's Peak to Elephanta*.[30] In this text many of the themes later developed in 'Narayan' were established: the depiction of native life in utopian terms, the conception of India as a 'wisdom land', and the connection between these and character, laying the basis for a unique critique of masculinity, industrial civilization and imperialism. Ceylon, and to a lesser degree India, are here represented as pastoral idyll, where life was lived in a natural and rhythmical way, fostering the free development of warm relations between people. The tropical climate, furthermore, encouraged more open attitudes towards the body, and with these a sense of harmony with the physical environment. The cultural traditions of the subcontinent were an inextricable component of this very different complex of societies, the key features of which were figured around the rejection of instrumental rationality in favour of reflective spiritualism.

The promotion of feminine values, and the representation of Ceylon and India as a locus of these, is a central concern of the narrative. Descriptions of the people (almost without exception male) which undermine notions of European superiority are extremely revealing. The following passages are particularly significant for their evocation of the body. If in dominant representation the male body is hard and phallus-like, here it is almost feline, and Carpenter does little to disguise his desire:

> The Tamils are mostly slight and graceful in figure, and of an active build. Down at the docks [in Colombo] they work by hundreds, with nothing on beyond a narrow band between the thighs, loading and unloading barges and ships – a study of the human figure . . . mostly they excel in a kind of conscious grace and fleetness of form as of the bronze Mercury of Herculaneum, of which they often remind me. (p. 14)

With respect to the Singhalese:

> In character . . . [they] are more like the Italians, easy-going, reasonably idle, sensitive, shrewd, and just a bit romantic. Their large eyes and tortoise-shell combs and long hair give them a very womanly aspect; and many of the boys and youths have very girlish features and expressions. They have nearly always grace and dignity of manner, the better types decidedly handsome . . . (p. 17)

The open revelation of desire for the brown male body departs sharply from the conventional negotiation of a narrative course, characteristic of the action genre, which advocates the desire to be a man without admitting the desire for other men. The hard body, the neglected body, the body as machine; these are the predominant tropes with which the (male) identifies in this fiction yet (ostensibly) falls short of desiring. Carpenter subverts this representational economy, by expressing his desire for a brown 'Mercury of Herculaneum', especially, it would appear, if he were effeminate.

Later in the narrative a Singhalese youth is described, like Ganesh and indeed like a famous self-description of Carpenter's, as 'of the usual sensitive clinging type' (p. 91). This is a position directly oppositional to the 'cult of manliness' prevalent in English middle-class society during this period. Emotionality and feminine sensitivity are positively valued in this world-view, and a move is made by which the binarisms around which sexual difference is structured are unsettled, if not quite reversed. Rahman reminds us that to be characterized as 'feminine' by Carpenter was to be praised, for in his conception possessing a feminine nature meant that one was more suited to love, and homosexual men, essentialized as men who had certain feminine attributes, 'may have an important part to play in the evolution of the race'.[31] Ceylonese and Indian masculinities are represented in this narrative as sharing with the homosexual these characteristics.

Part of the lure of the East for Carpenter, especially in his rebellion against Victorian values, was India's religious and philosophical system.

Two features of this system appealed in particular. One was the (absurdly exaggerated) notion that Hinduism is largely grounded in sex-worship, represented by the androgyny of Siva and translated into everyday life in the form of free and open attitudes towards sexuality. Astrology, as a component part of Hinduism, was a 'glimmering embodiment of the deep lying truth that the whole universe conspires in the sexual act, and that orgasm itself is a flash of the universal consciousness' (p. 192). Bakshi has correctly pointed out that Carpenter's experience of the Hindu festivals to which he was privy was erotic, although we might add that their spontaneity and the physical display which they encouraged appealed to his sense of freer human relations.[32] The other feature of Indian philosophy which Carpenter sacralized was the practice of the yogis, whom he saw as training themselves to suppress the immediate and material in the quest for the loss of ego and therewith attainment of higher forms of consciousness. The Gnani whom he adopted as a guru and whose outlook he proselytized is described in the following terms: 'His gentleness and kindliness, combined with evident power . . . his entire serenity and calm. . . [it was] as if the ordinary barriers which divide people were done away with' (pp. 183–4).

The transcendence of the rational in Hindu thought is central to Carpenter's critique of the Western over-valuation of the intellectual and the worldly, which he termed 'self-consciousness', and which he saw as based on the separation of 'man' from nature and of men from each other. India and its traditions were instructive in the progression towards a future time – which he termed the stage of 'cosmic consciousness' – in which 'men' would be in harmony,[33] much as they were in the stage of primitive communism which he saw as the natural (precolonial) state of the subcontinent. This was a state in which community had not been eroded by the urbanization and individualism of modernity and in which intimate relations between men were not tabooed as they were in the West.

The destabilizing of sexual difference which we have noticed was extended in *From Adam's Peak* to the cultural lines drawn by the Raj, its dependence upon a masculinist demarcation of the white community from the native. Anglo-Indians are lamented in the text, seen as corrupted and shrivelled by a political and economic system which propels them into inward-looking groups isolated from their environment, and into positions of hostility towards those whom they ruled. Imperialism becomes anathema to the democratic vision which informs the text. Referring to the 'insuperable stiffness' which characterized British native relations in Ceylon, the narrative naively decries that 'a perfect social amalgamation and the sweetness of brethren dwelling together in unity are things still rather far distant in this otherwise lovely isle' (p. 20). The British could not entertain the notion of associating with the Ceylonese on term of 'equality and friendship' (p. 34) and as a consequence were 'the chief losers by this insular habit' (p. 35). The English looked 'bored and lonely' (p. 35); prisoners themselves of an unjust and inhuman system. These tendencies were found to be even more marked in India. In a passage which reveals that Carpenter was aware of the politics of his position as privileged tourist, he reflects on the subservient manner in which he is treated by certain natives, which he finds

> a strange experience, impressing one no doubt with a sense of the power of the little mother-country ten thousand miles away, which throws its prestige around one – but impressing one also with a sinister sense of the gulf between man and man which that prestige has created. (p. 268)

The economics of imperialism also corrupted native society, encouraging the development of commercial and urban classes parasitic upon the productive agricultural majority. Subjugated races faced with the oppressed classes at home a common plight at the hands of industrialism and the imperialism it spawned. Noticing cotton goods and tin products in a bazaar, Carpenter painfully recalls that he had

> seen these knives and scissors . . . being manufactured in the dens of Sheffield by boys and girls slaving in dust and dirt, breathing out their lives in foul air under the gaslights, hounded on by mean taskmasters and by the fear of imminent starvation. Dear children! if you could only come out here yourselves, instead of sending the abominable work of your hands – come out to enjoy the sunshine, and the society of these brothers and sisters whose skins are dark by nature rather than by art! (pp. 45–6)

Idealization was not, however, the only lens through which Carpenter viewed the Indian subcontinent. There is a markedly split quality to his response to the place, the peoples and their cultures. If his general position departed radically from mainstream colonialist representation, there remains a residue, in *From Adam's Peak to Elephanta* at least, of that conventionality of outlook which he was generally at pains to reject. On the poor and outcaste in India, for example, he wrote the following, recalling the influence of racial theory:

> It is curious, but I'm constantly being struck by the resemblances between the lowest castes here and the slum-dwellers in our great cities – resemblance in physiognomy, as well as in many unconscious traits of character, often very noble, with the brutish basis well-marked, the unformed mouth, and the somewhat heavy brows, just as in Meunier's fine statue of the iron worker ('puddleur'), but with thicker lips. (p. 56)

This implicit reference to racial conceptions of human development is significant, for it reveals something of the limitations of Carpenter's project. There is an ambiguity in the descriptions of the Ceylonese male form which we noted above and which it was argued unsettled accepted notions of European superiority. These are taxonomic as well as sub-versive, indicating an unstable synthesis of racial theory with the homo-sexual idealization of the Hellenic form. The legacy of racial theory which these passages reveal brings to mind the ambivalence in the text's critique of the negative stereotypes current during this period, yet also its dependence upon similar representations. Thus references to the Hindu character adhere to aspects of the long-standing colonialist tendency to feminize a subject-people, feminization here standing for passivity and fecklessness, a stance which jars with the more considered attempt to problematize sexual difference noticeable in other parts of the text and in other narratives by Carpenter. Hindus are characterized by their 'passivity and want of animal spirits' (p. 44), and in a passage which is incomprehensible outside an imperial context we are informed that

> many of these Indian and Cinghalese races love to be servants (under a tolerably good master); their feminine sensitive natures, often lacking in enterprise, rather seek the shelter of dependence. And certainly they make, in many instances and when well treated, wonderfully good servants, their tact and affectionateness riveting the bond. (p. 54)

A marked tendency to essentialize the subcontinent and to locate its culture and traditions in the realm of the spiritual is also present in the narrative; a form of reverse orientalism. If in mainstream orientalist thinking the exotic other is devalued, here aspects of the society are highly prized. Oriental values remain alternative to those pertaining in the West, however, and in Carpenter's case Ceylon and India, as for the orientalist mainstream, becomes the West's contrasting other. In this case, though, it is the West which is devalued and which is the principal object of criticism. The notion that East and West represent opposite poles in the field of human potentiality permeates the text at many levels.

Carpenter finds much in India which repels, however. The Gnani is spiritually rich yet adheres to absurd disproved conceptions of the material world; religious festivals, however devout, entirely lack taste or dignity; and the well from which life springs in one society is incomprehensible to the other, a clash whose drama is played out in the tragedy of British rule. Indian tradition thus encouraged passivity and an other-worldly orientation. These were admirable, but as they stood seemed to be as narrow as the Western over-emphasis on the worldly. The West promoted an 'ideal of life . . . to have an almost insanely active brain and to be perpetually on the war path with fearful and wonderful projects and plans and purposes' (p. 165), but the East presented no ready access to a clear alternative.

If British society was moribund through corruption, Indian society was historically, even racially, so. 'The native, in keeping with his weaker, more dependent nature, is cunning and lazy', Carpenter writes; 'his vices lie in that direction rather than in the direction of brutal energy' (p. 55). Caste and arcane academicism had stultified India's traditions, and the exaggerated concern with higher consciousness had encouraged a lack of social and human interest which permeated religious teachings and the practices of many of those to whom people turned for spiritual guidance. In the universal quest for cosmic consciousness, therefore, a re-enlightened West, and not the East, would guide the way. The East was of the past, whose lessons could be taught to modern man. In common with colonial thinking of the time the East itself could animate nothing, this position being rather awkwardly yoked to a forceful critique of imperialism and an attitude hostile to Western-style modernization.

Many of these ideas were taken up, and revised, by E. M. Forster. For Forster the idea of male fraternity was a critical alternative to socially prescribed masculinity. He saw that individualism, control (over the self and over others) and aggression were foundational to male power in society as well as to the will to power in general. Furbank has noted the influence Carpenter had on Forster, quoting from the 'Terminal essay' to *Maurice*, to the effect that the novel's gestation was accredited to a pilgrimage to Carpenter's residence at Milnthorpe in 1913.[34] It was as a believer in the 'love of comrades' that Forster turned to Carpenter, as he put it, 'in my loneliness'. The oft-quoted passage describing how Carpenter's lover George Merrill touched him above the buttocks and how the feelings 'seemed to go straight through the small of my back into my ideas, without involving my thoughts',[35] has led a number of commentators recently to trace the thematic influence of Carpenter beyond *Maurice* to Forster's major novels, arguing that a homosexual sub-text may be found below the ostensible heterosexual surface in works such as *Howards End*.[36] My concerns are not to trace Carpenterian resonances in Forster's Indian narratives, but to indicate the central position occupied in these of an understanding of personal relations, and how this is used to criticize and to marginalize dominant masculinity, and how it provided a platform from which imperialism could be opposed.

In Forster's texts we find none of Carpenter's advocacy of male relationships as the credo of a new age. As a man who did not 'believe in Belief',[37] Forster saw personal relationships as something of an antidote to politics traditionally understood, rather than, as they were for Carpenter, the ground from which a new society could be built. They are 'something comparatively solid in a world full of violence and cruelty' (p. 65); a crucial release from the pressures to conformity in modern society, whether these be in the form of mass industrialism or the arrogance of state power. As he famously – for some, treacherously – declared in 1938, 'I hate the idea of causes, and if I had to choose between betraying my country and betraying my friend I hope I should have the guts to betray my country' (p. 66). As for those whom Forster would count as his friends, these would be people who were 'sensitive and would want to create or discover something', who did 'not see life in terms of power' (p. 67). Seyed Ross Masood became for Forster, and came to represent to him, that ideal friend, who 'lived by his emotions and instincts and . . . [whose] standards were those of good taste'.[38] A man whose 'temperament was aesthetic', Masood was memorialized by Forster in the following terms:

> There never was anyone like him and there never will be anyone like him. He cannot be judged as ordinary men are judged. My own debt to him is

incalculable. He woke me up out of my suburban and academic life, showed me
new horizons and a new civilisation, and helped me towards the understanding
of a continent. (p. 285)

It is clear from this revelation, as we shall argue, that Forster's understanding of India was a heavily personally invested one. Forster once
criticized Masood for the excess of his emotional display as they parted at a
Paris railway station after holidaying together. Masood's response was that
Forster was treating the emotions as if they could be parcelled out, 'like a
sack of potatoes'. Reflecting on the incident, Forster later wrote:

> I spoke as a member of a prudent middle class nation. But my friend spoke as an
> Oriental and the Oriental has behind him a tradition not of middle class
> prudence, but of kingly munificence and splendour . . . as regards the resources
> of the spirit, he may be right. The emotions may be endless.[39]

Like the cross-class relationship Forster romanticized in *Maurice* and the
greenwood into which the characters sought refuge from a homophobic
and class-conscious society, or the construction of Italy in *Where Angels Fear
to Tread* or *A Room with a View*, through Masood's influence India was to
become for Forster a site in which friendship was promoted and the values
sympathetic to this were nourished. India became the positive other to the
middle-class, academic and rationalistic Englishness of which Forster was
undoubtedly a part but from which, as an artist but above all as a
homosexual artist, he sought refuge.

The imaginary construction of India as a place of escape, and the
conflicts this presented Forster as a middle-class Briton are played out in
The Hill of Devi. Forster's letters from Egypt, where he spent part of the First
World War with the Red Cross, are full of the evocation of India, to which
he unfavourably compared Alexandria. In one to Masood, dated 1916, he
wrote 'Here there is only the pseudo-East – the pretentious, squalid,
guttural Levant – and I shut my eyes to it on purpose, lest it spoil my
pleasure in the true East, to which I shall one day return'.[40] Forster had once
written to Masood in terms which indicated his desire to escape the
conventionality of his life:

> Dearest boy if you knew how much I loved you and how I long to be alone with
> you . . . . Let us get away from the conventional world and let us wander
> aimlessly if we can, like two pieces of wood on the ocean and perhaps we will
> understand life better.[41]

Masood had later written to Forster that 'you are the only Englishman in
whom I have come across true sentiment and that, too, real sentiment even
from the Oriental point of view' (p. 107). He urged the older man to
cultivate *Tarass*, that faculty possessed by every 'true and well bred
Oriental': the capacity to enter the feelings of another and absorb the
atmosphere of a place (p. 107).

If India was the true East – the land of humanity, grace and cultural depth – it was also an economically backward society in which social distinctions were rife and which was decidedly not of the modern world.[42] India in this construction becomes a place where human relationships could be forged and where they were respected, but it could also be a land of despotism where social corruption was rife. In *The Hill of Devi* these become dichotomous images of India: one an imaginary India, a greenwood,[43] and which the narrative equates with the personality of the Maharaja of Dewas Senior, Sir Tukoji Rao III; the other, the sense of shock and disappointment, the feeling of distaste and of the overwhelming foreignness of India. As Forster quipped, 'One could apply to India what Michelangelo said of death – that the fact of it kills but the thought of it vitalizes and brings strength'.[44]

The conflict which these perspectives suggest is never resolved in the narrative. The fantasmatic construction of India leads Forster to overlook certain implications of his employment by the Maharaja, notably his position as the white sahib in an absolutist feudal state. His rationalistic rejection of much of what he saw around him, however, is much closer to the Anglo-Indian view which he despised as the perspective of those who saw 'life in terms of power'. In the remainder of this section we will examine these tensions.

'Life here will be queer beyond description' (p. 31), Forster wrote soon after settling in at Dewas in 1921, his second visit. In the 'Alice-in-Wonderland' Kingdom, 'one was always going to be wrong' (p. 11) and there was little that would be 'clear-cut'. It is precisely this queerness which attracted Forster. Significantly, in a letter dated 1 January 1913 (his first visit) in which he described a wedding banquet held in the Court, Forster's enthusiasm at the erotics of cultural cross-dressing bursts from the page:

> Baldeo [Forster's servant], much excited by the splendor that surrounded us, was making the best of my simple wardrobe . . . enter the Rajah, bearing Indian raiment for me also. A Sidar (courtier) came with him, a very charming boy, and they two aided Baldeo to undress me and redress me. It was a very funny scene. At first nothing fitted, but the Rajah sent for other garments. . . . My legs were clad in Jodpores made of white muslin. Hanging outside was the youthful Sirdar's white shirt, but it was concealed by a waistcoat the colours of a Neapolitan ice . . . and this was concealed by . . . a magnificent coat of claret-coloured silk, trimmed with gold . . . cocked rakishly over one ear was a Maratha Turban of scarlet and gold . . . I carried in my left hand a scarf of orange-coloured silk with gold ends, and before the evening ended a mark like a loaf of bread was stamped on my forehead in crimson. (pp. 7–8)

It would be inappropriate to apply to this episode the concept of 'double mimesis' as Silverman develops it with respect to T. E. Lawrence – his attempt through the adoption of Arab dress to mimic the other to the point where 'they might be prompted to imitate him back'.[45] There is little evidence in *The Hill of Devi* that Forster sought in his companions any imitation of himself and, unlike Lawrence, in Dewas he was not in a comparable position of power with respect either to the Maharajah or the other central figures at the court. Parallels do exist none the less. Like Lawrence, Forster was here attempting to take on through dress the 'psychic coloration'[46] of the other, the garments defining not only the body beneath them in terms decidedly un-middle class and much more attractive than in reality, but indicting also a desire to transcend his identity and to claim one appropriate to the values he admired and which he had projected on to Dewas. Dewas was transgressive in this scene, the formlessness, the sensuality and the decadence representing the polar opposite to the English prudence from which Forster was largely in retreat and which he saw as responsible for the acute sense of guilt he felt as a result both of his recent unproductiveness as a writer and of his homosexuality. Dressed as of the court, Forster could become at one with his surroundings, casting off his English identity and assuming one more in keeping with his new role as the Rajah's secretary. Dewas provided Forster with the opportunity to lose the self which he despised, and to locate and experience what Masood had termed *Tarass*.

The personality of the Maharaja (whom he called Bapu Sahib) became for Forster this society in microcosm and representative of the capacity for *Tarass*. Centred on his capacity for human feeling and the abiding importance with which friendship was regarded by him, the parallels between Forster's construction of Bapu Sahib and Masood are striking:

> Affection, all through his chequered life, was the only force to which Bapu Sahib responded. It did not always work but without it nothing worked. Affection and its attendant arts of human warmth and instinctive courtesy – when they were present his heart awoke and dictated his actions. (p. 22)

Always 'sweet and understanding' (p. 68), the Maharaja was an icon to Forster for his belief in the heart over reason. As he was to comment, 'to remember and respect and prefer the heart, to have the instinct which follows it wherever possible – what surer help than that could one have through life?' (p. 71). On his arrival at Dewas the Maharaja had telegraphed Forster's over-protective mother, reassuring her that he was in 'safe hands'. Forster's commentary runs as follows:

> I was indeed safe. In no essential did he ever fail me. Quite often I did not understand him – he was too incalculable – but it was possible with him to reach a platform where calculations were unnecessary. It would not be possible with an Englishman. (p. 33)

At the end of his experiences in Dewas Forster came to reflect upon a theme that was to prove central to his later understanding of empire and its future. If only the English had been capable of extending to Indians the friendship which was intrinsic to the colonized culture the political vulnerability of the Raj would not then have been so marked. It was now, he concluded, far too late (pp. 98–9).

If the chaos and muddle of India is a key to its attraction for Forster, that same lack of order and of certainty is the cause of considerable frustration. His disgust at the inefficiencies of the court, 'the idleness, incompetence and extravagance' (p. 38), his distrust of certain aspects of the elusiveness of the Hindu character, and his repulsion at the aesthetics of the Gokul Ashtami festival, at which there was 'no dignity, no taste, no form' (p. 64), are all marked. There was a deep-seated unease in Forster's attitudes towards Dewas; a sense that it disappointed. Significantly, in the light of what we have argued about his early enthusiasm to take on an Indian identity, he was later to say, with some vehemence, 'though I am dressed as a Hindu I shall never become one' (p. 64). In the end he expressed relief at leaving what he was to come to term the 'untidy anthill' (p. 85), and travelled to Hyderabad to be with Masood. The prudent Forster was to write:

> I have passed from Hinduism to Islam and the change is a relief. I have come too into a world whose troubles are intelligible to me. Dewas made much ado about nothing and no ado where a little would have been seemly. (p. 98)

Far more revealing of Forster's divided response to Dewas, and of the guilt attendant upon his imaginary representations of India, is the suppressed narrative of an experience critical to his life at Dewas. 'Kanaya' tells the story of Forster's sexual longings in India and how he attempted to ingratiate himself with several servants, later to his considerable embarrassment and shame. Forster feared that he had become the object of gossip within the court, and of derision to the Maharaja, Dewas taking on a more sinister or threatening character than in the 'official' *The Hill of Devi.* He decided to approach the Maharaja, who pleaded ignorance of Forster's sexuality, presumably untruthfully. Forster is at pains in the text to convince the reader (and himself) that in fact the Maharaja was unknowing of his proclivities, thus revealing his acute need to locate in the personality of His Highness those attributes he so cherished. The narrative response to the Maharaja's equanimity about the episode, notwithstanding his real distaste for homosexuality, is to make of this something of a case study in how friendship will broach difference, displacing criticism. His Highness arranged an alliance for Forster, a court barber, who was paid to visit him regularly. 'Kanaya' is a confession of the guilt Forster felt as a result.

Forster's guilt is caused by the stridency of his sexual longings, and by the feeling that he had failed or been disloyal to the Maharaja. Above all, the point of 'Kanaya' is to confess that he had taken advantage of the young barber, by using his position as the white secretary to the despotic Maharaja to secure his affections. 'Kanaya' speaks of the culpability which Forster felt as a result of having sought in feudal India the release from self and middle-class drudgery which led him to the East. It also reveals his shame at having, as a liberal and a humanist, omitted to take serious account of the Maharaja's political position as despot in his assessments of him and indeed, as crucial to his appeal to Forster and of the broader need which his interest in India addressed. Significantly, the narrative reveals that Kanaya was 'terrified of H.H., whose severity towards his class seemed notorious' (p. 319). Yet Forster projected on to the boy and others like him a hostility which is quite absent in his other writings, and which led him, unlike anywhere else, to resort to racial categories in his indictments. Certain indiscretions by the boy provoke in him a savagery which cuts at the heart of his ethic and reveal his own investments in power:

> I hesitated not but boxed his ears . . . He fell on the carpet and kissed my feet, praying for mercy, and his sobs floated all over the Palace . . . . He had been such a goose . . . . What relation beyond carnality could one establish with such people? He hadn't even the initiative to cut my throat . . . he scratched at my fly-buttons like a squirrel, in the hope of inducing an erection and free pardon. I said 'No' coldly. (p. 323)

Throughout this piece, in part because it was written to be read by a Bloomsbury audience, but largely because it gives expression to the unresolved contradictions central to the Dewas experience, poorer Indians are referred to in the language of Anglo-India. Two other examples stand out in this respect: 'Naidu had always attracted me a little, despite that damnable willowiness that makes an Indian's body as unsatisfactory as his mind' (p. 322), and, recalling a mistaken liaison, Forster was to comment 'he wasn't even the right sais, but another rather like him whom I had mistaken, never knowing these little Indians apart' (p. 317). Similarly, he stated that he could not get to know the barber-boy 'for the reason that there was nothing to know as a rule' (p. 320). The critical passage in the narrative appears towards its end:

> he kept on coming until the end of September, when I left. I resumed sexual intercourse with him, but it was now mixed with the desire to inflict pain. It didn't hurt him to speak of, but it was bad for me, and new in me, my temperament not being that way. I've never had that desire with anyone else, before or after, and I wasn't trying to punish him – I knew his silly little soul was incurable. I just felt he was a slave, without rights, and I a despot whom no one could call to account. (p. 324)

Forster was here seeing life in terms of power, that approach he so despised in others. If earlier cross-dressing had enabled him to lose his English identity, he had also lost that Englishness which he admired, as a citizen of 'the fag-end of liberalism'.[47] I have suggested that an aspect of the attraction which Dewas held for Forster was its extremely tenuous link to the modern world, and that under the protection of an absolutist (and benign) monarch could be secured a greenwood in which his fantasies regarding friendship and male to male communion could be indulged. 'Kanaya' indicated Forster's knowledge that this greenwood gelled little if at all with his democratic commitments. What the story also reveals, however, is his acute dis-ease regarding the consummation of homosexual relations, themes we find pursued in many of the suppressed homosexual love stories.[48]

Hostility is the vehicle through which Forster expressed his ambivalent feelings towards that from which he sought escape, and towards the very desire to escape. To work towards the 'ruination' of dominant masculinity, to use Silverman's expression,[49] or to seek for a space where that was possible, is a fraught exercise for a subject whose implication in a culture in which precisely the opposite is expected is marked by social and class position, and for whom such a course would carry tremendous costs. A very 'stern' entry in his diary of his first visit to Dewas, following a passage in which Forster found it 'impossible to resist him [the Maharaja] or India', depicted the state as a 'land of petty treacheries, of reptiles moving about too cautious to strike each other. No line between the insolent and the servile in social intercourse. . . . *Is there ever civility with manliness here?* And is foreign conquest or national character to blame?' (p. 12; emphasis added). In a provocative reading of *Maurice*, John Fletcher has suggested that the projection of desire on to a working-class lover enabled the upper-middle-class homosexual to reconcile sexual outlawry of a kind threatening to dominant masculinity without the loss of virility which such a course might otherwise entail.[50] In taking as the object of desire a working-class man, straightforward, 'manly' and unintellectual, the middle-class subject could attempt some reconciliation of his cultural investment in the manliness tradition with his more deeply personal interest in the transgression of this. An 'Alice-in-Wonderland' kingdom, which was also absolutist, could arguably perform a similar function. The transgressor is powerful and virile in a conventionally phallic sense, by virtue of the vicarious participation in the despot's power which is enabled through a privileged entry into his service; yet at times those disturbing aspects of the court in whose life one has become involved can be attributed to a lack of manliness in the culture. As I have indicated, to a significant extent the severity, or conventionality, of the judgement made in this respect can be attributed to the feelings of guilt attendant upon the subject's implication in the feudal order to which he is by conviction opposed.

In Forster's major work, *A Passage to India*,[51] the conflicts we noticed in the Dewas memoir have largely been resolved, and the expression of a homosexual sensibility is enabled in ways which avoid self-hatred. *A Passage to India* is pre-eminently a considered text. The novel represents the crowning achievement, as it were, of the narrative tradition which has been the subject of this chapter. *A Passage* has been criticized for its timorous avoidance of the issues of power at the basis of British rule (Stone), yet also praised as an enabling model for Anglo-Indian fiction which was allegedly henceforward freed from the need to express support for the Raj (Mukherjee). For many readers it is the text's investments in the conventions of orientalism which are among its most striking features (Parry, JanMohamed, Chakravarty, Herz).[52] The significance of the homoeroticism present in the text, most notably in the relationship between Fielding and Aziz, and also revealed through the deployment of images such as the naked coolie in Fielding's garden during the tea-party at which Godbole sings for Mrs Moore and Adela, and the punkah wallah in the trial scene, have been well noted by Suleri.[53] This, of course, signals in crucial respects the critical ground which the novel occupies with respect to masculinity. My concern is to argue that in this narrative the critique of imperialism and of dominant masculinity come together as they could not in a Dewas memoir, and as they were never fully resolved in Carpenter's writings. Although not entirely successful in its departure from the colonialist tradition it criticizes, it proposes none the less a richly complex deconstruction of the phallic economy which underwrote the Raj.

The significance of *A Passage to India* is its subversion of the Anglo-Indian masculinist stereotypes. Forster may have been facetious when he argued that his purpose in writing the novel was not political, for the import of his themes is profoundly troubling of the colonial and gender stereotypes central to the genre, bringing into sharper focus themes which were developed in the letters collected as *The Hill of Devi*. The attributes of character deemed by the dominant fiction as appropriate to the Raj are undermined through the portrait of model Anglo-Indian men and women as seriously deficient in almost every respect. The notion that India could prove a testing ground for British character is also subverted by the admittedly orientalist construction of India as unknowable, but also through the treatment of the British as aliens huddled together in a defensive community isolated from Indian life, 'which shares nothing with the city except the overarching sky' (p. 10). The shallowness of the British is contrasted to the cultivated leisure of Aziz's friends, who listen to poetry with delight, 'for they took the public view of poetry, not the private which obtains in England' (p. 16); and next to whom the concerns of the club with its stiffness and pantomimes looks banal. Also exposed as prejudiced is the common representation of the Indians as childlike and in need of strong paternal direction, the narrative following this line to some degree but also taking pains to depict the circle around Aziz as self-sufficient and independent, as indeed is the world of the Native State of Mau, the subject of the final section. As the central episode in the novel, the alleged rape and its consequences, the common image of Indian manhood as violent and sexually licentious is brought into the open and confronted. The alleged rape itself, though clearly implicated in a misogyny which would make the man the victim, does call into question the racially motivated sexual fears enflamed by the colonial situation and does indicate some knowledge of the position of otherness inscribed in the woman, even if this latter insight is more implicit than developed.[54]

The novel frees no character and no group from criticism, even as it embraces the inevitability of difference. In this the contrast with the earlier writing and with Carpenter's travelogue must also be drawn. There is little of the commitment in *A Passage* to a conception of the world which would assign India to the past or, indeed, which would invest in it a spiritualism unobtainable elsewhere, as if the West and India were on opposite ends of a continuum with time's arrow moving in the West's direction. If the British are tribal, they also exercise some respect for the rule of law; Fielding may be free from prejudice but he cannot extend to Aziz the warmth which the latter expects, and in the end betrays his convictions; Adela is full of enthusiasm for India, yet is naive and shallow; Mrs Moore has heart but runs away when she is needed; Godbole has spiritual knowledge, but his beliefs are arcane and insufficiently human in concern; Aziz himself has *Tarass*, if only at the expense of petulance and inconstancy. Similarly, no perspective is privileged in the narrative: the Muslim, Hindu and rationalist; each has value but also limitations. The need for a wider and embracing view, in this respect, would appear to be the text's central point.[55]

There is another key departure from *The Hill of Devi*. As Heath has argued, *A Passage* is extremely demanding: 'When the unknown universe of India invites, we should *not* seek our image in the "mirror of the scenery"; or, if we fail to see accustomed beauties, we must have the courage not to cry . . . or to break down.'[56] Forster in this work is thus mocking the very projection on to India of expectations, or the seeking in India for a space – a greenwood – from which to escape, which he had himself attempted in Dewas and which is a key colonialist move found in both the dominant genre as well as in that here under examination. This strategy is viewed as deluded and as calculated to disappoint:

> How can the mind take hold of such a country? Generations of invaders have tried, but they remain in exile. The important towns they build are only retreats, their quarrels the malaise of men who cannot find their way home. India knows of their trouble. She calls 'Come' through her hundred mouths, through objects ridiculous and august. But come to what? She has never defined. She is not a promise, only an appeal. (p. 135)

This representation of India as unknowable is, of course, a key orientalist trope; but the effect to which this is put in the narrative is to undermine the assurance with which India can appeal to the Western imagination. In this respect *A Passage* breaks with the tradition with which we have been occupied. Unlike Carpenter or the Forster of *The Hill of Devi*, in this novel the image of India as a space within which concerns unable to be explored in the West could be expressed, self-discovery achieved or the sense of self abandoned, is deconstructed. The naivety with which Adela Quested, 'the queer, cautious girl' (p. 25), conceives of India in these terms, seeking out 'the real India' (p. 27), is also blindness and contributes to her breakdown. In the end her 'desire to see India' decreases; 'There had been a factitious element in it' (p. 85).

Perhaps signalling above all its clearest break with other narratives is the more measured position from which the ideal of friendship is advocated. Friendship, the importance of the ideal and its notable absence across the racial divide is a critical theme, yet – as much a consequence of human limitations as of political – the concluding line pronounces 'No, not yet . . .

not there' (p. 317). The relationship between Aziz and Fielding starts promisingly. In the famous 'collar-stud' scene, the two meet while Fielding is dressing, in circumstances therefore which were by Anglo-Indian standards illicit, and which – almost but not quite – subvert the boundaries between the legitimate and deviant expression of male affection and friendship:

> They shook hands, smiling. He began to look round, as he would have with any old friend. Fielding was not surprised at the rapidity of their intimacy. With so emotional a people it was apt to come once, or never, and he and Aziz, having heard only good of each other, could afford to dispense with preliminaries. (p. 64)

Fielding breaks his collar-stud, and Aziz lends him his own, anxious to please. The friendship is thus apparently sealed by the intimacy of the exchange:

> 'But I always thought that Englishmen kept their rooms tidy. It seems that this is not so. I need not be so ashamed.' He sat down gaily on the bed; then, forgetting himself entirely, drew up his legs and folded them under him. 'Everything ranged coldly on shelves was what *I* thought. I say, Mr Fielding, is the stud going to go in?' (pp. 64–5)

Later in the novel the bond between the two will be further cemented by Aziz sharing with Fielding his sense of loss for his deceased wife, after awkwardness caused by Fielding's unannounced arrival at Aziz's squalid rooms. Aziz shows Fielding a photograph of his wife. This is a second moment of intimacy:

> they were friends, brothers. That part was settled, their compact had been subscribed by the photograph, they trusted one another, affection had triumphed for once in a way. He dropped off to sleep amid the happier memories of the last two hours – poetry of Ghalib, female grace, good old Hamidullah, good Fielding, his honoured wife and dear boys. He passed into a region where these joys had no enemies but bloomed harmoniously in an eternal garden, or ran down watershoots of ribbed marble, or rose into domes whereunder were inscribed, black against white, the ninety-nine attributes of God. (p. 119)

The friendship is not, alas, to blossom. Politics intrudes, as do personal characteristics, but so does race. Aziz, '[l]ike most Orientals', 'overrated hospitality, mistaking it for intimacy' (p. 141), and Fielding's sense of self, his capacity to 'travel light', meant that he was happy to 'pass on serenely'[57] rather than to engage personally. In these scenes the complexity of Forster's position is revealed; his departure from, as well as his dependence upon, colonialist representation laid bare.

What is especially crucial in marking this novel out as the major contribution towards the counter-tradition we have been examining is the location at its centre of the caves and the negation which they represent. The presence of a narrative voice which resists, indeed rejects, determinacy, control and closure is also important in this context.

In the light of contemporary feminist theory, the caves can be read as morphologically feminine, but in a sense radically at odds with the tradition which feminized the Indian landscape either as a trope to signal the white man's right of entry, or as emblematic of the masculine fear of loss of control. The caves in *A Passage* are feminized in the sense that they 'depict as female that force which disrupts phallogocentric representation and Western patriarchal values'.[58] The caves reduce all sound to an incomprehensible echo; all signifiers are severed from signifieds, rendering the former meaningless. Note how in the following passage the ready description and calibration of the caves is shown to be hollow:

> The caves are readily described. A tunnel eight feet long, five feet high, three feet wide, leads to a circular chamber about twenty feet in diameter. This arrangement occurs again and again throughout the group of hills, and this is all, this is a Marabar Cave . . . the visitor . . . finds it difficult to discuss the caves, or to keep them apart in his mind, for the pattern never varies, and no carving, not even a bees' nest or a bat, distinguishes one from another. Nothing, nothing attaches to them, and their reputation – for they have one – does not depend upon human speech.
>
> They are dark caves. Even when they open towards the sun, very little light penetrates down the entrance tunnel into the circular chamber. There is little to see, and no eye to see it. . .
>
> Nothing is inside them, they were sealed up before the creation of pestilence or treasure, if mankind grew curious and excavated, nothing, nothing would be added to the sum of good or evil. (pp. 124–5)

Masculinist attempts at mastery or control and the logocentric desire to grasp meaning are shattered by the caves, and in this respect they are distinctly antithetical to the values of the dominant discourse, with its valuation of fine distinction and measurement as a means to practical exploitation of the natural world or utilization of this for human purposes.

Underlining the critique of order and control which the caves posit is the central placement in the narrative of negation and negativity – in language, theme and structure.[59] With respect to language, it is noteworthy that

> One can . . . list the key words of the text and recover the novel in epitome: sky, arch, arching, arcade, echo, echoing, silence, not, dream, ghost, death, heat, darkness, rocks, stones, mud, mystery, muddle . . . . But against all these one must set the one word that tolls most emphatically through the text and is repeated more than any other, nothing . . . [60]

Thematically, as we have argued, the novel cautions against the predominance of any one world-view: mystical, aesthetic or rationalist. It is most active in its discrediting of the life of sense perception and positive knowledge, the cornerstones of Western epistemology and central to the West's denigration of the non-Western other. Multiple India unsettles Mrs Moore's apparently mature perception of life, and the meaning – or, rather, meaninglessness – of the caves we have already noticed. With respect to structure, it is significant that the trial, as the conventional centrepiece of the drama, turns on an apparent misperception and the issues in dispute are never settled. Rather than effecting narrative closure as would be expected, the trial and its aftermath are followed by the indeterminacies of the incomprehensible festival at Mau, and the final irresolution of the friendship between Aziz and Fielding is the subject of its closing pages. It is also noteworthy that Bette London has found the narrative voice to be hysterical; fragmented and decentred, 'a shifting, slippery, implacable voice that seems to take its timbre from whatever voice it happens to be near',[61] reinforcing the novel's embrace of multiplicity and rejection of certainty. The text in these respects subverts 'that struggle for dominion which is implicit in the struggle for language and meaning – the struggle to keep man at the centre of the universe' (p. 58). What I am arguing is that Forster is asserting in allegorical form that there is a close relationship between the desire for domination and a form of gender subjectivity and state of being in the world which is masculine in the phallic sense. The text stands for the view that the movement beyond relations based upon dominance requires the termination of a form of masculinity which Forster, as a homosexual, had suffered as one of its many others. Carpenter's subversion of the mappings of male desire is certainly more overt than Forster's, but Forster's use of the caves dramatically exposes the futility of the masculine fantasy of control and order.

We have briefly canvassed the argument that the texts with which we have here been concerned might be regarded as in some respects essentially homosexual. There might be such a case to be made about *A Passage* in a more significant sense than could apply to any of the other narratives notwithstanding their more open revelation of homoerotic desire. It is possible to read the absence at its centre, epitomized by the caves, as standing for the 'mappings of secrecy', so imperative a part of the modern experience of homosexual definition, as this has been explored by Sedgwick.[62] She has argued that

> a whole cluster of the most crucial sites for the contestation of meaning in twentieth-century Western culture are consequentially and quite indelibly marked with the historical specificity of homosocial/homosexual definition, notably but not exclusively male, from around the turn of the century. Among those sites are . . . the pairings secrecy/disclosure and public/private. (p. 72)

She goes on to claim that towards the latter years of the nineteenth century the possibility of representing sexual knowledge as same-sex desire was energetically repressed, to the point where the 'secret' or the 'undisclosed' became charged with sexual – especially homosexual – meaning. For the subject from the turn of the century onwards, the very thematics of knowledge and ignorance, 'of innocence and initiation, of secrecy and disclosure, became contingently but integrally infused with one particular object of cognition: no longer sexuality as a whole but, even more specifically, now, the homosexual topic' (pp. 73–4).

The caves as secret, India as unknowable, that nothing is as it seems – these are all tropes used by Forster with deftness and power and which are utilized to deconstruct conventional masculinity, as a subjective position and as an epistemological and ontological category. This is animated by and reflects, I would argue, the particularly charged meaning which secrecy and indeterminacy took in a society where sexuality was, by the time he was writing, central to identity and where the closet was crucial to the homosexual's survival and its signs read with increasing self-confidence by a community which was, during the last years of his life, able to 'come out'. The caves are, I am suggesting, the metaphor of the homosexual outsider.

A Passage to India does not depart entirely from the themes of colonial fiction. There are many instances where the narrative follows well-charted channels, deploying racist, and sexist, stereotypes, no more so than in the rather belittling way in which Aziz's endearing qualities are articulated, or in the crafting of Adela as prude. It is also notable that the Empire itself, as distinct from the impersonal and inhuman form it took, fails as stridently as we might wish to emerge as irredeemable, and in this respect Carpenter's critique goes further. These limitations apart, the subjective and intersubjective superstructure of British rule in India, as an instance of a system where personal relations were distorted by the search for power, are isolated and are interrogated as anathema to the generosity, tolerance and intimacies which were, on Forster's account, the distinguishing features of a civilized life.

In conclusion, we might ask how we should assess the achievement of the writing which has been the subject of this chapter. Reading these texts through our contemporary lenses, we find it relatively easy to dismiss Carpenter and Forster for the dependence of their work on colonialist assumptions, albeit deployed to ends rather different from those of the mainstream. In a different context, both of these men might be criticized for their exploitation of opportunities relatively unselfconscious of the position power which enabled each of them to do so. In this they are seriously compromised. Yet what is important about this writing is its working through of the linkages between sexuality, gender construction and the will to dominance which underwrote unjust political and personal relationships. A thoroughgoing critique of conventional masculinity is here presented, an extraordinary achievement at a time when that particular gender construct was at its high-water mark. The critique of this masculinity sustained for these men a disidentification with the normative order more generally, and from this, in a tentative way, the colonialist hierarchies of difference were provoked into disarray. We should take proper account of the strength of the case they variously made for the political relevance of the personal, themes which were not to become fashionable until the late 1960s and which now occupy a place on the scholarly, as well as the critical, agenda. It is this which marks out their perspectives as important to any critical reading of the processes of political domination in the world, not just to students of colonialism but to any reader anxious to understand the interrelations between gender and sexuality and power. The work here considered is therefore recommended to those working in the growing field of critical international relations theory, where gendered readings of power are, if not quite in their infancy, still to be much developed.

Note

1. John Drew, *India and the Romantic Imagination* (Delhi, Oxford University Press, 1987), preface.

2. See, for example, Gail Ching-Liang Low, 'His stories: narratives and images of imperialism', *New Formations*, 12:Winter (1990), 97–123.

3. Representative examples are R. Kipling, 'William the Conqueror' in *The Day's Work Part 1* (London, Macmillan 1899), pp. 237–88 and M. Diver, *The Hero of Herat* (London, Constable, 1912).

4. A third candidate would be Joe Ackerley, whose slighter work will not be considered here. See Joe Ackerley, *Hindoo Holiday: An Indian Journal* (London, Chatto and Windus, 1932).

5. P. Fussell, *Abroad: British Literary Travelling between the Wars* (New York, Oxford University Press, 1980).

6. Ibid., p. 5.

7. J. Dollimore, *Sexual Dissidence: Augustine to Wilde, Freud to Foucault* (Oxford, Clarendon Press, 1991), p. 339.

8. See especially G. Dawson, 'The blond bedouin: Lawrence of Arabia, imperial adventure and the imagining of English-British masculinity' in M. Roper and J. Tosh (eds), *Manful Assertions: Masculinities in Britain since 1800* (London, Routledge, 1991); G. Dawson, 'The public and private lives of T. E. Lawrence: modernism, masculinity and imperial adventure', *New Formations*, 16:Spring (1992), 103–18; and Kaja Silverman, *Male Subjectivity at the Margins* (New York, Routledge, 1992), ch. 7.

9. Dawson, 'The public and private lives of T. E. Lawrence', pp. 103–18.

10. See Dawson, 'The blond bedouin'.

11. Silverman, *Male Subjectivity at the Margins*, ch. 7.

12. Quoted in Dollimore, *Sexual Dissidence*, p. 334.

13. Silverman, *Male Subjectivity at the Margins*, p. 316.

14. D. Spurr, *The Rhetoric of Empire: Colonial Discourse in Journalism, Travel Writing, and Imperial Administration* (Durham, NC, Duke University Press, 1993), chs 3, 8 and 11.

15. R. Kabbani, *The Fiction of Imperialism: Europe's Myths of the Orient* (London, Pandora, 1994), p. 11.

16. J. Butler, *Gender Trouble* (New York, Routledge, 1990), p. 29.

17. H. Bhabha, *The Location of Culture* (London, Routledge, 1994), ch. 4 ('Of mimicry and man . . . ').

18. Butler, *Gender Trouble*, p. 34.

19. R. Aldrich, *The Seduction of the Mediterranean: Writing, Art and Homosexual Fantasy* (London, Routledge, 1993), p. 10.

20. See, for example, G. Steiner, 'Eros and idiom', ch. 5 of *On Difficulty and Other Essays* (New York, Oxford University Press, 1980); also the reviews of E. M. Forster, *Maurice*, collected as 'Two valedictory reviews' in P. Gardner (ed.), *E. M. Forster: The Critical Heritage* (London, Routledge and Kegan Paul, 1973), pp. 475–90.

21. H. Cixous, 'Sorties' in E. Marks and I. de Courtivron (eds), *New French Feminisms* (Brighton, Harvester, 1981), pp. 90–8. See also for a representative sample of recent queer

theory, M. Warner (ed.), *Fear of a Queer Planet: Queer Politics and Social Theory* (Minneapolis, University of Minnesota Press, 1993).

22. See R. Hyam, *Empire and Sexuality: The British Experience* (Manchester, Manchester University Press, 1990), especially pp. 35–9 and ch. 4, for examples.

23. On the importance of Whitman to the definition of a fledgling homosexual consciousness see E. K. Sedgwick, *Between Men: English Literature and Male Homosexual Desire* (New York, Columbia University Press, 1985), pp. 182–3; and R. K. Martin, *Hero, Captain and Stranger: Male Friendship, Social Critique, and Literary Form in the Sea Novels of Herman Melville* (Chapel Hill, University of North Carolina Press, 1986), introduction. With respect to the evocation of the exotic East, Whitman's 'Passage to India' was central. See W. Whitman, *Leaves of Grass* (Philadelphia, McKay Publishers, 1900).

24. Sedgwick, *Between Men*, pp. 205–6.

25. Quoted ibid., p. 206.

26. E. Carpenter, *Towards Democracy. Complete in Four Parts* (London, Allen and Unwin, 1915), pp. 440–2.

27. 'Empire', ibid., pp. 466–7.

28. E. Carpenter, 'Narayan' in *Sketches from Life in Town and Country and Some Verses* (London, Allen and Unwin, 1918).

29. See T. Rahman, 'The literary treatment of Indian themes in the work of Edward Carpenter', *Durham University Journal*, 80, NS vol. 69 (1987–88), 81.

30. E. Carpenter, *From Adam's Peak to Elephanta: Sketches in Ceylon and India,* revised edition (London, Allen and Unwin, 1921)

31. Rahman, 'The literary treatment of Indian themes', p. 78.

32. P. K. Bakshi, 'Homosexuality and orientalism: Edward Carpenter's journey to the East' in T. Brown (ed.), *Edward Carpenter and Late Victorian Radicalism* (London, Frank Cass, 1990), pp. 151–77.

33. Rahman, 'The literary treatment of Indian themes', p. 77.

34. P. N. Furbank, *E. M. Forster: A Life,* vol. 1: *The Growth of the Novelist (1879–1914)* (London, Secker and Warburg, 1977), p. 257. See also T. Rahman, 'Edward Carpenter and E. M. Forster', *Durham University Journal*, 69, NS vol. 48 (1986–87), 59.

35. Quoted in Furbank, *E. M. Forster: A Life,* vol. 1, p. 257.

36. See, for examples, D. Altman, 'The homosexual vision of E. M. Forster', *Cahiers d'Études et de Recherches Victoriennes et Édouardiennes*, nos 4–5 (1977), 85–95; E. Langland, 'Gesturing toward an open space: gender, form and language in E. M. Forster's *Howards End*' in L. Claridge and E. Langland (eds), *Out of Bounds: Male Writers and Gender(ed) Criticism* (Amhurst, University of Massachusetts Press, 1990), pp. 252–67; W. Stone, ' "Overlapping class": Forster's problem in connection', *Modern Language Quarterly* 32:3 (1978), 389; W. Stone, 'E. M. Forster's subversive individualism' in J. Herz and R. K. Martin (eds), *E. M. Forster: Centenary Reevaluations* (London, Macmillan, 1985); and J. Fletcher, 'Forster's self-erasure: *Maurice* and the scene of masculine love' in J. Bristow (ed.), *Sexual Sameness: Textual Differences in Lesbian and Gay Writing* (London, Routledge, 1992).

37. E. M. Forster, 'What I believe' in *Two Cheers for Democracy* (London, Edward Arnold, 1972), p. 65.

38. E. M. Forster, 'Seyed Ross Masood' in *Two Cheers for Democracy*, p. 285.

39. Quoted in R. W. Noble, ' "Dearest Forster" – "Dearest Masood": an East–West relationship', *Encounter*, 56:6 (1982), 64.

40. Quoted in Furbank, *E. M. Forster: A Life,* vol. 2: *Polycrates' Ring (1914–1970)* (London, Secker and Warburg, 1978), p. 64.

41. Quoted in R. Bharucha, 'Forster's friends', *Raritan*, 5:4 (1986), 107.

42. G. K. Das, *E. M. Forster's India* (London, Macmillan, 1977), p. 3.

43. See J. Birje-Patil, 'Forster and Dewas' in G. K. Das and J. Beer (eds), *E. M. Forster: A Human Exploration. Centenary Essays* (London, Macmillan, 1979).

44. Cited in editor's introduction, E. M. Forster, *The Hill of Devi and Other Indian Writings* (London, Edward Arnold, 1983), p. xix.

45. Silverman, *Male Subjectivity at the Margins*, p. 312.

46. Ibid.

47. E. M. Forster, 'The challenge of our times' in *Two Cheers for Democracy*, p. 54.

48. See especially E. M. Forster, 'The Life to Come' and 'The Other Boat' in *The Life to Come and Other Stories* (London, Edward Arnold, 1972), at pp. 65–82 and pp. 166–97, respectively. For a penetrating analysis, see B. Rosencrance, *Forster's Narrative Vision* (London, Cornell University Press, 1982), p. 177.

49. Silverman, *Male Subjectivity at the Margins*, ch. 6.

50. Fletcher, 'Forster's self-erasure', p. 74.

51. E. M. Forster, *A Passage to India* (London, Penguin, 1974).

52. See Stone, '"Overleaping class"', pp. 386–404; S. Mukherjee, *Forster and Further: The Tradition of Anglo-Indian Fiction* (Bombay, Orient Longman, 1993), p. 2; B. Parry, 'The politics of representation in *A Passage to India*' in J. Beer (ed.), *A Passage to India: Essays in Interpretation* (London, Macmillan, 1985), pp. 27–43; A. JanMohamed, 'The economy of Manichean allegory: the function of racial difference in colonialist literature', *Critical Inquiry*, Summer (1985), 66, 73–7; S. Chakravarty, *The Raj Syndrome: A Study in Imperial Perceptions* (Delhi, Chanakya Publications, 1989), pp. 118–22; J. Scherer Herz, *A Passage to India: Nation and Narration* (New York, Twayne Publishers, 1993).

53. S. Suleri, *The Rhetoric of English India* (Chicago, University of Chicago Press, 1992), ch. 6.

54. For a full discussion of these issues see J. Sharpe, *Allegories of Empire: The Figure of Woman in the Colonial Text* (Minneapolis, University of Minnesota Press, 1993), p. 118; and B. Silver, 'Periphrasis, power and rape in *A Passage to India*' in L. Higgins and B. Silver (eds), *Rape and Representation* (New York, Columbia University Press, 1991).

55. D. Schwarz, *The Transformation of the English Novel 1890–1930* (London, Macmillan, 1989), pp. 134–35.

56. J. Heath, 'A voluntary surrender: imperialism and imagination in *A Passage to India*', *University of Toronto Quarterly*, 59:2 (1989–90), 277.

57. Ibid., p. 115. See also G. Cavaliero, *A Reading of E. M. Forster* (London, Macmillan, 1979), p. 153.

58. For a reading which makes connections in this regard, see F. Restuccia, 'A cave of my own: E. M. Forster and sexual politics', *Raritan* 9:2 (1989), 124. Also illuminating is J. Meyers, *Fiction and the Colonial Experience* (Ipswich, The Boydell Press, 1973), p. 49.

59. G. Beer, 'Negation in *A Passage to India*' in Beer (ed.), *A Passage to India: Essays in Interpretation*, pp. 49–58; see also M. Tinsley, 'Muddle et cetera syntax in *A Passage to India*', ibid., pp. 71–80.

60. Herz, *A Passage to India: Nation and Narration*, p. 89.

61. B. London, *The Appropriated Voice: Narrative Authority in Conrad, Forster and Woolf* (Ann Arbor, University of Michigan Press, 1990), p. 58.

62. E. K. Sedgwick, *Epistemology of the Closet* (Berkeley, University of California Press, 1990).

CHAPTER NINE

Women in colonial Africa: agency, theory and literature

PAM STAVROPOULOS

That disciplinary international relations would appear belatedly to have acknowledged gender issues should give no cause for complacency to those expecting a paradigm shift.[1] Entrenched approaches predominate, and many scholars remain resistant – often overtly so – to the implications of a gender analysis. That the international itself might be constructed in ways deeply marked by gender categories eludes all but the most marginal scholarship. Where gender does appear within international relations, so often the work falls into one of three general categories: that which gestures towards, rather than takes serious consideration of, the questions at stake; that which directly engages core issues in international relations such as power and security, but works within the parameters of such categories and reinscribes them as central, rather than providing a more fundamental rethinking and critique; and that which is feminist-informed, but which tends to be self-referential and bracketed apart from the disciplinary mainstream. Rather than express surprise at this imperviousness, we should regard it as largely symptomatic of the definitional boundaries of the discipline. International relations has made its own the relations between states and has been principally preoccupied with the systemic or the structural. Questions related to the personal or to cultural particularity, or the relations within or between societies as distinct from states, have fallen outside its purview.

An unfortunate legacy of this disciplinary lacuna is the neglect of colonialism and imperialism in international relations, a neglect which, as Phillip Darby maintains in the Introduction, effectively displaced experiences and processes that shaped the futures of peoples and societies in Africa and Asia. It is no surprise, then, that questions surrounding female agency in colonial contexts have scarcely figured at all. Yet they are suggestively explored in other fields, as for example feminist and postcolonial scholarship, from which the international relations discipline is decreasingly able to insulate itself. This chapter addresses the topic of women and agency in colonial Africa with reference to recent theoretical debates, and uses fictional narratives as its principal example. It is argued that both domains suggest rich sources of insight for the discipline of international relations, not despite but because of the fact that their ostensible concerns are so contrasting.

The theoretical approach I advance – one which I argue to be of great potential relevance to students of international relations – is predicated upon a 'politics of the everyday'. With reference to some short fiction by African women writers, I will consider the potential of this methodology as one means by which the silences of the international relations discipline regarding women, agency and colonialism might begin to be articulated. My attempt to combine such disparate material and approaches – social theory and imaginative literature – invites a degree of scepticism. But the topic of women and agency in colonial African contexts is itself multifaceted. If it is conceded that this is a topic which cannot be detached from the processes of international relations, but which the discipline of international relations is ill-equipped to address, this in itself comprises a powerful argument in favour of more eclectic and less orthodox approaches. As a prelude to my argument, and by way of situating the discussion, I begin with consideration of the dimensions of my topic, and why the interplay of these facets necessitates a more wide-ranging methodological approach than might initially seem to be warranted.

To speak of women and agency in the variegated situation of colonial Africa is to enter – and be implicated in – complex political terrain. In addition to the contextual diversity, and the many differences among women, the notion of 'agency' is highly contested. Thus if each is conceptually challenging in its own terms, their combination is especially problematic. In their pioneering collection _Women and Colonization_,[2] editors Mona Etienne and Eleanor Leacock argued that acknowledgement of colonial exploitation 'does not preclude recognition of the colonized as capable of acting to influence their own destiny'. But they were also forced to concede that '[w]ith respect to women . . . a "double standard" prevails'.[3]

At one level, assumptions about the 'passivity' of women have long been challenged. Yet they remain deep-rooted in Western perceptions (including Western feminist perceptions) of non-European women, and of African women in particular. At the same time, it is clearly simplistic to embark on an analysis which is predicated, however implicitly, on any automatic replication of the 'Western'/'non-Western' dichotomy. Although endogenous and exogenous critique frequently differ radically, prior assumptions of irrevocable antagonism between them must be rejected.

Consideration of female agency in colonial Africa brings the dilemmas of cross-cultural analysis to the surface, and highlights how the intersections of gender, race and class both challenge and enrich attempts to resolve them. The colonial period comprises a suggestive focus in that it facilitates insight into the construction of contemporary relations between Africa and the West. It is also suggestive because it constitutes a moment in which the varying capacity of women to exert influence over their diverse situations was in major respects circumscribed. Thus while such breadth of context poses theoretical problems at one level (in that the limits of generalization are now well understood), it is precisely the differences colonialism subsumes among and between European and African women which I want to highlight. To the extent that the discipline of international relations has always been addressed to large 'macro' processes, consideration of the diverse and the particular is also salutary.

A focus on colonialism's issues immediately challenges any conception of women as a homogeneous group. Most broadly and obviously, differences between the experiences of European and African women were stark. The axis of race is pertinent because in a structure predicated on racial divisions, a white skin conferred privilege irrespective of material differences. Thus European women who in their own countries could not afford to employ servants found themselves able to do so in the colonies – an advantage which was enjoyed at the expense of African women as a group.

But to highlight the different experiences of colonialism by different groups of women is not to argue that all general characterizations of the phenomenon of colonialism are illegitimate. This should be reassuring to conventional proponents of the international relations discipline, who, in areas other than gender, accept that the workings of colonialism were not uniform. To the extent that 'the age of empire' (1870–1914) comprised part of an even broader process by which European powers attempted to consolidate political, economic and social control over the non-European world, the relationships it catalysed need to be understood in a wider sense than sole focus on the local ('micro') level can allow. A key point here – and one which pertains simultaneously to gender, economic and political reconfigurations – concerns the introduction of the public/private dichotomy entailed by the colonial state.

In her analysis of women and capitalist transformation in Africa, Kathleen Staudt discusses ways in which 'the domestication of women' under colonialism 'became a "mark of civilization" for people to strive for'.[4] In so doing, she substantiates in the broad field of Africa what feminist analysis has consistently established in relation to a range of otherwise diverse situations: the centrality of the public/private dicho- tomy to the consolidation of male power. In introducing and attempting to impose this artificial delineation on African societies, European powers simultaneously reconstituted colonial economies and the gender relations which sustained them: 'Once a moral and legal foundation of male authority was established [under colonialism] women were defined out of policy and political reality.'[5]

As precolonial work patterns were disrupted, women's labour was no longer recognized as such. Hence economic reliance of indigenous women on men increased. But proceeding on this basis, some scholars concluded that women had lost all capacity to act or to influence, and this view has proved surprisingly resilient. Consider, for example, the recent contention of one critic that under colonialism 'we see African women dependent and subservient in every aspect of their existence, in secondary or insignificant economic roles, without political clout, in every way dominated by men'.[6] This unequivocal reading is illegitimate in that it forecloses the existence, and even possibility, of agency. As Staudt argues, 'Attention to the overarching conception of the state, particularly the colonial state . . . should not divert analysts from attempting to understand the ways in which indigenous peoples received, manoeuvred, and accommodated themselves to the new institutions in which they were ensnared'. Unfortunately, many analysts have been 'diverted' from the methods by which even the most circumscribed situations were mediated, traversed and in turn influenced by those who are 'ensnared'.[7]

At the other end of the spectrum, however, there are problems with attempts to restore and, in fact, celebrate, female agency when they disregard structural constraints. In seeking to redress the deterministic bias of earlier approaches, contemporary critiques mostly emphasize that 'human subjects are never passively "shaped" . . . but actively engage with, and creatively interpret'[8] the contexts in which they are enmeshed.

Outside the discipline of international relations, there is now an extensive literature attuned to explication of the manifold ways in which people manoeuvre within, creatively improvise with, and covertly contest the power relations by which they are also constrained and even constituted. Yet the 'restoration' of agency entails corresponding and recurring dilemmas. To what extent is such an emphasis compatible with simultaneous emphasis on oppression?

Within feminist analysis, such questions are particularly acute. As has been observed, feminist theory has 'long grappled with the problem of documenting women's position as victims of their culturally constructed subordinate status while also celebrating women's strength and creativity in resisting that subordination'.[9] To what degree do inequitable gender relations undermine the very conception of female agency as such? How far can women's 'resistance' to asymmetrical power relations be emphasized before jeopardizing the also important reality of female subordination? Such questions are complicated and compounded by increasing recognition that gender inequity is far from being the only axis of oppression, and that it must be in the light of the dimensions of race and class, from which it cannot easily be separated, but with which it does not neatly correspond.

Recognition of the nexus between (and tensions within) the dimensions of gender, class and race complicates feminist discussion of 'agency' in several ways. At one level, it can lead to the converse problem of over-compensation, and to the simplifications, distortions and coerciveness of attempts to recognize 'agency' at all costs. Such a response, as I have suggested, is often apparent in Western feminist critique which attempts to rectify a long unacknowledged ethnocentrism. But it is also a question for 'Third World' feminist writers, who, in wanting to reclaim the agency which has traditionally been denied them by Western critics, are clearly cognizant of the dangers of emphasizing it too much.

In view of the obvious discrepancies of experience between Western and non-European women, Western women's 'complicity' in colonialism has become a prominent theme of contemporary recuperative scholarship.[10] Much of this critique is nuanced and sophisticated in exploring the contributions to, but also in some respects subversions of, colonial rule by European women. Yet there are senses in which the elusive dimensions of agency remain problematic within the 'complicity' school of writing on colonialism. To what extent does explicit or even implied reference to European women's contribution to empire both suggest a homogeneity of experience among European women, and deflect attention from the male dominance of colonialism *per se* (i.e. its extremely gendered character)? However nuanced the conception of 'complicity', its deployment suggests connotations that the category cannot comfortably contain, and which seem to elide the very complexity being conceptualized. Even more revealingly, preoccupation with the 'complicity' of Western women reinscribes the dichotomy between 'European' and 'African' women, and, although with clearer conscience this time, again robs the latter of their own agency and capacity to influence.

In the absence of corresponding attentiveness to ways in which colonial contexts were mediated by African women, the recuperative dimensions of Western women's 'complicity' readings risk being lost. There is also a latent danger in such readings that the varying activity of Western women under colonialism comes to be seen as either accommodatory or subversive, so that a further binary risks re-enshrinement. If critics are to avoid replicating the very distortions they are ostensibly contesting, attempts to address the agency of African women under colonialism must be especially attentive to the complex dynamics of accommodation and resistance. This is because the inequities and impositions of colonialism were such that degrees of accommodation were frequently necessitated even as they were simultaneously subverted.

In contending this, I am not asserting that the categories of accommodation and resistance should be or even can be conflated – a claim which would entail problems of its own. Nor am I contending that both dimensions are necessarily always discernible in the attempts of African women to mediate the constraints to which colonialism subjected them and which they in turn influenced. My point is that unless both axes of focus are preserved, efforts to elucidate the agency of African women under colonial rule become detached from the power disparities in which they were embedded.

It is arguable that the challenge of adequately portraying the intersections of agency and constraint also disrupts some of the more familiar categories and concepts by which such complexity is represented. In the reading of Arlene MacLeod,[11] 'women's struggle is limited by the constraints of existing social discourse', such that 'the categories we use to think about consent, resistance and protest may need to be reworked'. In a provocative paper which reconceptualizes Gramsci's notion of hegemony to take account of the complexity of consent in the context of gender relations, MacLeod argues for the need 'to think beyond the dichotomies of victim/actor or passive/powerful toward the more complicated ways that consciousness is structured and agency embedded in power relations'. For MacLeod, this task assumes added urgency in that it problematizes 'some of the unresolved methodological dilemmas of writing about women and power in the Third World'.[12] To be persuasive, then, analytical approaches need to address both the dimensions of accommodation and resistance, and their interrelationship. Outside the discipline of international relations, there now exist pioneering critiques of 'colonized African women' which engage with both these dimensions, and which explode static conceptions of female 'passivity'. In her confronting account of Igbo women – an account which also exposes the myopia of much Western feminist criticism, and which addresses the pre- and postcolonial periods in addition to the colonial context – Ifi Amadiume[13] establishes the assertiveness of such women as it operated within the often extreme constraints imposed by colonialism. Indeed, Amadiume highlights the fact that Igbo women of eastern Nigeria have been 'universally recognized as the most militant of women' – a recognition which, revealingly, was accorded 'only after both peaceful and violent mass demonstrations, riots and finally open war with the British colonial government in 1929'.[14]

In the different world of colonial Zambia, and in her consideration of Bemba women, Jane Parpart[15] likewise probes the dual dimensions of agency and structure, and the interplay of accommodation and resistance. Parpart reveals the categories of 'accommodation' and 'resistance' to be less fixed than often imagined. With skilful mediation of her own position and an awareness of power asymmetries, Parpart shows how constraint could sometimes become opportunity. In the process, she establishes what less careful theorists of colonialism have failed to recognize: that Zambian women 'often succeeded in defending their interests even in hostile circumstances'.[16]

In such accounts, the theoretical challenge of apprehending agency is not detached from consideration of the large 'macro' processes by which individual initiative is always conditioned. It is attentiveness to the dynamics of this nexus which renders contemporary explorations of female agency so potentially valuable to the discipline of international relations, in which individual subjects – particularly colonized females – have been subsumed by the force of global processes.

How, though, might such explorations be introduced to the international relations discipline, when there exist so few precedents for cross-fertilization between gender studies and international relations *per se*? Clearly it is necessary to go beyond consideration of particular accounts, however nuanced and suggestive these may be. In what follows, I discuss a methodological approach which I consider to be especially beneficial in addressing the 'micro'/'macro', 'agency'/'structure' dynamic – a politics of the everyday. I will consider the potential of this approach with reference to fiction by African women. My aim is to show that this material offers much to the discipline of international relations in areas in which it is recognized as being deficient. I also argue that the methodology of a politics of the everyday might serve as an avenue by which such insights could be made accessible. My approach is addressed to the challenge – and, as I see it, the necessity – of combining different levels of analysis. Notwithstanding increased relaxation of disciplinary boundaries, attempts to relate levels of analysis which are often (if artificially) kept discrete remain problematic. In the discipline of international relations, the 'subjectivist' realm of imaginative literature has traditionally had little place. Yet I will argue that from the 'politics of the everyday' approach I explicate – an approach which is concerned with creative negotiation of power disparities – enlarged possibilities emerge for exploration of the different 'levels' at issue.

As Brah has argued,[17] there are two broad levels through which diversity might be conceptualized: the social structural level (which circumscribes social position, and thus has 'a crucial bearing' on the shaping of life chances); and the experiential dimension of daily life (which is necessarily more personalistic, and variously – even contradictorily – manifested). Though interrelated and interdependent, these dimensions cannot be 'read off' from one another: 'Whilst the former describes a social division, the latter draws our attention to human subjects as complex beings who are sites of multiple contradictions, *and whose everyday praxis may reinforce or undermine social divisions.*' In Brah's view, it thus becomes essential 'to examine the loci of power which produce and sustain specific forms of subjectivity'.[18] This is a task, I argue, to which a politics of the everyday as portrayed in fiction would seem especially suited.

The suggestive potential of fiction as an alternative window on 'reality' was recognized long before it was theorized. As one critic has noted, although it may be 'theoretically hazardous to draw neat parallels between fiction and life, in practice we often do read fiction as an illumination of, and commentary on, real-life predicaments'.[19] Recent work – for example, social constructionist methodological approaches, feminist (and other) deconstructions of 'objectivity', and the genre of 'faction' – has also considerably challenged the boundaries between 'fact' and 'fiction', implying the artificiality and reductionism of attempts to delineate them rigidly. A politics of the everyday is thus far from the only approach to see in fiction a rich source of insight, though it is arguably distinctive in some of the perspectives it brings to bear.

More specifically, the potential benefits of drawing on fiction in cross-cultural projects have been recognized for some time. In the minefield that is intercultural studies, literary texts are considered valuable in two major ways: in challenging familiar and unexamined assumptions and thus raising the spectre of anomaly; and in facilitating insight into the values, beliefs and conflicts of a culture which is unfamiliar.[20] Of course, mere exposure to unfamiliarity is no guarantee that reappraisal will occur; there are not only political, but also perceptual and cognitive reasons why the 'novel' – in both senses – is interpreted in light of previous expectations and prejudice. But the 'subjectivist' realm of fiction can stimulate affective and emotional capacities in ways which theoretical texts mostly do not. To the extent that intersubjectivity – the 'dialectical relationship between the subject and object of research' – is addressed, the domain of fiction assumes a potential political importance to which a politics of the everyday approach can also contribute.

Of what, then, does a politics of the everyday consist, or rather, what distinguishes the variety I endorse from the many which might be described loosely in this way? Attentiveness to the dynamics of everyday interactions is promising for several reasons. One of the most potentially enabling features of this approach for our purposes is its implicit revising of the 'insider'/'outsider' relationship. African women writers have contested modes of analysis which, while ostensibly redressing a long-standing ethnocentrism, replicate the biases and paternalism of established methodologies. Correspondingly, international relations theory is recognized to be heavily ethnocentric.[21] By focusing upon everyday transactions against their broader socio-economic backdrop, a 'politics of the everyday' approach is attuned to the numerous individual and group interventions which are neglected by many contemporary methodologies.

Although informed by contemporary currents of thought, a 'politics of the everyday' approach also challenges the underlying assumptions of many of them. For example, the current postcolonial concentration on representation is revealed to be in some respects narrowing. In suggesting the extent to which modes of portrayal are intimately linked to structures of dominance, an emphasis on representation is, of course, valuable. Among other things, it affords recognition to what might be termed the 'unofficial' exercise of power. But in light of the mutuality and (at least) 'two-way' dimensions of power relationships, it is insufficient to focus simply upon representation. Corresponding consideration must be given to the nexus between representation and resistance. Failure to explore the latter is not only to perpetuate Eurocentric approaches to a range of topics and encounters, but to deny the struggles over representation which always exist. By focusing on the reception and uses of 'representation' – by problematizing consumption, which is viewed as a creative and dynamic process rather than a passive and static function – a politics of the everyday circumvents, even dissolves, this dilemma.

As Michel de Certeau[22] has declared, 'the presence and circulation of a representation . . . tells us nothing about what it is for its users'. Indeed, through their dissection of the mechanisms of imposition, theories of representation perpetuate the very dominance they expose. By contrast, a 'politics of the everyday' approach, as elaborated by de Certeau, and on which I draw here, seeks 'to bring to light the clandestine forms taken by the dispersed, tactical, and makeshift creativity of groups or individuals already caught in the nets of "discipline"'. For de Certeau, the tactics of consumers (perhaps most significantly in the context of colonialism, but also in 'the use made by the "common people" of the culture disseminated by "elites"') comprise no less than 'the network of an antidiscipline'. As elaborated in *The Practice of Everyday Life*, his work suggests that in order to find out what a 'representation' comprises for those at the misconceptualized 'receiving end' of it, 'we must first analyse its manipulation by users who are not its makers'.[23]

The restoration of agency – via a focus on subversive capacity – is in stark contrast to approaches which, while exposing power disparities, are unable to forfeit the notion of victimhood. Of course, an approach which dispensed entirely with this concept would be as suspect as those which enshrine it. Clearly there exist inequities which no amount of attentiveness to 'agency' can conceal. Nor would a credible politics of the everyday even attempt to do so. As with the previously noted approaches of Amadiume and Parpart, it is precisely in its negotiation of power disparities that a politics of the everyday has much to contribute.

How, then, are power disparities negotiated; by what means and methods does this occur? De Certeau's distinction between a strategy and a tactic is suggestive here. A strategy is 'the calculation or manipulation of power relationships that becomes possible as soon as a subject with will and power . . . can be isolated'. It is predicated on 'a place that can be delimited as its own and serve as the base from which relations with an exteriority composed of targets or threats . . . can be managed'. By contrast, a tactic 'is a calculated action determined by the absence of a proper locus. . . . *The space of a tactic is the space of the other*.'[24] Lacking the means to 'keep to itself' (to maintain distance, foresight and self-collection), the tactic 'must play on and with a terrain imposed on it and organized by the law of a foreign power'.[25]

But tactics are also inventive, and even ingenious. Though accommodationist where necessary, they constitute modes of resistance and not only of the stronger force or party:

> Many everyday practices (talking, reading, moving about, shopping, cooking, etc.) are tactical in character. And so are, more generally, many 'ways of operating' . . . clever tricks, knowing how to get away with things, 'hunter's cunning', maneuvers, polymorphic simulations, joyful discoveries, poetic as well as warlike.[26]

Even in the seemingly most unpromising circumstances, people do not passively accept their situations. Such situations are themselves transformed through utilization of the material at hand, makeshift creativity, poetic ways of 'making do' (*bricolage*). The most circumscribed contexts do not preclude – even open up – 'spaces for games and tricks', the often subtle exploitation of which renders people 'unrecognized producers, poets of their own affairs'.[27]

The political nature of the everyday is also a valuable feature of the framework I am explicating. To the extent that individual subjects are viewed against the wider processes which influence them, 'micro' dimensions are not detached from 'macro' ones. Yet this is a politics which treats participants seriously. Consumers are recognized in their complexity; in attempting to surmount the many obstacles to their daily existences, they are more than besieged ciphers engaged in battles of wits with nameless forces. Indeed, their creative uses of such obstructions – their negotiation of them – explode the notion of consumers as 'passive' at all.

For all these reasons, I want to argue that this politics of the everyday is not only interesting, suggestive and potentially useful, but particularly so for consideration of agency in the context of international relations. In addressing the 'actor' perspectives so often unexplored in traditional methodologies, in exploring the 'space' in which subversion and 'acceptance' of dominant practices occurs and is negotiated, and in preserving the agency of anonymous 'others' in whose names, even today, Western critics still unthinkingly speak, a politics of the everyday has much to recommend it. And it is the realm of fiction which is an especially fertile one for analysis, for in fiction these daily negotiations which I am privileging are habitually explored with great creativity.

In what follows, I will refer to some short fiction included in *The Heinemann Book of African Women's Writing*, edited by Charlotte Bruner.[28] Since I will draw on four of the stories in this collection, this obviously precludes detailed appraisal of any particular one. To the extent that the 'politics of the everyday' approach I am proposing is explicitly attentive to diverse elements, *bricolage* and creative use of materials at hand, brief reference to diverse fictional contexts is probably more appropriate than the sustained consideration of particular stories which might otherwise be attempted. But in the light of my thesis about the potential of such material for the discipline of international relations, it is important to highlight that I will be as concerned with the potential limits of a 'politics of the everyday' approach as with its possibilities (thus suggesting that the benefits of a conceptual marriage may not all be one-way). The short stories of African women writers will be shown to be suggestive in both these regards.

The first story to which I will allude is 'Saltless Ash', by the Nigerian writer Zaynab Alkali. Amsa, the young protagonist of this story, knows that she will be married young, being 'well prepared, as any free-born Betadam woman should be, to shoulder her responsibilities'. Nevertheless, she is 'ill prepared for the fate that awaited her'. Instead of being betrothed to someone 'young and single', she is promised, at age 13, to a man 'almost as old as her own father'. At 14, she becomes second wife to the head of the Turabe clan – 'an enviable position to many Turabe women' – and by the age of 30 has borne him eight children.

This brief description might seem to convey a scenario in which the possibilities for female agency have been, and remain, limited. Yet Amsa 'has her foot squarely placed on the man's neck', as the saying of her people goes. For although she is 'softly spoken and not given to expressing her opinions freely', Amsa's 'ways [are] quick and calculating, alert and cunning'. This means that she can achieve her own ends 'through matrimonial diplomacy', and 'wriggle out of tight situations'. So, too, can Yabutu (the wife twenty years her senior), who despite advancing age and declining attractiveness has also employed ways of achieving her ends and protecting her interests:

> She had kicked aside all conventions in order to acquire economic independence. In different ways, the two women devised methods with which to fight for their rights as people, and none of the methods went down well with the old man.[29]

In contrasting ways, and often in collusion, both wives are subversive; able to accommodate and challenge the potentially constraining situations in which they coexist. The story revolves around the attempt of their husband to marry a new wife, an attempt which has been foiled by the two women in the past and which is foiled again in this instance. During the course of the story there are several references to the old man's foolishness. We are told 'he stomped out of the room, more like a spoilt child than an enraged adult', in response to which Amsa has 'a good laugh'. Previously she has laughed uproariously, thinking that 'men are foolish, empty idiots'. At one point her husband challenges her, 'Can't a man tell his wife what to do without argument? . . . who is the master in this house?' while 'Amsa's insides rippled with laughter which she dared not express'.

'Saltless Ash' amply and eloquently confirms the capacity of the female protagonists not only to manipulate their situations, but to make great play with constraints. Strikingly apparent in this story is the enjoyment of subversion in the circumventing of authority, not only on the part of the younger wife, but by the older, less attractive and seemingly more vulnerable wife, who is also able to influence events which concern her. The language in which this story is expressed is similarly evocative of the 'politics of the everyday' approach I have outlined. Amsa's ways are 'quick and calculating, alert and cunning'; she is given to 'manipulative strategies'. While at one level authority is 'accepted', it is simultaneously negotiated, played with and subverted.

The second story on which I will draw, 'Mother Was a Great Man', is also by a Nigerian writer, Catherine Obianuju Acholonu. In many ways this story similarly explores female agency. It also provides an interesting fictional counterpart to Amadiume's admonishment of Western critics who failed to grasp that sex and gender in West Africa need not necessarily correspond – a point also highlighted by Sekai Nzenza in the next chapter. As apparently her name suggests, Oyidiya is 'the woman that resembled a man'. Her husband Nekwe – with whom she 'had almost exchanged roles' – 'was not the manly type': 'Was it not she, Oyidiya, who had to stand on her feet and defend her family whenever another family challenged it? How often did she have to defend her husband against his fellow men?'

But Oyidiya has become 'very old, and she had suffered a lot, chasing after a male issue which had always eluded her'. As the first daughter of an Igbo family, she had enjoyed position and status. In contrast to other girls of her age, she had grown up 'with the exuberance and freedom that was allowed only to boys'. Thus there is great irony – an irony felt keenly by Oyidiya – in the fact that 'she who had been a highly desired daughter' now risked forfeiture of anticipated privileges 'because she had no male issue'. The story relates her only partially successful attempts to acquire a son. For while she finally does gain a male child (via her second *wife* – Western critics take note!), the boy is 'a cheat, a liar, a thief' and 'a glutton', and at the time of the setting of the story is about to be executed for armed robbery. This induces great guilt in Oyidiya, and shatters her peace of mind: she had 'indulged in excesses for which she was now paying. . . . She, Oyidiya, had gone too far. She had not accepted her lot. She had forced the hand of her *chi*. And now this was the result.'[30]

'Mother Was a Great Man' is a complex and challenging story, conveying the veneration of African women which yet does not absolve them from the cultural imperative of producing a son. The story is ambiguous in its mediation of these 'realities'. How are we to view Oyidiya, whose death signals the end of the story? Her expressed regret and suffering over 'not accepting her lot' are arguably more than counterbalanced by the determination and relentlessness with which she has always attempted to orchestrate and improve her family's fortunes. As one who exploited every avenue in pursuit of her goals – and who, if she 'lost' in one sense, seems triumphantly defiant in another – Oyidiya defies easy categorization. For all her self-recrimination, she is certainly no orthodox 'victim'.

The third story I want to draw from – 'Regina's Baby', by Jean Marquard – presents a contrast in its evocation of differences among women. Marquard, as a white South African, necessarily has a vantage point different from those of the countless women who were directly oppressed by the colonialism of apartheid. Through the conflict and unease Mrs Jackson experiences in relating to her black maid, Regina, 'Regina's Baby' explores and dissects a privileged white female subjectivity.

The passage from which I quote evokes Mrs Jackson's perceptions of Regina's room, to which she has gone, in arrested empathy, to tell Regina of the death of her baby daughter. It is a room, we are told, which reminds her of the 'impersonal, odourless, virginally bland' cubicles of the boarding-school she attended. But despite this superficial similarity, there is a more significant difference. For while the school cubicles had 'carried the message of an essential abdication', Regina's room, by contrast, conveys 'an aura of intense, furtive life, the vivid smell of personal activity'. The careful neatness

> is only the surface. There is another kind of life in the room, a smokiness of corporate energy; the evidence, dense but invisible, of bodies other than Regina's tiny frame. She has women friends but she also has men in here.[31]

In the sense of the covert, intangible but extremely potent 'uses' to which something assigned and imposed can be put (becoming, in the process, 'something else'), this passage strikingly actualizes the politics of the everyday I have discussed. Vividly conveyed is the vibrancy of Regina, and her ability to transform with vitality the austere and bleak domain she is obliged to inhabit. Also vividly conveyed is the sense of unease and disquiet she instils in her white mistress, who senses 'something threatening' as a result. That this sense of threat to the objectively powerful party is seemingly induced unwittingly – as an unintended by-product, as it were, of Regina's attempt to 'make do' – is both illustration and powerful confirmation of a politics of the everyday in action.

I now want to move to a story which I feel to be more ambiguous in its affirmation of the insights of a politics of the everyday. This story – 'Lakshmi's Gift', by Ananda Devi – is written by an Indian woman from Mauritius. It dwells in unremitting detail on the hardships of the protagonist: 'worn out' by work in the fields and 'endless cycles of pregnancies'. As a result she has been drained of almost all animation. Shanti's physical surroundings are a sad reflection of her mental and bodily exhaustion:

> And the house, with its bare, austere interior, on whose walls no shred of fantasy hung, no breath of folly, where no secret double life, no caprice, could hide; the house that has become a prison, cramping her personality, curbing her smallest desires. A relentless routine with no place for pleasure or rejoicing.[32]

This description is unequivocal; the possibility of 'subversive space' is precluded. There are references to Shanti's 'shattered illusions and spirits, dampened by her daily life'. Almost the only anticipation is that of old age, 'with its prospect of an existence as uniformly ugly, grey, colourless as a shroud of rain, without a single well of happiness from which to drink deeply a strong desire to live. Wherever she looked, wherever she turned, she saw the same lowering horizons, drained of colour, cloudy, heavy with a lucidity too bitter for rebellion or rejection of the inevitable.'[33] To see in such descriptions any joy in subterfuge, possibility of ruse or capacity to mediate is surely to impose a reading that the text explicitly precludes. This is not only despite but because of the hope that still kindles in Shanti annually as she awaits a visit from the goddess Lakshmi.

It is possible to read 'Lakshmi's Gift' as a tribute to its protagonist's enormous inner reserves; even, though somewhat ambiguously, to the eventual rewarding of them. But I would argue that this particular story illustrates the limits of an approach which stresses the capacity of individuals and groups to 'use' the contexts which constrain them. There is something qualitatively different about Shanti's 'resistance', which is in sharp contrast to the joyful manipulations and subterfuges of the two wives in Alkali's 'Saltless Ash', to the robust ploys of Oyidiya in Obianuju Acholonu's 'Mother Was a Great Man', and to the covert vibrancy of Regina in Marquard's 'Regina's Baby'. To focus on Shanti's resilience is surely to come close to adopting such language and sentiments as 'the triumph of the human spirit', and a determination to recognize it which illegitimately de-emphasizes the human toll exacted.

This brings me to a pertinent critique of methodological approaches which – to slightly reword a criticism made by Lila Abu-Lughod[34] – risk 'romancing resistance'. Abu-Lughod spent a decade doing fieldwork among Egyptian Bedouin women, and herself considered ways in which storytelling, jokes, songs and poems comprise modes of female resistance. Yet she is also concerned about 'the implications of studies of resistance for our theories of power', in that some such studies (even when sophisticated) betray 'a tendency to romanticize resistance, to read all forms of resistance as signs of the ineffectiveness of systems of power and of the resilience and creativity of the human spirit in its refusal to be dominated'.[35] There are aspects of this critique which do not apply to the 'politics of the everyday' approach I have discussed. The very dependence of 'spaces for games and tricks' on the repressive contexts which generate them ensures that the links between 'power' and 'resistance' are not severed by de Certeau. Nevertheless, and as my reading of Ananda Devi's story 'Lakshmi's Gift' suggests, there is a sense in which Abu-Lughod's critique reveals a weakness to which 'politics of the everyday' approaches are vulnerable.

It is this potential vulnerability which also raises the possibility that disciplinary international relations may in turn furnish perspectives which enhance a politics of the everyday. For while I have been at pains to establish that emphasis on the negotiation of power disparities ensures that 'micro' dimensions of social reality are not detached from 'macro' ones (and that this is precisely the ground on which the politics of the everyday I elaborate has much to offer the international relations discipline), prime concern with creative negotiation of such inequities is problematic as well as salutary. This is because it can entail a blurring of, and shift of focus from, the real and continuing power disparities which, though never ignored by the approach I am discussing, tend, as a corollary, not to be emphasized by it. Conversely, it is with the 'larger', 'impersonal' forces which tend to circumscribe individual action that the discipline of international relations is concerned. In their respective axes of emphasis – the (necessarily) 'micro' bias of a politics of the everyday and the (necessarily) 'macro' bias of a discipline which privileges international processes – a politics of the everyday and the discipline of international relations may not only be contrasting, but in important respects complementary.

As part of the wider scholarly project in which the dualisms of agency/structure, micro/macro and subjective/objective are being contested, the need for methodologies attuned to the relationship between these dimensions is imperative. De Certeau is adamant that the 'politics of ploys' which should be developed must address the public aspects 'of the microscopic, multiform, and innumerable connections'[36] between small-scale 'tactics' and the 'strategies' they subvert (as well as accommodate). To contend that delineation of such 'connections' is not, in his approach, as clear as it needs to be is to highlight that, of itself, no single methodology can address all the levels of analysis necessary for such linkages to be apprehended. It is also to highlight the as yet uncharted potential of exploration of a politics of the everyday within the context of the international relations discipline.

Within the discipline of international relations, and as a corollary of the long-standing silence on gender issues, questions of 'the everyday' and of the agency exercised by individual subjects have scarcely been recognized, much less addressed. In contrast, this chapter has begun to explore these issues as they pertain to women and colonialism. It has been argued that consideration of the questions surrounding female agency in the context(s) of colonialism is salutary not only for what it reveals of the differences between women, but for its discrediting of the perception that colonized women were themselves silent in the face of European incursion.

During the course of my analysis, I have drawn on diverse material. Such eclecticism of approach has been necessary, since in the absence of wide-ranging and nuanced methodological perspectives, attempts to delineate female agency will fail to address a crucial dynamic. Thus it is not enough to highlight the work of individual scholars such as Ifi Amadiume and Jane Parpart, important though it is that such critique is brought to the attention of receptive students of international relations. Raising broader theoretical and methodological questions is preparatory to any work within international relations which seeks to overcome the discipline's continuing silence on gender issues.

The dynamics of the 'micro'–'macro' relationship, as of the 'agency'–'structure' relationship, present perennial and formidable conceptual challenges. This is especially so in the case of international relations, where the structural has received such heavy emphasis. Partly because of the long-standing predominance of 'realism', the realm of the everyday has been excluded from consideration. Given the similar neglect of gender and female agency, a 'politics of the everyday' methodology suggests one possible corrective, even as such an approach may itself need refining in light of the new insights its application to international relations studies will yield.

The immediate relevance of such a synthesis is not the issue here. We cannot know in advance what the short-term and longer-term benefits might be to a discipline which has so marginalized and excluded the dimensions that would be systematically explored by the approach I propose. My point is that the acknowledged lacuna within the discipline of international relations regarding gender, agency and the everyday requires urgent redressing, and that application of a politics of the everyday suggests one avenue through which recuperative efforts might be pursued.

Notes

1. For an introduction to the neglect and diminution of gender in international relations see Rebecca Grant , 'The sources of gender bias in international relations theory' in Rebecca Grant and Kathleen Newland (eds), *Gender and International Relations* (Buckingham, Open University Press, 1991), p. 8; J. Ann Tickner, 'Hans Morgenthau's principles of political realism: a feminist reformulation', ibid., p. 28; and Fred Halliday, 'Hidden from international relations: women and the international arena', ibid., p. 158.

2. Mona Etienne and Eleanor Leacock (eds), *Women and Colonization: Anthropological Perspectives* (New York, Praeger, 1980), p. 17.

3. Ibid., p. 17.

4. Kathleen Staudt, 'Women's politics, the state, and capitalist transformation in Africa' in Irving Leonard Markovitz (ed.), *Studies in Power and Class in Africa* (Oxford, Oxford University Press, 1987), p. 194.

5. Ibid.

6. Irving Leonard Markovitz, 'The consolidation of power: woman's role in political and economic transformation', ibid., p. 189.

7. Staudt, 'Women's politics', p. 201.

8. Anthony Elliott, *Social Theory and Psychoanalysis in Transition: Self and Society from Freud to Kristeva* (Oxford, Blackwell, 1992), p. 258.

9. Maureen Mahoney and Barbara Yngvesson, 'The construction of subjectivity and the paradox of resistance: reintegrating feminist anthropology and psychology', *Signs*, 18:1 (1992), 44.

10. See for example Nupur Chauduri and Margaret Strobel (eds), *Western Women and Imperialism: Complicity and Resistance* (Bloomington, Indiana University Press, 1992); Margaret Strobel, *European Women and the Second British Empire* (Bloomington, Indiana University Press, 1991); Margaret Jolly, 'Colonizing women: the maternal body and empire' in Sneja Gunew and Anna Yeatman (eds), *Feminism and the Politics of Difference* (St Leonards, Allen and Unwin, 1993), pp. 103–27; and Helen Callaway, *Gender, Culture and Empire: European Women in Colonial Nigeria* (London, Macmillan, 1987).

11. Arlene Elowe MacLeod, 'Hegemonic relations and gender resistance: the new veiling as accommodating protest in Cairo', *Signs*, 17:3 (1992), 553–7.

12. Ibid., p. 537.

13. Ifi Amadiume, *Male Daughters, Female Husbands: Gender and Sex in an African Society* (London, Zed Books, 1987).

14. Ibid., p. 13.

15. Jane L. Parpart, 'Sexuality and power on the Zambian copperbelt: 1926–1964' in Jane L. Parpart and Sharon B. Stichter (eds), *Patriarchy and Class: African Women in the Home and the Workforce* (Boulder, CO, Westview Press, 1988), pp. 115–38.

16. Ibid., p. 134.

17. Avtar Brah, 'Questions of difference and international feminism' in Stevi Jackson (ed.), *Women's Studies: A Reader* (New York, Harvester Wheatsheaf, 1993), p. 30.

18. Ibid., p. 33; emphasis added.

19. Susan Rubin Suleiman, 'On maternal splitting: à propos of Mary Gordon's *Men and Angels*', *Signs*, 14:1 (1988), 40.

20. Lothar Bredella, 'How is intercultural understanding possible?' in Lothar Bredella and Dietmar Haack (eds), *Perception and Misconception* (Tübingen, Gunter Naur Verlag, 1988), p. 21.

21. See, for example, K. J. Holsti, *The Dividing Discipline: Hegemony and Diversity in International Theory* (Boston, Allen and Unwin, 1985), p. ix; and Steve Smith, *International Relations: British and American Perspectives* (Oxford, Blackwell, 1985), p. x.

22. Michel de Certeau, *The Practice of Everyday Life* (Berkeley, University of California Press, 1984).

23. Ibid., p. xiii.

24. Ibid., p. 37; emphasis added.

25. Ibid., p. xxx.
26. Ibid., p. xix.
27. Ibid., p. 34.
28. Charlotte H. Bruner (ed.), *The Heinemann Book of African Women's Writing* (Oxford, Heinemann, 1993).
29. Ibid., p. 27.
30. Ibid., p. 9.
31. Ibid., pp. 118–19.
32. Ibid., p. 86.
33. Ibid. pp. 87–8.
34. Lila Abu-Lughod, 'The romance of resistance' in Jackson (ed.), *Women's Studies*, pp. 102–4.
35. Ibid., p. 103.
36. De Certeau, *The Practice of Everyday Life*, p. xxiv; emphasis added.

CHAPTER TEN

Women in postcolonial Africa: between African men and Western feminists

SEKAI NZENZA

Recently, I returned to the village in south-east Zimbabwe where I was born. After the usual greetings, my mother told me that everyone was well except for my brother's wife, Mai Shuvai: 'She has not spoken for two days, neither has she moved nor eaten anything.' My nursing experience prompted me to walk the few yards to my sister-in-law's house. Mai Shuvai sat with her back resting against the wall and her legs outstretched, arms folded and eyes fixed into the fireplace. She did not look physically ill nor did she appear to be in pain. Her face was expressionless. My efforts to greet her received no response. We all watched her for some time until my mother suggested that we leave her until the next morning.

Outside, my brother whispered that he had always suspected that his wife was possessed by a bad spirit and if she was not possessed, then she was simply in need of a psychiatrist. My mother replied that her illness could not be treated by Western doctors. At dawn, my mother walked across the river, returning just after sunrise with VaKariwo, my grandfather's sister, now in her late eighties.

A few hours later, VaKariwo summoned all the village elders and most close relatives including my aunts, uncles, cousins and their wives. She then ordered three women to carry Mai Shuvai out of her hut. Mai Shuvai made no effort to help the women lift her. They placed her on a mat where she sat with her eyes looking straight past her husband into the distance. What if there was something terribly wrong with her? What if she were to suddenly lapse into a coma? How could we get her to the hospital 200 kilometres away, given the lack of any form of transport and given the fact the daily bus had already left for the city in the morning?

I resigned myself to the fact that we might be waiting for a tragedy to happen in front of our eyes.

VaKariwo then ordered my brother to kneel down in front of Mai Shuvai and called her by the totem of her ancestors. My brother complied but Mai Shuvai did not speak or move. Then my three uncles were asked to do the same but to no avail. VaKariwo sat cross-legged and took her snuff quietly for some minutes, contemplating the problem. Everyone waited in dead silence. Then VaKariwo looked through the group of people and pointed at me. She summoned me to stand up.

'You are the sister-husband', she said. 'Speak to your wife. Tell her that as human beings we make mistakes. Ask her what troubles her so. You are her sister-husband: speak to your wife.'

Not fully understanding what it all meant, I did as I was told. To my surprise, Mai Shuvai quickly rose up from her stupor. There was no mistaking the anger in her voice. She confronted my brother and screamed 'Why have you cheated me? Why do you want to take another wife?'

VaKariwo chuckled to herself quietly. The people listened, obviously relieved to know that there was nothing physically wrong with Mai Shuvai. Mai Shuvai then gave a long speech, saying how she valued her relationship with her husband and how she had always believed that he was a good Catholic and would not take a second wife given the fact that he had six children to look after. VaKariwo thanked Mai Shuvai and told her to sit down.

Some of the men mumbled that such a situation did not warrant a *bopoto*.[1] The men then asked my brother eagerly about who the new wife was going to be, but the younger women shook their heads in disapproval.

'Not these days', said one woman. 'You cannot take a second wife. What if she has AIDS? And how is he going to support her in this drought?'

'If you do not shout out your anger, the noise within will suffocate you', VaKariwo said. 'We thank you for letting us know your grievances. Your silence has been heard. In the old days, I would have said that your noise has been too loud. But these days, we cannot tell you what to do because we cannot feed your children. This is a matter between yourself, your mother-in-law and your husband.'

My mother agreed and everyone dispersed. Mai Shuvai then shook my hand and humbly asked about my health in the manner that Shona wives use to demonstrate respect for their husband's sisters.

I can almost hear many African literary critics agreeing with the men in my village: Mai Shuvai has made too much 'noise'[2] on a simple matter. Some Western feminist theorists may not even hear Mai Shuvai's message. Distancing myself a little from the story, I am immediately faced with the question of interpreting it.

Finding what might be an appropriate model presents something of a dilemma, for notwithstanding the confident pronouncements of the committed that issues of gender, race and cultural difference can readily be negotiated, I find as an African woman that the obstacles to understanding remain significant. More often than not, cultural sensitivity is only a matter of gesture. The difficulty is compounded by the problems and possibilities of high theory which at present is the chosen mode of articulation. On the one hand, I recognize its enabling potential and the fact that it cannot be shut out of African thinking. On the other, it is very distant from our experience and it is, after all, understood only by a small elite, largely in the Western world.

I want to argue that African women are caught between two opposing streams of thought – between masculinist African national discourse and that of white Western feminist scholarship. It is my contention that the two dominant paradigms do not enable us to comprehend the ambiguities of African women's cultural identity. Under the rhetoric of racial and cultural retrieval, the African writer has relegated gender to the margins. Similarly, in the name of feminism and sisterhood, the white feminist has universalized her own experience and in the process has appropriated the experiences of African women, thus silencing them. The first part of this chapter attempts to trace patterns of gender representation in the writing of African males and identify areas that circumscribe women as well as to acknowledge roles or situations which empower them. The second part addresses the current debate about the relationship between African women and Western feminists. I will then focus on selected novels by Flora Nwapa and Buchi Emecheta and argue that, contrary to the purported extremes of submissiveness or assertiveness of African women, they have always had distinctive modes of speaking which indicate a more 'in-between' position. Modes of speaking, I will insist, can be best understood if we follow the perceived rituals of womanhood such as marriage, motherhood, polygamy and economic independence. Throughout these rituals, the issue is not that the women have been silent, but that they were not heard or understood. In addressing the literature of African women, I will ponder the nature of African women's aesthetics. To what extent do African women subvert the dominant African nationalist discourse? What are the issues that concern African women and how do these issues differ from those which preoccupy Western feminists? In what ways do women negotiate matters of resistance and agency? I should emphasize that I do not pretend to settle these issues. However, I hope to add to the current argument by highlighting the fact that African women are 'making noise'. While the noise of the 'subaltern' may not be recognized for what it is, if we listen carefully to the nuances of meanings it will become apparent that the women are in fact speaking, and in different voices. We will notice that the voices vary across regions, ethnicities, languages and class. None the less, they do carry the historical marks of colonial and patriarchal domination and therefore have certain features in common.

In his commitment to cultural retrieval, the African male writer aimed to correct the distorted images of Africans in colonial literature, history and anthropology. However, because of insensitivity to the issues of gender involved, the quest for national cultural identity was carried out in masculine terms. Apart from perpetuating the gender stereotypes in colonial literature, the African male writer also created new mythical images of womanhood. The significance of this for international relations should be noted immediately. As a consequence of the processes of imperial intervention and denigration, a new patriarchal order was ushered in. In their desire to set right the wrongs visited upon African societies, male indigenous writers, unintentionally no doubt, subordinated African women to wider racial and cultural interests. Their writing was widely read throughout the continent, and it was years before its loaded politics came to be appreciated. African literature thus served – and continues to serve – as a conduit between the international, the African and the local.

In tracing patterns of representation of women in male literature, the lack of women characters in African fiction during the late 1950s and early 1960s presents a problem. An overview of the novels written during this period, from Chinua Achebe to later writers such as the Zimbabwean Shimmer Chinodya, reveals that women appear in novels as appendages to the men – with a few exceptions, such as Cyprian Ekwenzi's *Jagua Nana* and Nuruddin Farah's *From a Crooked Rib*.[3] If the novel constituted a kind of masculinist retrieval of self, how are we to interpret women's roles when the women are absent? Since the African woman always appears attached to a male hero, we can to some degree trace her pattern of development by focusing on her interaction with the hero. But this approach has obvious limitations because it emphasizes the dominant role of men and presents women simply in their role as subordinate partners. It is my claim that even in these novels the women should be seen as far more powerful than has usually been the case. Tentative glimpses may be had of the distinctive and separate worlds of African women. In ways not always intended by the male novelists themselves, women's voices emerge: falteringly, quietly and not unproblematically; but never is woman silenced. This has eluded most commentators and leads us, if not to reject the received interpretation of the nationalist novel as patriarchal, at least to revise our assumptions that women characters are voiceless and passive. I would therefore like to move beyond the patriarchal hero and attempt to enter the separate world of women. It is pertinent to recall, in this context, that understandings of womanhood differ from culture to culture. For example, Mwangi Ruheni's portrayal of motherhood in a Kikuyu home in postcolonial Kenya differs from Achebe's images in precolonial Nigeria. Historical and cultural specificity are therefore important considerations to bear in mind. In the following section I will examine the roles of African women in novels with village settings, especially Achebe's *Things Fall Apart* and Elechi Amadi's *The Concubine*.[4] Although my principal concern is with these two novels, I will, where appropriate, also reach out to other novels in search of examples illustrating particular points.

Before I analyse images of women in Achebe's and Amadi's novels, a brief historical background to the popular image of woman as mother is necessary. Colonial imagination presented African women as symbols of negative sexuality and debasement. Furthermore, the African woman represented metaphoric images of the continent – passively waiting to be conquered, raped and dominated. Allegorical linkages between woman and the continent also gained appeal during the Negritude movement. But no longer was woman a symbol of debased sexuality but, instead, of Mother Africa – nurturing, long-suffering and forgiving. Negritude writers attempted to reclaim Africa's past as if African traditions had been static before and after colonialism. The Mother Africa trope, as Florence Stratton has argued, pervades much of African male literature.[5] Images of woman as a symbol of the state meant that the role of women as women was never fully realized; her everyday experiences were dismissed from view as trivial, or not noticed at all. When woman is not representing the state, she becomes woman as mother – a pillar of strength and stability. Thus, a conception of the traditional village woman remains the bedrock of much writing about Africa. In *Things Fall Apart*,[6] Achebe set a precedent by creating a hypermasculine hero who seems to exercise complete power and dominance over his wives. Whenever women appear, they are seen performing traditional roles associated with the feminine. In fact, there is a separate world of women which seems to revolve around the private sphere. Yet, despite their confinement to small, peripheral spaces and roles, there are intimations that women were not as passive as portrayed in the main lines of the text.

In writing *Things Fall Apart*, Achebe set out to restore history, voice and subjectivity to the African. He succeeded in doing just that except in terms of gender. We see very little of the women. Okonkwo is portrayed as an aggressive 'man of action, a man of war. Unlike his father, he could stand the look of blood.' The position of women as victims of Okonkwo's power is illustrated when he beats his wife for 'mumbling something about guns that fail to fire'. That Okonkwo is a hypermasculine figure has been discussed by several feminist critics.[7] Although I would agree, to an extent, that Chinua Achebe's portrayal of women is sexist, I want to argue that Okonkwo's dominance has been exaggerated. By focusing on Okonkwo's masculine strength, we run the risk of ignoring some aspects of male weakness or insecurity which are not so explicit.[8] In one of his essays, Achebe quotes an Igbo proverb which says: 'Where one thing stands, another will stand beside it.'[9] Seen in this light, as Obioma Nnaemeka has noted, Okonkwo is a complex man imbued with both feminine and masculine principles.[10] His dominance cannot survive without his acknowledgment of the 'female principle'. Achebe tells us that Okonkwo, totally obsessed with his power, offends the female gods three times. First, he offends the Earth Goddess by beating his wife in the Week of Peace. Second, he infuriates the Earth Goddess by killing Ikemefuna, a child under his guardianship. Third, he accidentally kills a man during a festival, and retribution for this crime involves a period of exile in his motherland. It is during his period in Mbanta that Okonkwo's uncle teaches him about the values of motherhood and the philosophy of suffering. Long suffering is part of the process of motherhood. Although we do not have images of women deriving power and status from motherhood, we do know that motherhood defines self-worth. One such example is shown by Ekwefi in her desire to have a child. Ekwefi prays hard and loses three children before she is 'rewarded' with Ezinma.

Although most representations of women in the novel show them in a subservient position, Achebe's depiction of Chielo clearly indicates that women can transcend their given roles through the medium of religion. Despite Okonkwo's masculine attributes, he recoils in fear one night when he and Ekwefi follow the goddess Chielo. Chielo carries Ezinma to visit the goddess. Agbala and Okonkwo and Ekwefi follow. At one stage, Okonkwo pauses to listen:

> But at that very moment Chielo's voice rose again in her possessed chanting and Ekwefi recoiled, because there was no humanity there. It was not the same Chielo who sat with her in the market. . . . It was a different woman – the priestess Agbala, the Oracle of the Hills and Caves.[11]

In another incident, we are reminded that motherhood and the position of senior wife accord women with power and status. Consider, for example, the ceremony at Nwakibie's house. After Okonkwo had tasted the wine, his host, Nwakibie, specifically asks for his first wife, and when she appears, the other three wives wait for her to drink the wine before they do. Achebe's description of Anasi is particularly striking:

> Anasi was a middle-aged woman, tall and strongly built. There was authority in her bearing and she looked every inch the ruler of the womenfolk in a large and prosperous family. She wore the anklet of her husband's titles, which the first wife alone could wear.[12]

Polygamy is taken here as unproblematic, and women appear to be comfortable in their respective places as junior wives. A sense of order and a recognition of male power exists between Nwakibie and his wives. To judge from the ceremony at Nwakibie's compound, it is quite clear that there are separate worlds for men and women. Yet we do not know what happens in the women's rooms or the women's world. Without knowledge of their thoughts and experiences we can only say that in polygamous households the senior wife, at least, enjoys power, and that the status of all the women is enhanced by age and motherhood. The women may have been discontented with their situation but to argue that they are victims can only be based on an assumption.

In *The Concubine*, Amadi, like Achebe, presents a cohesive precolonial society where gender relationships are structured by tradition, propriety and orderly behaviour. Motherhood determines a woman's position in society, while love and sex are kept in their respective spheres as prescribed by traditional practice. Unlike in Western society, there is no room for romantic love, because 'if a woman could not marry one man she could marry another'.[13] In addition, a woman's display of 'excessive or fanatical behaviour' is 'frowned upon and even described as crazy'.[14] We are given the impression that Ihuoma, the main protagonist, is well adjusted to the demands of her society. Patriarchal dominance is accepted as normal and natural. In fact, descriptions of Ihuoma reveal almost more about Emenike, her husband, than about herself as a person. We are told that at the age of 22 she is a mother of three children, calls her husband 'my Lord' and her plump features show that she is 'enjoying her husband's wealth'. In many ways, Ihuoma and Emenike's relationship epitomizes a romantic ideal. But, after Emenike's death, it is revealed that Ihuoma is not simply a beautiful woman but that she is the wife of a jealous Sea King who brings evil and death to all her suitors. Amadi's transformation of Ihuoma from a submissive mother to a threatening, mysterious and mythical *femme fatale* is ambiguous and contradictory. None the less, one significant point emerges from this characterization: Ihuoma is not what she appears on the surface. In fact, Amadi makes clear that Ihuoma had always been a restless individual. Nor does she reveal her feelings, even towards Ekwueme:

> Whatever she felt was safely locked up in her mind. Not even her mother could probe into the depths and wrench her secrets. She had admitted to herself that she liked Ekwe very much. But what woman does not like a man? Her liking for Ekwe was not frantic or sudden. It had grown over a long period. Since it did not take her by surprise, she was able to keep it firmly under her control.[15]

In essence, Ihuoma's mind cannot be penetrated because not only does she not express her thoughts, but her power over men is linked to the supernatural. At first, Amadi appears to suggest that in 'normal' circumstances women are submissive and nurturing mothers. But Ekweume's second wife, Ahurole, represents another contradictory image of womanhood. Ahurole reacts to her forced marriage to Ekweume with bouts of sulking, anger, sobbing and laughter. She constantly engages in 'irrational and childish' arguments with her husband. Finding no explanation for such 'stubbornness' in a young girl, her family assume that Ahurole is possessed by an *agwu* or evil spirit. So far, Amadi's attempts to represent African womanhood have pointed to two individuals whose identities are ambiguous. As such, the reader gets the impression that even in precolonial society, women attempted to speak, and when they did so there was an element of the extraordinary, linked to some supernatural influence. More importantly, women had the capacity to transcend given roles, although, as mothers, these roles appear to be limited.

Another significant theme emerging from the male-authored text is the relationship between the hero and his mother. Quite often, there is an account of the hero's journey from the city back to the village. In the city, the hero experiences the alienation and disillusionment associated with colonial or postcolonial modernity. Restless and lost, he returns to the village, where his mother has been patiently waiting for him. The mother's allegorical role is described by Chidi Amuta in terms of the longing for a romantic and 'pristine' maternal 'breast' which has been destroyed by colonialism.[16] Amuta's account appears to fit the situation of several heroes in African fiction. For them, the mother figure symbolizes Africa – nurturing and unchanging. For example in *No Longer at Ease*,[17] when Obi returns home after some years in England he romanticizes about his mother. Despite her ill-health and the task of raising eight children, Obi's mother remains a symbol of the stability of village values. Similarly, in *Jagua Nana*, Jagua returns to the village and is warmly welcomed by her mother: 'Mother. Sweet and trusting and so kind. She had aged terribly, suddenly, she was speaking to me as if she had *known* that Jagua would return one day, and for good.'[18] Images of 'sweet' long-suffering mothers are to be found in other African novels. The mothers' modes of resistance against the oppressive patriarchal colonial and/or traditional systems are not so explicit.

I would also like to draw attention to other areas of resistance so far neglected in the study of African novels. Women as grandmothers are invested with power and wisdom in African societies. My story at the beginning of this chapter is intended to exemplify this fact. In Ngugi wa Thiongo's *Petals of Blood*,[19] Nyakunia is a pillar of strength for Wanja, Karega and Munira. She is a storehouse of oral history and of the tradition and culture of Old Ilmorog. Through Nyakunia, the power and wisdom of old age is celebrated. In Charles Mungoshi's *Waiting for the Rain*,[20] Matandangoma and Old Japi are respected and listened to by the community. Mungoshi says the inspiration for creating a grandmother like Old Japi came from memories of his own grandmother: 'She had this herd of goats and cattle. She would kill, sell everything by herself. She lived alone. . . . She had a terrible range of vocabulary. She had a terrible mouth.'[21] Mungoshi also presents another way through which women could exercise power: that of spirit possession. Like Chielo in *Things Fall Apart*, Matandangoma speaks with authority when under spirit possession. The dual attributes of her role as grandmother and as a spirit medium accord Matandangoma a position of power despite her gender. Thus, although women may appear silent and submissive in the canon of African literature, beneath the surface of many of the texts their position is a good deal less circumscribed.

Then along comes the Western feminist critic. Now it should be said that Western feminists have worked to recover the voices of African women in African literature. The amount of work done by Western women is commendable. Moreover, they have been at the forefront of gender criticism of the predominantly male canon. None the less, with respect to the theorizing of African women's literature from a specific Western perspective, I share Achebe's concerns when he argues that 'We are not opposed to criticism but we are getting weary of all the special types of criticism which has been designed for us by people whose knowledge of us is very limited'.[22]

In line with the contemporary interest in issues of positionality, and as questions of speaking and silence continue to gain momentum, we should open up the debate about who should be speaking for African woman. To what extent can Western feminist critics distance themselves from their own Anglo-Saxon, American or European cultural values and interpret the African woman's experiences? Do not such critics run the risk of projecting their own views and values on to African woman? What are the origins of the authority which accords the Western feminist the right and power to represent, interpret and give meaning to African cultures whose history, language and social organizations are vastly different from her own?

There is also the colonialist trap of reading one particular event in a text and regarding it as anthropological and representative of a community or a society. This mimesis does not apply only to literary criticism. Achebe's *Things Fall Apart*, for example, has been translated into many languages, and has come to serve as an insight into all African cultures for non-Africans, as if these cultures were monolithic or homogeneous. In the same vein, critics have a tendency to ignore the historical and cultural specificity of African women's situations. Commonality in gender alone should not provide authority to speak for African women. Speaking about and on behalf of marginalized women can all too easily give rise to power relations of domination. Linda Alcoff reminds us that within feminist circles, speaking for others is becoming increasingly problematic. For Alcoff, the practice of privileged people speaking for or on behalf of less privileged persons has actually 'resulted [in many cases] in increasing or reinforcing the oppression of the group spoken for'.[23]

The critic's insensitivity to cultural particularity of gender relations can also lead to a misreading of the texts. For example, in reading novels by African writers, the feminist often exaggerates the power of men. Stratton is one prominent critic who does so consistently.[24] Referring to both *Things Fall Apart* and *The Concubine*, Stratton sees the narratives as 'thoroughly misogynistic' and as working to 'reinforce patriarchal ideology'.[25] Like many other feminists, Stratton reads conceptions of patriarchy from a specifically Western feminist perspective. She justifies this approach on the premise that 'despite specificity in its manifestations [it has] a cultural constant: patriarchy'.[26] Indeed, for Stratton 'all historical societies are patriarchal'.

However, Stratton does not ask what African women themselves think of Western feminist interpretation of their worlds. For African women, Western feminism (in its many varieties) emanates from the experiences of white middle-class women whose main concern is gender discrimination. Yet for many African women, gender exploitation is not the only form of oppression. There are, perhaps, more immediate and pressing concerns: poverty, illiteracy, inadequate health, lack of water, malnutrition and AIDS. In this context fighting patriarchy may appear rather abstract. Overcoming male dominance is indeed important, but 'first things first'.[27] And did we not neglect the fight against traditional patriarchy because we gave priority to national independence? I am not suggesting that challenging patriarchy in postcolonial Africa is not important. To the contrary, I am asserting that the solidarity we are getting from our sisters in the West may be silencing us, and notwithstanding that it is well-intentioned, it may be a form of cultural imperialism.

It is by now a truism that the relationship between researcher and the object of study is one of power and privilege. In her essay 'Under Western eyes', C. T. Mohanty uncovers how universalistic claims of womanhood produce relations of power and dominance between Third World women and Western feminists. We must take note of her recommendation that Western feminist scholarship begin to examine its role in the relations of power and knowledge production.[28]

Under traditional feminist paradigms, issues of race and difference are subsumed by the category of gender. Glossing over racial differences is a recurrring problem in Western feminism. There is a common assumption that by virtue of taking an interest in, or writing about, African women, one becomes culturally neutral or non-racial. Yet if race and gender shape the identities, privileges and cultural beliefs of African women, why should the same differentiation not apply to white women? As Ruth Frankenburg has observed, 'whiteness is a location of structural advantage, of race privilege'.[29] It may be the case that white feminists no longer allow race to determine the way they view African women's history and literature but for African women the idea of whiteness is still linked to various forms of dominance despite the claims of universal sisterhood. Furthermore, by universalizing women's experiences, the Western feminist marginalizes African women in what bell hooks has called 'the commodification of otherness'.[30] And we should note that colonialism is not a matter of the past: African women still feel its effects in their everyday life. It must also be recalled that it was usual in much Western feminist scholarship to portray African women under colonialism as weak and powerless.[31] This 'victims approach' works to silence those whose interests it purports to advance.

By asking who should be speaking, I hasten to add that I am not suggesting that the study of African women is the territory of African women only. Rather, I am proposing that anyone who theorizes about African women must first learn to appreciate the cultural differences that exist within Africa and between Africa and the Western world. More importantly, the critic needs to acknowledge the differences and distances between African women's concerns and those of their Western counterparts. Those with a limited experience of the African world need to be cautious in interpreting it. I therefore share Soyinka's belief that the rejection of difference by Western critics subjects Africans to 'a second epoch of colonialization' whereby African cultures are universalized by 'individuals whose theories and prescriptions are derived from the apprehension of *their* world and *their* history, *their* social neuroses and *their* value systems'.[32] Such hegemonic dominance also applies to mainstream Western women's theorization of African women's experiences.

Let us now turn to the writing of African women themselves. What do they contribute to the question of African women's passivity and silence? We have seen how traditional cultures have commonly been perceived to have been grossly patriarchal. The absence of women has also been attributed to the privilege accorded to African boys during the colonial era. Even when girls gained access to schools, missionary and colonial educationists expected them to enrol in non-academic courses; in classes such as sewing and cooking. Western hegemonic discourses tend to regard education as a metaphor for voice. The assumption is that if a woman cannot write, she is silent and powerless. In her introduction to *Unwinding Threads: Writing by Women in Africa*, Charlotte Bruner argues that a woman who dares to speak out through writing 'often goes against traditional values'.[33] What Bruner forgets is that writing was not a traditional value. Ten years later Bruner, in her introduction to *The Heinemann Book of African Women's Writing*, refers to the stories included as 'exceptional'.[34] Bruner celebrates the emerging voices of African women and implies that as a result of her efforts as an editor African women are no longer lost within 'a bleak desert or isolated jungle'.[35] Yet African women have always spoken in oral narratives, song, poetry and dance. By ignoring the historical and cultural contexts within which African women speak, Western feminists risk perpetuating the perceived silence of African women. In my story at the beginning of this chapter, Mai Shuvai's strategies for resistance are negotiated through silence as well as speech. Shall we therefore say she is a passive victim of patriarchy because we do not recognize her silent protest as a legitimate 'voice' of resistance?

Clearly, literature is a powerful tool of resistance. Literature is a way through which memory can be rewritten. However, it is incorrect to assume that women have no voice simply because a written tradition does not exist or cannot be found. The effect on African women is that their role as transmitters and custodians of cultural practices is simply erased. The unwritten is important in its own right but it also contributes to the written. Women writers like Buchi Emecheta record that they were inspired to write by the stories told to them by village women. Emecheta recalls how women told stories as they sat 'peeling egusi (melon seed) or tying the edge of a cloth or plaiting hair for hours. . . . I saw it and I used to sit with them. I liked the power those women commanded as story-tellers.'[36]

In what follows I argue that African women writers are rewriting history within the specific context of their people; their novels, narratives, short stories and poetry are informed by the conditions of their everyday lives. By engaging in literary activity, African women are finding ways of encompassing their experience and introducing a gender-specific politics of difference. In this respect, women's writing represents a continuity with non-literary modes of speech, inscribing in a written medium many of the concerns and issues which women have always articulated. What we find outlined in this writing are some of the subversive strategies which women have deployed in their uneven and at times none too successful negotiation with patriarchal authority. Without doubt what emerges, however, is that from a women's perspective, patriarchy is neither taken for granted, as the male writer would have us believe, nor as unidimensionally oppressive as Western feminists have asserted. Let us look at this women's world, at issues of motherhood, independence, community and the power of men. I will focus on Buchi Emecheta's *The Joys of Motherhood* and Flora Nwapa's *Efuru* and *One Is Enough*.

Released in 1965, *Efuru*[37] was the first novel to be published by an African woman. For the first time in African literature, the reader was given an insight into what Gay Wilentz has called 'a woman centred oral literature'.[38] This is the women's world we only partially glimpsed in Elechi Amadi's *The Concubine* or Achebe's *Things Fall Apart*. *Efuru* focused on the everyday lives of Nigerian women of the 1940s and early 1950s. When it first appeared it was harshly criticized by male Africanists, among them Durosimi Jones and Eustace Palmer, who dismissed it as a simple novel of women's 'gossip'.[39] Another critic who misread this novel was Kirsten Holst Petersen, who disposed of the book by saying that it presented 'a small, repetitive, uneventful and suffocating world' of women.[40]

The heroine of the novel is Efuru, a beautiful village woman who elopes with her first husband. Contrary to traditional female roles, Efuru chooses to become a trader instead of a farmer. Marriage and freedom of choice appear to be compatible until Efuru's husband deserts her. Soon afterwards, Efuru loses her only child and she is forced to return to her father's house. After a short period as a single woman, Efuru marries Gilbert, who later takes a second wife after Efuru fails to conceive. Her failure to be a mother is attributed to her role as the worshipper of Uhamiri, the Goddess of the Lake. At the end of the novel, Efuru leaves Gilbert after he accuses her of adultery.

In *Efuru*, Nwapa's concerns are with motherhood, marriage, polygamy, economic dependence and choice. Critics have interpreted *Efuru* in varying ways. Florence Stratton reads Efuru as a 'feminist' novel which frees Efuru from the traditional prescriptions of gender. Lloyd Brown observes that Efuru 'elects a course suitable to her needs without breaking her relationship with her community'.[41] Stratton and Brown therefore agree that Efuru exercises choice. But in terms of her association with the deity, Efuru does not exercise choice: she is simply chosen by a supernatural power. Like Chielo in *Things Fall Apart*, chosen women are usually ordinary people living in the community. But their link to the deity accords them a powerful status in religious matters. As a worshipper of Uhamiri, Efuru claims a new identity distinct from that of mother or wife.

The issue of motherhood is given paramount importance in *Efuru*. What emerges in the novel is that the relationship between husband and wife is of less importance than the relationship between mother and child. In a village context, a childless marriage is not acceptable but is also not usually a ground for divorce. It is common practice that the senior wife agrees to her husband's taking a second wife. When Efuru fails to have a child, she suggests that her husband take a second wife. When both Efuru and Gilbert are unhappy with Nkoyeni, the second wife, Efuru then takes her maid, Ogea, to be Gilbert's wife. Efuru's status as senior wife accords her power and status. Although she does not have children, she is regarded as a mother to the children of both Nkoyeni and Ogea. Multiple mothering or the sharing of mothering emerges frequently in the novel. For example, Efuru's close friend, Ajanupu, is involved in the care of Efuru's child from the time it is born until it dies. As in Achebe's novel, polygamy is not regarded as problematic or oppressive to women. In fact, the idea of a second wife in *Efuru* is suggested by Efuru herself.

The narrative does not clearly indicate whether the heroine was content with her position as a childless single woman. It seems Nwapa invested Efuru with religious qualities so the society could not condemn her for not being a mother. On the other hand, Efuru could have remained single and independent as she had been before. In fact, when she returned from her husband's village, the community welcomed her back and blamed the husband for being irresponsible. But the lingering unresolved question is whether Efuru finds satisfaction, despite the fact that she is not a mother. The novel ends by suggesting that Efuru's identification with the Woman of the Lake meant that she was happy and content. That may well be the case for women with supernatural powers, but how far is it possible for others?

Nwapa's other novel, *One Is Enough*,[42] is set in postcolonial Nigeria, a very different environment from that of Efuru. In this novel the main issues are motherhood, marriage and economic independence. When Amaka's marriage to Adizua does not produce children, Amaka's mother-in-law announces that her son has two children by his second wife. Although Amaka is angry that her husband took a second wife without her knowledge, she does not condemn polygamy as an institution. She demands recognition as a senior wife. When she fails to be reconciled with her husband, Amaka makes a decision to denounce her marriage and move to the city an as independent woman.

Male writers characteristically associate women with debased sexuality once they are in the city. Such women thus stand as symbols of a fallen Africa. Nwapa, in contrast, does not present her heroine in these terms. For Nwapa, the decision to be a prostitute in order to survive economically is not a moral issue. Amaka exploits her sexuality when she deliberately tempts Father McLaid. To enhance her economic security, she joins the Cash Mama Club whose membership is based on wealth and status. Most of the women in the club are unmarried mothers or widows from the Biafran Civil War. At first, it appears as if Amaka is content to be single and economically independent. But after she becomes pregnant we realize that she is unfulfilled and troubled by her barrenness. By rejecting marriage to Father McLaid, Amaka demonstrates that she values motherhood more than marriage. She states her position clearly:

> I do not want to be a wife any more, a mistress yes, a lover, yes of course, but not a wife. There is something in me in that word that does not suit me. As a wife, I am never free. I am a shadow of myself. As a wife I am almost impotent. I am in prison, unable to advance in body and soul. Something gets hold of me as a wife and destroys me. When I got rid of Obiora, things started working for me. I don't want to go back to my 'wifely' days. No, I am through with husbands. I said farewell to husbands the day I came to Lagos.[43]

This much-quoted passage has been viewed by many feminists as representing an African feminism. Susan Andrade argues that Nwapa reflects a 'female/feminist' individualism which separates Amaka from the patriarchal restrictions of Igbo society.[44] Although this is largely true, it is not the case that Amaka wants to free herself from the community. In fact, Amaka is not against polygamy, nor does she denigrate the tradition that valorizes motherhood. In fact, Amaka is grateful that Father McLaid has assisted her 'in proving to the world that I am a mother as well as a woman'.[45] In this respect, being a mother becomes the symbol for being a woman. I would differ with Kirsten Holst Petersen's assertion that Amaka's gratitude to the priest shows a sense of inferiority. Holst Petersen even goes so far as to suggest that Amaka's independence seems precarious because she chooses to be a mother.[46] Like some other Western feminists, Holst Petersen universalizes a view that motherhood is oppressive to a woman's sense of identity. Yet we should still ask whether to be economically independent and to be a mother signifies a specific self-identity. Amaka may have escaped to the city but she maintained close connections to her village. For instance, she returns the dowry to her husband, as is the accepted custom when a woman leaves her husband. Furthermore, she shares her mother's delight that the twins will remove the shame of barrenness. In many ways, Nwapa succeeds in creating a self-determined individual in Amaka but contradictions in formulating a fully self-realized identity remain. Tradition and modernity interrogate one another here; the assertion of individual identity is bounded by the power of collective culture. In her depiction of this hybrid experience, Nwapa speaks for many contemporary African women.

Similar female-centred themes as those evident in Nwapa's two novels also appear in Buchi Emecheta's *The Joys of Motherhood*. But, unlike Flora Nwapa, Emecheta uses the theme of motherhood in ironic terms. Critics of *The Joys of Motherhood* have often ignored the impact of colonialism on the two central characters, Nnu Ego and her husband Nnaife. Emecheta begins the novel by clearly stating that 'The year was 1934 and the place was Lagos, then a British colony'.[47] Working as a servant for a British doctor, Nnaife is forced to suppress his own male identity and perform duties often regarded as feminine such as washing and ironing.[48] Nnaife appears not to complain even when his white master dehumanizes him by calling him a 'baboon'.[49] While Nnaife seems to come to terms with his role as a servant, Nnu Ego cannot handle the loss of her husband's manhood under the colonized–colonizer relationship. Nnu Ego's fight against domination is targeted not against her husband but against the white people for whom he works. Her anger is particularly directed against the white woman whom she calls a 'shrivelled old woman with ill looking skin like the flesh of a pig'.[50] When Mrs Meers threatens to impose a Christian marriage on Nnaife and Nnu Ego, Nnu Ego challenges the system which has 'robbed a man of his manhood without knowing it'.[51] Emecheta's description of Nnu Ego's capacity to speak against imposed cultural practices is significant:

'You behave like a slave. Do you go to her [Mrs Meers] and say, "Please, madam crawcraw-skins, can I sleep with my wife today?" Do you make sure the stinking underpants she wears are well washed and pressed before you come and touch me? Me, Nnu Ego, the daughter of Agbadi of Ibuza. Oh, shame on you! I will never marry you in church. If she sacks you because of that I shall go home to my father. I want to live with a man and not a woman-made man.'[52]

Secluded from the master's eye or seen from a distance, Nnu Ego and the cook's wife, Cordelia, are acutely aware of their subjugation. 'If the masters treat them badly, they take it out on us', Cordelia reminds Nnu Ego.[53] However, the women appear to hold their ground much better than the men. Through their resourceful use of 'the women's fund', they provide economic support for each other. However, the situation becomes more difficult for Nnu Ego when Nnaife takes Adaku as a second wife. It is not that Nnu Ego is opposed to polygamy as such; in the village she would have no problem with it. But the city is different because a second wife causes economic hardship and urban values are such that a senior wife is not accorded proper status.

The two women, Nnu Ego and Adaku, represent the tensions and contradictions arising out of a woman's search for an identity in a period of tremendous flux. While Adaku is seen as a failed mother because she had given birth to girls instead of boys, she rejects the traditional image of a good mother and wife. In many ways her marriage is not an insurmountable barrier to self-discovery. She makes a conscious decision to become a prostitute: 'I want to be a dignified single woman. I shall work to educate my daughters, though I shall not do so without male companionship.'[54]

In comparison to representations of prostitutes in the male novel, Emecheta does not denigrate Adaku for making this choice. Also in significant contrast to the male novel, the city is not a place of cultural debasement for women. Instead, it offers them channels for individual and economic fulfilment. Nnu Ego remains there for a time to pursue a wifely ideal of self-sacrifice. In the end, she returns to the village, where she dies alone by the side of the road. For Emecheta, traditional motherhood means pain and hardship; Nnu Ego fades away. But rebellious action also has its costs: Aduka is ostracized. Emecheta captures the plight of urban women but she does not suggest what they can do about it. It is significant that Nnu Ego is acutely aware of her subjugation as a mother and as a woman. Nnu Ego asks:

'God, when will You create a woman who will be fulfilled in herself, a full human being, not anybody's appendage? . . . After all, I was born alone, and I shall die alone. What have I gained from this? . . . When will I be free? I am a prisoner of my own flesh and blood. Is it such an enviable position? The men make it look as if we must aspire for children or die. . . . But who made the law that we should not hope in our daughters? We women subscribe to that law more than anyone. Until we change all this, it is still a man's world, which we women will always help to build.'[55]

How Nnu Ego becomes aware of her condition without influence from the 'outside' world or from other women remains unclear. For Florence Stratton, Nnu Ego's words are the novel's strongest 'feminist statements', an assertion which begs the question of just whose feminism is being spoken of. I am not sure whether Emecheta herself knows. If she did, she might have offered Nnu Ego some avenue for empowerment. Instead, Nnu Ego remains a helpless victim of patriarchy and motherhood. She claims power of the supernatural to deny women children only after her death. But during her life she does not act to change her situation. There is, however, a clear message from Emecheta's ambiguous novel: motherhood itself is not the problem; what is damned is the patriarchal tradition that romanticizes motherhood as the only way to find personal fulfilment. In my reading, Emecheta invests Nnu Ego with a Western feminist consciousness which fails to hold. As I suggested earlier, universalizing gender experiences obfuscates the African woman's mode of resistance. Like the African male writer, the female writer may also find herself projecting the silent victim motif on to the African woman. At the same time she demonizes manhood.

Apart from themes of motherhood, childlessness, polygamy and economic independence, female solidarity emerges as a dominant feature in most novels. Women appear to enjoy the companionship, love, care and support of other women more than that of their husbands. In *Efuru*, for instance, village women find it 'disgusting' when they see Efuru swimming with her husband one year after her marriage. It seems that romantic love and male company are surpassed by motherhood and female company. Thus, Efuru has Ajanupu as her friend and confidante, and Amaka is paired with Adaobi or her sister. In the absence of a close friend, there is always a woman or a female relative to offer support and protection. Such close companionship between women has been misunderstood, at least in part, by Western feminists like Katherine Frank. According to Frank, African feminist novels

> embrace a resolution of a world without men: man is the enemy, the exploiter and the oppressor. Given the historically established and culturally sanctioned sexism of African society, there is no possibility of a compromise, or even a truce with the enemy. Instead, women must spurn patriarchy in all its guises and create a safe, sane, supportive world for women: a world of mothers and daughters, sisters and friends. This of course amounts to separatist feminism.[56]

Frank's argument is interesting, but it represents a partial reading of the literature in two respects. First, close friendship between women does not necessarily signify a desire to live in a world without men. In fact, as we have seen, having a husband is highly regarded in the societies under discussion. Second, Frank's conclusion is based upon the manner in which African women writers represent male characters. Like female characters in novels by male writers, the male characters are not accorded much voice.

In their attempt to reclaim womanhood, African women writers tend to have emasculated men. In *Efuru*, for example, Adizua's friends consider him 'stupid' for working in the fields alone while his wife shuns farm work. Despite a good marriage and one child, Adizua deserts his wife and no explanations are given for his disappearance except that he is with another woman. Adizua's mother then tells Efuru that Adizua's behaviour is not unusual: his father had been similarly irresponsible. Efuru's second husband appears to be caring at first, but he also disappears for some time, and when he returns Efuru discovers that he had been imprisoned and that he has fathered a child without her knowledge. Towards the end of the novel Gilbert is near death after Ajanupu crushes his head with a mortar, 'for she was a strong woman'.[57] Nwapa's treatment of violence against men is taken for granted. Likewise, in *One Is Enough* Amaka's mother-in-law denigrates Amaka's husband, Obiora, by referring to him as 'stupid' and 'useless'. Like Efuru's husband in *Efuru*, Obiora's weaknesses are very similar to those of his father. Such lack of manliness is demonstrated physically as well, as is shown in the fight between Obiora and Amaka. Amaka assaults him with a hammer, leaving him sprawling on the kitchen floor. Clearly, Nwapa enacts a world of powerful women by emasculating men. In this respect, she rejects the concept of women's physical weakness often seen in the male novel.

In *Things Fall Apart*, for example, we are constantly reminded that a man who does not perform the duties required of a man can be mocked as a woman. Ironically, powerful female characters in some African women writers' work also deride weaknesses in men as feminine. In *The Joys of Motherhood*, we expect Nnu Ego to sympathize with her husband for the abuse of his manhood under his white master. Instead, Nnu Ego seems to blame him for being 'feminine'. Another example of the feminization of men involves complete role reversals. Consider Catherine Obianuju Acholonu's story, 'Mother Was a Great Man'. The protagonist is Ada, a girl 'who grew up with the exuberance that was only allowed to boys'.[58] As a senior wife, Ada is described in masculine terms pitted against a feminine husband:

> Nekwe, her husband, was a man who surpassed every woman in beauty. He was tall and skinny, with a skin as ripe as udala fruits; and, as if to crown his beauty, Nekwe even had mbibi, patterns on his face and arms . . . to enhance beauty . . . Nekwe was not the manly type.[59]

After Nekwe's death, Ada considers herself a 'full man' and consults her husband's relatives about marrying a wife. In her quest for a son, Ada proceeds to 'marry' a young woman and she orders a man to have children with the woman. Like other senior wives or mothers-in-law, Ada follows the traditional custom of giving privileges to boys and not to girls. Gender relationships in this context are both complex and ambiguous because, as a 'husband', Ada exercises dominance over both the young woman and her husband. The son, we are told, is not only irresponsible, he is a 'cheat, a liar, a thief' and a 'glutton' who is soon sentenced to death for armed robbery.

From another perspective, the feminization of men can be seen to build upon the traditional role of women as senior wives, grandmothers or mothers-in-law. In these contradictory categorizations, perhaps the concept of power within an African extended family should not be measured in comparative terms. To be a woman does not necessarily mean that one takes a subordinate position. Each person, man or woman, occupies certain positions of power in a hierarchy which allows them status *vis-à-vis* other members of the family, again both male or female. Any straightforward dismissal of the extended family as grossly sexist or as backward or overwhelmingly oppressive therefore needs modification. It is this, above all else, which eludes Western feminism.

A further instance of this neglect of female power is demonstrated by the relationship between mothers and their sons. The revered position of the mother-in-law confuses the structures of traditional patriarchal dominance, as they are commonly interpreted. Mothers are very protective and supportive towards their sons and dictatorial towards daughters-in-law. By taking a strong role in their sons' selection of wives, mothers participate in the oppression of women. It seems the main role of the mother-in-law is to restore male authority as reflected in the desire for her son to have children, sons in particular. There is never any possibility that sons might be infertile. It is always the woman who is barren where a couple is childless, and mothers-in-law reinforce this thinking. For example, in *One Is Enough*, Obiora's mother denigrates Amaka and accuses her of barrenness. To prove that her son was not sterile, she brings home a woman who has had two children with Obiora. In *Efuru*, the village women encourage Gilbert's mother to find another wife for him when they suspect that Efuru may be barren. Recognizing the power of their mothers as decision-makers and strong participants in the affairs of the family, sons regard them with respect. The idea of 'Mother is supreme' brought out in *Things Fall Apart* applies to a number of mother–son relationships. My story at the beginning of this chapter also shows the power of mothers in making decisions with respect to a particular incident in the relationship between a young man and his wife. Although the dominant role of women as mothers-in-law or mothers is important in terms of subversion of male power, their participation in the oppression of other women should also be raised.

But modes of challenging these cultural structures are themselves problematic. Does one impose a specific conciousness on other people's cultures? To use my situation as an example, I am regarded by my sister-in-law as a 'sister-husband'. She is submissive to me and I am protective of her as a husband would be. (While there may be other African cultures similar to mine, I can speak only of the Shona people of Zimbabwe.) I am a sister-husband to my sister-in-law, subservient to my father and uncles, subservient to my aunts and grandmothers and dominant over my young brother by virtue of my age. As I grow older, I will expect levels of respect to increase from both men and women in my village. If I did not have children, my mother would regard it as a personal shame and the village people would blame Western education for my barrenness. Would I be content to be a single black African woman? If not, how would I like to be identified?

In our criticisms of international feminism, we should be cautious of finding ourselves entrapped in essentialist positions. Writing of boundaries between 'us' and 'them' can be extremely misleading. Almost all the African women writers I have referred to in this chapter have travelled or lived abroad. In her essay on African and Western feminisms, Christine Sylvester observes that African women writers are 'world travellers' in the sense that we willingly choose to cross the boundaries of our countries.[60] Like Western feminists travelling in Africa, we have had the benefit of seeing and internalizing cultural differences. Such journeys, argues Sylvester, have enabled us to achieve 'plural identities' and 'ambivalencies'. We are, in some ways, cultural hybrids, caught between two worlds. As she rightly argues, the attempt to articulate who we are requires an 'empathetic cooperation' across differences. In other words, a dialogue between Western feminists and African women will help us understand the differences within ourselves as women. But how far is it possible for us to see ourselves in 'them', as Sylvester suggests, unless we have more assurance? Are we not in some ways alienated from both worlds? Hence the contradiction in a writer such as Emecheta, who at one point claims that she is a feminist with a small 'f', only to reject the whole notion of feminism at another. In 1994, when asked why she is not a feminist or why she rejects the label, Emecheta replied:

> I have never called myself a feminist. Now if you choose to call me a feminist, that's your business; but I do not subscribe to the idea that all men are brutal and repressive and we must reject them. Some of these men are my brothers and fathers and sons. Am I to reject them too?[61]

The Nigerian critic Molara Ogundipe-Leslie declares herself to be a feminist and attributes Emecheta, Bessie Head and Ama Ata Aidoo's rejection of feminism to fear of intimidation by African men. But Emecheta's opposition to Western feminism cannot be dismissed simply on this basis. The word 'feminism' is indeed laden with ambivalences and contradictions for African women. Obioma Nnaemeka's conception of African women's liberation moves the debate further when she argues that African women do not reject oppressive indigenous traditions altogether; rather, they exercise freedom within the limitations of tradition. As such, they 'attest to the elasticity of their cultural worlds'.[62] Nnaemeka further locates African women writers as being at the 'edge' of two cultures and therefore having a sense of anxiety.[63] This condition of nervousness, argues Nnaemeka, is characterized by the women's fear of writing about issues of female liberation because doing so may result in harsh male criticism. In my view, however, it is not so much that women are nervous because of possible repercussions, it is more that they are uncertain about their sense of place. bell hooks sees the edge as a position of advantage: 'We looked both from outside in and outside out. We focussed our attention on the centre as well as the margin. We understood both.'[64] As I see it, African women are pulled between past and present, tradition and modernity, the centre and the periphery. Theirs is a space of tension and opportunity but it will take time to feel comfortable about it.

What is important is that African women steer some intermediate course between African patriarchy and transplanted Western feminism. Such a course will draw on the strengths of traditional values and the opportunities opened up by education and modernity. Silence should no longer be interpreted as submission to male domination, and the specificities of our historical and cultural backgrounds should no longer be erased. The validation of the experiences of African women within a more sympathetic framework can add much to the current debate on gender, identity and difference in postcolonial studies. If we look at the everyday lives of women in the novels, it is clear that African women are beginning to formulate their own discourses of empowerment through the written word, amplifying what they have always done in non-literary modes such as dance and story-telling. In time, this new power of speech will inevitably demand recognition from the dominant hegemonic discourses, whether these be African male literary criticism or Western feminism.

Notes

1. In Shona culture *bopoto* means shouting in anger. One performs this shouting only occasionally, when one has been offended over a long period of time.

2. The term 'noise' is used here as direct translation from Shona. It means being angry about an issue that one feels passionately about.

3. Cyprian Ekwensi, *Jagua Nana* (London, Heinemann, 1971); Nuruddin Farah, *From a Crooked Rib* (London, Heinemann, 1970).

4. Chinua Achebe, *Things Fall Apart* (London and Ibadan, Heinemann, 1958); Elechi Amadi *The Concubine* (London, Heinemann, 1976).

5. Florence Stratton, *Contemporary African Literature and the Politics of Gender* (London, Routledge, 1994), pp. 39–57.

6. Achebe, *Things Fall Apart*, p. 9.

7. See, for example, Carole Boyce Davies and Anne Adams Graves (eds), *Ngambika: Studies of Women in African Literature* (New York, African World Press, 1986), pp. 241–6.

8. Here I follow Obioma Nnaemeka's reading. See Obioma Nnaemeka, 'Feminism, rebellious women and cultural boundaries', *Research in African Literatures*, 26:2: Summer (1995), 52–110.

9. Chinua Achebe, 'Named for Victoria, Queen of England' in Chinua Achebe, *Hopes and Impediments: Selected Essays 1965–1987* (London, Heinemann, 1988), p. 44.

10. Nnaemaka, 'Feminism, rebellious women and cultural boundaries', p. 99.

11. Achebe, *Things Fall Apart*, p. 92.

12. Ibid., p. 18.

13. Amadi, *The Concubine*, p. 5.

14. Ibid., p. 4.

15. Ibid.

16. Chidi Amuta, *The Theory of African Literature* (London, Zed Books, 1989). See his chapter on African traditional culture.

17. Chinua Achebe, *No Longer at Ease* (London, Heinemann Educational Books, 1963).

18. Ekwenzi, *Jagua Nana*, p. 176.

19. Ngugi wa Thiongo, *Petals of Blood* (London, Heinemann Educational, 1986).

20. Charles Mungoshi, *Waiting for the Rain* (Harare, Zimbabwe Publishing House, 1975).

21. In an interview with Flora Veit Wild in Harare. Quoted in Special Writers Section, *Gweru*, 6 (1994), 12–14 (p. 13).

22. Chinua Achebe, 'Where angels fear to tread', *Nigeria Magazine*, 75 (1962), 61, quoted in Nnaemeka, 'Feminism, rebellious women and cultural boundaries', p. 59.

23. Linda Alcoff, 'The problem of speaking for others', *Cultural Critique*, 18:Winter (1992), 5–31 (p. 7).

24. See Stratton, *Contemporary African Literature and the Politics of Gender*.

25. Florence Stratton, 'Periodic embodiments: a ubiquitous trope in African men's writing', *Research in African Literatures*, 21:1 (1990), 111.

26. Stratton, *Contemporary African Literature*, p. 115.

27. See Kirsten Holst Petersen, 'First things first: problems of a feminist approach to African literature' in Bill Ashcroft, Gareth Griffiths and Helen Tiffin (eds), *The Postcolonial Reader* (London and New York, Routledge, 1995), pp. 251–4.

28. Chandram Talpade Mohanty, 'Under Western eyes: feminist scholarship and colonial discourses' in Chandra Talpade Mohanty and Ann Russo (eds), *Third World Women and the Politics of Feminism* (Bloomington, Indiana University Press, 1991), pp. 51–80.

29. Ruth Frankenburg, *White Women, Race Matters: The Social Construction of Whiteness* (Minneapolis, University of Minnesota Press, 1993), p. 1.

30. See Ann du Cille, 'The occult of true black womanhood: critical demeanour and black feminist studies', *Signs*, 19:3 (1994), 591–638 (p. 602).

31. For a classic case see Maria Rosa Cutrifelli, *Women of Africa: Roots of Oppression* (London, Zed Books, 1983).

32. Wole Soyinka, *Myth, Literature and the African World* (Cambridge, Cambridge University Press, 1976), p. x.

33. See the introduction in Charlotte Bruner, *Unwinding Threads: Writing by Women in Africa* (London, Heinemann, 1983).

34. Charlotte Bruner (ed.), *The Heinemann Book of African Women's Writing* (London, Heinemann, 1993), p. xxi.

35. Ibid, p. x.

36. Obioma Nnaemeka, 'From orality to writing: African women writers and the (re)inscription of womanhood', *Research in African Literatures*, 25:4 (1994), 136–57 (p. 140).

37. Flora Nwapa, *Efuru* (London and Ibadan, Heinemann, 1966).

38. Gay Wilentz, *Binding Cultures* (Bloomington, Indiana University Press, 1992), p. 3.

39. Durosimi Jones and Eustace Palmer, review of Flora Nwapa's *Efuru* in *Journal of Commonwealth Literature*, 3 (1967), 127–31.

40. Kirsten Holst Petersen, 'Unpopular opinions: some African women writers' in Kirsten Holst Petersen and Anna Rutherford (eds), *A Double Colonization: Colonial and Post-Colonial Women's Writing* (Sydney and Oxford, Dangaroo Press, 1986), p. 113.

41. Lloyd Brown, *Women Writers in Black Africa* (Westport, CT, Greenwood Press, 1981), p. 22.

42. Flora Nwapa, *One Is Enough* (Enugu, Tana Press, 1981; first published 1966).

43. Ibid., p. 127.

44. Susan Z. Andrade, 'Rewriting history, motherhood, and rebellion: naming an African women's literary tradition', *Research in African Literatures*, 21:1 (1990), 91–110 (p. 99).

45. Nwapa, *One Is Enough*, p. 127.

46. Holst Petersen and Rutherford (eds), *A Double Colonization*, p. 113.

47. Buchi Emecheta, *The Joys of Motherhood* (London, Allison and Busby, 1979), p. 7.

48. Ibid., p. 56.

49. Ibid., p. 50.

50. Ibid.

51. Ibid., pp. 186–7.

52. Ibid., p. 51

53. Ibid., p. 50.

54. Ibid., p. 170.

55. Ibid., pp. 186–7.

56. Katherine Frank, 'Women without men: the feminist novel in Africa' in Eldred Durosimi Jones, Eustace Palmer and Marjorie Jones (eds), *Research in African Literature Today: 15* (London, James Currey, 1987), p. 15.

57. Nwapa, *Efuru*, p. 112.

58. See Catherine Obianuju Acholonu's short story, 'Mother Was a Great Man' in Charlotte Bruner (ed.), *The Heinemann Book of African Women's Writing*, pp. 7–15.

59. Ibid., p. 8.

60. Christine Sylvester, 'Africa and Western feminisms: world travelling and the tendencies and possibilities', *Signs: Journal of Women, Culture and Society*, 20:4 (1995), 941–76.

61. Buchi Emecheta during a lecture at Georgetown University, Washington, DC, 8 February 1994. Quoted in Gwendolyn Mikell, 'African feminism: toward a new politics of representation', *Feminist Studies*, 21:2 (1995), 405–24.

62. See the argument by Obioma Nnaemeka, 'Feminism, rebellious women and cultural boundaries', pp. 81–112.

63. Ibid.

64. bell hooks, *Feminist Theory: From Margin to Center* (Boston, South End Press, 1984), p. 12.

Afterword

PHILLIP DARBY

The chapters in this book do not lend themselves to a conclusion in the conventional sense. Their purpose has been to bring together a range of perspectives on how the Third World figures in or is erased from global politics and, in so doing, to widen our conception of the arena of the international. Despite the connections between the individual chapters, it would be wrong to attempt to plot the position of the Third World in relation to the First on the basis of an implied consensus or to suggest agreement between the contributors about the prospects for change. Although international relations as an academic subject has been a designated point of reference throughout the book, it has not been given the kind of detailed treatment which would provide grounding for proposals for disciplinary revision. Rather than attempting at this point to give the book a singular stamp, I want to reflect on some of the themes which have been developed and to consider their implications and possibilities. It is our collective view that no purpose is served by simply reviewing each of the chapters in turn. Nor do we think it useful to clutter these concluding observations with citations to the individual contributors.

Beginnings, Edward Said has written, powerfully influence what follows them.[1] They do so, however, in different ways from origins which are more determining. According to Said, 'an origin *centrally* dominates what derives from it'.[2] Said's comments are revealing, but his analysis is rather too literary and his understanding of origins too theological to be pursued here. The epigraph he chooses for his study, however, has a direct applicability: 'Doctrines must take their beginning from that of the matters of which they treat' (Vico, *The New Science*). Overwhelmingly, the scholarly and more general paradigms which are applied to the Third World begin in Europe or the West and have their origins in European or Western experience and history. The very phrases employed to tell the story of subjugation and incorporation – 'the expansion of Europe', 'the expansion of international society' – signal the mindset. Thus the familiar is re-inscribed, in terms of both description and prescription. Once set up, the circuit has proved hard to break.

Such is undoubtedly the case with disciplinary international relations, which has remained true to its origins to an unusual degree. One strains to think of a single area within the discipline which can be said to have been fundamentally influenced by practices in or perspectives of the South. Much the same is true of those ancillary international doctrines – development, democratization and economic liberalism – which the discipline takes up when circumstances seem propitious. Although insufficiently acknowledged, the vistas of the good life held out to the South and the politics of change imposed when possible upon the South still draw much of their sustenance from classical political economy. Globalization theory looks ahead, more than behind, and it emphasizes how different the world is becoming. Yet its world is very much that of late modernity, postindustrialism and new cultural forms. It takes up from where imperial studies left off and ventures where international relations fears to tread, but the future it unfolds depends on a past it takes for granted. With its origins in Western sociology, globalization explicitly and implicitly privileges processes and ideologies which emanate from the West. Recently its universalism has been tempered by some recognition of local particularity and adaptation but still, in most versions, its theorizing sweeps above and across the Third World instead of engaging with it.

Of the major intellectual formations considered in this book, only two – dependency and postcolonialism – break with the predominant pattern. Both can make claim to having Third World origins and both embody a radical sensibility, directed to changing the global order. Yet it is apparent that strong beginnings and right intentions are not enough. Dependency is now discredited, at least if taken in literal terms. Postcolonialism is increasingly ensconced within Western academia and bears little relation to scholarly, let alone lay, thinking in most parts of the South. In addition, there is a feeling that, in its contemporary forms, there is more interest in reflecting back on Western bodies of knowledge – what does post-colonialism tell us about postmodernism? – than in articulating Third World concerns and perspectives. It has been argued here that both discourses are in need of revamping: the one brought forward to encompass the structural globalism of contemporary capitalism; the other led back to confront the material conditions of Third World life.

To contend, as we have, that international studies in its various formations needs to be more aware of the dangers of privileging Western standpoints and Western power and of neglecting non-European sources and experience is not without its own difficulties. How far the Western scholar, even of the most committed cast of mind, can engage with the culture of the other without in the process writing in the self and thus marginalizing or silencing the other has been much debated in postcolonial theory. What appears from one perspective to represent attempts to expose and dismantle hegemonic constructions can be understood from another as interventionist practices. These issues have been taken up with respect to the position of African women and the role of Western feminisms in Chapters 9 and 10, and it is apparent that there is no easy resolution. Nor should it be assumed that a greater familiarity with Third World issues would in all circumstances lead to more progressive appreciations. It has been the practice of late to emphasize the historical limits of Western knowledge of the Third World. This is certainly warranted. It is worth remarking, however, that British policy-makers during the period of empire knew much more about Asia than did American policy-makers in the United States' period of ascendancy afterwards. The British were therefore led to scale down their objectives and to act more through intermediaries, and were perhaps more successful as a result. There is also a line of argument which runs that at least in terms of advice and directives, the South is presently receiving too much attention, not too little. On one account, the promotion of good governance and the market economy represents a recolonization of subject peoples;[3] better a period of neglect to provide a space for the South to take initiatives of its own.

With these cautionary remarks being borne in mind, the question becomes one of how studies of international society might be made more responsive to the situation of the Third World and the evident need for far-reaching change. This is in fact the central problematic of the book. In different ways, each of the chapters has taken up the challenge, and to some degree our collective response is embedded in the structure of the book itself. Let me now, in summary fashion, draw out the major themes of argument and indicate areas of contention.

In the Introduction the commitment was expressed to a fuller exchange between different formations of knowledge. It should now be apparent that each discourse has its own distinctive viewpoints and concerns, and the tendency is for others to be pushed to the sidelines or actually discounted. The result is the creation of different worlds. Which issues are taken to be important and the construction placed on particular events are therefore likely to depend upon what one reads to a much greater extent than formerly. It may also be that the divergence associated with whether one's orientation is international or domestic has been widening. The chapters on democratization and partnership hint in this direction. The situation has worsened, the felt need to engage with material which is different from or opposed to one's own has diminished as discourses have multiplied and become more specialized. When the issue is put thus, it is perhaps natural to assume an openness to dialogue which we like to think of as a mark of academic enquiry. But can we assume that the problem is basically an intellectual one, which can be addressed through multidisciplinary courses, publishing outlets, conferences and so on? I do not think so. Closure is also a matter of interests and psychological predispositions. On the first point, there are issues of funding, jobs and personal advancement tied to academic competition and in some instances there are relations with outside interests also. In the case of international relations, we have suggested that the discipline's proximity to established centres of power requires much closer interrogation than it has received to date. With respect to the latter point, I have in mind the security associated with territorial preserves, the attraction of badges of distinctiveness and the wish to have no truck with the old (or the new). When I discussed this with a colleague who works at the intersection of politics and psychology, he mentioned a painting he had recently seen entitled 'Thirty-nine Desires and One Belief'. This, he said, only partly in jest, struck about the right balance as to how people approach politics.[4] It is also useful to recall that those sharing a degree of commonality often have the greatest difficulty in engaging. Clearly, such issues cannot be taken up here but they point to the need to focus much more on the viewer as well as on what is viewed.

Extending this material to develop a related theme, throughout the book we have attempted to express a scepticism about too much fixity – fixity of position, of approach and with respect to concepts. No doubt in places we too have allowed commitment to override caution in this regard, but the range of possibilities opened up by the different bodies of knowledge considered here and pursued in the narratives which accompany them should itself be a warning against a canonical approach. Although it is not explicitly argued as such, what emerges from our analysis of the various discourses is that each has about it a sense of being the revealed word – and this despite their evident differences in approach and chosen paradigms. In short, all are too sure of their bearings. Within each of these discourses naturally there are divisions, but these seem only to affirm certitude and to enclose thinking the further. Consider the case of international relations. Until the advent of postmodernism, the historical development of the discipline could be sketched in terms of the shifting lines of debate between realism in its various forms and the family of doctrines which comprise liberal internationalism. This schism, which hardly expressed the diversity of scholarly thought, nonetheless structured the discipline and defined its major concerns in a way which made it unresponsive to other agendas or ideas from the outside. Its influence can be seen in the often cavalier way in which considerations of order, stability, regime type and the significance of the end of the cold war are extended to the Third World. Mind you, it is altogether unlikely that a melding of realism and liberalism, as has been advocated recently, would at this stage make much difference.[5]

No one would doubt the virtues of confidence, but in the light of contemporary concerns with indeterminacy and multiplicity, and given the disarray about how to approach political and economic change in the Third World, circumspection is also needed. Over ten years ago, Tony Smith observed that the field of Third World studies was in a state of crisis.[6] This was perhaps an exaggeration but it throws into relief the sense of assurance on the part of the global discourses that they have the ground covered. The story of the Hottentot Venus reminds us to be on our guard against notions of normalcy and conceptions of the natural order, and of the ease with which they can be invested with the stamp of scholarly authority and internationalized as established doctrine. The way in which fears of the 'wild man' and of original evil were visited upon the Mau Mau and associated with the forests of the Aberdare Mountains is a cautionary tale about the propensity of anxieties about the self to be transposed to others and relocated 'out there'. Again, the psychological becomes relevant, and it needs to be approached in its cultural and historical context. Richard Johnstone has written a fascinating study of the novelist's desire for certainty of belief in the aftermath of the Great War. He explores the way communism and Catholicism were singled out as the alternative cures for the 'sickness of a generation'.[7] Surely there are insights here which need to be followed up.

There is a further problem about what we might call the grand narratives of the international and it is that they work from the top down – and often very little down at that! By this I mean that their frames of reference are in the first instance or in largest part global, their foundational paradigms are of the system. Only subsequently and secondarily do they examine the particular, the domestic and the local, and even then usually for purposes of illustration. Such is the pattern with international relations, with globalization and with dependency. How far postcolonialism is of a similar ilk is arguable, but certainly note should be taken of its selectivity with the particular and the trend over several years to accent the general and the global.

One of the central concerns of this book has been to demonstrate that so often accounts of what happens on the ground in the Third World do not conform with the story as told from above. This emerged repeatedly in the critiques of the three discourses in Part I; it figured large in the rationale of Part II; it was developed in Part III through reference to the politics of the everyday. The dangers associated with unrelieved reliance on theorizing from above should by now be clear; in summary, it tends to privilege the centre, essentialize the phenomena under investigation and downgrade agency. It seems also – and this requires special emphasis – to heighten the sense of certitude in the story being told and its completeness. The point is persuasively made in Gyanendra Pandey's essay on the Hindu–Muslim 'riots' in Bhagalpur in 1989.[8] Pandey argues that we should pay close attention to the moment of violence, and he does so by examining pamphlets and poetry and by drawing on his personal impressions. Piecing together 'fragments', he suggests, is often the best we can do, and the very word serves to underline the provisionality and incompleteness of our analysis.

Pandey's work on the construction of communalism in India is not usually associated with international studies but reference to it here serves to underline the insistence throughout the book on the need to expand the conception of what is international beyond established categories of thought. That need is acutely evident in disciplinary international relations, where much is declaimed to this effect but it is mostly disregarded in practice. Postcolonialism, through its reconceptualizations, has gone furthest in this direction, although the international, as such, has not figured prominently in the discourse's theorizing. It has been a fundamental premise of the book that the traffic in ideas and values and the processes of global exchange and domestic intervention are an integral part of world politics. They cannot be apprehended, in any adequate way, by studies of the interaction of states or when the political is separated from society and culture. This means nothing less than that the notional boundaries separating different areas of study must be rejected. From the earliest imperial contacts, raising issues such as the significance of race or the meaning of modernity, to the contemporary structures of global capitalism and the spread of consumerism, we have argued that the international has been constituted and re-formed as much by developments excluded from the world of formal diplomacy and foreign policymaking as by matters included within it. We have attempted to show – as in the chapters on democratization and partnership – that established international doctrine is very often qualified or contradicted by sources not customarily understood as international.

More than this, we have placed especial emphasis on questions of subjectivity and on the politics of identity. A stage has now been reached where the formal relations between designated international actors cannot be considered apart from the intersubjective relations of ordinary people expressed in their everyday lives. R. B. J. Walker puts the point well when he observes 'The state is within us as much as we are within it'.[9] One manifestation of such connectedness discussed in Part II is the way perceptions of identity can be driven by the significance of place; in the case considered where the forests of Kenya became repositories of cultural memories of darkness and evil, although not seen as such at the time because the spatial assumptions of international relations and defence studies were of a different kind. Our main focus, however, has been on the global movement of ideas about gender and sexuality in Part III. The conviction which ties together the three chapters in this part of the book is that the externalization of the construction of a dominant masculinity and later the circulation of the family of feminist perspectives about liberation from patriarchy raise important questions about cultural imperialism, new forms of internationalism and the relationship of the local to apparent global behavioural trends. There is room for different views about the significance of homosexuality to a greater appreciation of cultural difference, or about the ethics, the implications for agency and the evidentiary supports of Western feminist interventions in non-European societies. The position taken here is that personal rethinking about gender and sexuality can trigger challenges to other elements in the established domestic and international order. What can no longer command support, in our view, is the position that whereas gender and sexuality have their uses in critically reviewing the lexicon of high politics, they do not constitute matters of international relations in their own right.

Despite the book's elevation of identity politics and the weighting attached to the role of the discursive, these twin contemporary preoccupations have not been allowed to displace a concern with the material conditions of global life. Whatever one thinks of the present eclipse of Marxist thought, it has had a most unfortunate effect of shifting the centre of gravity of debate away from the role of material interest. Nowhere is this more apparent than within the body of postcolonial studies. Homi Bhabha's preoccupation with '[t]he work of the word'[10] has led Benita Parry to counter that what Bhabha offers is the '[t]he World according to the Word'.[11] Here we have attempted to ensure that the word (and the subjectivity of self) is situated in the social and the material. No discursive realignment can dispose of the economic pre-eminence of the West or of the reach and potency of the global processes associated with its technology, culture and military power. In several points in the book attention has been drawn to the difficulty of striking a balance between reconceptualization and an expansive conception of agency, on the one hand, and the limits of manoeuvrability imposed by material circumstances. If there is reason increasingly to weight the former, the process is slow and uneven. Moreover, as I suggested at an earlier stage, there is no reason to assume that the social optimism associated with the politics of knowledge and representation is equally appropriate in all the diverse areas which fall within the domain of the international. Beyond this, we can claim no collective position. The contributors to the book each have their own views and it is proper that they are expressed in the individual chapters.

There is one final thought which relates back to the title of the book. Why, it might be asked by those working in the new discourses or basically engaged with the Third World, attempt to bring disciplinary international relations into the picture? Would it not be better all round to leave international relations to its own concerns? After all, its evident commitment to disciplinary boundaries and its lack of receptivity, even hostility, to many of the approaches favoured by the new discourses hardly augurs well for productive exchange. Moreover, its links with established power compound the constraints of disciplinary orthodoxy and give international relations' politics a very different leaning from, say, post-colonialism or cultural studies. There is also a feeling that international relations' capacity to co-opt, to appropriate contending perspectives to its own design, could blunt the edge of alternative approaches to the situation of the Third World in global politics. Such, it might provocatively be claimed, has been the fate of feminism, which has been domesticated within the discipline and has come increasingly to concern itself with established reference points such as the state and security. The realist chorus seems to run 'We are all good feminists now.'

Such claims may well be overstated but they are not without truth. Yet it is precisely international relations' influence and its assurance that it holds the keys to understanding global politics which makes dialogue so necessary. Whatever its shortcomings, the discipline has highlighted many of the major impediments to the processes of global change, and they need to be addressed if the radicalism of the new discourses is to bear directly on the problems of the Third World. In this respect, being at the edge should not constitute an end in itself, for such a position is surely destined for continued marginalization and ineffectiveness. Rather, the edge needs to engage the centre and draw it out; it needs to inscribe its perspectives and insights as no longer marginal to the prospects for social change and global transformation. Merely ignoring the centre and the mainstream will continue to shield peoples and experiences at the edge from view.

Notes

1. Edward W. Said, *Beginnings. Intention and Method* (New York, Basic Books, 1975).

2. Ibid., p. 373; original emphasis.

3. See, for example, Yash Tandon, 'Recolonization of subject peoples', *Alternatives*, 19 (1994), 173–83.

4. The colleague is Graham Little.

5. See for instance Charles W. Kegley Jr, 'The neoliberal challenge to realist theories of world politics: an introduction' in Charles W. Kegley Jr (ed.), *Controversies in International Relations Theory: Realism and the Neoliberal Challenge* (New York, St Martin's Press, 1995), p. 17.

6. Tony Smith, 'Requiem or new agenda for third world studies?', *World Politics*, 31:4 (1985), 532–61 (p. 532).

7. Richard Johnstone, *The Will to Believe: Novelists of the Nineteen-Thirties* (Oxford, Oxford University Press, 1982).

8. Gyanendra Pandey, 'In defence of the fragment: writing about Hindu–Muslim riots in India today', *Representations*, 37:Winter (1992), 27–55.

9. R. B. J. Walker, 'From international relations to world politics' in Joseph A. Camilleri, Anthony P. Jarvis and Albert J. Paolini (eds), *The State in Transition: Reimagining Political Space* (Boulder, CO and London, Lynne Rienner, 1995), p. 23.

10. Homi K. Bhabha, *The Location of Culture* (London and New York, Routledge, 1994), p. 125.

11. Parry, 'Signs of our times', p. 9.

Index

UNIVERSITY OF WARWICK LIBRARY

Date of Return

UW 9716874 2